God's Mirror

God's Mirror

Renewal and Engagement in French Catholic Intellectual Culture in the Mid-Twentieth Century

Edited by **Katherine Davies** and **Toby Garfitt**

Fordham University Press | New York 2015

Fordham University Press also publishes its books in a variety of electronic formats. Some content that appears in print may not be available in electronic books.

Visit us online at www.fordhampress.com.

Library of Congress Cataloging-in-Publication Data is available from the publisher.

Printed in the United States of America

17 16 15 5 4 3 2 1

First edition

Contents

Acknowledgments vii

Introduction 1
Katherine Davies and Toby Garfitt

1 **"Catholicisme ondoyant": Catholic Intellectual Engagement and the Crisis of Civilization in the 1930s** 28
Michael Kelly

2 **Paul Valéry and French Catholicism: Recognizing the Context of Renewal** 50
Paul Gifford

3 **A Strange Christian: Simone Weil** 69
Florence de Lussy

4 **Jean Grenier and the "Spirit of Orthodoxy"** 88
Toby Garfitt

5 **Charles Du Bos's Catholicism and His Politics of Sincerity in Interwar France** 104
Katherine Davies

6 **From *Mystique* to *Théologique*: Messiaen's "*ordre nouveau*," 1935–39** 129
Stephen Schloesser

7 **Rethinking the Modernity of Bernanos: A Girardian Perspective** 162
Brian Sudlow

8 **"Into the Catacombs of the Past": Women and Wartime Trauma in the French Catholic *Ressourcement* Project (1939–45)** 186
Brenna Moore

9 ***La Relève* and Its Afterlife: A Current of Catholic Renewal in Twentieth-Century Quebec** 210
Joseph Dunlop

10 **Louis Massignon: A Catholic Encounter with Islam and the Middle East** 230
Anthony O'Mahony

Notes 253
List of Contributors 337
Index 341

Acknowledgments

We are grateful to the President and Fellows of Magdalen College Oxford for hosting and supporting, through their Annual Fund, the conferences held in 2010 and 2011, at which most of these chapters were presented, and to the Director of the Maison Française d'Oxford for hosting one of the sessions. Our thanks must also go to all of the participants at the conferences who provided important comments and such rich discussion, from which this volume benefited.

God's Mirror

Introduction

Katherine Davies and Toby Garfitt

> As body, man is a being whose condition it is always to be communicated; indeed, he regains himself only on account of having been communicated. For this reason, man as a whole is not an archetype of Being and of Spirit, rather their image; he is not the primal word, but a response; he is not a speaker, but an expression governed by the laws of beauty, laws which man cannot impose on himself. As a totality of spirit and body, man must make himself into God's mirror and seek to attain to that transcendence and radiance that must be found in the world's substance if it is indeed God's image and likeness—his word and gesture, action and drama.
>
> Hans Urs von Balthasar, *The Glory of the Lord*

> We understand that there is a dialectic of realism . . . such a realism consists not as a doctrine, but rather as an effort; and it purports less to resolve problems than to first see them clearly. It is the presence of this notion of a dialectic that explains . . . "toward the concrete." The concrete will never be the given for the philosopher. It will be the pursued. It is only in the absence of thought that the concrete can reveal itself to us.
>
> Jean Wahl, *Vers le concret* (*Toward the Concrete*)

The "existential" register unites what might only be seen as irreconcilable: the theological aesthetics of Catholic theologian Hans Urs von Balthasar and the "philosophy of the concrete" espoused by the Jewish-born agnostic philosopher Jean Wahl. Writing nearly thirty years apart in this instance, roughly at the beginning and the end of the period under study here, Wahl and Balthasar nevertheless emerge as particularly useful interpretive "signs" of Catholic intellectual culture *in transition* in mid-twentieth-century France in their respective encounters with the question of human existence.

Balthasar's theological aesthetics represented a blow struck at the intellectualization and conceptualization of faith—neo-scholasticism being a prime target—which tended, he believed, to treat God as simply an object of knowledge. His approach provided the foundation for a theology that could do justice to the global experience of faith and the fullness of God's glory, which the human ambition "to know" could not. Beauty answered Balthasar's call for a more integral vision: "Beauty is the word that shall be our first. Beauty is the last thing the thinking intellect dares to approach, since only it dances as an uncontained splendour around the double constellation of the true and the good in their inseparable relation to one another."[1] Beauty sanctifies and gives both truth and the good their power by engaging the holistic nature of faith. The primal and archetypal expression of beauty is God's self-revelation in the world—the Incarnation of the Word.[2] It is this taking of form that is the focus of Balthasar's theological aesthetics and, more especially, how we "see the form" of God, of revelation and faith, and how human beings, as forms, relate to created reality.

"Faith is participation in the free self-disclosure of God's interior life and light, just as the spiritual nature of the creature means participation in the unveiled-ness of all reality."[3] Here, Balthasar's contemplative "seeing the form" shows itself as leading to action. One is both a "communicated body," "a response," and "expression" and an active participant in God's reality in one's "word and gesture, action and drama." Balthasar thus reengages the material and the embodied: "His theology sacralises, through Christ, the historical and concrete, giving back soul to the historical and concrete."[4]

Toward the Concrete, Wahl's 1932 work on Alfred Whitehead, William James, and Gabriel Marcel, called for a shift from idealism to a new realism: Inspired directly by Heidegger's phenomenology, Wahl searches for the "concrete" in his emphasis on the immediate, immanent character of human beings' encounters with the world—the "sentiment of our existence in the midst of things."[5] Wahl's three case studies are all characterized by a "dialectic between thought and its object that refuses to lose touch with the real":[6] The dialectic expresses an "active oscillation" of elements (between, for example, transcendence and immanence) that does not "suppress oppositions but rather maintains them."[7]

Although Wahl and Balthasar are clearly distinct from one another (not least in their different perspectives on transcendence), there is nevertheless a striking resonance between Wahl's realism and Balthasar's theological aesthetics, a resonance that speaks to a broad transition. An orientation rather than a doctrine, Wahl's existential dialectic did not resolve problems but rather rendered them visible. It was characterized as a movement *toward* the concrete rather than attainment *of* the concrete—the concrete is not a given but the "pursued." Wahl's concrete reveals itself only in the absence of thought; in other words, he insists on the irreducibility of being to *knowing*.[8] In a similar fashion, Balthasar's concrete was that which was born through beauty rather than simply the logic of truth. What emerges is a shared concern for the aesthetic—the extraintellectual, the revelatory and transformative. Both Wahl's realism and Balthasar's aesthetics can be understood as subjective insofar as they reveal the life of feeling and objective insofar as this life of feeling is real.[9]

This volume brings together a series of impressions or snapshots of French Catholic intellectual culture in the mid–twentieth century caught up in its process of transition—whether by virtue of participation in, resistance to, or mediation of that transition—in which the drive for the human, for being, and for the concrete or real was so often crucial. This is the story of a transitional Catholicism that creatively managed the task of making oneself into "God's mirror."

Renewal and Engagement

Historiography on twentieth-century French Catholicism broadly follows a narrative that typically heralds the transition from a pre-1914 right-wing, antimodern, and theologically ghettoized Catholicism to a post-1945 progressive and intellectually "avant-garde" Catholicism.[10] The present collection provides a new dramatization of French Catholic intellectual culture by exploring some of the many and varied modes and expressions of Catholic renewal and engagement during the mid–twentieth century and in doing so, casts a new light on the historiographical narrative of reconciliation between the Catholic Church and the modern world.[11] The focus is on unraveling the contours of a Catholicism that was in transition by investigating the subtleties of tensions and conflicts that were negotiated during this period and that constituted and informed typologies of renewal and engagement.

On a basic level, renewal refers to the constellation of efforts to revivify a Catholic culture, which have been lumped together under the label of *le renouveau catholique*. But here, renewal, as well as designating the "fact" of the flowering of Catholic thought and culture, is more especially explored in its "form"—is it a matter of renaissance, reappropriation, reimagination, or reconfiguration? For example, the late nineteenth-century renaissance of Thomism, instigated by Pope Leo XIII, was hardened into a profoundly antimodern enterprise by Pius X, who was attempting to circumscribe orthodoxy in the wake of the modernist crisis.[12] In this form, Thomism proved itself a powerful partner for the integral nationalism of Maurras's Action française.[13] The interwar years witnessed an unraveling of this collocation. Jacques Maritain's intellectual and cultural enterprise, for instance, came to promote Thomism, especially after his move away from Action française, as explicitly *modern* in its inexhaustible fecundity and thus precisely in its ability to adapt to and contain the modern world. At the same time, Maritain's particular strain of neo-Thomism faced competing renewals from transcendental Thomism, which broadly colluded with the legacy of Kantian metaphysics in its emphasis on the knower's projection on the real, and the excavation of the *historical* Aquinas, which ultimately fed into a relativization of the neoscholastic Thomistic system.[14] Renewal, then, also asks questions about the nature of its self-presentation in its relation with the modern world.

A purposely wide approach is taken to "engagement," too, in terms of the object and subject of engagement and in terms of its form. The contributions here range in detailed focus from the engagement of individual Catholic thinkers to groups and periodicals or journals; from the connections and interactions between philosophical, theological, and cultural issues on the one hand, to social and political engagements on the other; and from engagement marked by adaptation and dialogue to resistance and aporia. Moreover, engagement is conceived hermeneutically in different ways. It may be in terms of the internalization of "external" debates within a distinct discursive space or in terms of the relationship between two discrete parties or identities; it may be read analogically insofar as a non-Catholic subject reflects and inflects Catholic thought and engagement, or it may be conceived as an affective mode of survival. Of course, we cannot conceive of engagement without an appreciation of its actors.

The "Catholic intellectual" has been the focus of a growing body of scholarship over the past fifteen years.[15] While some tend to privilege the papal condemnation of the right-wing nationalist royalist Action française in 1926 as a decisive turning point for Catholics, others have placed the censure of 1926 within a broader trajectory of the "birth of the Catholic intellectual." Philippe Chenaux presents the condemnation of Action française and the crisis it provoked as the "Dreyfus affair" for Catholics; the papal interdiction disentangled Catholicism from its traditionally right-wing identity and freed up a space ordained to pluralism within the church. Hervé Serry has taken a longer view: It was the separation of church and state in 1905 that created "a specifically Catholic space for intellectual debate," and it was the continuous struggle—the stresses, strains, and adjustments that Catholic writers experienced in consequence of the tension between the liberty of literary creation and the pressures of the ecclesiastical hierarchy—and experimentation with positions involved therein that formed the Catholic intellectual. It was only in 1945, however, a year after the formation of the Christian democratic Mouvement républicain populaire, that the identity of the Catholic intellectual was structurally cemented, with the establishment of the Centre catholique des intellectuels français, whose objective was to create a community of thought between Catholic intellectuals and to diffuse their ideas through the newly created Mouvement international des intellectuels catholiques.[16]

The interrogation of "engagement" thus involves exploration of its conceptualizations, its methodologies and tools, its spaces, and its effects. The figure of the Catholic intellectual and the travails involved in its development inform the possibilities of Catholic engagement. The contributions to this volume are all broadly underpinned by a concern for how the Catholic intellectual reflects and takes a position on the relationship between the church, personal faith, and the world and on the necessarily problematic relationship between intellectuals and the magisterium.

Periodization

Cholvy and Hilaire, and Fouilloux, among others, have identified the period between the 1920s and the 1960s as a "golden age" of French Catholicism.[17] Much of the scholarship specifically on Catholic intellectuals has hitherto tended toward a focus on the first three decades of the century, when the Catholic renewal had largely been seen as a success, or singularly on the postwar period.[18] This volume offers something different in its particular periodization. It serves as a bridge by ranging from the twilight years of the 1920s and the political paralysis and crises of the 1930s, to the occupation years, and through to the postwar years of progressivism, Christian democratic efforts, and the run-up to Vatican II. Although there is certainly no claim to comprehensiveness or perfectly even treatment across these decades, the range of focus here illuminates the continuities and discontinuities during these critical years. Moreover, it interrogates the nature of change and how best to understand its makeup and processes, including consideration of the roots of such a transition, the tensions contained therein, and the role of political or social changes that may accompany, reflect, or contribute to theological, philosophical, and cultural shifts.

The late 1920s and, more critically, the 1930s were a rich time for the reconfiguration of Catholic identity and engagement and a reconfiguration of the forms of renewal of Catholicism. Historians have described the 1930s in France not only as a period of social, political, and economic crisis but also a time of cultural, psychological, and moral crisis. France faced a series of domestic and international crises: the economic depression after 1929 (France maintained "relative immunity" from the world crisis until 1931);[19] the right-wing riots of 6 February 1934; entanglement in Mussolini's Ethiopia conquest in 1935; the Spanish Civil War of 1937; disillusionment with the Popular Front government; the anguish of the Munich agreement; and the tragic slide toward war. Catholic intellectuals became as much embroiled as their secular counterparts in the turmoil of the 1930s, visible in their assent to political manifestos via the proliferating Catholic press, such as the Dominican *La vie intellectuelle* (1928), *L'aube* (1932), and *Sept* (1934).[20] This periodical and journal press was critical to the development of new Catholic political positions and specifically to an "opening to the left," which included those progressives close to Communism, certain Christian democratic strains, and some of those in the amorphous group baptized as "nonconformist," such as Emmanuel Mounier, who inaugurated his personalist revolution through the pages of his influential journal, *Esprit*.[21] Mounier in particular nailed his colors to the mast in Catholic renewal by responding to the "crisis" of civilization. Critiquing the worn-out *désordre établi* (established disorder) of capitalism, bourgeois values, and materialism, he pushed for a spiritual revolution involving the rehabilitation of human beings and the community.

Moving into the German occupation years of World War II, scholars have identified Catholicism as a key "structural factor" that can explain the depth of the French crisis of 1940–44 and the subsequent debates over how the Vichy regime ought to be remembered.[22] The ideological cleavages and complexities of collaboration and resistance are well-trodden scholarly terrain, but for Catholics especially, their relationship with Vichy was, to say the least, complicated.[23] The increasing split between democratic Christians and more conservative Catholics during the 1930s contextualizes the path of resistance chosen by some and the political acquiescence or active collaboration with Vichy chosen by others. Initially the great majority of Catholics followed the lead given by bishops and welcomed the Vichy "National Revolution," grounded largely on Christian moral values. Former militants of the Fédération nationale catholique, such as Philippe Henriot, easily found official positions in Vichy, but Resistance leaders emerged from the Catholic youth and labor movements and also religious congregations, evidenced, for example, by the founding of the clandestine Jesuit journal *Témoignage chrétien* in 1941.[24] The postwar contours of Catholicism make sense only in the context of the war years and choices made at that time. On an immediate political level, for example, Catholic Resistance warranted integration into the new Fourth Republic, which was grounded on the shared antifascist struggle. The Christian Democratic Party (Mouvement républicain populaire, or MRP), which gained immediate electoral successes, arose from the French Catholic Resistance; Georges Bidault, who had been chairman of the Conseil national de la résistance, was a founding father of the MRP and held several high ministerial positions.[25] On a cultural level, it has been argued further by Michael Kelly, "the Occupation was, in effect, the making of the French Catholic intellectuals"; it was their making because Catholic intellectuals in the Resistance were not only revealing their dissent from Vichy but also dissenting from the teaching of their church.[26] Indeed, Fouilloux argues that the clerical and lay elite that emerged from the Resistance played a major role in the push for liturgical and ecclesiastical reform, contributing to the movement that eventually led to the Second Vatican Council of the 1960s.[27] But it would be false to simply conflate the political and religious chronologies of the postwar period: If there was a degree of alignment between Catholic participation in the Resistance and the move toward the *nouvelle théologie* movement that took off properly after the war, there was certainly no guarantee of correlation between neo-Thomism and support for Vichy. For example, although the Roman neoscholastic Réginald Garrigou-Lagrange—dubbed the "sacred monster of Thomism"—was an enthusiastic supporter of Vichy, Maritain's Thomism led him in the exact opposite direction of resistance.[28] Philosophical and theological differences (or resemblances) did not always correspond to those of a simple right or left political orientation; it is sufficient to say that the heterogeneity of Catholic intellectual engagement forged during the war is clear. The creation of the Centre catholique des intellectuels français (CCIF) in 1945 is testament to the vibrancy of postwar Catholic intellectual culture. The CCIF rendered faith in a secularized society intelligible. Fighting against a political and cultural context of exclusivism, the CCIF encouraged dialogue between Christians and nonbelievers and engaged in key debates of the fourth and fifth Republics, such as the construction of Europe, and its work was equally central to theological renewal in its defense of liberty of research and conscience, anticipating the efforts of Vatican II. In its own image, the CCIF presented Catholicism as "open."[29]

This particular periodization of Catholic intellectual culture allows for a more explicit exploration of the shifting norms and values of political and social commitments in relation to their cultural, theological, and philosophical fault lines and for a more explicit consideration of the ways in which change was effected.

Common Themes and Creative Tensions

A major part of the story told here is the relationship between French Catholicism and the modern world in the twentieth century. A great deal of scholarship has been devoted to the construction of a self-consciously modern Catholic identity. For example, Jean-Dominique Durand's work on *Les Semaines sociales de France, 1904–2004* (2006) examines the laic institution of Christian social education and its development of a model of engagement that mediated between Catholic adaptation to modernity and the Christianization of modernity, while Stephen Schloesser's *Jazz Age Catholicism: Mystic Modernism in Postwar Paris, 1919–1933* (2005) casts postwar Catholicism as the "truest expression of modernity" by virtue of the successful creation of Catholic modernisms or "mystic modernisms" in the literary, artistic, and musical realms. The present volume does not foreground the relationship between Catholicism and modernity so explicitly; moreover, this is not the space for adding to the cottage industry of scholarship on the conceptualization of modernity, the modern, and modernization. However, the traces of this confrontation underpin several of the contributions, especially in terms of the radical subjectification of reality in the secularization narrative, long acknowledged as a constituent element of modernization, and in terms of the new "temporal" quality of modernity.

Jürgen Habermas allows us to engage with some of the productive tensions Catholicism might entertain in its dialogue with the modern world. Habermas argues that modernity can be understood as a forward-looking consciousness that generates a reflexive awareness, a privileging of the present standpoint within the horizon of history as a whole that in turn accelerates the expectation of a future of difference because of the scarcity of time.[30] The distinctly modern self-consciousness of the desire for "newness" means that there is a need to differentiate modernity's historical legitimacy from an orientation to past times: It "has to create its normativity out of itself."[31] Of course, on a basic level, modernity's general rejection of tradition to authorize its identity naturally places it at odds with Catholicism. But delving beneath the superficial, the contributions here illustrate how the notion of reflexivity and the urgency of the present in fact become increasingly essential for many Catholic intellectuals not only to assert their relevance in the world but also to shape the possible ways in which modernity could be managed creatively; Catholicism was not a subculture but rather an active participant in the substantive intellectual landscape, and it could maintain this imaginative role by virtue of heeding the special relationship of the present to God, the embodied of the Incarnation, our human existence *in time*.

In dialogue with the modern world, Catholicism necessarily came face to face with the epistemological restructuring involved in the secularization process. Louis Dupré provides a useful framework to define this restructuring: first, the substitution of the explicitly "modern" idea of culture as humanity's need to create its own nature for that of the ancient model of cultivating an already existing potential; second, the disruption of the analogy between God and people, whereby people are now left to claim meaning for reality; and third, the disappearance of transcendence—here modernity becomes arguably more than the sum of secularization motifs such as the decline in religious faith and/or practice and the retreat of religion from the public space.[32] Historicizing the relation of modernity and Catholic intellectual culture during the mid–twentieth century, we perhaps see less a concern for secularization in terms of the separation of a temporal and supernatural realm and more an inflected concern for the often-unresolved tensions of the dialectic of immanence and transcendence and the fate of the deified Enlightenment subject, whose role was to constitute objectivity. The cluster of effects that make up a concern for authenticity of the self, for fragmentation, self-alienation, and disunity, could yet inform new typologies of Catholic renewal and engagement.

The contributions to this volume all share the same intellectual and cultural parameters. The tensions, resonances, and contradictions or confrontations within and between each dramatization operate in relation to the same problems to be solved and questions to be answered. Certainly, this level of commonality might well be said to derive simply from their shared historical circumstances—Catholic intellectuals were reacting to their context. But to take this view would be to overlook the reality that these manifestations of Catholic renewal and engagement were not simply hermetically sealed efforts (although Catholicism of course does have its own internal logic and is thus also not a simple reflection of culture in toto); rather, they were indicative of how Catholic intellectuals were creating, as well as participating in, the intellectual landscape.

Particular dimensions of this historicized Catholic imaginary repeatedly rise to the surface and can be rendered visible by a vocabulary. What follows is a—by no means exhaustive—sketch of those "signs" that capture something of the nature of the renewals and engagements. But these signs are "uncivilized": They are uncivilized because not always traceable in linear, transparent, or logical fashion but rather often submerged, messy, and aesthetic in kind.[33] There is an intertextual or interdiscursive quality to the method of exploring this transitional Catholicism insofar as we might speak about how the recurrence of particular words, phrases, and practices indicates a familial relationship; they suggest shared iterations of theological, philosophical, political, and cultural determinants, which are themselves "texts" that wield transformative potential. Building up an image of French Catholic intellectual culture and the creative tensions at play, the volume offers a focus on those modifiers or hinges of Catholic faith and engagement.

The "Human"

In 1926 François Mauriac defended Christian humanism, the very example of a "hyperhumanism," of which Christ was the emblematic figure.[34] A concern for the "human" or the "person" is a fundamental identifier for the renewal and engagements of Catholicism in transition in the mid–twentieth century.

From the vantage point of an unbeliever, we are invited to consider the relation of the "human" to religion. Paul Valéry performs something of an intellectual history or sociology of religion in his interrogation of how "divine things" are made tangible through people's desire (as Gifford argues). In unraveling the divine through an anthropocentric lens, the human is given a particular power as the creative center. This reading raises, in acute fashion, the question of how the "human" positions itself in Catholicism.

Jacques Maritain is perhaps the clearest example, in terms of depth and breadth of influence, of a "spokesperson" for Christian humanism as elucidated in his *Humanisme intégral* (1936). Maritain's personalism was founded upon the classic Thomist distinction between the individual and the person. Although individuation is required by existence, we are more than individuals; we are also human persons endowed with intellect and will and can transcend matter, and thus we are to be thought of as "whole" spiritual beings.[35] Individualism becomes a problem only when individuality does not submit to the person. Maritain's attacks on the Cartesian spirit are familiar enough. In his work *Religion and Culture,* Maritain highlighted the poverty of modern humanism, which he defined as "political and economic physicism," and he saw in it the estrangement of people from themselves: "[Youth] is strolling in its own humanity as in a museum: it sees its heart in the show-cases . . . We are exotic to our very selves." [36] Maritain explained that the common good could be achieved only through the communication of human *persons*; dialogue cannot be entrusted to individuals shut off from one another but can be effected only through love, which is sourced in the metaphysics of personal intersubjectivity.[37] Kelly's chapter delves into Maritain's emphasis on the human and its efficacy for a new mode of engagement. The role of the Christian in the temporal realm was to ensure it was a place fit for fulfilling the potential of the whole human person, and this Christian humanism was later crystallized in Maritain's development of human rights, albeit with a modulation of vocabulary. Further afield, Maritain's humanism was a formative influence in the development of a vibrant progressive strand of Québécois Catholicism in the resituating of nationalism below the Christian notion of the person (Dunlop).

However, the human person as developed by Maritain was only one explicit, and conceptually rigorous, dimension of Catholic renewal and engagement. To unravel some of the more elusive appropriations and rejuvenations of the human, we must turn to the slippery questions raised by the notion of human subjectivity and its relation to ontology. In his 1934 work, *Sept leçons sur l'être* (*Seven Lessons on Being*), Maritain made a distinction between scholastic philosophers on the one hand, whose quest for the object of metaphysics operated on the level of intelligible intuition, and modern philosophers on the other hand—he makes specific reference to Gabriel Marcel here—who seek to constitute "existential ontologies," insofar as being is the object of an experimental intuition of a concrete encounter, an affective experience that remains in the same category as the psychological or moral experience.[38] This distinction captures something of the different views of the role of the human in Catholic intellectual culture. The net must be cast wider, then, for examples of what the Catholic turn toward the human could entail. The human in protoexistentialist garb, which was opaque and experimental, signaled a shift away from a notion of the human that could be managed or contained by an intellectual schema, such as the neo-Thomism of Maritain. Garfitt's and Davies's contributions focus on the experiential problems of the human person and the implications for engagement and faith in the life and thought of Jean Grenier and Charles Du Bos, respectively, exploring the tensions that arise from a natural dependence on one's psychological subjectivity rather than on the intelligible intuition of being. If epistemology is not a condition of ontology—"realism is lived by the intellect before being recognized by it"—as Maritain would have it, interior observation is left in abeyance.[39] But we see precisely a concern for what the subjective core must serve: Grenier's "truth" "has been commanded by a temperament," and Du Bos's "truth" is his aesthetic-ethical self, mediated by his particular practice of sincerity.

Action

A fundamental point of debate of this broad intellectual preoccupation with humanism was the notion of action and its relationship between thought and being. The Weberian distinction between an "ethics of conviction" and an "ethics of responsibility" provides a particularly pertinent descriptor of a developing Catholic attitude of engagement. The former means that one feels responsible only for "ensuring that the flame of pure conviction . . . should never be extinguished," whereas the latter designates a wider responsibility involving an "account of the foreseeable consequences of one's actions."[40] It is the rather more open-ended and ethically driven approach of responsibility that embeds Catholics in their actions; open-ended because it allowed for a flexibility of the nature and type of engagement in accordance with the changing circumstances and demands of the world, given that "eternal values are embodied in material forms," and ethically underpinned precisely because fidelity to engagement was a fundamental fidelity to eternal values (Kelly). Reconciling a purity of means with efficacy in achieving one's end was critical to the task, which can be conceived in terms of a type of sincerity and a type of ontological exigency. The embodied nature of the human person called for a coordination of one's thoughts and actions to ensure that avowal matched real feeling, for instance (Davies), and in Gabriel Marcel's terms, action was intrinsic to existence. Concrete situations, as a fact of human existence, necessitate choice, and we can choose to open ourselves up to being or to close ourselves off in any situation (Kelly). The role of action in Catholic intellectual engagement was thus indicative of how freedom of moral choice increasingly became the order of the day rather than assent to and approval of a preformulated set of rules and obligations. Although action for some of the intellectuals in this volume meant intervention in the political and social realms, for others, problems of ideological commitment and its lived reality necessitated a withdrawal from direct political action precisely in order to restore the spiritual meaning of action (de Lussy).

The "Concrete"

The Catholic (and indeed non-Catholic) protagonists in this collection are all directed, in their own particular ways, "toward the concrete," to use Jean Wahl's expression. Gabriel Marcel observed that there was "something inexhaustibly concrete at the heart of human reality."[41] Specifically, he understood the concrete to be "the primacy of the existential over the ideal" and related to "incarnate being, i.e. to the fact of *being in the world*."[42] In Catholic terms, the "concrete" could be an emphasis on the embodied and the incarnational truth. Privileging of the "concrete" is problematic insofar as its meanings exceed containment by such a reference, but it is a useful descriptive term to indicate the many-sided postwar preoccupation with realism: Olivier Messiaen's shift from the "mystical" to the "theological" register is an affective internalization of the uncertainty and disorder of the sociopolitical terrain and the corresponding desire for concrete stability that theological truth could provide (Schloesser); the concrete is harnessed in Georges Bernanos's search for value that cannot be "instrumentalized or reified" following the horrors of the First World War (Sudlow), and the spiritual was sought in its concrete and more "real" form, which, for many, could be located on the left (Kelly). A Heideggerian-inspired philosophical turn to the concrete, denoting the self in the given world of things, which substantiated the life of feeling by virtue of its reality, was articulated in the Catholic realm in terms of a delicate attention to the concreteness of the present, a "sacrament of the present moment" (Davies's Du Bos) and a self-surrender to "live beyond oneself, *each day*" (Garfitt's Grenier). The concrete could also be an operation of grounding the self, not necessarily by facing the realities of war head-on but rather by drawing on and internalizing the "mystical" texts of the faith to coordinate and structure the self on the solid, "real" ground of truth, precisely because it was spiritually and emotionally nourishing in its emphasis on the authenticity of faith (Moore).

Questioning Orthodoxy

For some, the theological orthodoxy of Thomism was precisely that which anchored the "concrete" by bringing a solidity and reality to the "marvelous" (Schloesser). However, for others, a turn toward the human and/or the concrete went together with a dissatisfaction or an unease with the straitjacketing of the conceptual, intellectualizing system of neo-Thomism. Many of the contributors identify this questioning of the unified metaphysics of Thomism as central to a revivification of Catholicism. The rigidity of form, the inflexibility of the citadel, was critiqued by many: according to Marie-Madeleine Davy Thomist theology was like "assisting at an autopsy of a cadaver" (Moore); for Valéry, Thomist scholastics was a philosophy with a "raison d'État, a goal, a political will" (Gifford); for Du Bos, Thomism risked alienating other truths (Davies); Grenier was a "believer who does not want to subscribe to an orthodoxy" (Garfitt); Massignon was decidedly anticlerical and distanced himself from neo-scholasticism (O'Mahony); and rebellion against Thomism was accompanied by a decline in certain Catholic social institutions, which phased out confessional identity (Dunlop). Distancing oneself from what was often seen as the lifeless edifice or outworn architecture of Thomism entailed bringing "life" back into Catholicism. And this was recognized often in terms of a reconfiguration of the forms of renewal, by an emotional, affective engagement with the sources of the faith, for example (Moore).

The traction of the engine of Thomism was analogically related to the ideologically watertight party-political line. The shifts at work in the means of renewal were reinflected in the refusal to be tied down by particular forms or typologies of engagement. This was a move away from a zero-sum game in politics and faith. Surrendering completely to a political line could often deform the purity of thought (Garfitt). There was a reconfiguration of what engagement could be, and to this end, Catholic intellectuals were experimental, and their efforts not easily contained by a preformulated order or itinerary. The limit point of this loosening of dogmatic strictures and formulaic structures may well be illustrated by the absolute freedom of conscience of "the strange Christian," Simone Weil (de Lussy).

Engagement

Catholic intellectual engagement very often came to be characterized by a refusal to be caught by current forms and instead involved flexibility and ambiguity. Mounier's term "ondoyant," picked up by Kelly, points succinctly to the function of oscillation or the dialectic of balance and disequilibrium that was deeply set in many Catholic intellectuals. Even though this form may seem suggestive of the powerlessness and fragility of Catholic engagement, it could, by virtue of its capacity for modulation, maintain a priority on the ethical imperative. Catholics could find themselves jostling for position within a "third-way" discourse, which was striking for the ideological range it embraced. However, the constellation of dispositions and outlooks was nevertheless characterized by a shared *ethicopolitical* imperative that involved: a certain degree of rejection of parliamentary liberalism and capitalist disorder, a disavowal of the extremes of Fascism and Communism, and a desire to rehabilitate spiritual values through the person—the renewal or establishment of the "new man."[43] Emmanuel Mounier can be placed within this broad, multidimensional movement, but there are countless other examples of the ways in which Catholic engagement could be reimagined in its "ondoyant" capacity, subverting simplistic heuristic categories of Catholic engagement. We see Bernanos engaging with political and cultural crises by a process of myth deconstruction and critique of violence underpinning the conditions of ossified bourgeois political and economic liberalism (Sudlow); we see how the shift can be made from a nationalist and rather narrow social Catholic militancy to an eclectic pluralism in terms of an open engagement with the changing demands of the political landscape (Dunlop); and we see how managing a path between fidelity to Catholicism and Islam by the convert Louis Massignon could be accompanied by, and in part make for, a distinct form of political engagement such as anticolonialism (O'Mahony). Bound up with so much of Catholic engagement was the tenuous issue of the relationship between means and ends. Notions of impartiality and "good faith" became markers of engagement for many Catholics (notably Du Bos and Grenier), and indeed an antipartisan approach, which followed an ethics of responsibility rather than conviction, was developed as an efficacious form of engagement in its capacity for communication and communion between people. Vacillation intrinsic in typologies of Catholic engagement was both problematic and powerful and can be found, as a kind of corollary, within renewals of faith itself.

What emerges so forcefully in this context is the "balancing" act at work—an exercise on parallel tracks with an "ondoyant" sociopolitical engagement—in situating one's "self" in faith. Some of the actors in this volume bear the burden of dislocation of the "self," but internal conflicts were also a creative energy for many Catholic intellectuals: They turn toward the disequilibrium and find within it the authenticity of the human. Garfitt's Grenier discovers the human in his fissures and fragmented form. Others, such as Davies's Du Bos, participate in this almost ascetic process, striving for an integral humanism rather than the Gidian self-divisive humanism of surrender to one's desires and acts. What unites these efforts is a heightened affectation of how the "human" dimension might serve to negotiate one's faith. This is addressed in rather more explicit terms in Sudlow's appropriation of Charles Taylor's tension between the territorialized or "buffered" self and an "openly immanent" self, which is conscious of its own psychology but is also fundamentally directed exogenously by God's grace.

But the "human" is also a hinge; it is an index for transcendence, for a movement beyond the anthropocentric veil. For Catholic intellectuals, the question of the human and humanity could ultimately be answered only by surrender to God, by renouncing the desire to smooth out or unify the tensions born of psychological egocentricity. In a way rejecting the burden of "completion" of the project of modernity, Sudlow observes that Bernanos dismissed autonomous subjects and abstract notions such as freedom of conscience and thus an interiority shaped by the modus operandi of the Enlightenment. In so doing, he directed himself singularly toward the divine. The turn to the "human" often involved a type of phenomenologically or existentially inspired turn in terms of a fruitful engagement with the anguish intrinsic to human existence and thus the need for salvation. Spiritual nourishment could be found in the mystery of anguish in the recognition that religious traditions—Catholicism, Islam, and Judaism—all shared in suffering and compassion as the root of human nature (O'Mahony). Suffering was fundamental to Simone Weil's life and thought; to the Greeks she owed her sense of the wretchedness of existence and the tragic destiny of the just person (de Lussy). A heightened sensitivity to despair and human solitude brought a sense of urgency and prompted a development of "coping strategies" for many Catholic intellectuals in the renewal of their faith. For example, Grenier considered the human as "a defeat accepted" and artistic creation his "means of coming to terms with the solitude of the islands," while Moore's women religious were confronted with their own "life boundaries" in the face of the trauma of war and thus turned to mystical texts to cope with the painful recognition of their finitude.

Renewal

Many of the Catholic actors featured in this volume were converts to the faith. Their respective journeys back to Catholicism were often painful, their itineraries often heterodox, nonlinear, and innovative. Being a convert allowed for a questioning of the a priori heritage and inherited beliefs. By ridding oneself of the shackles of uniformity and conformity and by crossing boundaries, new forms of renewal of the faith could be nurtured. This could include a space for "neo-Catholicism," for "Protestant Catholicism," and for an engagement for all citizens regardless of social status and freed from the confines of membership of particular parties. The most obvious exemplar of the development of new renewals of the faith might be recognized in the *ressourcement* movement, otherwise known as *nouvelle théologie* (new theology). Reengagement of theology with history and with the concreteness of reality was one of the key imperatives of nouvelle théologie, which entailed a critique of the orderly rationalism and conceptual framework of neo-scholasticism, the dominant theology of the church up until the Second World War. Nouvelle théologie, broadly speaking, involved a turn to the scriptural sources of faith, a reintegration of nature and the supernatural, and an approach to tradition as organically developing in history. The distinction between neo-scholasticism and nouvelle théologie has been articulated as the difference between "system thinking" and "reality thinking."[44] For those inclined toward "reality thinking," "revelation was in the first instance a living reality," and "faith was a reality made concrete."[45] There was a transition from a closed, defensive, and conceptual theological structure of the late nineteenth century to an open, assertive commitment to the "authenticity" of Christian faith on a human level. Many of the contributions to this volume engage with nouvelle théologie, some implicitly and others explicitly, some in terms of a "prehistory" of developments, others in terms of direct interrogation of the movement.

The freedom of expression, of conscience, and of research propagated through the efforts of the CCIF in the postwar years had its corollaries and antecedents. For example, the postwar "New Catholic Left" was flexible and fluid in its approach to engagement in terms of entertaining exchange with Marxists and the existential avant-garde (Dunlop). Dialogue with difference and the "other" was instrumental in reconfigurations of faith, whether in terms of engagement with the Jewish roots of Catholicism and retelling or rediscovering a Christian history that salvaged it from complicity in violence (Moore) or in terms of reimagining or mediating the relation between religions—Catholicism and Islam—which could shine a direct light on the development of the church's ecclesial self-understanding (O'Mahony).

Summaries of Chapters

All contributions to the volume, which include literary and cultural commentary, political analysis, and theological and philosophical reflection, embedded within their historical contexts, are integrated around the dual themes of renewal and engagement. They illuminate, in their own particular ways, the conditions, factors, and concrete possibilities for revivifying Catholicism and taking seriously the idea of humankind being God's mirror in the world. They refine our understanding of the forms and contents of Catholic engagement and, indeed, what is thinkable as "engagement." While some of the contributors focus on discrete moments, a particular decade, or specific individuals, others take a broader view. These different approaches allow for close comparative readings of chapters with respect to particular personalities, debates, or ideas and for broader contextualization of key themes throughout the twentieth century.

Kelly's chapter opens appropriately with a conspicuous treatment of the development of a new concept of engagement forged by Catholic intellectuals in the crucible of debates and experiments of the 1930s. The "crisis of civilization" of this decade informed the development of a new humanist concept of engagement, which he traces through the voices of Jacques Maritain, Gabriel Marcel, and Emmanuel Mounier. Kelly's contribution clearly shows the importance of the 1930s as a precursor to, or the seedbed of, a broader, inclusive, and flexible means of engagement, which emerges afresh today as strikingly effective. Gifford's placement next to Kelly is propitious in his framing of the contours of a Catholic faith in transition from an alternative, veiled standpoint. He leads us through an experience on the threshold of "divine things," not by way of an orthodox Catholic but rather by way of the revelatory agnosticism of Paul Valéry, who acts as a witness to the "sea change" produced by the "forces of modernity," that broad crisis of culture and civilization, of which the "hidden nerve point" is the declared or so-called death of God. Sharing the same mind-space as a modulating Catholicism taking shape in the 1930s, Valéry provides sharp insight, precisely by virtue of his position outside of the fold, into the themes and directions taking shape within the womb of French Catholic tradition.

Both an "insider" and an "outsider," the figure of Simone Weil illuminates the possibilities of Catholicism through her moving search for a form of engagement congruent with her life and thought. De Lussy explores Weil's inner transformation and the tensions at play that brought her tantalizingly close to Catholicism. From Weil's struggles with the rigidity and "totalitarian" jurisdiction of the magisterium and her absolute commitment to free thought to her Hellenic route to religious awareness and refusal of the distinction between the profane and the sacred, de Lussy highlights how the heterodox and modernist Weil called forth a Christianity that was embodied, open to the world, and fully *engagé*. Weil invites us to recognize the possible fault lines along which Catholicism could be renewed and reenergized.

Garfitt and Davies take on engagement and renewal through the intimate excavation of personalities whose anguished negotiations of intellectual identity, it could be suggested, were anticipatory of and reflective of the equivocal nature of engagement and, specifically, the turn toward the "human" therein. Garfitt's portrait of Jean Grenier, a sympathizer with the Catholic tradition, dissects the problem of ideological certainties and commitments in the project of intellectual engagement through his 1938 volume, *Essai sur l'esprit d'orthodoxie* (*Essay on the Spirit of Orthodoxy*). Garfitt traces the intersections of Grenier's concern for the "human" and his rejection of programmatic orthodoxies of the modern world, whether in their political or religious forms. As an example of a "pure intellectual in a time of upheaval, who yearns to be free to explore the furthest limits of philosophical, religious, literary and artistic thought," Grenier perceived keenly the danger of ideological commitment as "losing the ability to think."

Davies's account of Charles Du Bos, literary critic and convert, addresses his notion and practice of sincerity, a sincerity that rendered visible the often painful mediation between the temporal and spiritual self, between ecclesiastical orthodoxy and the autonomy of the individual and writer. The experiential, aesthetic-ethical nature of Du Bos's faith often placed him at odds with the conceptual thinking of interwar neo-Thomism, and informed his particular fidelity to sincerity, which was manifest in his spiritual life, his literary work, and which was arguably capable of underpinning pluralist engagement. The fundamental tension between Du Bos's quest for authenticity and the irreducibility of the real to intellectual concepts, and a dutiful education in neo-Thomism, is suggestive of the fruitful reconfigurations of faith and intellectual engagement born of tensions of interwar French Catholicism.

Taking a step further toward the implications of mutual interactions between cultural enterprises and political commitments in Catholic intellectual culture, Schloesser interrogates the ways in which cultural-theological realignments could be reflective, and constitutive of, new typologies of engagement in response to the human and spiritual demands of the historical moment. Schloesser explores how the moment of Olivier Messiaen's turn from the "mystical" to the "theological," a shift Schloesser identifies around 1935, can be understood in terms of Messaien's maintenance of the "marvelous" in an "ordered" fashion amidst the political demands of the time. Third-way politics pushed for spiritual rehabilitation and a "new order" beyond the Left and Right in the 1930s and were inflected by Messiaen's commitment to music that served the concrete, stable order of Catholic dogma, by way of Thomas Aquinas, rather than the "vagaries of the mystical."

Sudlow's concerns with Catholic engagement emerge in the form of a critical reading of Georges Bernanos, a reading which raises fundamental questions about the relationship between aesthetics and politics: the heuristic devices and tropes Bernanos harnesses for his polemical works open up what is thinkable for Catholic engagement and renewal. Whilst acknowledging Bernanos's stylistic modernity, Sudlow argues that the critical consensus about the modernity of his political writings is too dependent on hegemonic social and cultural theories. Harnessing the theoretical work of René Girard to read Bernanos's *Scandale de la vérité* (*The Scandal of Truth*), *Nous autres Français* (*We French*) and *Les enfants humiliés* (*The Humiliated Children*) Sudlow highlights Bernanos's fundamental preoccupation with desire, possessiveness, imitation, and violence, and myth. In this light, Bernanos's challenge to the modern world is rooted not in an alternative view of modernity, but in a commitment to the timeless values of truth and innocence.

The chapters by Moore, Dunlop and O'Mahony chart the development of Catholic engagement in terms of the heterodox, the progressive and eclectic pluralism, and interreligious nourishment and dialogue. Moore's exploration of the heterodoxy of the "turn to the sources" (*ressourcement*) project casts a critical light on how the traditionally marginalized and 'other' could be constitutive of new forms of Catholic intellectual engagement and renewal. Moore delves into the intuitive and imaginative engagements of female religious French intellectuals—principally the medievalists Marie-Thérèse d'Alverny and Marie-Madeleine Davy, and the memoirist Raïssa Maritain (wife of Jacques)—who introduced into the mix of *ressourcement* an interpretation of Christianity stressing its complex, heterodox nature, including its dialogue with Judaism and Islam, the possibilities of re-configuring its history, and how it was an emotional inflection and response to political trauma.

Dunlop and O'Mahony too take on the nature of the evolution of Catholic engagement across the interwar through to the postwar years, each by illuminating particular tensions, formations and effects of engagement in terms of Catholic faith and the church's self-understanding. Dunlop explores the twists and turns of Catholic identity through the engagements and faith of those involved in the Québécois Catholic journal *La Relève*. Dunlop's account illustrates something of Kelly's "ondoyant" engagement in practice: the journal had its roots in traditionalist French Canadian nationalism and militant social Catholicism and wielded a disdain for Western cultural degeneration, but the emphasis gradually shifted from nationalism to personalism and the "new Christian humanism" in the later 1930s and early 1940s, and into the postwar period, *relèvistes* championed a greater openness of eclectic pluralism and progressivism, which would play a prominent role in Quebec's Quiet Revolution from the 1950s into the 1970s. These shifts, Dunlop maintains, reflect at once the destabilizing of traditional markers of Catholic engagement and faith and their rejuvenation.

O'Mahony investigates interreligious dialogue, and the rich possibilities of religious renewal and political engagement this entailed, through the figure of the French Catholic convert and Islamic scholar Louis Massignon. A central figure in Catholic intellectual culture and the Arab world from the interwar years through to Vatican II, Massignon was a formative influence by virtue of his multiple roles and experiences; soldier-diplomat, leading scholar of Islam and the Muslim World, politically engaged, religious activist and Greek Catholic priest. Massignon sought to create new thought within Christian theology on Islam and wished to find a space for Muslim belief within Catholicism. Massignon's interreligious dialogue was personal—his studies of Islamic mysticism contributed to, and were informed by, his own spiritual journey; it was ecclesiastical—he opened up pathways between the church and Islam; and it was political—he played a critical role in Muslim policy-making in France.

With the exception of Massignon, the Catholic intellectuals discussed here were not ordained priests or religious professionals (Massignon was a married Greek Catholic priest, ordained in the Melkite Church in 1950). Major figures of the ressourcement or nouvelle théologie movement, such as Gilson, Chenu, Congar and de Lubac, are mentioned infrequently, although Urs von Balthasar has been a useful reference point. Our focus has been upon lay people, creative artists, academics, thinkers—all of them thinkers—who were faced with the practical problems of understanding and expressing their faith in a rapidly-changing modern world. They were not so much concerned with exploring the possibility and nature of Christian philosophy or Christian art,[46] but rather with identifying and defending those values that corresponded to, and would sustain, a true humanity in the full Christian sense of the word, understood in Balthasar's terms as God's mirror in the world. They often engaged just as much with non-Christian figures like Marx, Gide, or Heidegger as they did with Aquinas or his modern interpreters, and the sources and resources (both of which are implied in the term "ressourcement") which they exploited were rich and varied. They resisted narrow party-political definitions of orthodoxy, although many of them can in fact be considered as champions of Catholic orthodoxy.

Pascal famously called a human being a "roseau pensant," a thinking reed. The intellectuals studied here were concerned, each in their own way, to be a thinking mirror, reflecting the Gestalt of God (again Balthasar's expression: the original title of *Seeing the Form* was *Schau der Gestalt*). In an age when the "concrete" was unavoidable and yet at the same time always just out of reach (according to Wahl), the temptation was to adopt a form of engagement that paid insufficient attention to transcendent values. As Jean Rimaud noted in his review of Grenier's *Essai sur l'esprit d'orthodoxie,* "what one calls engaged thought often ceases to be thought." The subjects of the following chapters may not always have found perfect solutions, but they engaged honestly, faithfully and productively with real issues, and their experience repays study, not only with respect to a particular historical period of Catholic renewal, but in terms of the perennial vocation of the Christian embodied consciousness.

1 "Catholicisme ondoyant": Catholic Intellectual Engagement and the Crisis of Civilization in the 1930s

Michael Kelly

The Emergence of Catholic Intellectuals

Catholics have often struggled to achieve recognition in France as legitimate intellectuals with a distinctive voice and valuable ideas to contribute. To a large extent, this is a result of the difficult interface between religion and politics. However, key Catholic figures in the interwar period worked with great tenacity to address the problems and dilemmas that rendered the interface difficult, especially the tensions between the spiritual and temporal realms and between a long-term conception of civilization and short-term political objectives. In the process they developed a complex but workable concept of engagement, based on a notion of the human person, which provided a flexible and humanistic basis for political commitment. Primarily because of this flexibility of commitment some political actors considered Catholics to be *ondoyant*: inconstant, volatile, or ambiguous in their alliances. The capacity to sway in different directions was, however, integral to the concept of engagement. This chapter examines the circumstances in which the concept was developed to confront the crisis of the 1930s. It suggests that, in contrast to the later Sartrean model, this Catholic humanist concept of engagement is capable of surviving the crisis of the intellectual in France and offering viable foundations for a sustainable conception of citizenship.

The emergence of Catholic intellectuals in France has been illuminated by recent debates on the decline of the French intellectual. Toward the end of the twentieth century, the French model of the intellectual entered what appeared to be a terminal crisis. The crisis was at times elegiac and at times bitterly acrimonious, and it took place almost entirely within the public domain. From the 1980s onward, the deaths of major figures like Sartre, Beauvoir, Barthes, and Foucault were accompanied by gloomy musings on whether this marked the end of an era. The century ended with a series of dismal obituaries for the familiar figure of the French intellectual as such.[1] For various reasons, intellectuals appeared to have lost the status and authority accorded to them by earlier generations. But just as Hegel's owl of Minerva "spreads its wings only with the falling of the dusk," bringing understanding as the day is ending, so efforts were deployed to understand where the figure of the intellectual had come from and why it now appeared to be in decline.[2] As a result, the history of the intellectual became a major growth area in historical scholarship at the turn of the century, just as the subject under investigation was passing into memory.[3]

As part of these debates, an anxious discussion took place about the distinctive nature and status of Catholic intellectuals.[4] It was sparked by an article in *Le monde* about their apparent silence in recent years, and a number of contemporary issues were cited to account for it. The issues included disagreements with the Vatican on social policy in areas such as contraception, divorce, and homosexuality. They included dissensions on Rome's generally conservative political orientation, disquiet over the authoritarian governance of the church, and dismay at the apparently deliberate deterioration of relations with other religions. The result of these disagreements, it was argued, was that some Catholics were silent because they did not wish to disagree publicly with the church's teaching, and others were silent because they did not wish to articulate Catholic views that ran counter to the mainstream views of the liberal intelligentsia. Although these arguments carried some conviction, a number of cultural historians suggested that the dilemmas facing Catholic intellectuals in the 1990s were already inherent in the difficulties Catholics had experienced in gaining recognition as intellectuals earlier in the century.[5]

By common consent, Catholic intellectuals emerged into public view during the interwar period, which, with the benefit of hindsight, now appears as a golden age of French intellectuals. Jacques Julliard and Étienne Fouilloux argued that the "late" arrival of Catholic intellectuals stemmed from a combination of blockages in France and in the church.[6] In the specific French context, Catholics were unwilling to associate themselves with the strongly secularist positions adopted by the leading progressive figures, to whom the name "intellectual" was originally applied as a pejorative term. This was the inheritance of the "two Frances" approach, in which Catholicism was "a general portmanteau of the past: Monarchism, Bonapartism and Counter-Revolution."[7] The republic, on the other hand, represented progress and the achievements of the French Revolution. The Dreyfus case has been generally accepted as the founding moment for French intellectuals, and to a large extent the Dreyfusards were aligned against the great institutions of France: the state, the army, and the church. In these polarized circumstances it was difficult for Catholics to associate themselves with the *intellectuels*. The difficulty was compounded by the fact that the most prominent Catholic writers took an anti-Dreyfusard stance, which was adopted, for example, by all members of the Académie française, with the sole exception of Anatole France.

Catholics were also blocked from acting as intellectuals by the church. Rome did not at this time grant intellectual authority to lay Catholics to speak on behalf of the community of believers. This was still very firmly the pastoral role of the clergy. The role of the laity was to accept clerical guidance and not to develop their own independent views. The force of this prohibition was demonstrated by successive papal actions against modernism and democracy and by the condemnation of even modestly reformist initiatives, such as Marc Sangnier's *Sillon* (The Furrow) movement, which was banned in 1910 for its involvement in democratic politics. As a result, most educated Catholics tended not to take a deep interest in issues of social doctrine. Instead, they focused their efforts on approved charitable works rather than on the principles behind social intervention.

A significant exception to this pattern was to be found in people who had come to the church later in their life. Not surprisingly, the most prominent Catholic intellectuals of the early part of the century were in fact converts.[8] Writers like Jacques Maritain, Gabriel Marcel, Charles Péguy, and Paul Claudel were strongly drawn by the intellectual attraction of Catholic ideas and did not take them for granted in a way that those who had grown up in a Catholic milieu were likely to do. These converts subsequently provided a spur to the younger generation of Catholics to explore the intellectual inheritance of the church and to engage in public debate in their capacity as Christians.

The decisive event in drawing Catholics into the role of public intellectuals during the interwar period was a breakdown of the long-standing identification of Catholicism with right-wing politics. The most important representatives for Catholics on the right were anti-Republican groupings, among whom the monarchist movement, Action française, led by Charles Maurras, emerged as the most influential force in the aftermath of the Dreyfus case.[9] As its influence increased after the Great War, some members of the church hierarchy became concerned that its political leadership of French Catholics might be replacing their own spiritual leadership. Pope Pius XI published a condemnation of the Action française movement in 1926, placing its newspaper and Maurras's works on the church's Index of Prohibited Books, which Catholics were forbidden to read. Shortly afterward, priests were instructed to withhold the sacraments from any Catholics who refused to dissociate themselves from the movement. In the furor that followed, many prominent Catholics decided to break publicly with it and explore different directions.

At issue was the relationship between religion and politics. Based on the demography of its supporters, Action française increasingly presented itself as the political representative of France's Catholic community. The Vatican's condemnation sprang from its anxiety that the temporal authority of the movement was intruding on the spiritual authority of the church. This was symbolized by Maurras's often-repeated slogan, "politique d'abord" (politics first). The Vatican interpreted this to mean not only that political action was more urgent than religious observance but also that political leadership should take precedence over religious guidance in the lives of practicing Catholics. This was not acceptable to the church.

The Catholic-monarchist alliance known as *l'intégrisme* (fundamentalism) was irrevocably fractured, opening up a space within which the relationship between Catholicism and politics could be openly debated and therefore a space in which the Catholic laity could begin to function as public intellectuals. The most energetic of the Catholic intellectuals newly freed from political bondage was undoubtedly Jacques Maritain. A friend of Maurras and a professor of philosophy at the Institut catholique in Paris, Maritain at first attempted to mediate between the movement and the Vatican but rapidly moved to accept the pope's ruling and undertook to explore its consequences. In doing so, he faced the challenge of providing a philosophical grounding for political action rooted in Christian doctrine. The first formulation of this was presented in his book *Primauté du spirituel*, translated as *The Things That Are Not Caesa's.*[10] In it he endorsed the pope's action and reversed Maurras's slogan by affirming the primacy of the spiritual, that spiritual authority took precedence over political action. However, this reversal did not mean that spiritual leaders should dictate specific political programs, which would turn the church into a political party. Rather, the church should establish a framework of spiritual guidance on which the faithful could draw. In this way, Maritain introduced an explicit but indirect relationship between faith and politics, one that left the individual a degree of leeway. Previously, the main choice for Catholics was whether to involve themselves in political activity of a right-wing conservative nature. But now, he argued, the choice was both whether to become involved and what kind of politics to be involved in. In recognizing that people should be able to make their own political choices, Maritain provided a starting point for a concept of engagement. In the short term, this was a largely theoretical shift that did not produce any major political changes. The implications became clear only in the crisis of the 1930s, when Catholic intellectuals were compelled to make urgent political choices.

A Crisis of Civilization

Most historians of the interwar period agree that the decade before the Second World War was a time of crisis, especially in France. Several have in fact taken crisis to be the defining feature of the period.[11] In the French context, there was a widespread agreement that the crisis was both economic and political. The economic crisis was clear for all to see. The French economy was at a peak of prosperity in 1929 at the moment of the Wall Street crash, and it was two years before the full impact of recession was felt. When it came, the economic crisis proved deep and enduring, bringing with it a trail of unemployment, industrial action, bankruptcies, and destitution in town and country.[12] France did not recover to its previous level of economic activity until the postwar boom of the 1950s.

For France, the economic collapse coincided with a series of political crises. The final decade of the Third Republic was characterized by a fragmentation of the center parties, which had governed for the previous fifty years. Their decline was accompanied by an upsurge of movements of the extreme Right and Left, which sparked a rise in confrontations in the city streets. Protests were fueled by growing public revulsion against endemic corruption, symbolized by the Stavisky affair, a large-scale financial scandal involving the issue of fraudulent bonds, with connections to leading government politicians, and the death of the perpetrator apparently while in police custody. It triggered a series of mass demonstrations, especially in Paris, in February 1934. In foreign policy, France floundered in face of the rise of Nazism and Fascism in Europe and the rise of national liberation movements in its colonies. Taken together, these developments contributed to a general sense of crisis, which was widely shared in France and has been amply echoed in the historiography of the period.[13] The rapid succession of major political crises during the 1930s is one of the reasons that writings of the period must be read in the context of their date, especially after the international turning point of Hitler's rise to power in 1933 and the national turning point of the riots of February 1934.

So serious was the economic and political crisis that many French intellectuals at the time believed that it must be of much more fundamental import. For them it betokened a crisis of civilization that called into question the beliefs and values on which European civilization was based. This was not a new fear since the notion had come to prominence in the aftermath of the Great War. Otto Spengler's *Decline of the West*, first published between 1918 and 1923, was the classic exposition, among many others across the continent.[14] In France it was Paul Valéry who articulated the sense of fragility that pervaded European culture, with his essay of 1919 on the crisis of the mind, which memorably began with this diagnosis: "We civilizations now know that we are mortal."[15] Europe, he suggested, might face the same fate as the ancient civilizations of Elam, Nineveh, and Babylon. As the economic recovery of the 1920s took hold in France, these portents of decline and fall were largely set aside, and the intellectuals of the 1920s began to take a more optimistic view. However, with the onset of the international economic crisis at the end of that decade, conditions deteriorated in the early 1930s, and many intellectuals denounced the political, social, and economic conditions that had brought on the crisis, once again arguing that the problems were more fundamental and more long term.

This view was especially attractive to the younger generation, who had been too young to fight in the Great War. For Marxist intellectuals like Paul Nizan and Henri Lefebvre, the 1930s were marked by a crisis of capitalism, one of the recurrent crises inherent in the capitalist mode of production.[16] For Fascist intellectuals like Drieu la

Rochelle and Bertrand de Jouvenel, it was a crisis of the modern world, caused mainly by the liberal democracy that had led the West into decadence.[17] For Christian intellectuals like Emmanuel Mounier and Paul Ricoeur, it was a crisis of civilization, brought about primarily by the abandonment of spiritual values.[18] There were clear points of intersection between these different analyses. They were sufficiently evident to persuade *La Nouvelle revue française* to publish a "cahier de revendications" (list of demands) in late 1932, edited by the Swiss literary critic Denis de Rougemont.[19] In it, young intellectuals presented their critique of the contemporary world from a number of ideological perspectives, ranging politically from the Far Right to the Far Left, and through a variety of centrist or noncommitted positions. De Rougemont was at pains to draw out their shared refusals alongside the differing remedies they proposed. However, after the review was published, several of the contributors found that they had been presented in embarrassing company and dissociated themselves from the exercise.[20] This amalgamation proved particularly uncomfortable for the Catholic thinkers, who were courted at different times during the period by leading representatives of both Marxism and Fascism.

Commentators have subsequently suggested that a degree of commonality existed between the intellectuals of this generation, based on their desire to reject the inherited world order and search for radical solutions to its problems.[21] This was clearly the case in 1932, though of course they all had different views of what those problems were. Broadly, for the Left, the key problem was the ownership of the means of production, whereas for the Right, it was a problem of leadership. For the young generation of Catholics, it was a problem of beliefs and values. What these young intellectuals did have in common was a concern to translate their very broad diagnosis into actions that could produce change in the basic structures of Western society. For the Left and the Right, their program of action was already largely sketched out and could be expressed as a social and political revolution even if they had radically different conceptions of the form it should take. The Catholics, on the other hand, had no distinct program of action to which they could adhere.

Certainly, there were authoritative sources for the analysis of social issues. Catholics could refer to papal encyclicals on pastoral doctrine, particularly Leo XIII's influential *Rerum novarum* (1891) and Pius XI's recent *Quadragesimo anno* (1931). In fact, both of these encyclicals were regarded with suspicion on the political Right. Despite their condemnation of socialism and prescription of very moderate social change, both encyclicals offered a degree of recognition to the criticisms of capitalist society made by socialists. *Rerum novarum* specifically addressed the "condition of labor," and its detailed consideration of working conditions contained some sharp rebukes to employers. For example, it suggested, "The first concern of all is to save the poor workers from the cruelty of grasping speculators, who use human beings as mere instruments for making money."[22] The reaffirmation of Leo's strictures by Pius XI was not widely welcomed in conservative circles since he agreed that "the conditions of social and economic life are such that vast multitudes of men can only with great difficulty pay attention to . . . their eternal salvation."[23] The "ruin of souls" was identified as the chief disorder of the modern world; a "moral renovation" was needed to address it; and the role of the laity was essential to "reconstructing the social order." *Quadragesimo anno* confirmed the value of the different social action programs and charitable initiatives that had been established in the late 1920s. It also confirmed some of the political prohibitions, especially against the more extreme forms of socialism. But it did not provide a blueprint for translating social teachings into political action. Although it emphasized the need for bishops to train, support, and respect the laity, it did not offer a concept of political engagement beyond the expectation that lay activists should strive to implement Catholic teachings in their various activities. To a large extent, this may be a reflection of the nature of encyclicals. As a general rule, these papal letters were addressed to the senior clergy: "All Patriarchs, Primates, Archbishops and Bishops of the Catholic World." *Quadragesimo anno* was innovatory in extending the greeting to "All the Faithful of the Catholic World," though the mode of address is still to a clerical audience.[24] As a result, the advice was specifically destined for the pastoral leaders of the church, recommending how they should guide the faithful. It was not framed to address the concerns of lay Catholics, whose context would be substantially different. There was therefore an unfulfilled need for laypeople to be able to address their own concerns within a coherent framework for decision making. In other words, a concept of engagement was needed.

A Concept of Engagement

In order to develop a workable framework of guidance for lay decision making, it was necessary to develop Maritain's assertion of the "primacy of the spiritual," which had opened the door to engagement. Maritain's own thinking was summarized in his book *Humanisme intégral* (1936), translated as *True Humanism*, which sought to define a new relationship between the Christian and the world.[25] Writing against the backdrop of the upsurge of left-wing alliances that led to the Popular Front government, he drew a sharp distinction between the spiritual and the temporal, suggesting that it was a principal tenet of Christianity that religion, culture, and civilization were separate realms. Drawing on the teachings of Saint Thomas Aquinas, on whom he was a considerable authority, Maritain argued that religion has essentially spiritual aims, whereas culture and civilization have temporal purposes. Clearly, the spiritual can illuminate and nourish the temporal, but in the earthly realm, the watchword was "render unto Caesar the things that are Caesar's." This clear distinction was, in his view, "a major advance for freedom of the spirit."[26] He emphasized that the role of the Christian in the temporal realm was not to turn it into the kingdom of God but to make it "the place for a truly and fully human life on earth."[27] This formulation marks a fundamental shift, which was pioneered in the early 1930s by Maritain, by the "personalist" group of Catholic thinkers, led by Mounier, and by the Catholic existentialist Gabriel Marcel. In brief, it took the concept of the soul out of social doctrine and replaced it with the concept of the human person. The aim of the Christian in the world was not to save souls, they held, since this belonged strictly to the spiritual realm. The aim was rather to fulfill the potential of the whole human person, enabling all people to live fulfilling lives on earth. The magnitude of this shift was not fully recognized at this period but gradually entered the mainstream of Catholic thinking and formed a central theme of the major encyclicals of Pope John XXIII and the Second Vatican Council. The encyclical *Pacem in terris* (1963), for example, declared that "every man is a person with rights and duties."[28]

The task of creating a concept of engagement based on the human person was complex, and many religious thinkers contributed to the process, in which Maritain, Mounier, and Marcel played major roles. Somewhat controversially for the period, both Maritain and Mounier accepted that their conception was humanist in the sense of putting the human person at the center of temporal concern but not in the sense of diminishing the importance of a transcendent spiritual realm. Maritain argued forcefully that "humanism is inseparable from civilization or from culture, these two terms being in fact synonymous."[29] In this sense, humanism was the philosophical stance that took seriously the fundamental values of civilization.

Maritain himself was careful to avoid any specific political commitment, though he had a number of proposals on long- and short-term aims that might be set and the means that might be adopted. In theoretical terms, he advocated a politics of saintliness, which would sanctify life in the profane sphere. In practical terms of the situation in the mid-1930s, his most crucial contribution was to draw a sharp distinction between two types of Christian political activity: "There is a very clear distinction to be drawn between the notion of political activity *carried out* (and legitimately carried out) *by Christians*, and the notion of political activity (falling within one or other school of thought) which is *of Christian inspiration*."[30]

Christians, he argued, might be expected to take part in a wide range of activities that are not unique to them and about which other Christians might have different judgments. In doing so, they act *en chrétien* since they are known to be Christians, but their choices commit only themselves. On the other hand, they may also participate in activities inspired by Christianity, working *en tant que chrétiens*, where more stringent spiritual requirements may apply since they are acting as Christian representatives and their actions implicate the church more broadly.[31] With this distinction in mind, he asserted the right and duty of individual Christians to engage in secular politics of different types following their own best judgment of how their endeavors would contribute to humanizing the world. On several occasions, this distinction was used by French Catholic activists to assert their right to work within organizations, particularly on the left and in the labor movement, where they would necessarily cooperate with non-Christians. In effect, it ensured permission for Catholics to participate in the Popular Front movement and therefore to enter mainstream political life.

The challenge for the intellectuals was therefore not so much to develop a new program as to situate themselves in relation to the available programs and negotiate a relationship with them. This was a principal source for the refusal of many Catholics to express a commitment to either of the polarized sides in French politics. The Right, from which the new generation was seeking to distance itself, was the traditional location of conservative Catholics. But the Left was largely terra incognita, except to the extent that it was traditionally hostile to Catholics. It was an unenviable choice, one that many refused to make. Their refusal was often expressed in the phrase "ni droite, ni gauche" (neither Right nor Left), which has had a checkered career in France. At one end of the spectrum, it was adopted by the nonconformists of the 1930s' *ordre nouveau* movement and in technocratic circles, expressing a critique of democracy and a withdrawal from parliamentary politics.[32] At the other end of the spectrum, it became a slogan for a range of Far Right movements, including Fascist groups, which sought to overthrow the Republican regime.[33]

In between were a range of Catholic-inspired groups that were attempting to find an elusive "third way" between the traditional Right and Left. Emmanuel Mounier and the review *Esprit* set out to develop a philosophy that would provide a theoretical framework for these groups and in particular for a newly founded group, La troisième force, led by lawyer Georges Izard and medieval historian André Déléage. In this context, the slogan "neither Right nor Left" might be linked to a wide range of political positions, but for Catholics in particular, it reflected primarily a sense of exploration, without at this stage knowing precisely where that might lead.

Mounier's approach was laid out in the first issue of *Esprit* in October 1932, where he presented a programmatic analysis, whose title, "Remake the Renaissance," indicated the civilization scope of the crisis.[34] He reiterated Maritain's assertion of the "primacy of the spiritual," and at first glance, his analysis was broadly compatible with the approach of "neither Right nor Left": "Right, Left, we should write the history of this universal system of bookkeeping and show how a diffuse movement of opinion is slowly forcing all spiritual values into one of the two columns. There are Right-wing virtues: honor, moderation, prudence, and Left-wing virtues like boldness and peace."[35]

Virtues and vices existed on both sides, he argued, and each side had taken advantage of its monopoly of particular virtues to justify the corresponding vice. So the love of one's own land and history was used on the right to justify nationalist fanaticism, while the desire for justice was combined on the left with antispiritual metaphysics. This has since been taken by commentators, like the late Tony Judt, to indicate "a curse upon both houses," balancing any criticism of the Left with criticism of the Right.[36] However, this was not Mounier's purpose since he concluded that "for three quarters of its life, the spirit was domiciled on the Right and lived on the Left."[37] He suggested that spiritual values should be sought where they actually lived, on the left, rather than at their official residence, on the right. His priority was therefore to dissociate the spiritual from the reactionary. He argued that the spiritual had been monopolized by the Right for too long and that the result had been to mask the real aims of conservatism, to distract the Left from identifying its real opponents and to starve the spiritual forces of dynamism and innovation.

The solution, in Mounier's view, must be to prepare a moral revolution. This concept of revolution was an explicit echo of Charles Péguy, who declared that "the revolution will be moral or else it will not be."[38] At the limit, for Péguy, any revolution had to be primarily moral. Mounier also implicitly echoed Pius XI's call for a fundamental moral renovation. However, he was careful not to place himself explicitly under the authority of the pope since his purpose was to take a step beyond Maritain's focus on the Christian in the world and offer a more inclusive approach. His aim was to provide a framework that would have relevance to a wider audience than just Catholics and would allow Catholics to engage with non-Catholics and even nonbelievers in political action on the left. In so doing he began to develop a notion of engagement that was available to all people.

In the context of the period, Mounier's position had a particular novelty in linking political action with personal choice, where previously it would have been associated with religious obligation or collective interest. France was accustomed to seeing politics in terms of confrontations between Catholic and secular forces or between the bourgeoisie and the working class. The duties of engagement would then fall "naturally" according to the religious or social position occupied by an individual. However, Mounier's step of basing engagement in the moral choices of the human person meant that the first task of (moral) revolutionaries should be to transform themselves, transfiguring their own lives in the light of eternal values rather than simply following the options of their peer group. Consistent with this, he argued that the appropriate forms of action should above all show a personal example and bear witness to the truth. The aim of all commitment, Mounier argued, should be to promote the dignity of the human person and to build a society composed of communities in which persons may flourish and achieve spiritual growth.

In broad outline, Mounier's proposal to remake the Renaissance provided a framework for the future political positions of the influential personalist movement in France. However, in the short term, it left a lot of questions hanging, not least the question of who might implement the personalist revolution in practice. He rapidly discovered that the shifting configurations of political movements were driven more by pragmatic considerations of organization and electoral impact than by doctrinal inspirations. At a very early stage, *Esprit* parted company with the original *Troisième force* grouping with which it had been linked. Most members of the grouping had little appetite for doctrinal reflection and were much more preoccupied by alliances and relationships with other compatible groups on the center left. *Esprit* continued under Mounier's direction to explore the philosophical underpinnings of political engagement, but within a year and a half, the rapidly changing political environment plunged the journal into urgent and difficult political choices, which gave a sharper edge to the issue of engagement and put *Esprit*'s principles to the test in practice.

Events did not allow much time for adjustment as the political crisis of the Third Republic deepened and became more polarized. The turning point came with the confrontations of 6 February 1934, when a protest march turned into an abortive attempt to overthrow the National Assembly and ended in several deaths. This was followed by demonstrations and counterdemonstrations which crystallized into two opposing sides, defining themselves variously as republican and antirepublican, democratic and antidemocratic, Left and Right. In this increasingly polarized context, Catholic intellectuals were compelled to elaborate a concept of engagement that could provide a coherent framework for urgent political choices while at the same time affirming more fundamental long-term beliefs and moral values.

In the aftermath of February 1934, Mounier reworked his theory of engagement. He argued that engagement was both a fundamental dimension of the human person and a basic duty: "[A] person proves themselves by their engagements."[39] He therefore emphasized the need to be aware of the embodied nature of the human person, pointing out that all people are involved in the "established disorder" of the world regardless of whether they like it. People should not seek to evade their responsibility, he argued, but should attempt to align all of their thoughts and actions in a coherent direction. In the same way, he suggested, eternal values are embodied in material forms, and the ways of protecting them must change as the material world changes, with the implication that the duty of commitment to change is always accompanied by a duty of fidelity to values. Ultimately, he argued, it is more important that people bear witness to their fidelities than that they achieve success in particular ventures. As a result, he proposed "a technique of spiritual means," drawing from Maritain's politics of saintliness and strongly influenced by the example of Gandi's campaign of nonviolent action.[40] His aim was to define the kinds of action that would be robust and at the same time spiritually acceptable and to suggest ways of reconciling purity of means with efficacy in achieving one's ends.

Mounier's formulation was designed to appeal not only to a Catholic readership but also to a wider range of sympathizers. It was intended to assist Catholics and others to work together in the broad popular movements of the Left, which led to the election of the Popular Front government of 1936. In practice, his ideas percolated through several Catholic groups, which merged and blended with other centrist and center-left formations and played a minor role in the Popular Front. In the long term, they entered the mainstream of French political debate and offered a transferable model for a wide range of political and social involvements.

No doubt, many Catholics were not adept in exercising their newfound political options and had yet to find their sea legs in the choppy waters of the early 1930s. The rapid political changes and the complexity of major issues led Catholics to shift their alliances and allegiances, often to the annoyance of their partners. The criticism was recognized by Emmanuel Mounier in an essay of 1937, where he noted that Benito Mussolini had reportedly been exasperated by the lukewarm support offered by some leading Catholics and had given a stern warning to "a certain wavering Catholicism with which, one day or another, we shall settle accounts in our own way."[41] Mounier pointed out that Catholics might well share a political position with a particular party on one issue but be opposed to them on others. Moreover, he believed it was important not to be deterred by the fear of being tarred with a single brush but at the same time to be vigilant against conniving with policies that they could not publicly endorse. In particular, Mounier recognized that Catholic participation with left-wing movements could be seen by those movements as less than wholehearted, while at the same time depicted by opponents as supporting a program of atheistic communism, which the pope had condemned. He called on Catholics to be courageous in opposing both of these misrepresentations: "It would then be possible for this intelligent and creative Catholicism to 'sway' with a serene mind, and to sail past Scylla, which does not tempt it, without wrecking its boat on the abandoned hulks thoughtfully placed along its course by the inhabitants of Charybdis."[42]

Negotiating around the Scylla of the Right and the Charybdis of the Left was a difficult task in the 1930s and continued to dominate debates on Catholic political engagement in France for several decades. Ultimately, it stemmed from a tension between on the one hand fidelity to long-term values and on the other hand action in the political context of the immediate present. Both dimensions are constitutive of the concept of engagement, as it was developed by Maritain and Mounier.

Phenomenology of Engagement

With all its tensions, this conception of engagement broke new ground in placing the human person at the heart of political action. In the process, it reopened the question of what effect the process of action might have on a person's innermost being. The relationship between being, thought, and action had been explored in detail by Maurice Blondel, whose thesis of 1893 was widely known.[43] However, the most influential Catholic exploration of action and the person during this period was provided by the philosopher and dramatist Gabriel Marcel, whose study of "Being and Having" addressed the issues of engagement in the most intimate areas of human experience.[44] Marcel was not closely involved in political activities, though he did frequent Maritain's weekly discussion meetings and was involved in the discussions around the establishment of *Esprit*. He did occasionally sign petitions, such as Mauriac's appeal for the people of the Basque country after the bombing of Guernica.

Whereas Maritain emphasized the freedom of the person with respect to action, Marcel emphasized the ambiguities of the two terms and their complex interrelation. In his phenomenological analysis, he suggested that the nature of the self was ultimately indefinable by itself and that the nature of things inevitably remained mysterious to the self except insofar as they were possessed. However, he argued that the process of possessing created a bond between the self and the thing and that things exercise a power over the self in exact proportion to the extent of one's attachment to them. In summary, he noted an intention to "examine, more closely than I have done as yet, the nature of the relative dependency of being and having: our possessions swallow us up."[45]

In a 1935 essay Marcel suggested that a similar logic was in play in the relationship between persons and their actions. He suggested that the nature of an action is to produce changes and that this includes changes in the actor. However, the changes are not confined to the moment of doing something but are attached to the actor indefinitely: "[I]t is of the essence of the act to engage the agent."[46] In undertaking an action, he claimed, it is as though the person has signed an admission in advance, which includes responsibility for all of the subsequent consequences. The essence of persons, he argued, is to confront their situation, considering and evaluating it, exposing themselves to risks and assuming the responsibility. In return, actions are the way in which persons connect with themselves and overcome alienation.

The force of Marcel's argument was to situate engagement as a fundamental dimension of human beings. His point was that the scope of engagement extended to the whole of human life and was not confined to the realm of politics. In whatever realm action was carried out, it was both an ontological and an ethical requirement. Ontologically, action was rooted in the nature of being and was necessary for human beings to complete their own existence. Ethically, action was rooted in the nature of human community and was necessary for individuals to connect with other people. In Marcel's view, shared by Maritain and Mounier, action also engaged with the divine presence, which inhabits the core of human beings. In consequence, he argued, the obligation for human beings was not just to act but also to be always ready to act if called upon. Marcel placed a preeminent value on *disponibilité* as the availability of the person to answer God's call, to respond to his invocation, and to enter into dialogue and engage faithfully with him.

Marcel's reflections on the divine dimension of commitment were specifically Catholic, but there was a wider audience for his analysis of the dialectic of being and having and the interweaving of action with the human person. In this way, his contribution served to complete those of Maritain and Mounier. As a result, a broad consensus emerged among these three leading Catholic thinkers about the need for Christian involvement in the political events of the period. With the benefit of hindsight, the consensus comprised a fully developed theory of engagement, in which the vocabulary of engagement was fully present. It was put together under the pressure of economic and political crisis but sufficiently robust to serve in other contexts. It was an inclusive conception that was developed for the needs of Catholics but rapidly expanded to offer a humanistic approach to political involvement to which many non-Catholics could subscribe.

The Legacy of Engagement

The humanist conception of engagement was based on the understanding that human persons are intimately engaged in the society in which they live and that they are morally accountable for their actions and the consequences of their actions. They have a responsibility to make society more supportive for human development, and working to achieve this is a primary source of personal fulfillment. People should set a personal example of working toward human progress in morally acceptable ways, and their choice of short-term actions should be guided by their fundamental long-term values. In the case of Catholics, those values are the spiritual purposes of the church, but laypeople have the task of deciding how best to pursue them in the temporal domain, whether through specifically Christian initiatives or through their involvement in social and political activities in collaboration with others.

In the context of France in the 1930s, this conception was designed to provide Catholics and others with a wider choice of options for addressing urgent political and social issues arising from the conditions of crisis in which France found itself. It was particularly intended to enable Catholics to join or work with movements, including political parties, other than the traditional conservative groupings that had previously monopolized Catholic political expression. As a result, this understanding of engagement had two important characteristics that potentially made it sustainable in a wide range of social contexts. First, although it was developed by writers like Maritain, Mounier, and Marcel, it was intended for people of any social status and not confined to intellectuals. Second, although it recognized the importance of political movements, it did not define action in terms of membership of particular parties. Both of these characteristics were inherent in the context of the 1930s, when Catholic writers and artists were seldom regarded as intellectuals and parties were a limited part of the political landscape. In fact, significant influence was exercised by movements, newspapers, coalitions of groups, and other configurations, potentially providing a wide array of forms of engagement from which individuals could choose.

By virtue of its high level of generality, this was a broadly permissive concept that enabled Catholics in particular to explore a wide range of political options. It also set political choices firmly in a relative perspective, subordinate to the fundamental human and spiritual values they should serve. In summary, it was a concept that opened doors—and then kept them open. Engagement was not designed to lock people into particular choices, beyond the point at which they served a deeper moral purpose. The concept of fidelity was highly valued but was reserved for fidelity to long-term values. The permissive nature of this engagement represented a step beyond the rejection of political commitment that was articulated in Péguy's much-quoted dictum that "everything begins as mystical and ends as political."[47] Writing in the disillusionment of the fallout from the Dreyfus case, Péguy was defending the "mystique" of fundamental values that he took the Dreyfusard cause to represent but rejecting the political purposes that were being pursued by Jean Jaurès and other leading figures in the republican campaign. His dictum was generally interpreted as a rejection of politics as such, regarding it as a tainted activity to avoid. The new concept of engagement took a more balanced view, seeing politics not as a degradation of the spirit but as the necessarily imperfect embodiment of spiritual values in the temporal realm. The task was to choose between the different temporal lines of action. Conversely, this was the basis for Mussolini's complaint about the wavering and inconstant nature of Catholic support. Specific commitments were always provisional and always revocable, and only long-term engagement to fundamental values was unconditional and irreversible.

Engagement or commitment became part of the political vocabulary of the 1930s. In the postwar period, which some historians have named "les années Sartre," it became virtually synonymous with the intellectual in France.[48] And yet, the Catholic conception was always a broader humanistic one, available to all citizens rather than belonging only to an intellectual elite. As a result, the decline of the classical model of the French intellectual does not entail the end of engagement in its broader sense. On the contrary, it may well be the condition for a renewal of engagement as a vital part of modern citizenship.

The polarized world of France in the 1930s was a difficult environment in which to develop a humanist conception of engagement. But the conception proved sufficiently robust to survive the Second World War and the acute polarizations that followed. It was undoubtedly less comfortable than the dominant form of Sartrean commitment, which was largely an all-or-nothing conception tailored to the confrontations of the Cold War. Nonetheless, it endured long enough to provide a framework for the subsequent movements of détente and reconciliation. It may be that the decline of polarizations was a factor in precipitating the crisis of the French intellectual, and if so, it is unlikely that the humanist conception of engagement will be fatally damaged by the crisis. On the contrary, it is quite likely to prove its value in the multipolar world of the twenty-first century, where complex choices and shifting alliances appear to be the norm.

2

Paul Valéry and French Catholicism: Recognizing the Context of Renewal

Paul Gifford

It must be something of a paradox to identify the sociopolitical and intellectual context of the renewal of French Catholicism in the third and fourth decades of the twentieth century by appealing to an agnostic intellectual, a poet, thinker, and public writer who, in the preceding period, observes the church, its beliefs, practices, and behavior—closely, to be sure—but with unfailing skepticism and consistently from the outside, looking in. Yet Paul Valéry, precisely because he does *not* belong to the household of Catholic obedience, sharing neither its philosophic mind nor its Christian faith, while still operating in the same sociopolitical context and the same cultural mind space, which he navigates in often contestatory dialogue with Catholics and with the church, does furnish singular resources for our act of recognition.

Dissenting, Valéry stands back from religious tradition (and from the very notion of a revealed truth, handed down and received), which gives him a distance and a perspective by which to see the larger picture of the great sea change in which French culture, and European culture more generally, are engaged, and because he does so in jealously guarded independence of judgment, he measures acutely the ineptitude or inaptitude, in times of radical change, of the traditional edifice of faith. His own parallel and rival construct of spirituality, moreover, is based on a very radical critique of *relligio* in general and of Catholic neo-Thomist orthodoxy in particular—a more truly searching critique, in my view, than that of Nietzsche. For all these reasons, Valéry offers a sort of "negative way" toward understanding. He acts as a strangely prophetic witness or *révélateur* of the phase change or "turn," whose genesis the present volume seeks to retrace and examine in its initial stirrings.

This chapter will, I hope, give some sense of what that transition consists, how it arises, and what birthing process is at work. We must first see how Valéry occupies a common social space and a common cultural mind space with two generations of French Catholics and how, within it, his own parallel and rival construct of spirituality is set up in opposition to theirs. It will then be possible to see how this involves a wide-ranging contestatory dialogue with a number of Catholic figures, with the church, with its social vision, its mind forms, its gospel, and its proclamation.

A Shared Social Space: Old-Style and New-Style Catholics

Valéry was superbly connected. Reviewing Michel Jarrety's monumental 1,366-page biography, I found myself inclined to speak of the "poet who knew everyone."[1] He knew, or at least met, and interacted with at some level, a stunning array of the leading figures of his time—secular writers, philosophers, artists, politicians, scientists, generals, and musicians (of course)—but also (which is what most interests us here) mystics, spiritual seekers, clerics, monks, theologians, Catholic thinkers and novelists of all shapes and sizes. The latter group included nearly the entire range of luminaries of the French Catholic intelligentsia of the time.

One of the first was Huysmans, who got him his early meal-ticket job as charge hand at the Ministry of War in the 1890s and through that circle the right-wing, anti-Dreyfusard fraternity (he also came across Péguy but did not take to him, no more than to leading anti-Dreyfusards—there are in the *Cahiers* strongly negative appreciations of Bourget, Barrès, and Maurras, too).[2] Through the *Nouvelle revue française* he came to know Claudel and, through him, Jacques

Maritain and Raïssa Maritain, together with various Thomists. Then there were his family connections, bringing him into contact with the lay Dominican order—"the third order of Saint Dominic"—to which they were committed, and through this connection, a large number of priests and religious: the RR.PP. Hurteaux, Sertillanges, Gillet, Rideau, Valensin, and Baudrillart,[3] to mention a few leading names; we also do not wish to forget his wife's parish priest, Abbé Bosson at rue Villejust (currently the rue Paul Valéry in the 16e arrondissement), who is represented, with a one-letter change of name, as Abbé Cosson in the *Lettre d'Emilie Teste* (1924).

Valéry was also private secretary to the Catholic director of the Agence Havas, Édouard Lebey, who—to Valéry's astonishment—cited the role played by his secretary's searchingly honest religious critique in his own return to the faith of his childhood.[4] Valéry himself, in 1927, made a retreat—out of aesthetic curiosity (this a souvenir of Huysmans and of his early symbolist "liturgism")[5]—at the Benedictine Abbey of Solesmes.[6]

After the First World War, at the height of his fame, this circle of acquaintances expanded hugely. He met socially other leading Catholics, such as Teilhard de Chardin, through the various Paris salons he then frequented or through the Abbé Mugnier, unofficial "chaplain of arts and letters" of Parisian "high society" of that time. At the Académie française, to which he was elected in 1927, he met others still such as the Abbé Bremond, instigator of the polemic on pure poetry. "Pure" in what sense? This was the hotly debated question: in the sense of a form of linguistic expression distilling purely the instinct of prayer? Or "pure" as a distillation of the musical properties of language? He met Bernanos in 1929, not long after the condemnation by Pius XI of Maurras's Action française, in the youth section of which the young Bernanos had once militated as a *Camelot du roi*.[7] He knew François Mauriac socially, and that connection was reinforced when, through Claude Mauriac, General de Gaulle, in 1945, called on him as one of the figures of continuity and resistance, capable of giving legitimacy to the government of the newly restored French Republic.[8]

Had Valéry not "resisted" morally? Indeed he had, despite his personal links to Pétain;[9] he had done so by adding his voice, in 1941, to a special issue of the *Revue philosophique*, published in Switzerland, by way of homage to the French Jewish philosopher Bergson. He stands in that volume alongside (among others) Péguy, Raïssa Maritain, Gabriel Marcel, and Emmanuel Mounier. And that special issue itself was inspired in part by the Vichy-defying tribute that Valéry himself had made earlier in officially associating the Académie with the grief of Madame Bergson.[10]

The arc traced by this first sketch of encounter and acquaintance is worth noting. It begins with Valéry's youthful and passing commitment on the "wrong" side of the Dreyfus affair at the end of the 1890s. Rather than of *engagement*, one should perhaps speak of his temporary immersion in the current of ideologically vectored right-wing nationalism, a force powerful at the time and which constituted for some French Catholics a deviant and violent form of sacrality. This was a confusion acutely present in all European societies, Catholic or not, at the high point of Europe's imperial power, and it is a persuasion to which French Catholics were more distinctly prone than some other European faith traditions because of an ideological cleavage, two centuries old, yet reactivated, and indeed reaggravated in its primal vigor, by the anticlerical Third Republic.

This was of course the seismic fault line imprinted into the French national psyche by the Revolution of 1789. Very typically, Catholics of the period 1871–1926 (and beyond) found themselves on the antiprogressive side of the barricades, where stood the representatives of authority and social order, and thus on the "wrong" side of nineteenth-century history. They were, ideologically, to a large extent, locked into the ethos and outlook of the ancien régime. (René Girard would today say that the Dreyfus affair was a capital example of political scapegoating, particularly grave because it substantially subverted large parts of French Catholic opinion and the judicial system of the nation.)[11]

And at the other end of the ideologicopolitical spectrum, we find the committed and resistencialist countermovement, in which Valéry joins with ethically and socially committed French Catholics against the military violence of occupation and anti-Semitism, albeit now imposed on France from outside, by Nazi Germany. There is something symptomatic, almost symbolic, about that trajectory: a first harmonic of the figure of sense we are seeking to uncover.

In his *Cahiers* we can find Valéry's commentary on the pivotal event on which that reversal of direction turns, the condemnation in 1926 by Pius XI of Action française: "Middle Ages, excommunication, carnival. But how many people have come to believe that Maurras was Pope, oracle, infallible!" (*C* X, 911). We hear in this note for the first time the long "hissing" anticlerically emitted from the accustomed vantage point pictured in "Ébauche d'un serpent" ("Sketch of a Serpent," Valéry's biblical parody in *Charmes*): that of the serpent entwined in the tree of consciousness and knowledge within the Garden of the Faith, but showing here, perhaps, unwontedly limited prescience of the strategic ferment at work. If we ask why this restriction of prescience, the ultimate answer, ironically enough, may lie in his lack of any framework of transcending hope. Valéry believed, like Maurras, albeit nostalgically and without illusion, in the immense inheritance of the sociopolitical edifice of the church in shaping European civilization; he did not however believe in the resurrection life of the church's faith proclamation. With Maurras, consequently, he here observes only an incident in the life of a "very beautiful but uninhabitable house," a house wrought solely by the human hands of yesteryear.

Here we have a substantial clue as to why the fundamental dialogue of the *Cahiers* could never exteriorize itself and achieve a voiced, incarnate form. None of his numerous Catholic acquaintances could have become the interlocutor of confidence of that one-man citadel or his Crusoe-like desert island of pure thought. Neither traditionalists (like Claudel) nor modernists (like Teilhard de Chardin) could have exercised this role.

This is clear enough in the case of Claudel. "It is true I am founded on a doubt, as you are on a faith," writes Valéry, recognizing two symmetrically inverse ways of being a "whole man."[12] Each would have sustained a discourse in principle antipathetic to the other, indicting the work and the subject at its center. Claudel certainly thought so. "As to the thinker"—he writes of Valéry—"I consider he gets into a blind alley. I preferred never to engage in discussion with him. That would serve neither him nor me."[13] And reciprocally so, from Valéry's point of view. So, despite mutual esteem between the two poets and the generally cordial social relations between them, the "closed system" of the pure thinker and the "closed house" of the man of faith absolute are essentially "non-communicating vessels."[14]

If Claudel is one limit case, Teilhard de Chardin, at the spectrum's other extreme, is still outside Valéry's circle of confidence. Valéry encountered him three times between 1928 and 1932—at the threshold of our target period—describing him as "the delightful Teilhard"—an epithet recognizing his personal simplicity and charm but also, no doubt, crediting him with scientific curiosity, independence of mind, a spirit of adventure: "He has made up his own religion" (*C* XVI, 3). However, Valéry's objection is immediate and characteristic: Teilhard is a teleological reader of evolution. "He makes an—entirely transformed—Christ into a sort of cosmic Self," and he posits "a God at infinity toward which one should tend" (*C* XIV, 716). But this is still, for Valéry, the shadow of a bankrupt Western metaphysics: "I said that what we need is a labor of the Einstein type to construct a God invariant" (*C* XXIV, 716). Against Teilhard's finalist model of convergence, Valéry's counterproposal posits an unlimited and open adventure: "I posit the zero of conscious existence from which we should diverge" (*C* XVI, 3).

So, once more we encounter an inverse symmetry of figures of sense, limiting the potential for dialogue. Valéry judges, accurately enough if we recall Teilhard's treatment at the hands of his own order and by the Roman hierarchy, that this Jesuit priest "is dicing with his [priestly] condition." His conclusion—"At bottom, they (intellectual priests) are seeking to make it to a new religious continent by swimming there" (*C* XIV, 716)—implies that the church has, in the hour of "modernist" crisis, suffered a sort of shipwreck.

Recognizing the Underlying Culture Crisis

The prior question however arises: How does this anticlerical and humanist of the Third Republic come to be, and in what sense is he any sort of interlocutor of French Catholic Christianity in the interwar period and in the period preceding it? What account does he give of the shared context of crisis and cultural change?

Had the possibility of any interlocutory role been mentioned to the professional establishment of French Valéry criticism forty or fifty years ago, it would have been greeted like a message from Nietzsche's prophetic madman. The most settled conviction of competent experts was that here was the purest son of the Enlightenment, a successor to Descartes and to Voltaire: intellectual factotum, symbol even, of the anticlerical Third Republic; notorious adversary of Pascal, whom Valéry describes brutally in his private notebooks as "the enemy of humankind" and as "the Adversary" (*C* XVI, 504). An agnostic, a skeptic, not so much an irreligious man (that, too, no doubt, on occasion) but perhaps even more an *areligious* one: a "modern" and even—if this slightly mischievous suggestion is in order—a "pre-postmodern" exemplar of Unbelieving Man.

Then between 1957 and 1961 came the publication in facsimile of his notebooks, the famous *Cahiers*: twenty-eight thousand pages of them, representing Valéry's experimental or "laboratory" work devoted to the analysis of mental functioning and of the making of the cognitive and creative products of the mind—his real œuvre as he saw it. This was the submerged part of the iceberg, and as it came to be surveyed, what appeared to those who had eyes to see was that Valéry is, in the reserved space of this private laboratory of reflexive thought, extraordinarily preoccupied with what he calls "divine things." Beginning in 1921, he actually projected a third Socratic dialogue, "Peri ton tou theou" (On Things Divine). If that successor dialogue to *Eupalinos* and *L'âme et la danse* (*Soul and Dance*) never saw the light of day, it was not from any deficiency of sustaining interest or any paucity of material. Quite the reverse: it was because the subject was too vast, too crucially important, too intimate, too delicate for its place and time. And so it was reabsorbed into that central laboratory of thought, into the reserved space-time of the *Cahiers*, and there pursued until his last day.

Almost literally so, in fact. For information—though this comes with a severe "health warning"—the last entry of the *Cahiers* reads as follows: "All odds of error, worse, all odds of poor taste and vulgarity are on those who hate. / The word love has been associated with the name of God only since Christ" (*C* XXIX, 909). One might draw from this empirically *last*, if not logically or teleologically *final*, word a searching reflection on a number of interesting things: on the extraordinary role attaching to *ultima verba* and the motif of the deathbed scene, attesting the fraught and conflictual ideological climate of Third Republic France; on the pointer it offers to the interpenetration of mortality and religion in Catholic France of the same, postromantic era; and even as offering a series of clues to the consequent shape and internal logic of Valéry's own explorations *peri ton tou theou*.[15]

But, with respect to mortality, Valéry points us, from the beginning, toward something even more revealing and fundamental. If we wish to understand the deepest sense in which he shares a changing cultural mind-space with a more slowly modulating Catholicism—the Catholic Church being, notoriously, like an oil tanker, it does not turn quickly!—we have to look at what puts divine things on Valéry's agenda in the first place and keeps them there so insistently until his last articulated moment. I refer to a psychic wound, fresh in his own time and still, despite the best "distract-disperse-and-downplay" efforts of postmodernism, unhealed in our own. I refer to that traumatic event in European culture—that *sea change*, that *shipwreck*, and that *eclipse*—generally known by the shorthand name given to it by Nietzsche, the "death of God."

Great artists, in the best hypothesis, are spiritual seismographs and imaginary modelers of things implicit and invisible. They register, and they can represent large-scale, underlying culture shifts.

"Shipwreck" is the title of a poem that is, in point of fact, highly *un*characteristic of Valéry in its tone and manner, one that he wrote (or, more accurately, rewrote) in 1909, having just completed his reading of, on the one hand, the complete works of Nietzsche (he reviewed these for the *Mercure de France* as they appeared in their French translation by Henri Albert between 1902 and 1909) and, on the other hand, Saint John of the Cross, whom he discovered by chance in the seventeenth-century French translation of the R. P. Cyprien of the Nativity.[16] Between two such poles, it was predictable that a certain spark of prophetic recognition might be generated. And here it is:

> What hour is this that shudders 'gainst the hull,
> What squall of darkness dislocating fate?
> What power impalpable rattles in the rigging
> The skeleton bones of all our deaths?
> . . . .
> I see the Christ lashed to the mast
> Dancing to death and foundering with his own;
> His bloody eye illuminates the scripture writ:
> A GREAT SHIP HAS PERISHED WITH ALL HANDS![17]

For a French symbolist poet this is fiery vodka; it sounds as if Valéry has been swallowing a lot of neat Nietzsche, possibly laced with a reminiscence of Wagner's *Flying Dutchman* or Rimbaud's "Le bateau ivre" (The Drunken Boat), perhaps even, for this poem was again revised after the First World War, of the "Wreck of the Deutschland."

And yet Valéry's own poetic voice had something similar, twenty years earlier. In 1888, as a seventeen-year-old schoolboy, not yet having read Nietzsche, he wrote a prose poem dedicated to Mallarmé. In it, as in a dream, the subject witnesses a funeral, which, so he is told, is that of *God*: "'Who is being buried?' I asked him—'God,' he said. And he too ran to rejoice before the funeral procession."[18] There follows a cataclysm of cosmic proportions:

Then it was that the Sun, after a last brightness, paled and disappeared. Something warned me it would not return and that we should not see it more. The moon itself had melted in the skies. The dark firmament no longer held stars. It was a cold dark hole. And at that moment I felt falling onto my hands from above a few icy drops like melting diamonds and I understood that all the stars had come loose and that I was witnessing the tears of Heaven flow.

. . . A great cry rent the air.

. . . A great wind stirred up the leaves that covered the Earth . . . And it seemed to me that this wind blew within me and extinguished my Being.[19]

This is far better writing, extraordinarily impressive, in fact, for a seventeen-year-old schoolboy, with its powerful symbolism of eclipse and apocalyptic disorder, its bold and subtle correspondences of inner and outer worlds, though if pressed, I might still be inclined to detect a hyperbole of the romantic heart and a form of the pathetic fallacy behind this presentation of an event in culture as an event in nature.

If we want the full Valéryan music of this particular score, it is to be found in the prelude to his masterwork, *La Jeune Parque*. In that poem of 1917, the heroine awakens shocked and trembling in a cold night wind, after some unnameable trauma, under a fateful night sky (though now the impossibly beautiful stars are back). "What grief awakens me; what crime by myself or upon me consummated?"[20] These lines actually register the ambiguity we have just noticed. Culture or nature? And is the human subject victim or perpetrator of the great Decease, perpetrator or victim of the great wound of diminishment it brings to humankind? Or are *both* things somehow true?

That God *once was* but has *now suffered decease* is not logically thinkable. That he did historically die, killed by men, but is *not* "deceased" in the metaphysical sense claimed by Nietzsche: This affirmation is, at the heart of the gospel, the paradox of orthodox Christianity. But there is an ambiguous intermediate sense with which

Valéry—and the whole of our modern culture with him (albeit less presciently)—has attempted to grapple: an *anthropological* paradox describing a form of consciousness and outlook of a given culture at a given time. A particular idea or set of ideas of God or perhaps the very category itself—an inherited notion of the divine or "the theistic hypothesis," perhaps, of Western reason—has, as we say, "gone dead on us." That is an entirely coherent sense and a very important one, every bit as awesome as Valéry suggests.

Furthermore, that hidden wound or trauma explains the radicality of Valéry's reaction. His idea—his great project—is to take back the entire nexus of questions and problems that make up the human science of divine things into the sphere of human-generated, mind-made, meanings and to give them back their proper place in the universe of representation and of the culturally conditioned productions of the social psyche. He proposes to ask how thought about divine things comes to be generated in our minds and what the religious function of the human psyche is and how it works, individually and collectively. He wants to rethink the whole process by which we ask religious questions and verify the legitimacy of our answers—are they intelligible, coherent, necessary? Are they "divine" or not? And what is this *value category* of the divine that we carry around with us? Can we do without it? What can we do with it for the greatest development of human potential?

His long odyssey of research is most profoundly described as the dialogue between a resolve to reexamine and, if possible, to refound the religious function in humankind—to constitute what might be called a generative anthropoetics of religion—and the existential or spiritual need to reinvent the form of its intentional movement, a "mysticism without God" ultimately open still to the discovery of metaphysical truth.

Seen in context, this very radical reaction, I would suggest, helps us discern the broadest and most comprehensive frame of reference of our inquiry about the nature and logic of the phase change germinating around 1930 within French Catholicism. The case of Paul

Valéry invites us to think in terms of a generalized crisis of culture and civilization, of which the hidden nerve point is the declared or so-called death of God.

"We civilizations know now that we are mortal," wrote Valéry famously in "La crise de l'esprit" (The Crisis of the Mind) just after the First World War.[21] His own diagnosis of the origins and antecedents of that crisis has to do with the shock of war and the crisis of science (increasingly a form of practical reason, in Kantian terms, placed in the service of power and its myths and itself an exercise of power rather than a form of understanding, of *conscience*, or of wisdom). It has to do with the advent of modern utilitarianism. Above all it has to do with the relentless rise of a critical, reflexive, and positivistic mind-frame, dissolving the fiduciary cement that had held together all of our Western constructions of sense and human meaning. "The debate is no longer between the religions, but between those who believe believing has any sense and the others" (*C* VI, 648).

Not everyone contributing to this volume will find Valéry's diagnosis of this problem sufficiently "incarnational," for instance, with respect to its relative inattention to socioeconomic factors. Others may object that Valéry observes a Catholicism fashioned overwhelmingly by Vatican I, whereas the changes of the period 1930–1950 are, immediately or more distantly, premonitory and/or prophetic stirrings of a church that would be substantially remodeled by Vatican II. Yet Valéry's profiling of the landscape and of his Catholic "other" are distinctly pertinent. Change is a function of the *felt need to change*. This need is established at least as much by what *precedes* as by what, in the landscape of the 1930s and '40s, accompanies change or conduces to it.

I would moreover suggest that Valéry offers us a variation on the theme of "violence and the sacred" that takes the measure, as other readings rarely do, of the cataclysmically transformed cultural landscape and the challenge of finding, in response to it, a new authenticity, a new balance, and a new assurance (today I would add, in Girardian mode, a new containment or exorcism of humankind's perennial, self-generated violence; hence also a Christian form of the sacred freshly and fundamentally distinguished from that of self-generated "archaic" or "natural" religion). It will be profitable, at all events, to ask of each of the voices questioned in this volume: "What grief awakens me? . . . What crime by myself or upon me consummated?"

Modeling the Catholic Other

The shared mind-space of this time of profound cultural crisis, because it is differently navigated by the church and its contestatory observer, produces a strongly critical-differential modeling of the "other." Space permits here only a cursory dip into what is in fact a large and substantial dossier, coresonant with insights that many other writers of the time have confided or analyzed out of their own parallel experience of the French Catholicism of this period. Were this anthology of testimonies to be constituted whole, it would make a precious contribution to anthropological understanding of religious and cultural change in the twentieth century.

Valéry is profoundly open to a sense of the value-led consecration of the energies of human spiritual potential. "Please know [he writes to a nun] that I admire *above all else* the strength of knowing how to choose between the Everything and the Nothing, when one has managed, as you have, to discern in oneself what can be *Everything* and what must be *Nothing*."[22] Yet his *Cahiers* declare the darker reverse of this same coin: a perpetual serpentlike hissing at the element of *negligo* he discovers in *relligio*—the publicly practiced religion of the tribe. (The Latin word, with its curious doubling of the *l*, suggests the impression of constraint or heavy binding that neo-Thomist orthodoxy and its regulation of moral space make upon Valéry, and indicates his fundamental agreement with the post-Enlightenment perception of religion—a perception formalized by Valéry's contemporary Durkheim at the origins of sociology—as the major bonding-and-binding agent of the social psyche.)

In raging or scandalized disappointment, the one-man order records privately the lack of everything that might, in his time, have made the French Catholics of his acquaintance interlocutors of confidence. He is withering on the dogmatism and intellectual dishonesty of the God-convinced. The believer always wants to be right (*C* XVII, 640). He makes truth the spouse of his private person (*C* XVII, 339). His faith cannot get by without a large dose of bad faith since it respects the inner convention of not listening to anything subversive of belief (*C* XV, 509). He uses mysteries and miracles to evade fair terms of engagement (*C* XXI, 427). Is he even faithful to his beliefs or conscious of what they entail?

I know of no Christian who has reflected on the Lord's Prayer, who has attempted to figure out what ideas, what state of mind, what knowledge sets this prayer supposes in its author: "Thy will be done." (*C* V, 264)

You people, Christians and others, you may perhaps believe in a God, but you make of Him only intermittent use, an indeterminate danger, an uncertain and finally capricious protector . . . . (*C* XV, 66)

Quite particularly inassimilable for Valéry are converts who bear witness in (literary) print—Christians whose prayer "concludes with a request to publish." He explains: "[M]y nature is very simple and I suppose they share it. If I believed, I would sink into contemplative expectation—and my mind wouldn't bother in the least about itself, its present knowledge and its powers" (*C* XIV, 170). Above all, the lack of charity of Christian believers "stupefies me" (*C* XXIX, 11). By this virtue—"the most rare, the most nonhuman"—Valéry declares that one recognizes a Christian "baptized or not" (*C* XV, 512). Yet here, too, the worm is in the fruit. Valéry's experience suggests that "Faith does the greatest harm to charity"; thus "an independent observer would have to conclude that statistically the second is in inverse proportion to the first . . . It's the deification of blackmail" (*C* XV, 413).

With respect to the official church, the litany of anathema becomes more acute, more obsessional. It models an ecclesial practice heavily dependent on theistic proofs, mysteries, and miracles and predicated on a form of apologetics that both sidesteps the challenge of the critical intellect and speculates ignobly on human weakness. The sin against intelligence and against any authentic sense of the divine—he considers—was committed on the "day the Church took as poisoned weapon the idea and the terror of death" (*C* XVII, 745). Since that day, "The Christian religion debases the divine by using and abusing the notions of death, hell, divine judgment and wrath, eternity and the devouring worm, and in failing to confess that man is closer to the divine when he laughs at all these filthy things than when he believes in them . . . it is the deification of blackmail" (*C* VI, 716).

Similarly, for the apologetic use of miracles as supernatural persuasion machines:

> A religion without "miracles" may be true.
> A religion with miracles must be false.
> They want to stun me.
> Astonishment as a means is unworthy of the god.
> The god is clear, honest—a stranger. (*C* VIII, 725)

False must be any religion presenting four capital marks of evident inauthenticity: mysteries, miracles, threats, and promises. "I do not believe in a God for whom I exist. / But if there is such, O Phaedrus, it is impossible for me to think that he should be satisfied to have reduced me by surprise, taken advantage of me by posing enigmas, checkmated me by the fear of punishments, or lured me by rewards" (*C* VIII, 758). There can be no doubt that the four marks of inauthenticity represent Valéry's direct, if negative, profiling of French Catholic "relligio" in the first half of the twentieth century.

A second, highly characteristic chapter of Valéryan contestation concerns "the Church and sexuality" or, perhaps more broadly, "ecclesiastical tutelage and human intimacy." Hence this indirect, fictionalized "confession":

> Gozon, at the age of 7 "troubled" by his confessor, a very old, very severe priest, crowned with curls of white hair, skull of ivory and parchment entirely wrinkled, chaplain to the Penitents . . . this saint asks him in confession: "Do you not look at yourself in the lavatory?" There was, therefore, something to see . . . He dashes off. . . . The awful idea of a hidden, eternal Witness, as if this God kept our immodesties for himself. "He knows your innermost thoughts." It is dreadful![23]

Or again, in the same vein of fictional autobiography, this time positing a feminine subject:

> Begins catechism classes and therefore becomes unbelieving. Yet she continues to go. She feels, hears herself told things that she cannot think, which represent for her mere words, to which nothing in herself responds. Answering no need, no idea, mediated by no experience of hers.[24]

Worse:

> He spoke and intoned, as one walks a wire. / A tone of voice so high-pitched that it was dangerously in peril—unbelievable! / The authority of the tone seemed super-added, as one warms up a dish from yesterday.[25]

Patriarchal, authoritarian, intrusive, divorced from experience, deeply mistrustful of human sexuality: these features of Valéry's profiling of the style of early century French Catholicism need to be added to his vision of a disastrously conceived apologetics operating on the "all-too-human" underbelly of humankind.

The most specifically Valéryan chapter concerns rather the opacity and inadequacy to the modern mind, at least as represented by its intellectual advanced guard, of Catholic *ontotheology*. The Thomist renewal officially promoted by the encyclical *Aeterni patris* (1879) and developing, broadly speaking, up to the Second World War is almost exactly contemporary with Valéry's lifespan. Claudel, the Maritains, and all of the writers of the Catholic revival of the prewar period belonged to the generation who discovered Saint Thomas with admiring enthusiasm, often with real passion. The Angelic Doctor allowed them to overcome the dichotomies and dualisms of secular rationalist tradition; he gave back to creation its divine value and to thought its catholicity, but at the price of making them speak in a language and a discourse of faith conceived and forged in the thirteenth century.

For Valéry, that was of course too high a price to pay. It is clear from the *Cahiers* that "the naive and clever arguments of Aquinas" struck him immediately as precritical, unscientific, and frankly out of date (*C* VI, 271). Then there were the impurities: "S[aint] Th[omas]. Attempts to compose all the absurdities in the Scriptures—[with] the honest but often unfortunate essays of Aristotle—and the subtleties of the Church Fathers" (*C* XIII, 667). Worst of all: "Thomist scholastics is a philosophy with a raison d'État. There is a goal, a political will" (*C* IX, 773). For Valéry, one might say, its official Thomist framing—almost as much as the appeal to mystery and miracle and the cult of the will to believe—puts the Catholic Christianity of that period outside the pale of intelligibility and acceptance.

But the invisible damage is much greater. Thomist ontotheology locks the Catholicism of this period into the great criticist and verificationist assault on Western metaphysics as such, of which Valéry is one of the great unsung pioneers (for instance, in relation to the theistic proofs, the so-called five ways of Aquinas, arousing a barrage of critical objection and persiflage). There is no more characteristically Valéryan place than the garden of "Ébauche d'un serpent," in which the serpent prowls in subversive parody and dissent, hissing acerbically at "the old and pure Being." The church, on this view, imposes the choice between the Tree of (eternal) Life and the Tree of (modern) Knowledge. Worse still, its attempt to marry Greek metaphysical reason with the Hebrew scriptures occults the very nature of the divine and the logic of Judaeo-Christian proclamation. This is, along with the lack of any kind of insight derived from text-critical hermeneutics (proscribed as dangerously liberal by the antimodernist reaction of the Roman magisterium), one of the things that most makes the gospels almost entirely unintelligible and/or objectionable to Valéry.

Conclusion

I leave to a present-day Catholic voice what seems to be the major figure of sense to be drawn from Valéry's negative profiling of early twentieth-century French Catholicism. Nicholas Lash, professor of divinity at Cambridge, puts it this way. Describing the "state of siege" that characterized the Catholic Church at the time of the proclamation of papal infallibility in 1870, Lash writes: "The theology of the Church was becoming rationalist, apologetic, absolutistic. Ideology of an institution seeking retrenchment within a fortified citadel, this theology proceeded from a defensive and peremptorily assertive spirit rather than from reflection; it feared pluralism, uncertainty, significant dissent."[26]

If we add to this theological dogmatism and this siege mentality the peculiarly sharp French temptations of right-wing ideology, including elements of nationalism, authoritarianism, and anti-Semitism—and in general a confused sacralization of money, power, influence, and other deviant sacralities—we obtain a fairly good readout of the nature and sources of a certain alienation from Christian authenticity, from the gospel.

The question then—and I take this to be our question in the present volume—is what are the sources and resources of a movement of *Exodus* from the Citadel? What are the antecedents and origins of a postwar turn from an ideologically armored but self-enclosed orthodoxy, a fossilized and immobile verticality—to a stripped-down but a more spiritually quickened and Christianly authentic commitment, operating preferentially in the horizontal plane, at the human and social level?

It may be that certain good clues to this process exist in the work of Simone Weil, who admired Paul Valéry and who resembles him in angelism, in the intransigence of the critique she directs against Catholic orthodoxy, in her Hellenic reference and her mathematical turn of mind, and in her sense of "attente" (waiting, expectation), mirroring Valery's "mysticism without God." Of course, to these Simone Weil adds grace, suffering and an awareness of the working-class industrial poor.

3 A Strange Christian: Simone Weil

Florence de Lussy

Simone Weil provides an excellent case study of the problems of commitment (*engagement*) in relation to French Catholic thought in the mid–twentieth century. Weil was a thoroughgoing intellectual for whom life and thought were inextricably linked. She was and is an uncomfortable figure. She lived her life as a kind of martyrdom, and she remains difficult to come to terms with even today.

Her strangeness stemmed largely from a combination of her family and cultural background, as well as her own psychological and personal qualities, but her education also played a determining role. She was a born militant, and as a spirited adolescent she was already strongly drawn to political and social commitment. Like many of her generation she responded enthusiastically to the ideas of Alain, the semiofficial philosopher of the Radical Party, whose philosophy classes she attended at the Lycée Henri-IV beginning in 1925. Having won a place at the select École normale supérieure in 1928, she lost no time in joining the Groupe d'éducation sociale, founded by a railway worker, Lucien Cancouët, which revived the tradition of the older workingmen's universities. She even persuaded her brother, André (later a famous mathematician and founder of the Bourbaki group), to attend meetings of the group.

After obtaining the *agrégation* in 1931, Simone Weil taught philosophy in various provincial towns. She maintained high intellectual standards, but her main interest was in fact the labor movement. Her political convictions colored her teaching, and she threw herself body and soul into militant trade unionism. Over a period of three years she built up an extensive network of contacts in that world and tried to develop them into a coherent force, but without success.

A trip she made to Germany in the summer of 1932, together with the information supplied by friends who were deeply involved in two periodicals, *La révolution prolétarienne* (at first a "syndicaliste-communiste" monthly, then a fortnightly, and described as "syndicaliste révolutionnaire") and *La critique sociale* (founded by Boris Souvarine, one of the founding members of the French Communist Party in 1920 but later an anti-Stalinist), convinced her of the stupidity of the struggles within European socialism. Weil's period of intense commitment ended with a dramatic farewell to the revolution in the form of a powerful article, "Are We Heading for the Proletarian Revolution?," written in August 1933, which distressed her friends.[1] In March 1934 she wrote to her friend and former classmate Simone Pétrement that she had "decided to withdraw completely from politics in all forms, except historical research."[2] That marked a clear, indeed brutal, exit from the political arena, in which she had been so active for three years, deploying all the resources of her youthful energy. Those years had revealed not only an exceptional strength of character and mind and remarkable powers of thought but also a certain breathless impatience.

The first act of the drama of Weil's packed life was now over. It had been very intense. We can already see the distinction between militant action proper, where ideological positions give rise to practical involvement in day-to-day events, and what might be called the margins of political action, what precedes and follows it. What precedes action is theoretical study and reflection, in her case on the alienation produced by factory work (as in her seminal 1934 essay, "Reflections Concerning the Causes of Liberty and Social Oppression"),[3] coupled with the actual experience of living the concrete reality of this new form of slavery (her months as a factory worker and the "Factory Journal," 1934–35).[4] What follows action is the quest for a form of inspiration capable of restoring to that action its spirit and its meaning, which were to inspire her final work, *L'enracinement* (*The Need for Roots*), written in London in 1943.

There were of course moments in the remainder of Weil's short life when the urge to take direct action welled up irresistibly—during the Spanish Civil War or the Second World War, when she was in Marseilles or London—and the thought of resistance action was very tempting, involving as it did the idea of sacrifice and maybe even of suicide.[5]

This is the background and the immediate context for the emergence of what, for want of a better term, we may call a religious awareness. They are absolutely essential if we are to understand Weil's development. She had already explored the idea and the practice of commitment, and they were to remain central: it was the focus of the commitment that was to change. What happened was that her thought took a different turning, assuming new risks, revisiting concepts that had hitherto seemed obvious and unproblematical, and thus opening itself up to be transformed. That was indeed the classical sense of the practice of "philosophy."

In this new phase, which brought Weil close to Catholicism, we notice not only the dominance in her thinking of the Greek rather than the Hebrew tradition but also the paradoxes to which that preference gave rise. Then there is the comparative failure of the conversations she had over a period of a year with Father Joseph-Marie Perrin, a Dominican priest, while she was in Marseilles after the fall of France in 1940. This was related to the growing difficulty she had in accepting the authority of the church. In this chapter I also touch on the extreme modernity of the positions she adopted, especially on the question of the relationship between the profane and the sacred.

The Path of Religious Awareness

The path Simone Weil took was a difficult one, but essentially it followed a straight line against the backdrop of a deepening pessimism, intensified by the months of factory work, which "killed her youth."[6]

The change she was undergoing was striking. Having been brought up as a complete agnostic in an assimilated Jewish family that had lost touch with any religious culture, she moved to an atheism that in 1933–34 could still be characterized as jubilant. In one of her letters to Perrin she even admitted quite openly that since the problem of the existence of God was one for which the data were simply lacking, the only sure method of avoiding a wrong solution was simply not to pose it in the first place (*WG*, 62). It is hard for us to conceive just how extraordinary this slow penetration into a totally new world—that of the things of God—was for this philosopher, who up to now had been steeped in Marxist thought. How on earth did she proceed? Very cautiously, is the answer, and in order to find her way in an area that was utterly foreign to her, she made use of the conceptual tools that she had at her disposal, namely those of a vast but non-Christian culture. She felt completely bereft. It was the religion of the ancient Greeks that enabled her to take the very first steps in her spiritual quest.

She began to be inhabited by a sense—a prephilosophical sense—that impressed itself upon her with increasing force: the sense of exile. The first elements of an adequate expression of this were provided by what she had read of the ancient Greek mystery cults, no doubt inspired by her friend Simone Pétrement. Pétrement specialized in the study of Gnosticism and had by then written the first version of what was to become her doctoral dissertation and was subsequently developed into her big book on the origins of Gnosticism.[7] Weil was no doubt specifically influenced by André Boulanger's 1925 book on Orphism, of which we have her personal copy.[8] Boulanger says the following, for instance: "At the origin of this religion of 'separate ones' (i.e., Orphism) is a pessimistic view of life, a sharp sense of the contrast between the wretchedness of man and the greatness of his aspirations."[9] Simone Weil wrote to her brother in early 1940 in very similar terms: "[C]ertainly they [the Greeks] had a painful conception of existence, like all whose eyes are open; but their pain had an object, it had a sense in relation to the happiness for which man is made."[10] It is clear that a decisive step had been taken. The same idea recurs in a text written the following year, "La science et nous" (Science and Us) with reference to Spinoza this time: "[H]uman beings are made, they feel, for something other than time and space; and being unable to avoid having them present to their minds, they feel themselves made at least to be masters of them, to inhabit eternity."[11]

It is then only one further step from this strong sense of the wretchedness of humankind to the tragic destiny awaiting anyone who tries to live a just life. There again it is Greek thought that shows the way. The figure of the just person suffering in Plato's *Republic* and that of the crucified Christ, so eloquently described in patristic apologetics, struck Weil as being obviously, indeed self-evidently, comparable. There is a beautiful text dating from 1937–38, "A Meditation on Obedience and Liberty," which represents a major exposition of her thought and articulates sharply and decisively her tragic vision of human destiny: "As for those who want to think, love, and transpose in all purity into political action what their mind and heart inspire them with, they can only perish murdered, forsaken even by their own people, vilified after their death by history, as happened to the Gracchi."[12]

As she was growing up, Simone Weil's choice of this Greek path, which gave a permanent coloring to her mental landscape, was all the more fervent because it was opposed to the Jewish tradition, which should by rights have been hers. That may be explained partly by her upbringing (her parents' agnosticism) and partly by the very negative comments of her teacher Alain on the God of the Old Testament, as well as by the anti-Jewishness of the Catholic Church in that period and indeed of much of modern philosophy since Kant, Fichte, and Hegel.[13] An alternative explanation is given by Edgar Morin (who invented the term "Judeo-Gentile" to signify the duality of Western Jews caught in the contradictions of assimilation), namely that for some people "universalist ideas involved losing the Jewish part of their identity in the adoption of a revolutionary internationalist identity."[14]

Weil's rejection of her Jewish heritage was twofold, covering both the biblical tradition of the Hebrew kings and prophets and the contemporary dimension. Thus in a fascinating if unacceptably extreme text on "Israel and the Gentiles," which she wrote in New York in October 1942 as an expansion of the first of her questions to Father Marie-Alain Couturier (the Dominican to whom she addressed her *Letter to a Priest*),[15] she inverted St. Paul's thesis of the primacy of Israel (with the Gentiles "grafted in" later), giving precedence to the Gentiles, in whom she saw a purer form of spirituality. In so doing, Weil was virtually espousing the position of the pagan Celsus as presented in Origen's treatise *Contra Celsum* (which she had certainly read, at least in part, and to which she refers elsewhere).

In another extraordinary outburst (as yet unpublished), written in London (where she was under no illusions about the horrors of Nazi anti-Semitism and the atrocities of the extermination camps) in response to a text on the Jews of France produced by a clandestine, extreme right-wing movement, she called for Jewish influence to be countered by the most dishonorable means, including deprivation of French nationality and the encouragement of mixed marriages.

The evidence of such extreme hatred of Judaism is bound to call into question the validity of Simone Weil's thought. Although it is widely admired for its power and lucidity in nearly all areas, it is clearly deeply flawed in some respects, and the image we have of her as a philosopher cannot but suffer as a result.[16]

Paradoxes

The paradoxes to which this complex situation led were multiple but all interlinked. They were all related to a certain conception of time.

Weil's thought displays an ahistoricism that corresponds to a cyclical conception of time. Time is no longer directional. She has a manner of privileging the category of timelessness, which leads her, for instance, to exalt the figure of the cosmic Christ rather than the historical Jesus, who lived and died in Judea at the beginning of our era. Of the historical Jesus, this strange Christian retained practically nothing but the details of the passion, though of course she accorded them immense importance. She believed firmly in the possibility of multiple incarnations, going so far as to draw up, in one of her New York notebooks, a "list of images of Christ" with no fewer than twenty-six entries (*OC* VI. 4, 224–25). Here the paradox is deepened by her own encounter with Christ, which she revealed to very few people but which testifies to an authentic experience of personal contact (the definition of a mystical experience). In saying that "Christ himself came down to me and laid hold of me" (*WG*, 21), Weil is echoing the words of Saint Paul in Philippians 3:12 (*katalambano*, lay hold of) and 2 Corinthians 12:2 (*harpazo*, catch up).

The category of timelessness is close to that of myth. Simone Weil undertook lengthy investigations into myth (with aims that were quite different from, indeed the opposite of, those of her contemporary Claude Lévi-Strauss). Her pitilessly logical mind was undoubtedly at the same time highly intuitive, and she had a remarkable gift for decoding the universal language of the collective imaginary. But occasionally she went too far. She espoused the Platonic idea of an original revelation, which led her to judge certain traditions by the yardstick of their putative connection with the knowledge derived from that original revelation and to suppose that some of it might have gotten lost in transmission.[17] Time was thus in danger of becoming directional again, but in reverse.

Her privileging of the timeless led logically to the adoption of heretical positions in favor of Gnosticism, Manichaeism, and even Marcionism (which she liked because of its fierce opposition to the Jehovah of the Bible). This is not the place to develop these views, but her rather exaggerated way of defending views that she knew to be controversial (especially in her *Letter to a Priest*) was in keeping with her natural impatience and independence of mind. Weil was quite capable of using her immense intelligence to argue at great length in defense of her views, refusing to give up. Obstinacy was one of her defining characteristics.

Objections to the Church

In this time of dreadful persecution, Father Joseph-Marie Perrin took an active interest in the fate of the Jews and did all that was in his power to help them, which earned him in 1999 the title of "Righteous among the Nations" (attributed by Yad Vashem, the official Holocaust memorial agency of the state of Israel). It was Simone Weil's Jewishness that appealed to Perrin, but she was after something quite different: not help against persecution but the chance to work in the fields. Their conversations started off on the wrong foot and involved quite fierce arguments. Weil's awkwardness and unease affected those around her, and Perrin was not exempt. She was probably "a stranger to any religious confession,"[18] and she was half-unconsciously playing a kind of game of advance and retreat, which was manifestly never going to produce a clear-cut resolution. Yet the difficulties they encountered were also related to the various problems and contradictions experienced by the Catholic Church on the eve of the war, especially in connection with the magisterium. These can be summed up briefly as follows.

Catholicism at the time was rigid and stifling.[19] Very little had changed since the Council of Trent (convened in reaction to the Protestant Reformation). The neoscholastic revival promoted by Vatican I had in many ways made it worse, and the crisis of modernism at the turn of the century had provoked a further clampdown. Simone Weil's position was that she did not recognize the Catholic religion in the traditional catechism. The *Letter to a Priest* begins abruptly with these words: "When I read the catechism of the Council of Trent, it seems as though I have nothing in common with the religion there set forth" (*LP*, 9).

The teaching of theology was controlled entirely by the thought of Saint Thomas Aquinas or, rather, by the neoscholastic tradition, as encouraged by Leo XIII in his 1879 encyclical *Aeterni patris* and vigorously pursued by theologians like Réginald Garrigou-Lagrange. People used terms like "absolute Thomism" and "state doctrine."[20]

Alternative interpretations were automatically suspect. The contributions of historicocritical study and of patristics were still considered controversial after the war, when the emergence of the so-called *nouvelle théologie* challenged the dominance of neo-Thomism.[21] Perrin naturally encouraged Simone Weil to read Aquinas. She was not impressed. She was not alone in this: another recent Catholic convert with no previous religious background, philosopher Gabriel Marcel, had a similar reaction.[22]

Her attitude to Jacques Maritain, that indefatigable promoter of the "angelic doctor," Aquinas, gives a perfect illustration of her reasoning. No doubt at the instigation of Perrin, she read Maritain's *Humanisme intégral* (1936) but was not converted to Thomism. In her last letter to Perrin, sent from Casablanca on 26 May 1942, on her way to New York (where Maritain was now living in exile, enabling them to meet and correspond for a while), she did not mince words:

> We are living in times which have no precedent, and in our present situation universality, which could formerly be implicit, has to be fully explicit. It has to permeate our language and the whole of our way of life. Today it is not nearly enough merely to be a saint, but we must have the saintliness demanded by the present moment, a new saintliness, itself also without precedent. Maritain said this, but he only enumerated the aspects of saintliness of former days, which for the time being at least, have become out of date. (*WG*, 98–99)

She was of course struck, as were many others, by the beauty and force of Maritain's spirited and very successful *À travers le désastre* (*France, My Country, Through the Disaster*), written for both the American and the French public.[23] But when, on her arrival in New York, she read his latest book, *Les droits de l'homme et la loi naturelle* (*The Rights of Man and Natural Law,* 1942), any admiration she may have felt for the author turned into fierce opposition. There were many reasons for this, including Maritain's picture of Antigone as the "eternal heroine of natural law." Weil reacted violently to this claim in one of the greatest essays from her London period, "On Human Personality": "It is extraordinary that Antigone's unwritten law should have been confused with the idea of natural right . . . The unwritten law that she obeyed . . . was the same love, extreme and absurd, which led Christ to the Cross."[24]

Another major stumbling block was the language used by the church. This had become fixed and formulaic, with the result that it was completely out of touch with the new generations of believers and in many cases actually unintelligible. There was a pressing need for a new hermeneutics, using the best critical tools available to interpret the sacred texts for the modern world.

For her part, Weil confided to a friend in Marseilles that she could not always understand what Perrin meant.[25] She evidently doubted his philosophical sharpness and indeed his general intellectual culture.[26]

Intellectual Pyrotechnics

This was the state of French Catholicism that Simone Weil the intellectual came up against, and it was a great shock to her. She desperately wanted to understand. For her, the intellect was sovereign and could make no concessions. She represented the "*fides quaerens intellectum*," which Anselm rejected, rather than the "*credo ut intelligam*," derived from Augustine, whom he preferred.[27]

Abstract thought came naturally to her, as to many born philosophers, but in Weil's case it was reinforced by a strong mathematical bent that she shared with her brother. She tended to cast everything, including theology, in mathematical terms. In that she resembled some of the forerunners of the Renaissance, like Nicholas of Cusa, whom she discovered toward the end of her time in Marseilles.[28] Her interest in mathematics also explains her enthusiasm for Pythagoreanism. The last section of her *Intuitions pré-chrétiennes* (*Intimations of Christianity among the Greeks*, 1951) is a pyrotechnic display of intelligence applied to dogma, a kind of cosmotheological poem or dream that evokes Cusa's "spiritual hunt" (*De venatione sapientiae,* 1463). Weil was not beyond claiming an element of genius for herself. In her final letter to Perrin in May 1942 she spoke of her attempt to find an analogy for a new revelation of the universe and human destiny, commenting that "it will take more genius than Archimedes needed to invent mechanics and physics" (*WG,* 46). However, her speculations are decidedly unorthodox, and there is at least a whiff of heresy about them.[29] The Catholic path now seemed to be definitively blocked. In these conversations and controversies, Weil, despite her abomination of the hair-splitting *pilpul* style of Talmudic exegesis, showed herself to be every bit as persnickety, obsessive, and obstinate. She was never prepared to back down if she thought she was right. She was never easy to talk to, although she was perfectly agreeable and indeed quite warm and friendly on the human level. Stanislas Fumet, who met her in Marseilles, commented half-severely and half-jokingly: "This avid philosopher scrutinized everything with such passionate objectivity!" They had spent an hour discussing Maritain and the question of slavery in Aristotle without Fumet suspecting for an instant that his interlocutor was the author of the remarkably impressive article on quantum theory to which he devoted an admiring review just a few months later.[30]

Simone Weil's main difficulties with Catholicism were centered on the very idea of the church and the jurisdiction that it claimed. She found it too reminiscent of what Plato called the "great beast" (which she equated with the beast of the Apocalypse). Her prejudice against it continued to strengthen, as can be seen in the progression of the language she used to describe it. She suggested that the power of the church could be seen as more totalitarian than that of empires such as the German Reich (*OC* VI.4, 249).[31] At the very end of her life, in London, she went even further: "If it is true that the gates of Hell have not prevailed, that can only mean that the true faith has survived in secret in a few hidden hearts—well hidden" (*OC* IV.2, 331).[32]

This virulent rejection of the Roman magisterium stems from a deep and powerful sense—both innate and acquired, as we will see—of the absolute freedom of conscience. Freewill is sovereign. Not that she had much difficulty with the basic doctrines of the faith (her personal experience of Christ and her love for him gave ample access to these mysteries), but she could not relinquish the critical examination of what she was being asked to believe. That critical examination was essentially philosophical in nature in that it was based on the systematic exercise of doubt, as she had learned from her revered teacher Alain.

Her conception of doubt was an extreme one, as can be seen from the preliminary remarks she makes in a letter to Couturier: "Among the opinions that are to follow there are some about which I am doubtful; but were it a strict article of the faith to esteem them false, I should regard them as being as serious an obstacle as the others, for I am firmly convinced that they are held in doubt by me, that is to say, that it is not legitimate to deny them categorically" (*LP*, 10). A little later she added this: "I look upon a certain suspension of judgment with regard to all thoughts whatever they may be, without any exception, as constituting the virtue of humility in the domain of the intelligence" (*LP*, 12). This is precisely Alain's position. She had recently reread his famous *Entretiens au bord de la mer* (*Conversations by the Seaside*, 1931), in which the theme of doubt appears frequently and almost obsessively in the ninth conversation: "I refuse ready-made thoughts. I judge them: that is what thinking is"; "Doubt is the salt of obedience" (which gives rise to the remarkable adage "to obey while refusing"); and again: "the true god, which is none other than refusal, sacred doubt, scruple."[33]

What a strange position to be adopted by this almost-Catholic, would-be-Catholic, young woman! With on the one hand her cult of free critical examination and on the other her thoroughly negative reading of church history, Simone Weil seems to embody the spirit of the Reformation, for these are essentially Protestant characteristics.

Two other major strands in Weil's thought might be adduced here, both featuring a contrasting pair of concepts where she accentuates the contrast. One is the opposition between sovereignty and suzerainty, as seen for instance in the struggle between the state and networks of interest. Here a central and indeed emblematic figure is Lawrence of Arabia, whose *Seven Pillars of Wisdom* she had read with admiration before the war. The other is the opposition between belief and mysticism.[34] I do not develop these here, but they provide the transition to the third and final part of this chapter, which focuses on the extreme modernity of Weil.

Weil's Modernity

The fact that Simone Weil seems to progress in fits and starts, with great enthusiasms, total rejections, and plenty of assertiveness, may well disorientate the reader. Yet we can discern a vision of great scope and modernity. Let us consider two main aspects: a way of looking and a way of operating (a *gaze* and a *praxis*, or an embodied philosophy and an embodied, committed Christianity). These two aspects, representing a kind of double quest or prayer, can be summed up in a single maxim: "Lose nothing of the profane world." On this point there is a striking parallel with the thought of the great Swiss theologian Hans Urs von Balthasar in his 1956 work, *The God Question and Modern Man*.[35] Balthasar explores the same territory as Weil and is sometimes very close to her. Both look at the modern world in a new way, opening up a connection with a transcendent reality.

An Embodied Philosophy

This is best seen in a letter Weil wrote in January 1941 to Déodat Roche, a leading expert at the time on the Cathars. In it she said: "A thought never exists fully until it is embodied in a human setting, that is to say, something that is open to the outside world, that is immersed in the surrounding society, that is in contact with the whole of that society, not just a closed group of disciples round a Master. Without the atmosphere of such a setting to breathe, a fine mind may indeed create a philosophy; but it can only be of a second order, and thought in such a case will attain a lesser degree of reality" (*OC* VI.4, 626). It is clear from this that the cast of Weil's mind led her to seek to make bridges between the philosophical and the religious and to try to understand their puzzling relationship, with the aim of reviving the Greek idea of "philo-sophia," which made no distinction between them.

The comparison with Urs von Balthasar can be usefully summed up under three headings: the dialogue between cultures, the decisive importance of their reading of Greek tragedy, and their interest in the church fathers. On the first of these, we have already seen the extraordinary *libido sciendi* that drove Weil in her attempt to embrace all of human knowledge. It is perhaps only in the area of mathematics that she outdid Balthasar, but one might suggest that she took the notion of implicitness (as in "Forms of the Implicit Love of God")[36] further than he did in relation to the seeds of the Word, which her ultrasensitive intuition detected everywhere.

Both thinkers were equally passionate about the contribution of the Greeks. Their arguments are remarkably similar, centering on the way the figure of the suffering righteous (just) man in Plato is enriched by that of the heroes devoured by their love for others—Prometheus or Antigone. Balthasar says that Aeschylus's *Prometheus* is a "religious event," while Sophocles's *Oedipus Rex* (which he compared to the *Antigone*) is "almost a liturgical drama."[37] Weil also gives considerable attention to the figure of Prometheus, but the key for her is the *tô pathei mathos* (wisdom through suffering) of Aeschylus's *Agamemnon*.[38] There is, however, a significant gulf between these two. If Balthasar hints at a kind of "inchoate Christology" in Greek tragedy,[39] Simone Weil is typically more outspoken in talking of "lines certainly inspired by the mysteries, and absolutely Christian."[40] Balthasar speaks of the fathers "taking over all the partial truths in paganism,"[41] whereas Weil takes the opposite tack: Augusto del Noce refers to the way she incorporates Christianity into Greek thought.[42] So, despite the remarkable closeness of their interests, the two thinkers adopt opposing positions.

The third area in which they can be compared is that of patristics, to the renewal of which they each contributed in their own way. The series "Sources chrétiennes" was founded in Lyons in 1942 by the Jesuits Victor Fontoynont, Jean Daniélou, Henri de Lubac, and Claude Mondésert, at a time when the church was still suspicious of patristic studies.[43] Daniélou wrote two books on Gregory of Nyssa, in 1942 and 1944, the first of which (*Contemplation de la vie de Moïse*) launched the series. These were followed by one on Origen in 1948, then one on Philo of Alexandria in 1958. Balthasar in fact got in first with a volume on Origen as early as 1938, followed by two on Gregory of Nyssa (1939 and 1942) and one on Irenaeus in 1943. Simone Weil was not far behind. She had already read Maurice de Gandillac's thesis on Nicholas of Cusa before leaving Marseilles and avidly devoured all the notes dealing with those church fathers or medieval theologians who challenged the magisterium and bordered on heresy (just as she always favored "irregular" thinkers).[44] Simone Weil returned to the fathers in the summer of 1942, while she was in New York, looking in particular at Justin Martyr, Clement of Rome, Clement of Alexandria, Irenaeus, Origen, and even Eusebius. Having never encountered them before, she read an impressive amount, devouring the somewhat austere volumes of Jacques-Paul Migne's mid-nineteenth-century series, *Patrologia latina* and *Patrologia graeca*, and also the English translations published slightly later in the twenty-five volumes of the Presbyterian *Ante-Nicene Christian Library*.[45] However, she favored material that seemed to support her own views, working with no method and nothing to stop her making silly mistakes and blithely ignoring all secondary material. Nevertheless, this almost frenzied curiosity betrays a remarkable intellectual energy that fiercely resisted any attempt at regimentation.

An Embodied Christianity

Weil's thought here rests on a circular argument, namely, that "all that exists is equally sustained in existence by the creative love of

God." The corollary of this is that "Christianity should contain all vocations without exception since it is catholic" (*WG*, 26). She is writing here to Father Perrin and using the word "catholic" in its etymological sense. She wanted to "show the public the possibility of a truly incarnated Christianity" (*WG*, 75–76). It is not surprising that she should have dreamed of renewing the social teaching of the church. Her experience of committed social action predisposed her to welcome any reform that favored openness in the context of an overly rigid magisterium. She therefore called for a Christianity that was open to the world and fully engagé (committed). This would take the following forms.

On the question of a fresh examination of the conditions of the workers, Weil was well placed to give a convincing testimony, and so it was natural for Perrin to introduce her to another Dominican, Jacques Loew, who worked as a longshoreman in Marseilles.[46] Loew became secretary of the Économie et humanisme movement in Lyons, which had been founded in 1941. Father Louis-Joseph Lebret, who launched the movement's review the following year, asked Simone Weil for an article on her experience working in a factory (published as "Expérience de la vie d'usine" [Experience of Factory Life] and based on a long letter she had written to Jules Romains in late 1935).[47] It should be noted that this kind of commitment provided no guarantee against dubious relationships with the government of the day: Lebret had some involvement with the Vichy régime, whose social ideas he shared and whose corporatist doctrine his center was intended to promote.

Another form of commitment is the idea of Christianity as a leaven in society, giving rise to a kind of invisible church, expressed through religious orders "without habit or distinguishing marks." She indicates this in one of her notebooks in February 1942 (*OC* VI.3, 65–66).[48]

It is then a short step from the notion of the invisible church to that of a "lay order," which was to have a great success in later years. Enzo Bianchi, the founder of a mixed ecumenical community in Bose in northern Italy in the 1960s, called himself a "lay monk." The Sant' Egidio community, founded by Andrea Riccardi in Rome in 1968, is another international association of laypeople.

This idea of interconfessional groupings growing in popularity leads on to that of the dialogue of cultures and their complementarity (through the exploration of what is implicit and explicit in each), to which Weil was deeply attached, and hence to interfaith dialogue, for which she fought doggedly. The *Letter to a Priest* is really a long development of this position, with all the oddities and excesses that have already been noted.

The problem of interfaith dialogue, still so controversial today, inevitably raises that of the missionary calling of the churches. Here again Weil spoke out fearlessly, believing as she did that missionary work had more often than not had a disastrous and destructive effect on other cultures. She had no hesitation in drawing attention to the scandalous link between the advance of the missionaries and that of the colonizing armies.[49]

In 2010 the four-hundredth anniversary of the death of Matteo Ricci, the pioneer Jesuit missionary to China, drew attention afresh to this question. It is generally recognized that a certain degree of sharing and mixing of wisdom and spiritual experience is beneficial and necessary, for "the Spirit blows where it wills." One term that has been put forward is that of polyphony.[50] Simone Weil would have approved.

More broadly, Weil invites us to redefine the relationship between the profane and the sacred, between the natural and the supernatural. She sees the latter in terms of a source of light and inspiration for the profane world, which allows her, without contradiction, on the one hand to evoke the happy days of the early Middle Ages, when "the supernatural did not mix with the profane, did not squash it, did not attempt to suppress it. It left it intact, and in so doing remained pure. It was its origin and its destination" (*OC* IV.2, 419). On the other hand, at almost the same time, she wrote this: "It is not a question of there being a Christian point of view and then other points of view, but of truth and error. This does not mean that what is not Christian is false, but that everything that is true is Christian" (*OC* VI.3, 395). She thus distinguishes the two domains quite sharply but proceeds to incorporate one to some extent into the other. This can be seen as a very modern way of recentering everything on what has been called "the authentically human."[51]

Conclusion

What conclusions can we draw about Simone Weil's relationship to Christianity and the church? She certainly exercised considerable freedom in relation to doctrine, not least because she insisted on remaining on the threshold of the institution, "at the intersection of Christianity and everything that is not Christianity" (*WG*, 76). She went as far as to proclaim that "the Catholic religion has never had a thorough philosophical spring-clean" and added: "In order to achieve that, it is necessary to be both inside *and* outside" (*OC* VI.2, 438).

What Simone Weil actually wanted was nothing less than a new religion.[52] That involved undermining two thousand years of Christian civilization, and she was fully aware that she was situating herself at the breaking point. Plowing up the ground in all directions, she was sowing the seeds of a revolution that was both specious (the absurdities in her thought, arising from her extreme assumptions, are all too obvious) and fruitful, for the sure-footedness of her introspective journey, which takes her to the summits of mystical thought, is extraordinarily impressive.

Yet one must also recognize two weaknesses that cast something of a shadow over what has been characterized as the "admirable" sublimity of Weil's thought (with reference to Ruysbroeck, known as "the Admirable"). In a lapidary phrase that sums up her indomitable will, Stanislas Breton suggests that she "prized her lucidity even more than her fervor."[53] Weil, in her closeness to the Flemish mystics, was so keen on the idea of self-annihilation (she invented the concept of "decreation")[54] that she has been suspected, while meditating on nothingness, of maintaining the self in a position of supremacy. If she heeded the injunction to obedience (which Urs von Balthasar characterizes as *Bejahung*, the act of saying "yes"), it was only once she had used up all the oil in the lamp of her will.

The second weakness that undermines her sublimity and leaves the reader frankly puzzled can be put in the form of a question. Why did this exceptional woman, who, as Balthasar said of Paul Claudel, "could breathe only in the air of the world-totality,"[55] cut off from that totality her Jewish brothers and sisters? This strange Christian is more than strange: she remains an enigma.

4 Jean Grenier and the "Spirit of Orthodoxy"

Toby Garfitt

In his studies of the major French literary periodical, the *Nouvelle revue française* (*NRF*), in the years leading up to the Second World War, Martyn Cornick has traced how "Jean Paulhan edited the *NRF* so as to prolong and develop its literary reputation, at the same time as taking calculated risks to 'shock the bourgeois' among its readership."[1] He draws attention to the remarkable way Paulhan, as general editor, "balanced the review, aesthetically as well as politically, around a centre of gravity that is identifiably radical-republican and liberal," showing how he aimed to place the *NRF* "at the centre of an oscillation between what he called the *saugrenu*—in other words, texts (not necessarily literary) which challenged the *status quo*—and the 'orthodoxe.'"[2] One article that deserves the adjective *saugrenu* (whimsical, apparently preposterous) was the opening piece in the April 1936 issue. It bore the title "L'âge des orthodoxies" (The Age of Orthodoxies) and was signed by Jean Grenier.

Jean Grenier was coming to play an important part in the life of the *NRF*. Previous examples of the *saugrenu* might be Panaït Istrati's polemical attack on Soviet repression in 1929, which Grenier felt was an excellent counterbalance to the increasingly pro-leftist articles of Julien Benda or the pieces by Raymond Roussel and Michel Leiris in 1935.[3] Grenier was clearly a valuable sounding board for Paulhan in such instances. He was also a source of provocative texts himself. A series of articles on India challenged conventional Eurocentric thinking, in line with Paulhan's own Orientalist inclinations.[4] Later contributions would help to counter not only the specifically pro-communist tendencies within the *NRF* but also its increasing politicization under the influence of people like Gide, Malraux, and indeed Gaston Gallimard (who formally handed over the responsibility for the *NRF* to Paulhan in January 1935).

Grenier was of course not simply a docile supporter of Paulhan, ready to be wheeled out when the left-wingers threatened to get out of hand. He was his own man, and like other contributors he was given the freedom to write what he liked. He produced a mixture of book reviews and more personal essays, with an important series of brief notes in the "Air du mois" section from 1934 on.

With the first round of voting in the general election due to take place at the end of April 1936, Paulhan's decision to publish the article then rather than a couple of months earlier, when he received it, was a calculated one. Daniel Halévy commented a little later that he had heard that it and the sequel had been hatched "in high secret councils."[5] Grenier's piece would undoubtedly challenge readers and offend many. Tensions were running high. The Rassemblement populaire or coalition of the Left had published its manifesto in early January, and at the end of that month Pierre Laval had been replaced as prime minister by Albert Sarraut, whose watchword had been "Communism, that is the enemy."

Grenier's article began with a penetrating analysis of the postwar period as constituted by three distinct phases, the "age of negations" (1917–24), the "age of heresies" (1924–32), and finally the "age of orthodoxies," in which commitment to a political creed was all-important. "What is urgent is to get oneself a faith, to join a party."[6] Many intellectuals had adopted Marxism not merely as an economic theory but also as a philosophical doctrine, indeed a quasi-theological dogma. Marx had never pretended to explain everything in life, but his writings were now being used as infallible scripture. Independent thought was being quashed, and any hope of true culture denied to those who had most need of it. "Socialism, instead of being a narrowing of the human spirit, should be a broadening of it."[7] The first part of Grenier's article ended with a passionate appeal: "Spread culture, yes; but now that unthinking conformism has triumphed in the middle classes, do not ensure the same happens among the workers."[8]

The second part moved away from politics to trace a parallel development in religion. In singling out neo-Thomism, Grenier was not attacking it for itself—any more than he had been attacking Marxism in itself. A reviewer in the *Mercure de France* pointed out that he could have said the same things about Fascism[9]—but in order to show the dangers that flow from any one individual tradition claiming to have a monopoly on truth, in religion just as much as in politics. "Nothing is more natural and legitimate than to be catholic or revolutionary; nothing is more objectionable than to try to make all human knowledge serve the purpose of justifying one's faith."[10] In a later book, *Le choix* (*Choice,* 1941), Grenier would name the leading neo-Thomist, Garrigou-Lagrange, expressing astonishment that the author of books like *Le sens commun: La philosophie de l'être* (*Common Sense: The Philosophy of Being,* 1909) should place such confidence in a so-called *philosophia perennis,* which was after all derived from a synthesis of Mediterranean civilizations and represented "rather an admirable order than a unified and coherent thought."[11] Grenier was himself always subject to the opposite temptation, that of the nondualistic philosophical religions of India and later China (he was to write an important book on Taoism[12]), although he did not refer to them in the *Essai sur l'esprit d'orthodoxie* (*Essay on the Spirit of Orthodoxy*).

On the sociopolitical side, Grenier of course knew that he would be accused of Fascism. In *Commune,* his former colleague at the *NRF,* Georges Sadoul, attacked him publicly as a "scourge" of Marxism.[13] Étiemble, who was at that time secretary of the Association internationale des écrivains pour la défense de la culture, sent Paulhan a detailed refutation of eight "errors" that he had detected in Grenier's article. He later recognized that his anger was fueled by the conviction of the absolute necessity of maintaining a united front against

Fascism and that in fact Grenier had been right.[14] The *NRF* itself was accused of selling out. It had been coming closer to the antifascist movement, but Grenier's article provoked a number of readers to cancel their subscriptions,[15] and in the first issue of *Europe* since Jean Guéhenno's eviction as editor in a Communist coup, Georges Friedmann labeled "L'âge des orthodoxies" a manifesto, implying that it signaled a new political stance on the part of the review.[16] It was more in the nature of a corrective: Paulhan, who wanted to defend the freedom of critical thought, was under pressure from Gide and Gaston Gallimard to take a harder political line, and Grenier's article helped to buck the trend.

What Grenier had of course not addressed was the worry that underlay Étiemble's criticisms, namely, the timeliness of his attack on ideological orthodoxies. He made no explicit mention of the dangers of Fascism or of the need to stand against it. He cast himself rather as the heir of the critic Albert Thibaudet, who had recently died. In an article titled "Thibaudet politique et moraliste," published in the special Thibaudet issue of the *NRF* in July, he praised the scrupulous impartiality of his illustrious predecessor and his refusal to be drawn into overemphasizing one factor rather than another (as between, for instance, the individual human agent and the cultural context) in his interpretation of historical events. "Truly Thibaudet has nothing to please simplistic minds." "The Age of Orthodoxies" would similarly offend the "simplistic minds." At the same time, Grenier was honest enough to recognize that Thibaudet's dilettantism could become embarrassing. "Intellectual dilettantism and butterfly-hunting take up too much room in his work . . . The most lucid and uncluttered intelligence cannot put off reaching conclusions."[17] But would he in his turn be able to rise to the challenge?

Who was Jean Grenier, and what circles did he move in?[18] Born in 1898, he had grown up in the provincial town of Saint-Brieuc on the north coast of Brittany. He had attended a private Catholic school, the Institution Saint-Charles, run by the Société de Marie or Marianists—not because of any religious convictions on the part of his family but because it prepared pupils for the prestigious naval school at Brest. As a young man he had formed a lifelong friendship with the writer Louis Guilloux, also from Saint-Brieuc, who remained faithful to his syndicalist background, and among his other friends he counted Jean Guéhenno, son of a cobbler like Guilloux, and, like him, strongly influenced by the left-wing idealism of Romain Rolland. Grenier's sympathy for left-wing causes was tempered by other friendships and interests. He went to Paris to follow the *classes préparatoires* for the *grandes écoles*, and among his fellow students in the *khâgne* at Louis-le-Grand were two fervent young Catholics, both destined to follow distinguished intellectual careers. One was Jean Guitton, two years younger than Grenier. More than twenty years later, it was to be Grenier who would recommend to Brice Parain that the *NRF* publish Guitton's first notes on the remarkable biblical scholar and spiritual guide Père Pouget. The other was André Festugière, then known as Jean, an exact contemporary and close friend of Grenier's, who became a major Dominican scholar of Greek thought.

After obtaining his *agrégation* in philosophy, though not yet a doctorate, Grenier taught in Algiers and Naples and then returned to Paris and worked for a couple of years as an editorial secretary to Gaston Gallimard at the Éditions de la *NRF*. By that stage he had gone through a period of somewhat cynical dandyism and had returned to the Catholic faith of his childhood, under the influence of people like Festugière and the flamboyant poet Max Jacob. At the same time he had been developing his interest in Indian philosophy with the idea of possibly writing a thesis on its links with Greek thought and art; his first articles for the *NRF* were on India, in 1930.

In that same year, 1930, Grenier spent two months as a *pensionnaire* (distinguished visitor) at the Château de Lourmarin in Provence. The idea was to set up the château as the Provençal equivalent of the Villa Médicis in Rome and sponsor a number of promising young artists and writers to come and work there. This would be the first year of the project, and Grenier, who was already familiar with Lourmarin through his good friend Henri Bosco, would fit the bill admirably. His fellow *pensionnaires* were to include the right-wing Catholic critic Henri Guillemin. Lourmarin indeed attracted people on the political right, and some of them were Grenier's friends, among them Noël Vesper (Noël Nougat), the Protestant pastor of Lourmarin, whose wife was shot at the end of the war for collaboration. Others, like Massis and Maurras, he did not know personally, but he insisted on admiring Maurras the writer publicly even when it was risky to do so. Gabriel Marcel later became a close friend, when they were both teaching in Montpellier in 1941.

For most of the 1930s Grenier was back in Algiers, teaching at the lycée, where his most famous pupil was Albert Camus. Although he was very present in the pages of the *NRF*, his physical contacts with the cultural life of Paris were limited to a few days a year. Any spare time that he had was taken up with his own creative writing, work on his thesis (now to be devoted not to India but to the thought of the nineteenth-century Breton philosopher Jules Lequier, who is often seen as a precursor to existentialism), and looking after his young family. Politics could not be ignored, of course. Emmanuel Mounier wrote to ask not only whether Grenier would contribute to *Esprit*, which had been launched in 1932, but also whether he would consider temporarily leading the new local group in Algiers while his ex-pupil Max-Pol Fouchet was recovering from illness.[19] Grenier declined the offer, but he was happy to give an occasional public lecture under the auspices of the *Esprit* group.

Grenier's own position was not dissimilar to that of Mounier's movement, with its emphasis on spiritual and human values, and when Mounier pressed him to publish in *Esprit* the same kind of notes that had been so successful in the "current trends" section of the *NRF*, he must have felt tempted to transfer his allegiance. The December 1934 issue of the *NRF* carried a two-page review by Grenier of the movement and its journal that is at least cautiously welcoming. Grenier saluted its spiritual basis but warned that there was a danger that it might follow the path already chosen by its sibling, La troisième force, that of revolutionary politics, and abandon all vestiges of the original "spiritual program." His association with *Esprit* over the next couple of years was to help him to explore a kind of practical commitment, which provided an important balance to the rather deliberately antipolitical pieces that continued to appear in the *NRF* and a valuable protection against the possible temptations of right-wing solutions.

One of these temptations came from his old mentor and long-term correspondent, Edmond Lambert. Lambert was afraid that Grenier was being seduced by left-wing ideas. The right course to follow was not to seek some kind of temporal remedy for a supposed *malheur* but rather to "live above yourself, *every day*." This sort of right-wing preexistentialism was very appealing to Grenier and was of course in line with the advice that Lambert had always given to his protégés, who included Louis Guilloux.[20] Grenier's openness to Lambert's strongly held opinions does not undermine the left-wing sympathies (and indeed credentials) that he had been developing during the early 1930s. His position can be distinguished from that of Henry de Montherlant, for instance, who, in response to Paulhan's call in the *NRF* that winter to "take [a] position," declared his intention of proclaiming in a lecture in Algiers in February that, on the contrary, "one must remain neutral."[21]

An essay written a few months earlier under the title "Sagesse de Lourmarin" (Wisdom of Lourmarin) reveals something of Grenier's struggles to face up to the current situation despite a tone of apparently apolitical lyricism. In the essay he discusses his strategy of "attachment" as an alternative to the impossible demands of absolute truth. A region of France or even an animal or an inanimate object can act as a sign of the absolute and inspire a genuine attachment, breaking the indifference previously associated with merely relative values.[22] Human beings and human society seem less attractive, however, and in this Grenier shows himself to be very different from his former pupil Albert Camus, who wrote as follows in a letter to him in 1938: "I cannot separate myself from those among whom I was born and whom I cannot abandon."[23] For Jean Guéhenno, of course, truth itself was defined as a function of humanity: "The truth that matters to me is an earthly one, fully human . . . It comes only from us . . . It is indeed *the* truth. The truth of human beings, of man."[24] Yet in a letter to Camus in 1947, Grenier makes an important concession: "As for me I continue to believe that the essential part of truth is neither social nor historical; I believe this less than in the past, having become aware of how exaggerated my position was and how much it was controlled by temperament . . . No, I have to resign myself to this: there is no *truth* for man that is not incarnated."[25]

People can organize themselves in order to "change life" (the title of a book by Jean Guéhenno published in 1961, adopted as a slogan by the protesters of May 1968). But Grenier found it hard to endorse the idea of human action. In one of his early letters to Guéhenno he denied "that the artist should be directly involved in humanitarian work,"[26] and he persisted in finding the cult of action ill founded and sterile when not actually dangerous, as is shown by his open letter to André Malraux about his novel *L'espoir* (Hope) (included in *Essai sur l'esprit d'orthodoxie* in 1938). Most people, according to Grenier, are not called to emulate the exceptional figure of the hero or indeed that of the sage, who each offer radically different solutions to the stark contrast between human and inhuman, between the "full" and the "empty."

What then did humanity mean to Grenier? In his first *Lexique* (*Lexicon* or *Dictionary*, Gallimard, 1955), the entry for the word *humain* offers not a definition but a question: "But first of all, what is man?" In his correspondence with Guéhenno he emphasized the metaphysical and indeed existential aspects of the human condition ("The religion of humanity gives only a partial satisfaction to human evil"), and in 1935 he mentioned his plan to write a book dealing with "human anguish and its relationship to the social question"—never completed but leading perhaps to *L'existence malheureuse* (*Wretched Existence*, 1957).[27] In an essay on the painter Georges Braque, Grenier claimed that "the human is measured by the extent of the sacrifice that must be made to give up a perfection . . . The human is, after the revolt of despair, a weakness that is accepted."[28] In 1955 he published a book titled *À propos de l'humain* (*About the Human*), which brought together several of his essays, and the final chapter, "Qu'est-ce que l'humain?" (What Is the Human?), dating from 1950, starts by rejecting both the attempt to provide an essentialist definition and the optimistic profession of faith in the future ("if man is nothing in himself, he is capable of becoming anything"), insisting that "the human oscillates between the vital and the cerebral without ever finding its point of equilibrium." "What is human is this reality of the in-between, this unforced friendship, this hidden link between one individual and others, this understanding, this complicity, this collusion, everything that sighs in tune with nature while not being confused with it." It is for that reason that Grenier rejected the programs and orthodoxies of the modern world, for "the human resides precisely in a crack that the 'total man' or the 'new man' hastens to fill up."[29]

At least Grenier tried to face up to the issue in the form of a second article, in which he offered a reasoned reply to his critics. "L'orthodoxie contre l'intelligence" (Orthodoxy Against Intelligence), which appeared in the August issue of the *NRF*, answered Friedmann point by point and concluded by drawing attention to an insinuation that was particularly painful because near the bone. Friedmann had suggested that Grenier's article represented "a refusal to take sides, an antipathy toward action that stems from a temperament unfitted for practical life."[30] Grenier's response is magnificent: "But those who possess such a temperament are quite ready to recognize their limits if they are honest about it; they may well be the first to suffer from them; they will perhaps commit themselves to action one day, as far as they can, and not on the side of the privileged. But it is not making things any easier for them when the first condition that is proposed is the acceptance of ideas which they see as quite unacceptable."[31] The crucial point is that "one can love only that which one believes to be true,"[32] so that intellectual terrorism is counterproductive. Grenier had discussed intellectual terrorism in an exchange of letters with

Paulhan in May and June, which was contemporary with the writing of "Orthodoxy Against Intelligence." Paulhan had sent him a summary of his own book *Les fleurs de Tarbes* (*The Flowers of Tarbes*, subtitled *Terror in Literature*), whose subject is of course very similar, though in the field of literature rather than politics.

Grenier's profession of faith in intellectual values was bravely saluted by Guéhenno in a letter that he sent the day the article appeared: "That all seems to me just right," wrote the man who had been forced to resign by the intellectual terrorists.[33] Paulhan also approved strongly, though he was not entirely sure about the personal element.

To the original two articles on orthodoxies Grenier added several other pieces, including lectures and an open letter to Malraux, in order to make the volume that was published by Gallimard in April 1938 under the title *Essai sur l'esprit d'orthodoxie*. Much of the emphasis was of course on social, political, and cultural questions, but Grenier did return to religion in the opening chapter, titled "What Is an orthodoxy?" Here he starts by borrowing a definition from the dubious nineteenth-century Orientalist and racialist Émile Burnouf: "Every orthodoxy thinks that it is the only correct one and the only true one."[34] An orthodoxy, then, is a doctrine of exclusion. It is a development from mere belief and appears to be "an inevitable consequence of every belief that is successful." It is marked by "crystallization," "stiffness," and intransigence. "It can maintain itself only by remaining immobile, for the smallest crack might bring down the whole edifice."[35] Grenier appears not to have encountered Newman's ideas on the development of doctrine or indeed the growing *nouvelle théologie* movement, or he would surely have mentioned them here. He did correspond with both Étienne Gilson and Jean Daniélou from 1943 on and indeed published Gilson's essay on the existential limits of philosophy in the important edited volume *L'existence* (1945), but he did not engage with them theologically. As for Jacques Maritain, he appreciated the presentation but took issue with the substance. In the original article Grenier had commented that thanks to "a mind as open and generous as Maritain's" the intransigence of Thomist doctrine had seemed less rebarbative, but "you find out that you were really a Thomist without knowing it."[36]

Grenier says that he understands perfectly well that humans fear loneliness above all things ("escaping from isolation is the first need of man"), and that is a strong reason for signing up to an orthodox system. His first book in 1933 had after all been called *Les îles* (*Islands*), which he later defined as "isolations." Nevertheless, "such conversions . . . are none the less suspect from the point of view of intellectual integrity, for one should not accept any idea, even one that promises to bring benefits, if one does not believe it to be true."[37] He then traces the process by which, in Marxism as in Christianity, scientific advances are first of all seen as contradicting orthodox belief and therefore ignored, then as dangerous and therefore attacked, and finally as invincible and therefore accommodated, while all the time the claim is made that orthodoxy has made no concessions and lost nothing of its authority. The two concrete examples he takes are both aspects of the evolution debate: the creation of the world, and species transformism. Christian thinkers tried unsuccessfully to appropriate elements of the ongoing debates on such subjects in a vain desire to show that a single overarching principle could account for every aspect of existence. "The Church," he says, "was wrong in trying to extend its competence and its jurisdiction to areas which might well not have come within the remit of the Catholic faith, and which in the end it decided to abandon to the sciences, but only after many inglorious struggles!"[38]

What did Christian readers make of this attack on ideological empire building? The first thing to say is that the historical circumstances of the publication of the original essay in 1936 and the volume in 1938 (after the collapse of the Popular Front in January of that year and at the same time as the eventual construction of a government of national defense under Daladier) drew attention to the comments on Marxism rather than those on Thomism, with most reviewers confining themselves to the first. Fouchet in *Esprit* looks more broadly at culture and society but does not directly address religion.[39] Raymond Christoflour in the *Mercure de France* quotes Péguy on the importance of "men of eternal salvation," who will keep alive the original faith, which can still illuminate the letter of necessarily dogmatic beliefs, but he is thinking more of Benda's *clercs*—*La trahison des clercs* (*The Betrayal of the Intellectuals*, 1927) than of specifically religious faith.[40]

Berdyaev, on the other hand, writing in his journal, *Put'*, takes the question of what he calls Christian totalitarianism seriously. "This sort of totalitarianism has nothing in common with Marxist orthodoxy nor with totalitarian states," he affirms:

> Spiritual truth is totalitarian and it relates to the human person . . . Christian totalitarianism, so very distinct from formal liberalism and individualism, presupposes freedom, as the setting of the verymost [*sic*] totalitarian truth . . . An orthodoxy, as the fullness and integral wholeness of truth, is not a given and cannot be bindingly obligatory with any sort of societies, even though religious, for it reveals itself upon the "pathway" and in "life." The book of Grenier leads toward these thoughts and in this is its merit.[41]

There is certainly a strong plea for the humanizing of orthodoxy in Grenier's *Essai*, but Berdyaev has interpreted it very much in his own sense and has not fully considered Grenier's criticisms.

It is a pity that the *Revue thomiste* did not manage to review the book before ceasing publication at the end of 1939, but an interesting if brief review by Jean Rimaud, author of *Thomisme et méthode* (1925), appeared in the Jesuit journal *Études*. After noting that Grenier's primary target does appear to be Marxism rather than any of the other orthodox systems he mentions, he makes the valid point that "the author is on the side of those he criticizes" and continues: "But he is a believer who does not wish to join the ranks of the orthodox." "For us," says Rimaud, "the interest of these pages is to make absolutely clear how 'committed thought' often ceases to be thought at all"; he concludes: "[T]his danger threatens us all; philosophy and science are not the handmaids of politics, and nor is theology."[42] This is a sympathetic and honest response that avoids falling into the trap of taking sides and recognizes the inner struggle of believers, religious or other, who wish to maintain their intellectual integrity at all costs.

On the whole, however, it was not until after the war that Grenier found a sympathetic hearing. Recent critics have been kind to Grenier, as indeed they have tended to be kind to Camus. Susan Suleiman, in a 1991 article on surrealist politics in the 1930s, calls Grenier's initial essay "one of the most acute analyses of the trend toward party orthodoxy, on both the right and the left."[43] Michel Onfray, the maverick philosopher noted for his libertarian views and for his attacks on all forms of religion, is outspoken in his praise of the "magnificent *Essay on the Spirit of Orthodoxy* which was . . . perhaps the first to lay the foundations of that libertarian left to which I aspire: while it is a critique of revolutionary messianism, of Marxist teleology, of the Hegelian dialectic used to justify negativity in history . . . it is at the same time a eulogy of a left-wing political program favoring those modern-day slaves: the poor, the workers, the excluded, the victims of liberal capitalism."[44]

But what was the extent of Grenier's commitment either to real sociopolitical action or to an intellectually respectable faith? He had claimed in his response to Friedmann that he "would perhaps commit [himself] to action one day, as far as [he could], and not on the side of the privileged."[45] His work with the *Esprit* group in Algiers was already an expression of commitment, and his simple, plain-spoken plea in the pages of the *NRF* in December 1937 in favor of the poor and the excluded he saw around him in Algiers, titled "Ils ont faim" (They Are Hungry)—written after all the pieces collected in the *Essai*—is another.[46] Fouchet was indeed in no doubt that the *Essai* itself was "a fighting book, in which a man commits himself."[47] For the most part, however, Grenier exemplified the anguish of the pure intellectual in a time of upheaval who yearns to be free to explore the furthest limits of philosophical, religious, literary, and artistic thought. The *Essai* may seem profoundly "untopical"—indeed

Grenier pointed out in the brief introduction that, although inspired by "topicality" (current affairs), the various pieces were written in reaction against it—and yet paradoxically that is what guarantees its perpetual freshness and relevance.[48]

He certainly continued to resist the blandishments of Catholic or rightist sociopolitical movements. His association with the Jeune France movement, for instance, was slight. Mounier identified him as a somewhat ambivalent prospect for this Vichy organization that had been founded in November 1940 by Pierre Schaeffer, with the encouragement of Mounier, in order to promote art, music, and culture in the context of the Pétainist "national revolution": Grenier, he noted, had an "excellent general orientation, but hitherto he has worked very much on his own."[49] There was to be a big rally at Lourmarin in September 1941. As a friend not only of Lourmarin but also of many of the participants in the rally, Grenier was eager to attend. Fouchet recalled later that they treated the rally as an "excellent way of using Vichy funds for anti-Vichy aims," and in the evening some of them went through the village shouting "Vive de Gaulle!"[50] Grenier said little about the day and had nothing further to do with the movement.

In terms of religious faith and commitment, Grenier equally continued to resist enrollment into any particular camp, while seeking always to push forward in his own exploration of the frontiers. In 1938 he and his family returned from Algiers and found accommodations to rent in Meudon, near Jacques and Raïssa Maritain. Early in 1939 Maritain contacted Grenier for the first time since 1933, inviting him to take part in two of his monthly group meetings at which the topic for discussion would be evil, in both the theological and the philosophical senses. For someone like Grenier, who owed his whole philosophical vocation to his early encounter with the problem of evil, that invitation must have been particularly tempting. On the other hand, he had already had hard words to say about the totalizing pretensions of neo-Thomism, and Jean Guitton, too, with whom Grenier had recently renewed his friendship, was strongly opposed to Maritain's crusading zeal. There is no evidence to show whether Grenier attended the meetings, but in either case he would have been encouraged to return to the question of evil, which was to become the main focus of his philosophical thought in the late 1940s and 1950s.

It was in fact in relation to the understanding of evil that he engaged in a lengthy controversy with Jean Paulhan, who could not accept the Christian views, however undogmatically expressed, that Grenier was putting forward in his book *L'existence malheureuse*. In a long letter, published posthumously as a small book, the key turning point in Grenier's argument comes as he considers the question of doubt:

> I admit the fact of our solitude—and everything I have written up to this point is simply the expression of that solitude. I have an extreme fear of being taken in and imagining that I have an *echo* . . . And yet what if I was deceiving myself in being afraid of being deceived? Is it not the case that I have often had the opposite experience, of trusting someone and then seeing that trust rewarded beyond my hopes? . . . What if . . . what if the call for help that is implicit in me were to receive a response? Or rather, if a call came to me from elsewhere, would I not be in danger of losing everything, simply through lack of patience?[51]

In the context of such a "call" representing the irruption of absolute value into human existence, human freedom (in the sense of contingency, independence, indetermination) undergoes the same kind of *dévalorisation* that individuals with a different attitude could apply to all of their actions. If the hand is the hand of love, then: "If it is withdrawn you have nothing left, for you are nothing except through that act of love."[52]

Grenier's extensive output displays a delicate and often uneasy balance between skepticism and the possibility of faith, between solitude and the possibility of love. That is a tension typical of the artistic temperament, and after the war he became increasingly known and respected as an art critic, to the point that, when he was finally elected to the Sorbonne, it was to a chair of aesthetics and the science of art. The preface to his *Essai sur l'esprit d'orthodoxie* declares that "To move from islands to orthodoxies is not progress."[53] It was essentially through artistic creation, his own and that of others, that he found an alternative means of coming to terms with the solitude of the islands, celebrated in despairing lyricism in his influential early work, *Les îles*. But there was never an easy resolution. "The Age of Orthodoxies" originally ended with a reference to Mallarmé's poem "Brise marine." If only it were possible to move forward into a new world where there were no guides and there to experience, "after so many useless reasons, a faith without system, after so many vain disputes, the sailors' song!"[54] Grenier suppressed the last clause before publishing the article in the *NRF*, restored it for the first edition of the book, and suppressed it again for the second in the 1960s. Though much less engagé than his pupil Camus, Grenier found, like him, that being an artist in the arena involved a constant balancing act.

5 Charles Du Bos's Catholicism and His Politics of Sincerity in Interwar France

Katherine Davies

> Sincerity toward oneself is, as everyone knows, the virtue of our generation.
>
> François Mauriac[1]

Taking his cue from François Mauriac, literary critic Albert Thibaudet contemplated the currency of sincerity in a 1929 article for the *Nouvelle revue française.* While stressing the polysemic nature of sincerity—its meaning slips and slides depending on the vocation and philosophical disposition of the subject—Thibaudet's commentary was indicative of the imaginative space it occupied in French intellectual life.[2] As a hinge for literary debate, the notion of "sincerity toward oneself" crystallized in no small part around the figure of André Gide. His sincerity lay in the cultivation and celebration of the conflicting dimensions of the self, the total autonomy of self-development, and freedom of expression.[3] Mauriac reproached the Gidian postwar generation precisely for honing a "so-called sincerity" that involved revealing the life of their instincts and reveling in abandonment to themselves.[4] For Mauriac, sincerity involved a constant effort toward self-knowledge and, with the clarity this afforded, a moral responsibility to order and regulate the self. It was precisely a refusal to intervene and "form" one's self that necessarily led to a deformation of the self.[5] Leaving to one side how Mauriac's Christian conception of humankind and the "humanist" conception of people peculiar to Gide obviously informed their understanding of sincerity, the tensions at play between these positions analogically reflect what was a central modifier in the formation of Catholic intellectual identity during the interwar years: the pull between obedience to ecclesiastical orthodoxy and the autonomy of the individual and self-expression. This chapter contends that the problem of sincerity overlay a Catholicism in transition; sincerity brought into relief the demands of a changing relationship of believers with themselves, and the tensions born of sincerity wielded transformative potential in the configuration of faith. Charles Du Bos (1882–1939), lauded literary critic and Catholic convert, lived a life marked by the requirements and the fruits of sincerity. His intellectual and spiritual journey, his literary criticism, and his sociopolitical engagement were directed, sometimes explicitly, at other times implicitly, by sincerity.

Du Bos was a key interlocutor in modern French Catholicism, counting among his friends and colleagues leading intellectuals such as Jacques Maritain, Gabriel Marcel, François Mauriac, André Gide, and Ramon Fernandez, to name a few. In 1927 he made his way back to the faith of his childhood at the age of forty-five, a journey that involved a commitment on two fronts: "drawing his faith into his life" and "drawing his faith into his thought."[6] Although Du Bos could manage the first by virtue of the ethical disposition of his soul, the second would prove to be a continual source of difficulty. Intellectualism was never to be an easy bedfellow, the conceptual "system thinking" of neo-Thomism in particular proving to be a difficult mold for a faith that was experiential, experimental, aesthetic-ethical, and deeply autobiographical. Du Bos's conversion can be understood only within the context of his lifelong concern for the inner life of the soul, developed through a *natural* spiritual experience afforded by his work as a literary critic.[7] Echoing Claudel's emotive cry, "someone within me who is more 'myself' than me," Du Bos sought the "truth" of the work of art that could bring him to that higher self by which he was united to all others.[8] Tracing the concentric layers of Du Bos's soul from the superficial "I" to the profounder "self" and finally arriving at the "God within one's self," that natural faith in God hidden in the soul, scholars for the most part have considered Du Bos's conversion to Catholicism a natural progression or maturation.[9] If indeed it was natural, tensions were not lacking in the transition, and in fact it was in the years after Du Bos's conversion that his preconversion commitments and his conversion itinerary could be the greatest source of tension in relation to the new set of intellectual and spiritual demands of Catholicism. It could be argued that the very fact of conversion prepares the ground for the challenge of these kinds of tensions and that some form of sincerity must inevitably be involved. However, even though Du Bos was only one in a wave of converts, peaking in the years from 1905 to 1915 and in the late 1920s, his particular notion and practice of sincerity was intrinsic to and nourishing of his faith.[10]

Lionel Trilling's work can be a helpful start here in unpacking the meaning of sincerity. He designates sincerity as the congruence between avowal and actual feeling and the avoidance of being false to others, which is predicated on such a fidelity to oneself, and he designates authenticity as the coincidence of feeling and expression in the absence of any attempt to shape one's feelings or regard for a relationship to the social world or self-representation.[11] Sincerity is about a relation to the public; authenticity disregards the audience. Another way of thinking about this is to consider authenticity as a matter of being true to oneself for its own sake; it is revelatory and has critical capacity, whereas sincerity implies some sense of duty or service by virtue of the demands made by ethical precepts on the self but which signify more than the self.[12] Without getting too involved in the semantics, it is important to note that those critics Thibaudet alludes to who harnessed the term "sincerity" do so in very particular, discrete ways, which included authenticity and sincerity in Trilling's terms and all the nuances in between. But what sincerity did "catch" at collectively was a concern for the purity of the self or conception of the human in French interwar intellectual life.

Although he avoided historicization of the notion of sincerity in his article, two points in Thibaudet's commentary do seem to hint at a subtly shifting ground and are suggestive of a modulation from what might be called an affective sincerity to an effective one. First, the sincerity of a writer, Thibaudet argues, applies to knowledge of himself insofar as he is interested in the production of a work: "[T]hinking matters less than saying, knowing matters less than doing."[13] The emphasis here is on the act of saying over the act of thinking. Second, Thibaudet observes that the writer is not sincere directly with himself but rather by intermediary, by way of the whole body of literature: "[P]erhaps true sincerity should be understood as a reality that is no longer individual but social, which is made up of the sum of contrasts in dialogue and a balance between all writers."[14] Sincerity emerges here as an intersubjective, communicative process; it is not so much an operation one "does" to oneself but rather a mode of being that is performative and relational. It might not be too much to suggest that Thibaudet's idea of sincerity here can be mapped analogically onto the intellectual landscape of interwar France in a number of ways that contextualize Du Bos's Catholicism and his politics of sincerity.

The place of sincerity in Du Bos's life and thought illuminates the constellation of tensions at work in a critical developmental phase of Catholicism. The role of sincerity in this transition operates within three broad contexts. First, the late 1920s, and the 1930s more especially, were a terrain ripe for a reconfiguration of Catholic identity and engagement and of the forms of renewal of faith. After the papal interdiction of Charles Maurras's right-wing, nationalist Action française in 1926, which reinforced the distinction between the temporal world and the supernatural order, a new space was carved out for pluralism and critical speech within the church. Scholars have focused on how this gave opportunity for new expressions of Catholic social and political engagement, but what will be made clear in what follows are the reconfigurations and tensions in faith itself and how they may have underpinned such new engagements. Second, scholars have observed the emergence of innovative interwar "realisms."[15]

The new philosophical efforts inspired by phenomenology and paving the way for existentialism, for example, encouraged a turn toward the concrete reality of life and the situational dimension of human existence. Accompanying this "philosophy of the concrete," humanist writers of all colors and hues championed conceptions of a "new man" in order to overcome an obsolete secular bourgeois humanism that they deemed inadequate to meet the needs and reality of the human person. Third and finally, *nouvelle théologie*, the movement that called for a return to the sources of faith, began to develop in the interwar years. *Nouvelle théologie* broadly entailed a critique of the orderly rationalism and conceptual framework of neo-scholasticism in its closed form of the late nineteenth century and an assertive commitment to the "authenticity" and experiential nature of Christian faith, operating on the human, social, and cultural level. The 1920s and '30s witnessed an "internal pluralization of neo-Thomism" that opened up a degree of space for the subject and the nonconceptual within the ranks of neo-scholasticism, and this was accompanied by a range of theological developments given over to reconnecting Catholic theology with the reality of the faith in concrete everyday life and to emphasizing the mystical dimension of faith.[16]

Du Bos's sincerity was informed by and reflective of these contextual layers, and in turn, the role of sincerity in his life and thought functioned as a multivalent "sign." It was centrally involved in his mediation of the relationship between the pressures of the ecclesiastical hierarchy and the liberty of the individual and writer and in the relation between his temporal and spiritual self. Within the management of such tensions, sincerity was for Du Bos a quest for unity of the self, a matching up of feeling and public avowal, and a fidelity to the historicity and emotion of his human self. Further, the particularities of Du Bos's path to conversion, involving as it did a struggle between his preconversion aesthetic-ethical self and his Catholic soul, only heightened his sensitivity to the call of sincerity. Two years after his conversion, it is revealing that Du Bos still confessed a strong attachment to his psychological and necessarily individual self:[17]

"I will never be able to completely eliminate the psychological dimension of my nature—and I am not even sure . . . that God would wish that I eliminate this aspect once and for all, for this vow would be equivalent to forbidding and suppressing my task here below in its personal capacity, to follow St Paul, it would annul my own 'gift' and 'graces.'"[18]

What follows deals with some of the strongest currents of this complexity.

Balancing Sincerity and Orthodoxy

Du Bos's relations with the theological modernist and literary scholar Abbé Henri Bremond, with his spiritual director, Abbé Jean-Pierre Altermann, and with his longtime friend and mentor, Jacques Maritain, are revealing of the conflicting influences and strains he experienced in terms of his Catholic identity.[19]

Du Bos had a long-standing admiration for the literary scholar Bremond, the "father of the history of spirituality in France," who can be placed alongside figures such as Maurice Blondel, Alfred Loisy and Édouard Le Roy in a roll call of the originators of Catholic Modernism.[20] Du Bos's admiration for Bremond was focused on his 1926 work *Prière et poésie* (*Prayer and Poetry*), in which poetry is deemed a profane mystical expression of the sacred. Du Bos insisted that his path to conversion was inextricably linked with his personal experience of this work: "I belonged . . . to the zone of *Prayer and Poetry*, what I am saying is that states of profane mysticism inscribed themselves in me from the beginning in the religious sphere, these states, more than anything else, may be . . . what brought me back to God."[21] His kinship with Bremond was invoked more broadly in terms of their mutual crusade against rationalism, what he described as the pathological desire to "classify, define, and also intellectualize."[22] Theirs was a perpetual unease with the primacy of intelligence and the conceptualizing activity demanded by neo-scholasticism, an unease that was self-fashioned as critical for Du Bos: "[T]he fundamental anti-intellectualism of my nature almost held the value of a postulate."[23] Homing in on Jacques Maritain's "strict adhesion to Thomism" and his work *Réflexions sur l'intelligence* (1924), Du Bos could thus react only with a mix of joy and surprise on discovering a point of common ground with respect to the essential role played by will in the concrete movement of intelligence toward the act of supernatural faith.[24] To be certain, Du Bos was not completely paralyzed by Maritain's Thomism. By virtue of his commitment to sincerity—here an intellectual and spiritual honesty to coordinate the self—he was compelled to think through the tensions he experienced in attempting to reconcile and balance Bremond and Maritain: Bremond was "the becoming," whereas Maritain was "being, metaphysical essence."[25] Bremond's work addressed those who were in the process of turning toward the faith, whereas Maritain nourished those who already had faith.[26]

Du Bos searched for reconciliation in other ways, observing that it is necessary to complete Maritain by his adversary Blondel.[27] This completion refers to Blondel's epistemology. Du Bos shared with Blondel the same reservations about the atomism of "notional knowledge"—a matter of fabricating representations and abstractions of concepts from singular givens—that claimed commensurability with reality.[28] "Explaining the most with the least": these words by Du Bos warn against the reductionism of notional knowledge in contrast to "real knowledge," which was neither image nor symbol but rather "living presence, effective action."[29] Blondel provided for an integral philosophy in which action is the condition of real knowledge: "[Real knowledge] is more universalizing, more realizable, more unifying, more intelligent and comprehensive . . . action is the completion of the idea, the proof of its sincerity."[30] Action does not preclude speculative objectivity then, but rather it completes it. Du Bos's natural affinity with Blondel turned around their mutual emphasis on the concrete lived experience of the subject.

In the quest for balance and completion, Du Bos committed himself, postconversion, to educate himself in Thomism. Moreover, Du

Bos's attraction to Bremond's pure poetry was dogged by the legacy of the papal condemnation of modernism. After his conversion, Du Bos faced a choice: either adjoin Thomist categories to his thought and deny the spiritual itinerary that had given him his faith or preserve his liberty of thought and risk falling into heresy.[31] But his efforts did not bear full fruit.[32] Maritain's Thomist metaphysics restricted precisely that which was indispensable to Du Bos's faith and the path he took to return to Catholicism: "Thomism, by its lines of demarcation so strictly and severely maintained . . . forbids interior observation any access to metaphysics."[33]

Du Bos's difficulties with neo-Thomism come into sharper focus during his time as coeditor of the short-lived Catholic journal *Vigile,* which he established in 1930 along with Mauriac and Altermann. The relationship between Du Bos and Altermann was complicated by the latter's "radical" Thomism.[34] Although Du Bos could concede that Maritain theoretically kept a space open to rethink Thomism and acknowledged the existence of views that might not be his own, Altermann, on the other hand, demanded that Thomist philosophy must be accepted unequivocally en bloc: "[I]n his case [Altermann] the mode of thinking is architectural, but the edifice has been constructed once and for all."[35] Likening the current state of theology to a "doctrine of the state" Du Bos struggled with the asphyxiating effects of Altermann's Thomism, which were suppressive and threatened to alienate all other truths.[36] Such effects spilled over into the editorial practices at *Vigile.*

Before the launch of *Vigile,* Du Bos had expressed a wish to welcome new authors and visions: "[T]he review, whilst being fundamentally Catholic, is open freely to those writers sympathetic to religious and spiritual life."[37] Indeed, *Vigile's* "mission statement" established the review as a forum for Catholic writers to "collaborate in perfect communion of faith, *according to the mode of expression proper to each individual* [my emphasis]," but it was precisely individual expression of religious life that Altermann "flatly refused."[38] This difference proved to be a continual source of tension—Du Bos went so far as to admit to Mauriac that, "for a long time already, *Vigile* has been nothing more than a cross for me to bear."[39] A case in point was Altermann's reservations about an article submitted by René Schwob, a Jewish convert.[40] Altermann expressed concern about opening the doors to intellectually ambiguous Catholics who failed to offer a guarantee of doctrinal and moral orthodoxy, and he was especially conscious of converts in the early stages of their journey to the Catholic faith. In Altermann's eyes, Schwob's particular difficulty lay in the fact that he dealt with subject matter that troubled his spirit and tormented his imagination—a sure indication for Altermann of the potential trouble of the newly converted Catholic. Altermann expressed extreme caution against publishing the entirety of Schwob's manuscript. The correspondence that ensued between Altermann and Du Bos involved negotiations about which parts of Schwob's article could be published and which parts were deemed inappropriate for *Vigile*. Altermann stood firm on the matter. Rather than allowing the fear of risking Schwob's feelings (an unfortunate but transitory result) to intimidate one's judgment, Altermann believed that to preserve the integrity of *Vigile* it was necessary to insist that the true virtue of charity complied with the morally correct administration of intellectual judgment.[41]

Du Bos was in a tricky position. On the one hand, he respected and admired Altermann for the clarity of his criticism and for the manner in which he could link an aesthetic faux pas to an internal deficiency of attitude on the part of the author in order to illuminate and remedy errors.[42] On the other hand, however, Du Bos was disquieted by the way in which he felt restrained as if by final jurisdiction: *Vigile* was as Altermann saw fit, and Du Bos believed that his own name on the editorial header of the journal was no more than a sign of simple obedience, which injured "sincerity quite seriously."[43] The tension for Du Bos was experienced most acutely as the feeling that the truth of orthodoxy, "prescribed" by Altermann, threatened his freedom.[44] It was a matter of principle for Du Bos that believers should express their religious life in all the particularities of their being.

Although Du Bos was thinking idiosyncratically, he also recognized the need to assert the subject's experience of faith and stand by one's expression: "I feel that I am the spokesperson for the best laic writers who are both believers and sincere."[45]

Sincerity as Unity

"Unity does not function in him as a means of self-explanation, but rather it serves to salve, by way of illuminating, a moral anxiety which continually invades him."[46] This observation strikes at the heart of Du Bos's motivation for interior observation. The drive for unity was not simply directed toward self-knowledge but was also a morally infused effort; there was a sentiment of duty and responsibility essential to the task, an imperative not always led by a theocentric priority. Before his conversion, Du Bos was committed to sincerity as the reconciling of discordances of the self, as the matching up of his emotional and mental life and his expressions: "putting my actions, words, and to the extent it is possible, my thoughts in accordance with the realities for which I live."[47] The notion of harmony implied the wish for a sense of control over one's self, and indeed Du Bos valued unity as a defining feature of his efficacy: "I am a unity that fares well, or a diversity that fares badly."[48]

Of course, Du Bos could not remain solely on the level of immanent activity of the individual after his return to the Catholic community, but his conversion did not facilitate an easy transposition to the absolute theocentric recognition of God as the center of man. Du Bos continued to be concerned with the "problem of the individual despite himself . . . the problem of the discontinuity of the soul."[49] The human dimension of his spiritual itinerary fed into Du Bos's emotional, experiential Catholicism and at the same time complicated his thoughts and feelings about sincerity. It was to the nineteenth-century liberal Benjamin Constant—"Constant is my human side"—that Du Bos turned for help with these issues and, he confessed, perhaps liberation of the human dimension.[50]

For Du Bos, Constant was the "authentic" man par excellence.[51] In 1932 and 1933 he mounted a heroic restoration of Constant by devoting a series of lectures to the study of his interior life, and their particularities are revealing of his own preoccupation with the virtue of sincerity. In these lectures (published posthumously), Du Bos identified two types of sincerity. First, there is the sincerity that consists in abandonment to personal preference or whim—no doubt a nod to André Gide—that costs nothing to the individual, which can inevitably risk becoming a vice. Second, there is Constantian sincerity, a true virtue of moral force and courage, which calls for daily "severity toward myself."[52] Practicing severity toward oneself was the mark of sincerity inasmuch as it involved taking responsibility not only for one's actions but also for one's feelings by playing the part of one's own "persecutor."[53] Sincerity as self-criticism was directed at, and directed by, in Paul Bourget's terms, a "nobility of the soul."[54] No stranger to the task of the (re-)discovery of the soul, Du Bos's reading of Constant illuminates his own concerns about the unity intrinsic to the soul. His diagnosis is revealing: "Constant is in time and his same tragedy is being in time because he endlessly submits to the offensive reversals of his nature and even his discontinuous soul, he has never been able to maintain an interior continuity."[55] Framing the problem in temporal terms, Du Bos noted that Constant was harassed by the eternal return of himself, his own "persecutor," such that to a greater or lesser extent there was always a gap or disjunction between his feelings and the "rightness" of those feelings.

Du Bos pays homage to Constant's practice of sincerity by adopting his subject's own language to describe this experiential process of self-criticism by drawing specific attention to its lyrical and somatic qualities.[56] "Prestissimo" is the spontaneous tempo of Constant; it depicts the fever of his enervated nervous system, a ceding to his passions, will, and desire, a sensibility that Constant believes his fever dictates. From the moment the fever subsides and the blood coursing through his veins decelerates, Constant enters into self-reflection, prestissimo dissolves, and "adagio" takes its place.[57] The slow, moderate tempo of adagio is a state of wakefulness to the self. In this mode of self-reflection, Du Bos takes sincerity beyond a moral quest to a movement toward God by recognizing himself as a created being among all others, a child of God:

> [W]e rise above ourselves, we purify ourselves of everything which is only personal or individual within us . . . only by the purification of the mind in the sphere belonging jointly to ethics and religion can we prepare the path by which we can accomplish the necessary work that is epitomized by the command of Saint Augustine—this command which, envisaged from within and in the human share that we have contributed to it, sums up entirely the religious life of our being: transcend yourself.[58]

This engagement with Constant was a therapeutic step for Du Bos, a step by which he hoped to unwed himself from the particularities of his feelings, actions, thoughts, and the never-ending quest to unify them and ground his humanism solely in humanity's fundamental relation to the divine.

Sincerity and the Battleground for Humanism

"Humanism: Its many faces and its essence—is a new humanism possible?"[59] This was the question that attendees of Paul Desjardin's famous decades—the annual literary, philosophical, and political forum for intellectuals at Pontigny—were invited to consider in September 1926. In the wake of the violence, the bloodshed, and the mourning of the war, a turn to realism was accompanied by a "fragmentation of the humanist imagination."[60] This was a disaffection with the existing notion of a liberal bourgeois humanism of the Third Republic, which espoused a project with man as "bearer and guarantor of his own dignity, equality, and freedom."[61] And yet, humanism was not renounced completely; rather, it was reworked and reappropriated. In the interwar years intellectuals across the spectrum, from Communists to nonconformists to Catholics, reclaimed the "true" humanism in ways that reflected their own particular positions.[62] Humanism continued to be a badge of identity and something to be addressed. Christian humanism, which found a spokesperson in Jacques Maritain and his 1936 work, *Humanisme intégral* (translated in the English as *True Humanism* in 1938), called for the necessary recognition of the transcendental dimension of human beings to achieve a fully *integrative* humanism—one that did not rest on psychological individualism but rather on an antianthropism that saw God as the center of humankind. Competing humanisms make for a complicated picture, too complicated to be considered fully here, but suffice it to say that certainly humanism challenged Du Bos to tackle those central human issues not fully addressed by inherited faith. Here especially, Du Bos was embroiled in the politics of sincerity in terms of pressing assumptions and revealing vulnerability.

In 1929 Du Bos had written to Gabriel Marcel about a critique he had received from the radical writer Emmanuel Berl concerning Du Bos's apparent betrayal of humanism. Berl considered that Du Bos was prone to "a certain idealism, a certain way of considering the absolute nature of conscience and the soul [which] turns its back on what seems to me to be human in the human."[63] Berl's Communist leanings may well have fed his castigation of Du Bos's idealism—it was not a "real" humanism, for "realist humanism has no enemies more dangerous than spiritualism or speculative idealism, which in place of the individual, real human being, places consciousness or the spirit."[64] This polarization of secular humanism and Christianity was well-trodden territory, but what Berl's accusation did was strike at the heart of Du Bos's Catholic identity. And, more broadly, it is indicative of how the "human" in humanism and the "real" were emerging as intellectual and cultural capital in the trajectory of Catholicism.

Berl's criticism was a direct riposte to Du Bos's famous work, *Dialogue avec André Gide* (1929). The *Dialogue*, as well as the ensuing debate it engendered between Du Bos and his friend and interlocutor, literary critic Ramon Fernandez, whose work on Gide was published in 1931, illuminates the Catholic confrontation with humanism. The strongest criticism contained in *Dialogue*—the *Labyrinthe*—concerned the so-called dangers of Gide's inversion of values: "It consists, essentially, in a displacement by which not only evil becomes good, but more disturbingly still, good becomes evil . . . that is the stroke of genius—so marvelously tailored—of the diabolical intervention in our time."[65]

Béatrice Didier's commentary on the exchanges between Fernandez and Du Bos about Gide highlights the stark difference in their respective responses to him: Where the humanist Fernandez was naturally led to meditate upon the "respiritualization" of Gide, Du Bos could only perceive Gide's "despiritualization."[66] Writing to Du Bos, Fernandez offered his own estimation of the ground that separated them: "Christian values carry a transcendent perfection which the Christian must somehow reach and imitate, while humanist values are discovered by a progressive deepening of the human spirit."[67] Identifying himself firmly with a secular humanism—an ascendant process of making and rediscovering the human being—Fernandez perceived the absence of the human in Du Bos because the Christian cultivates only the mimetic faculty and surrenders the self. Fernandez thus challenged Du Bos on the ground that his judgment on Gide—in this particular instance on the issue of Gide's pederasty—had been dictated by his religious convictions: "You do not leave the reader with the impression that the end of your *Dialogue* is not written under the empire of your beliefs . . . you cite Goethe before Saint Paul, but it would appear that it is Saint Paul who provides you with your point."[68] Du Bos responded by arguing that his judgments on Gide were established while he was an unbeliever and that his faith only clarified his earlier opinions.[69] Didier's account of this issue tends to gloss over tensions experienced by Du Bos retrospectively, once he had converted, between his theocentric self and his humanist, "aesthetic-ethical" self. She simultaneously supports Du Bos's claim that there was no strict relation of cause and effect regarding his return to the Catholic faith and the content and tone of the *Labyrinthe* section of his work and claims that Du Bos the critic was a "whole" person and would not be himself without his faith. Either Du Bos's Catholicism was intrinsic to his *Dialogue* or his aesthetic and ethical judgment (including a pointed discussion of Gide's pederasty) could be understood as formulated apart from his Catholicism. In any event it is, I would argue, through these tensions, or ambiguity of identity, of the Catholic and humanist dimensions that the virtue of sincerity was experienced by, and tested in, Du Bos.

"Gide the humanist may well be, if he wishes, the ultimate Gide, but he will never be the integral Gide."[70] Referring to Gide's sexual encounter with Mohammed (as Gide described it in his *Si le grain ne meurt* [*If It Die*]), Du Bos recalls how he was struck by that which followed the encounter when, "according to Gide's own expression, 'measure' is exceeded."[71] Writing to Fernandez, self-consciously donning a humanist "hat," Du Bos argued that humanism is nothing if not "measure and equilibrium."[72] Rather than admonishing pederasty primarily via a Paulinian rebuke, Du Bos sought to tease out the issue by suggesting that it was related to a failure of Gide's humanism. Fernandez's treatment of Gide was entirely silent on the values of measure and equilibrium in the context of physical love, and without these values, Du Bos argued, humanism degenerated into a kind of "sublime Epicureanism"; humanism must be founded on values in and of themselves rather than the pleasures to which they can lead. In this light, Du Bos could perceive Gide's night in Algiers in terms of an absence of moderation and discipline of the self: "[T]he 'lightness of the soul' corresponds to nothing other than the mechanism that triggers the same excess of sensual abandon."[73] Gide's celebration of frisson and divinization of the instant was analogous to his excess and self-abandonment; it made for a humanism that prioritized fulfillment of all desires. If the Catholic tenor of Du Bos's critique is rather more nuanced than his critics would have, his suggestion that Gide would never be "integral" illustrates how his Catholicism and his "humanist" perspective could bleed into one another. Several years later, in correspondence with Marcel, Du Bos reflected on the source of his ideas on integrality from his entrenched position in the Catholic community: "[I]t is the theocentric potentiality . . . that God placed in me from the very beginning, much more than a properly human element in my nature . . . which enables me to conceive of a notion of *man* as distinct from the *individual*."[74]

Sincerity as Authenticity

"A lingering scruple still forbids us to believe that reality can ever be purely rational . . . *the notion that existence should be the same as understanding* [my emphasis] strikes as cold and ghost-like as the dreariest materialism."[75] In 1933 Du Bos quoted these words of the British idealist philosopher F. H. Bradley. It is perhaps no coincidence that the year before had seen the launch of the new avant-garde journal, *Recherches philosophiques*, edited by Alexandre Koyré and Albert Spaier. Dissatisfaction with the intellectual armature of the Third Republic—the neo-Kantianism of Brunschvicg and Bergson's spiritualism—encouraged the emergence of a new philosophical impulse, inspired by phenomenology, neo-Hegelianism, and protoexistentialism, in the late 1920s and early 1930s. Those who inaugurated and participated in this new philosophical direction—the "generation of 1933"—found a home in *Recherches philosophiques*.[76] Du Bos cited Jaspers, Heidegger, and Marcel as key figures in the flourishing *Existenzphilosophie* current in Germany and France, an intellectual movement to which he felt the most "profound" and "original" minds rallied.[77] Du Bos was drawn to these philosophies of existence just as he was to Bradley's delicate truth. The extrarational, or "suprarational," which Du Bos preferred, struck a chord with his notion and practice of sincerity. Sincerity was not a matter of calculating the pluses and minuses of action or inaction or of a particular thought; rather, the extrarational was the mark and the worth of sincerity.

A critical figure in this new philosophical movement was Jean Wahl, who heralded an "antifoundational" realism in his 1932 work, *Vers le concret* (*Toward the Concrete*).[78] Examining the thought of Alfred Whitehead, William James, and Gabriel Marcel, Wahl offered a critical reexamination of realism and idealism in calling for a turn to the "concreteness" of lived experience and the immediacy and immanency with which we encounter the world. Du Bos's friend and confidant, Marcel, featured in Wahl's work as a key example of this style of thinking by virtue of his emphasis on the existential given of incarnation, on the human being as a being-in-a-situation and on the notion of participation—one is a human being among other beings. Wahl's manifesto "toward the concrete" was an orientation underpinned by Heidegger's phenomenological modus operandi: "to let that which shows itself be seen from itself in the very way in which it shows itself from itself."[79] The concrete denoted a strong sense of the self as given in the world of things, the irreducibility of the real to intellectual concepts, the privileging of intuition, and the importance of categories of feeling. Indeed, Wahl spoke of a realism that is subjective insofar as it is the life of feeling and objective insofar as this life of feeling is real.[80] Even though he did not explicitly align himself with this "philosophy of the concrete," earlier exchanges with Marcel, Maritain, and with Léon Brunschvicg in the intellectual forum Union pour la vérité (Union for Truth) in 1929, intimate the close affinity Du Bos had with the priority of the embodied and embedded human. In a meeting of this forum, titled "Le temps et l'éternité" (Time and Eternity), Du Bos distinguished himself from Brunschvicg's hyperidealist notion of eternity, which was stripped of any relation to temporality and the concreteness of life. Du Bos instead showed sensitivity to the situatedness of the person, much in keeping with Marcel's philosophy. Marcel stressed that transcendence did not involve an escape from human temporality; rather, it was founded upon *disponibilité* (availability) (though this should be distinguished from the more aesthetic and sensual form of *disponibilité* associated with Gide), a willing availability and openness to the ontological call of human personal participation.[81] Du Bos rallied to Marcel on this matter by arguing that the eternal could be grasped through a concrete encounter or communion with another.[82]

This intersubjective imperative appeared to run on a parallel track to the decidedly humanist, anthropocentric appropriations of Heidegger and Hegel in France in the 1930s.[83] Henri Corbin, who penned the first French translation of "Was ist Metaphysik?" (1929) in the avant-garde journal *Bifur* in June 1931, stripped Heidegger's *dasein* (being-in-the-world) of its spatial character as existence in the midst of things and instead rendered it as human reality (*réalité-humaine*), prioritizing the specific existence of the individual.[84] In a similar vein, Hegel was given the anthropological treatment by the Russian émigrés Alexandre Kojève and Alexandre Koyré, who prioritized the existential conflicts of the subject.[85] Wahl was integral to the humanistic appropriations of Hegel and Heidegger. In his 1929 work, *Le Malheur de conscience* (*The Unhappy Consciousness*) he perceived the "unhappy individual consciousness" as the motif of the Hegelian dialectic, an internal conflict that every individual experiences, and he highlighted how Heidegger's *Dasein* was an inflection of Kierkegaard's existential anxiety insofar as it designated those who, faced with despair, could either actualize their authentic existence or fail to do so: "being-for-the-death, the fundamental historicity of being."[86]

Du Bos's "suprarational" was decidedly idiosyncratic. His response to Bradley's lingering scruple, via the philosophies of existence, was to return first to his literary self. Du Bos turned to both Bradley and John Middleton Murry in the context of their insights on John Keats. Du Bos was drawn to two particular quotations: from Bradley, "the question still remains whether a truth which is also beauty or a beauty which is also truth, can be found by man," and from Middleton Murry, his use of Wittgenstein's "ethics and aesthetics are one."[87] These both allude to the intersection of Du Bos's natural and sacred forms of mysticism. Du Bos argues that the only response to Bradley's question would emerge in the collapsing of the terms "beauty" and "truth" because then they would be transcended by their same operation and become one. In the same vein, Du Bos found Wittgenstein prescient. Ethics and aesthetics were one insofar as they both exceeded logical referentiality; for Du Bos aesthetics represented the experience of all that made up the dynamic confrontation of his consciousness with truth.[88] The only term that could subsist in the union of beauty and truth, Du Bos argued, would be "this unnamed and unnamable divine attribute of which God lets us glimpse its refraction in the most sublime works of art."[89]

In the same journal entry, Du Bos's celebration of his aesthetic-ethical self was immediately tempered. Du Bos was conscious of his position within the wider Catholic lay and ecclesiastical community, and he felt compelled to make a distinction between his "aesthetic-ethics" and his morality as a Catholic. Du Bos defined ethics as "these life causes that Juvenal puts above life itself, these final justifications, infinitely variable from individual to individual, which each of us must achieve for ourselves, and in favor of which or to the benefit of which one is ready at any moment to leave one's life to the sense of brute fact, the incidental, the transient."[90] Morality, on the other hand, was "all the currency of those universally valid precepts to which the individual consents and by which he voluntarily limits himself to consider the existence of people beside himself."[91] There appears to be something of a political move here, uncharacteristic of Du Bos, to seal off an ethics by precept, which requires submission and self-giving, from the aesthetic-ethical, which is based on moral individualism. This continual to-ing and fro-ing was Du Bos's sincerity in practice: "I have always bathed, lived and prospered in experiencing the reality of mystery . . . I feel there is an infinite gap between showing and demonstrating: intuition shows, it makes us see; rational processes demonstrate . . . between intuition and truth there exists for me a place which I cannot renounce, for I have always lived by it and cannot live otherwise."[92]

Practice and Performance: Sincerity as Effectivity

Du Bos was certainly no natural political animal, but it is possible to locate him loosely within a Catholic third-way discourse, principally in line with Jacques Maritain's Christian humanist-democratic directive, which sought to forge a viable alternative to totalitarian statism and laissez-faire individualism, and facilitate a political community in which Christians and non-Christians could cooperate toward the common good. During the 1930s—sometimes called the "decade of manifestos"—Du Bos's refusal to defer simplistically to the left or the right and his honest engagement with the human situation are indicative of the intellectual disposition that underpinned the Catholic "third way."[93] Du Bos lent his name to a number of manifestos inaugurated by Maritain: "Pour le bien commun" (For the Common Good), which was launched in 1935 in response to the threats of the extreme right the previous year and marked a refusal to be embroiled in choosing between Fascism and Communism; "Pour la justice et la paix" (For Justice and Peace) the same year, which sought to tread the line between resisting conflict with Italy and condemning Italian aggressions as morally abhorrent; and "Pour le peuple basque" (For the Basque People) in 1937, which denounced the slaughter of noncombatants at Guernica on the premise that the Catholic people of the Basque country should be defended by all Christian people without distinction of party.[94] An anguished commentary on the Munich agreement in the autumn of 1938, in which Du Bos struggled with the "tragedy" of the tension between "peace" and "justice," is particularly revealing of how political issues impressed themselves upon him only by way of a *crise de conscience*, served by his sincerity.[95]

A case for testing the limits of the efficacy of sincerity arrived in the form of a debate at Pontigny in 1934 titled "The Desire for Justice: Does It Necessarily Lead to Revolutionary Action?" As director of this meeting, Du Bos was eager to draw some limits to ensure communication between believers and unbelievers. Above all, the meeting had to be marked by "good faith."[96] Du Bos recognized the singular "abyss" between the believer and the unbeliever insofar as the former must always be conscious of two worlds, whereas the latter will be attentive to only one. Referencing Maritain's work *Religion et culture* (1930), Du Bos believed that laying bare this distinction as a preliminary to any discussion would be essential for maintaining mutual understanding and respect. The incumbent task for the believer was to negotiate the paradox of fidelity to the eternal and an honest diligence to the anguish of daily life: "As a man, he is in time, and subject to all the vicissitudes of becoming; as a member of the mystical Body of Christ, he is joined to eternity . . . This sort of mediation between time and the eternal is for the Christian mind at once a sort of painful cross and a sort of redemptive mission."[97]

Du Bos's claim that "good faith is a union, it is *our* union [my emphasis]" suggests an imaginative space of conciliatory relations rather than a set of practical tools for negotiation, but he did hope to bridge the gap between believer and unbeliever more concretely by placing an emphasis on the *temporal* task of the Christian and thereby encourage shared work toward the common good.[98] Accompanying "good faith," Du Bos insisted that fruitful dialogue could be realized only by virtue of communicative purity. To avoid the rhetorical games of the "verbalism" that pervaded France, he called for a "maximum of clarity" from participants with respect to their usage of definitions in order to do justice to the complex, often contradictory realities at stake.[99] This was an appeal not only for lucidity but also for *parrhesia*, for frank speech. During the tortuous months of the Munich crisis in 1938, Du Bos's praise of Léon Blum illuminates the importance he placed on sincere speech. Quoting Blum, "I feel torn between cowardly relief and shame," Du Bos observed that "not only is this sincere speech, but it is *the* [my emphasis] expression of the situation."[100] By being true to himself, Blum was not false to another, and further, he was true to the historicity of the situation, the concrete reality. This emphasis on the concrete comes into focus in Du Bos's declaration: "[A]ny action which does not proceed from a thought does not merit the name action . . . any thought which does not translate into an action . . . does not merit the name thought."[101] There are hints of Blondel's influence here, but more broadly, Du Bos was aligning himself with those critics of Julien Benda's infamous tract, *La trahison des clercs* (*The Betrayal of the Intellectuals*, 1927), who admonished Benda for his hermetic sealing off of universal truth from the particularities of human affairs. Gabriel Marcel, for example, reserved his strongest criticism for Benda's fallacious joining together of the suprasensible or eternal and the abstract and general.[102] Du Bos shared Marcel's personal metaphysics of incarnation insofar as they both prioritized the manifest *human reality* of the concept.

And yet, Du Bos's directorial demands for sincerity of intention, for sympathy for an "other," and for transparent speech were problematic precisely because of the nature of the debate at Pontigny. Du Bos's attempts to cling to a commonality of form and stylistics could not compel consensus, and indeed it might lead to the realization that agreement could not be reached with regard to means and ends. Du Bos does not intimate that the aim of the meeting should be to achieve consensus as such. He argues that believers and unbelievers may diverge on definitions of justice and the means of action to employ justice, but they will not disagree about their love of justice or their desire to aid its implementation.[103] In this respect, perhaps the goal was simply to reach a mutual understanding of the differences at work amongst participants' means and ends.[104] However, as director and participant of the décade, Du Bos did call for certain norms of sincerity. He insisted that the director of any décade must surrender to a self-conscious doubling or splitting of the self, which he likened to the "severity to oneself" that Constant demanded. Du Bos designated this peculiar operation as "Pontignacian splitting," which involved serving the interests of the meeting independently of one's personal sentiment and opinions.[105] Du Bos's impartiality was driven by Constant's self-regulation: "[I]f one wants to achieve integral sincerity, it is necessary to argue the *for* to the same degree as the *against*, with no less objectivity and impartiality when oneself is at stake as when we examine the case of another."[106]

Writing to Marcel in March 1936, Du Bos confessed that in recent years he had lived by the words of the eighteenth-century Jesuit Père Jean-Pierre de Caussade: "the sacrament of the present moment."[107] The "present moment" demanded self-abandonment, a total surrendering to God's purpose and recognition of the transcendent in the individual moments of daily life. This conscious self-surrender to the holiness of the present was in stark contrast to the Gidian anarchic, nihilistic sense of abandon. The lingering question for Du Bos was whether tension might exist between such a surrender and the autonomy of the self required for real surrender. In the same letter to Marcel, Du Bos quotes from Lamennais to define this relationship: "one foot in the finite and the other in the infinite."[108] This division into two worlds to which the Catholic simultaneously belongs is, Du Bos insists, born of the divine Cross. "God helps us little by little to *live this simultaneity as simultaneity*: he makes the timeless reside in time . . . we discharge the least amount of evil as possible toward these two planes at the same time so that we are not wholly unfaithful in our reception of the 'sacrament of the present moment.'"[109]

Conclusion

"It must become a concrete attitude before existence—one unified response that engages the whole person, the inner light of a course of action in which the whole of life is engaged."[110] Father Jean Daniélou wrote these words in his 1946 article, "Les orientations présentes de la pensée religieuse" for the Jesuit journal *Études* to call for a reformulation of theology. One can imagine that Daniélou's emphasis on the necessary engagement of the whole person would have resonated loudly with Du Bos. The latter's death in 1939 prevents a genealogical examination of his relation to the *nouvelle théologie* movement Daniélou was so prominent in, but Du Bos's spiritual itinerary, although not definitively prescient, is at least suggestive of the murmurings of such developments in the interwar years. For example, Mettepenningen has described the first phase of *nouvelle théologie* in the 1930s as a rediscovery (*ressourcement*) of the *historical* Thomas. This was a rejuvenation of Thomism away from the theology of those who, according to Henri de Lubac, "make dogma a kind of superstructure," guard theology as "a system of truths and precepts," and practice their vocation "like curators in a museum."[111] The similarities are unmistakable: Du Bos had explicitly denounced theology that amounted to a doctrine of the state, he had lived with the burden of the architectural edifice of Altermann's Thomism, and he had struggled to fully integrate Maritain's Thomism into his life and thought. Du Bos's conversion experience, from aesthetics and deism to theism and finally to Christ the Redeemer, was subject centered, confessional, and situational. It is easy to see where his future sympathies might have lain. But retrospective analysis is not (and should not be) the aim here. Rather, this chapter has attempted to unveil the types of tensions at play that were formative of modern Catholic intellectual identity and to do so through the voice of Du Bos. Certainly, we cannot claim Du Bos was "representative" in any broad sense, not least because Catholic intellectuals were a multiform, heterogeneous bunch, but Du Bos's life and thought do shine a particularly effective and pertinent light on the constellation of developments of a Catholicism in transition mode, critically because his thought so often inflected those questions that were being asked of Catholics: how to reconcile individual expression with orthodoxy; how to revivify the temporal realm for Catholicism, and then how to determine what shape Catholic political and social engagements could take; intrinsic to these tasks was also the matter of how the "human being" should be configured. This list of questions is far from exhaustive, but they indicate some of the central issues at stake to which Du Bos responded via his lifelong quest for sincerity.

Du Bos's sincerity mirrored Daniélou's emphasis on the engagement of the whole person. It reflected and cultivated a modulating Catholicism. Engagement of the "whole man" or "the circle," as Du Bos would have it, could refer at once to what theology should serve and the daily Constantian task of severity toward oneself. Du Bos's politics of sincerity reflected his tensions with neo-Thomism; to engage the whole person required an appreciation of the living enactment and embodiment of faith rather than what he perceived to be the conceptual straitjacket of certain neo-Thomist "curatorships" of the faith. Indeed, Du Bos's faith was experiential, intuitive, and aesthetic-ethical by nature, and he lived the reality of mysteries. Whereas Thomism was in the camp of the "said" and the already constructed (with, albeit, some room for reformulation), Du Bos was part of the impulse in Catholicism that encouraged the "saying" over the said.[112] In other words, to be consonant with this impulse was to render Catholicism performative and experimental. In this light, a necessary element of Du Bos's Catholicism was a respect for the uncertain and the anguish this furnished. One of Du Bos's biographers, Michel Crépu, has said as much: Du Bos was caught between "a fundamental respect for the principle of uncertainty" and "a moral sense of the perfectible."[113] This principle of uncertainty was part and parcel of his spiritual release, and his delving into authenticity and the place of the "human" was on a track similar to those of intellectuals searching for the "new man" or a reconfiguration of human beings in the world. But Du Bos required a "severity toward oneself" to maintain his sense of the perfectible and his Catholic soul. Sincerity for him could of course never be a total abandonment to oneself; rather, it was a measured practice to wean him away from his own human "divinity" and move beyond the profane mystical experience of literature to God as the center of humankind. The divisiveness he experienced is expressed as the gap between soul and self: "I suffer from a sense of overflowing myself . . . by which one feels altogether enlarged and dispossessed . . . we touch here on the intrinsic difference that I have always felt between the soul and the person."[114]

Du Bos's politics of sincerity was precisely that: a politics insofar as his spiritual and intellectual life was marked by a continual to-ing and fro-ing that he had to manage but which, at the same time, allowed for a Catholicism that was centered on the concrete *and* the supernatural, the mystery of the Incarnation. Sincerity then was simultaneously a burden to and the nourishment of his Catholicism.

6 From *Mystique* to *Théologique*: Messiaen's "*ordre nouveau*," 1935–39

Stephen Schloesser

Consult any concert program, review, or advertising for the music of Olivier Messiaen: very likely some variation of the word "mystic" will appear as an identifier or modifier. Partly, this is simply modernity's lack of an appropriate category. One of the most recent examples is a book review that appeared in 2010 in the *Journal of the British Institute of Organ Studies*: "The title [*Messiaen the Theologian*] is perhaps (deliberately?) provocative: as the contributors demonstrate, Messiaen was profoundly influenced by certain theological traditions. Yet it is slightly implausible to ascribe to a composer the didactic, essentially word-based role of 'theologian'; 'Catholic mystic' might have been better."[1]

However, the question of categorizing Messiaen's music as either "mystical" or "theological" has been an ongoing historiographical question for several decades.[2] For example, Wilfred Mellers has written that all of Messiaen's music may be described "as 'mystical' in the dictionary sense, in that it is not only 'mysterious, occult, and awe-inspiring' but also seeks 'by contemplation and self-surrender to obtain union with or absorption into the deity.'"[3] On the other hand, Messiaen himself resisted the label. Often cited is this quotation from a 1979 interview, when the composer was seventy years old: "Personally, I deeply distrust this word [mysticism]. It doesn't suit me at all, and I'd like to say why not. As soon as one starts talking about mysticism, people think of a diseased state, of a neurotic who has vague sentiments and ecstasies. I don't like that; I'm a devout man and I love the sound, solid gifts of Faith."[4]

As primarily an intellectual historian, I myself feel that this argument at least partly results from not seeing these categories—that is, "mystical" and "theological"—as historical products, time-bound conceptual tools that are meant to do cultural work.[5] If we consider them as such, we can narrow down Messiaen's turn from the "mystical" to the "theological" to a fairly specific moment: most particularly around 1935, after he had completed the *Ascension* suite and begun working on *La nativité*.

Following the lead of musicologist Jane Fulcher and, more recently, French historian Philip Nord, I want to situate Messiaen's turn to the "theological" within the broader 1930s' nonconformist movement called the "ordre nouveau."[6] I suggest that Messiaen turned away from the discourse of the "mystical" because it conveyed a vagueness that was no longer appealing in a culture that was "dancing on the edge of the volcano."[7] In particular, I suggest that at least one indication of the shift in his thought and music is a turn from vague romantic notions of an incorporeal "soul" to Christianity's central doctrine of the resurrected "body."

1830–1930: Discourse of the "Mystical"

What did the words "mysticism" or "mystical" mean in the early twentieth century? As this is a massive topic, I merely offer some suggestive points here.[8] Although *la misticité* had been a synonym and pejorative term for the quietism condemned in the late seventeenth and early eighteenth centuries, it was not recognized by the Académie française as late as 1814.[9] By contrast, *la mystique* seems to have been a romantic invention of the 1830s and 1840s, a reaction to scientific positivism. Usages include the French translation of Joseph von Görres's massive five-volume study, *La mystique divine, naturelle, et diabolique* (*Mysticism: Divine, Natural, and Diabolical*); Dom Guéranger's even more massive fifteen-volume *L'année liturgique* (*Liturgical*

Year) (1841–1901), analyzing the liturgy from the historical, practical, and "mystical" perspectives; and Abbé Migne's many works, especially the *Dictionnaire des sciences occultes* (*Dictionary of Occult Sciences* [1846–48]), *Dictionnaire d'ascétisme* (*Dictionary of Asceticism* [1853–54]), and *Dictionnaire de mystique chrétienne* (*Dictionary of Christian Mysticism* [1858]).[10] The fin-de-siècle pejorative usage should also be noted (i.e., the association of the "mystical" with mental illness as physical "degeneration" in Jean-Martin Charcot's *Les démoniaques dans l'art* [*Demoniacs in Art*, 1887]); Max Nordau's monumental study of "degeneration" in 1894 (followed by Jules-Désiré-Gabriel Cloitre's gloss in 1902). Lucien Lévy-Bruhl, one of the founders of sociology, considered the mystical as the primary characteristic of "primitive [precivilized] mentality."[11] At the turn of the century, a second wave of literature occurred, indicating the emergence of a postdogmatic religiosity: note especially William James's *Varieties of Religious Experience* (1902); Baron von Hügel's *Mystical Element of Religion* (1908); Evelyn Underhill's comprehensive *Mysticism* (1911); and Arthur Waite's *Way of Divine Union* (1915).[12]

Here, as in so many political, social, cultural, and intellectual arenas, the impact of the Great War was decisive. In France and Belgium, a self-identified "mystic realist" generation, disillusioned by the Great War, engaged in a new wave of Catholic revivalist activity.[13] But that particular endeavor of Catholic revivalism needs to be seen within a much broader postwar intellectual and cultural enterprise. A sampling of postwar publications having to do with the "mystical" suggests promises implicit in 1920s' "mystical" discourse.[14] First, it was about *experience*, individual deeply emotional experience, and *not* theological or dogmatic concepts.[15] Second, in addition to being postdogmatic, the "mystical" was also largely postconfessional—Catholicism, Orthodoxy, Protestantism, Judaism, Islam, Hinduism, Buddhism—all were now studied as various expressions of the one "mystical" experience: what James had called the "varieties of religious experience."

With respect to Messiaen, one final note is essential: the publication, from the years 1928–36, of *L'orgue mystique* (*Mystical Organ*), an organ cycle for the entire liturgical year. This monumental work of fifty-one volumes was composed by Charles Tournemire, organist at the Basilica of Sainte-Clotilde and an early Messiaen mentor.[16]

1931–32: Messiaen and the "Mystical"

During the years 1931 and 1932, that is, when he was twenty-two and twenty-three years of age, Messiaen was immersed in the discourse of the "mystical." In March 1931 the word was used in the first public review of a Messiaen work. Reviewing *Les offrandes oubliées* (*The Forgotten Offerings*), this critic wrote that Messiaen was "a musician, an artist, a nature 'in depths'; and what pleases me best of all, a mystic." The work's two slow movements demonstrated that Messiaen was capable of representing "tenderness, sorrow, and the humanly perceptible part of the ineffability of his music and his mysticism."[17]

Indeed, the years 1930 and 1931 were remarkably prolific for Messiaen. Five works especially stand out in this "mystical" period: his *Diptyque pour l'orgue* (*Diptych for Organ,* composed in the spring of 1930; published in May 1931); *Les offrandes oubliées* for orchestra (composed in the summer of 1930; published in February 1931); *La mort du nombre* (*The Death of Number*) for two voices (a soprano and a tenor), violin, and piano (composed in the fall of 1930; published in May 1931); *Apparition de l'église éternelle* (*Apparition of the Eternal Church,* composed ca. 1931–32; published in 1934); and *Le tombeau resplendissant* (*The Resplendent Tomb*) for orchestra (composed in the summer of 1931; not published until 1997).[18] In the second half of his *Diptyque,* Messiaen depicts the "life of the blessed in eternity." Ten years later, Messiaen would recycle this work, score it for piano and violin, and use it as the final movement of the "Quatuor pour la fin du temps" (Quartet for the End of Time), premiered in a German prisoner-of-war camp. *La mort du nombre* involves a dialogue between two "souls"—the first soul is the soprano, the second the tenor. After the first soul sings his earthly plaint of loss, the second soul—

the soprano—comes to comfort him. I suspect that the two souls are meant to be those of Messiaen himself and his mother, who had died tragically young two years before *La mort du nombre* was composed.[19] All four of these works demonstrate Messiaen's trademark efforts throughout his life to represent timelessness with the artistic medium of time—music.[20] The 1931 reviewer's attention to the two slow movements from *Les offrandes oubliées* underscores this.

Four months after this review appeared, the titular organist at the church of La Trinité died—this provided a very rare opening of such a position in Parisian churches. Messiaen enlisted several senior organists, including Tournemire, to assist his competition for the position. In his letter of support, Tournemire wrote: "I am particularly concerned about the young and magnificent Christian artist, and a pure Christian *whose mysticism is well-balanced*: Olivier Messiaen."[21] After Messiaen successfully obtained the organist position, he was interviewed in October. In that interview he said: "[W]e have terribly neglected Gregorian chant: a source which is still living . . . I think it's above all in the mystic sense that this source can give life to our art . . . we must return to Charles Tournemire, whose *L'orgue mystique* washed clean of any sentimentality, also relies on the art of Gregorian chant . . . The only admissible way [of return] is . . . to rediscover the depths of the soul—the mystical soul—and faith." The interviewer's own quip capped off the session: "Olivier Messiaen seems to want to claim a kingdom for which there is little competition: that of the mystical composer."[22] Two months following this interview, Tournemire reciprocated with a brief but important review of yet another Messiaen concert in which he declared: "The very young composer Olivier Messiaen pursues a very pure ideal; *he belongs to the lineage of mystics*."[23]

Just as the following summer was about to begin, Messiaen, now twenty-three years old and titular organist at La Trinité, married Claire Delbos in June 1932. They immediately went off to the south of France for the summer months, during which Messiaen wrote one of his most popular works: the *Ascension* suite—initially for orchestra but later reduced for organ (with a completely new fast movement better suited to the organ).[24] The scriptural and liturgical quotations on which Messiaen's movements are musical commentaries are all taken from meditations for Ascension Day written by Dom Columba Marmion in the book *Le Christ dans ses mystères* (*Christ in His Mysteries*)—a work that is indispensable for locating the sources of Messiaen's ideas.[25] The epigraphs, however, are Messiaen's own words—and it is significant here again to see this romantic image of a disembodied "soul":

> Movement II: "Serene Alleluias *from a soul longing for Heaven.*"
>
> Movement III: "Outburst of joy *from a soul before the Glory of Christ* which is its own glory."[26]

With Messiaen delayed by other commitments and work needed to make money, three years elapsed between the initial composition of *Ascension* in the summer of 1932 and its premiere (both organ and orchestral) in the first half of 1935. During those three years, Messiaen's outlook underwent a significant change. The *Ascension* suite and its language of "souls" may be considered the last composition in this "mystical" style.

March 1933: A Musical Daniel-Rops?

What happened between 1932 and 1933 to effect this shift? A turning point is suggested in a curious review published on 1 March 1933. It is worth contextualizing that moment. In Berlin, the Reichstag fire had occurred two days before (27 February); the Reichstag Fire Decree, setting Hitler's dictatorship on fast-forward, was passed the next day. Franklin Delano Roosevelt's inauguration was to follow three days later (4 March). Put starkly: By the first week of March 1933, the postwar 1920s had definitively passed over into the interwar decade of the 1930s. This is the historical context in which to read the review of Messiaen's *Le tombeau resplendissant*.[27]

The reviewer (signed "F. D.")[28] began simply enough: "This new work, essentially romantic, testifies to the mystical aspirations of the author." But "F. D." then took a literary turn, comparing Messiaen's "mystical" vision to that of Henri Daniel-Rops, a brilliant young history professor seven years older than Messiaen. Daniel-Rops had begun his literary career with a book of essays published in 1927 titled *Notre inquiétude* (*Our Anxiety*).[29] The work was a response to a cultural conversation about whether the postwar generation was one that had been "born under the sign of anxiety" (Daniel-Rops) and was suffering a new *mal du siècle* (malady of the century).[30] Daniel-Rops wanted to distinguish between what he considered to be anxieties that were superficial and historically contingent (e.g., a result of wartime trauma) and "metaphysical" anxiety, the profound type of instability or "inconstancy" (following the thought of Blaise Pascal), from which the human condition cannot escape.

Whereas literary critics were arguing about the emotional instability manifesting itself in postwar literature, Daniel-Rops wanted to emphasize that the search for stability, although perhaps inevitable, is (again following Pascal) illusory. "For if it is true that in searching to create a new order the mind admits disorder, and if it pleases, that it would be vain to affirm that once this order is attained, it would be able to rest content with it."[31] Daniel-Rops praised metaphysical anxiety as the only one worth considering: "The foundations of the soul are reached only by means of anxiety. It alone indicates the meaning of great problems. . . . Anxiety appears to us formally as the only creator of art."[32] By contrast, he criticized the postwar modernist cult of machines and mechanism: "[H]ow mediocre does this humanity appear to us: while it knows only how to build machines, the notion of the absolute completely escapes it!"[33]

Daniel-Rops, who in the 1920s had left behind his childhood faith for agnosticism, nevertheless quoted at length the afternoon Sunday sermons preached at the Cathedral of Notre-Dame in Paris during the Lenten season of 1925, titled *L'inquiétude humaine: Le message de Jésus-Christ* (Human Anxiety: The Message of Jesus Christ)."[34] With respect to Messiaen, one quotation stands out:

> For the Christian, terrestrial life has no other meaning than that of a waiting for eternal life: *"And far from being troubled by the reproach addressed to Christianity for orienting ourselves in our entirety toward the beyond, I say that it is by this, and by this alone, that [Christianity] reveals itself to us as being the truth of life."*
>
> "Orient humanity in its entirety toward the beyond." Words profound in both meaning and influence, words that adolescent souls cannot hear without emotion. It is true that at the moment in which the intransigence of youth speaks alone in the heart of humanity, religion is willingly turned into this superhuman idea: a passionate waiting for the beyond, a constant desire for God, a renunciation of the earth in favor of heaven. The love of God appears alongside the first passion of the adolescent. However, very quickly, what we call reason takes up residence in the aging soul.[35]

Reading this passage, one finds it difficult not to think of both the passionate late-adolescent Messiaen, who was about to compose *Le tombeau resplendissant* (1931), as well as the composer in old age, who, just before dying, completed his final finished work, *Éclairs sur l'au-delà . . .* (*Lightning Flashes of the Beyond . . .*; composed in 1987–91).

Beginning in 1931, Daniel-Rops's writing, increasingly on Catholic topics, was advised by the philosopher Gabriel Marcel, newly converted to Catholicism in 1929.[36] (Daniel-Rops himself returned to practicing Catholicism in the early 1930s.) Both were members of L'Ordre nouveau, an intellectual movement later dubbed the "nonconformists of the 1930s," whose first manifesto for a "new order" was cosigned by Marcel in March 1931.[37] Catalyzed by the apparent catastrophic failure of republicanism and capitalism, these nonconformists sought a "third way" that would avoid the extremes of dualistic oppositions between individualism and collectivism, capitalism and communism, nationalism and internationalism.

In March 1932 Daniel-Rops published *Le monde sans âme* (*The World Without Soul*), a scathing critique of the cult of "machinism" and of mechanized industrial society, especially as represented in the United States, Henry Ford, and Taylorism.[38] This attack was set within a broader analysis of modern culture as one in which the cult of logical reason had "hypertrophied" and other nonrational (but not necessarily "irrational") mental functions—like "instinct" and "intuition"—had "atrophied." (In this respect, Daniel-Rops and the surrealists were of one accord in their attack on the cult of reason alone.)

In the book's first chapter, "Adieu à une inquiétude" (Farewell to an Anxiety), Daniel-Rops followed the argument he had made in *Notre inquiétude*. Postwar discourse over anxiety had grown tiresome. It was time to bid farewell to all the forms of anxiety except the eternal metaphysical one. Ironically, however, modernity had itself long ago bid farewell to this only true form of anxiety:

> True anxiety, the only one which is valuable in itself, is metaphysical anxiety . . . Every anxiety is vain which does not seek to transform itself into order, which, without hope, does not aspire to rest [from inconstancy] . . .
>
> Without doubt, we have become blind and deaf with respect to an immense number of phenomena with which our ancestors were able to establish some communication. To take an example from the material domain, the diminution in quality of our instincts is a significant fact . . . For almost three centuries, every action of humanity has replaced instincts and intuitions by rational volitions.[39]

Exactly one year after the appearance of *Le monde sans âme*, "F. D." quoted it in his review of Messiaen's *Le tombeau resplendissant*:

> [Messiaen] seems to feel with M. Daniel-Rops that "metaphysical" anxiety is "the only kind that is worthy in itself and which tends to transform itself

into order." [Messiaen] seems to regret, with the same philosopher (who joins Bergson, Massis, Mauriac and Ch. Gillouin), "the atrophy of certain instincts of ours" and to think that in recognizing the primacy of reason "we are rendered blind and deaf with respect to a great number of phenomena with which our ancestors knew how to establish valuable communications."[40]

By situating Messiaen not only alongside Daniel-Rops but also in the genealogical line of Henri Bergson (who had just published *Les deux sources de la morale et de la religion* [*The Two Sources of Morality and Religion*], 1932), Henri Massis (of the now-condemned Action française), the Catholic revivalist novelist François Mauriac, and Charles Gillouin (who had just published his *Journal d'un chrétien philosophe 1915–1921* [*Diary of a Christian Philosopher*] in 1932), the reviewer created the composer as a bold new "nonconformist."[41] For although these figures were in one sense political opponents—Bergson and Mauriac on the left; Massis and Gillouin on the right—all shared an opposition to the "primacy of reason," a trait that French republicans valued as their distinguishing mark, the heritage of Descartes's "clear and distinct ideas." The words of the late Sorbonne philosopher Victor Delbos (d. 1916)—who also happened to be Messiaen's father-in-law—are worth recalling: "Indeed clearness can be brought to bear on . . . concrete relations as well as on abstract concepts and their concatenation."[42]

An unmentioned yet implicit figure here might also be Jacques Maritain and his important 1927 work written to defend the pope's condemnation of Action française: *Primauté du spirituel* (*Primacy of the Spiritual*) (against Charles Maurras's *politique d'abord!* [politics first!], the slogan of the nonconformists was *spirituel d'abord!* [spiritual first!]).[43] However, opposition to the "primacy of reason" might just as well refer to the poet Paul Éluard. Messiaen was devoted to Éluard's surrealist attempts at dethroning "reason" and making a place for what the review calls those "phenomena"—irrational, antirational, or perhaps superrational—"with which our ancestors knew how to establish valuable communications."[44] Each of these figures extolled an alternative path countering mechanistic modernity and elevating the emotional over the rational.

"F. D." concluded that the "excesses" of Messiaen's *Le tombeau resplendissant,* "justified by the subject," might well have come as a surprise, explaining why "part of the audience applauded while another part booed." However, he insisted that Messiaen's work signaled a new generation's turn toward concerns more profound than their predecessors:

> Whatever one might think, it is necessary to recognize a sign of the evolution of the mind [or spiritual evolution: *l'évolution de l'esprit*] among certain young people, of which M. Daniel-Rops, cited above, is the torch. Judging, it seems, with the author of *Un monde sans âme* [*sic*], that revolutionary existence will consist in recovering a presently lost knowledge of the nature of the world and its laws, the sense of being, M. Messiaen has desired, against all the practices in honor since the manifestations of the impressionist school, to reintegrate the human being in music and to make him express his passions, this interior impulsion of which Huysmans spoke, the 'silent voice that the tumult of noisy machines cannot suppress in us," "the hope that does not define itself."[45]

By recalling the figure of Joris-Karl Huysmans, a primordial figure of nineteenth-century Catholic revivalism, "F. D." planted the young Messiaen in a long and venerable Catholic genealogy.[46]

Just a month and a half after this review, the same "F. D." published yet another review of the first performance of *Hymne au Saint-Sacrament* (*Hymn to the Blessed Sacrament,* 1932), a ten-minute work for orchestra described by Messiaen as "a song of praise to Jesus present in the Host."[47] In this April 1933 review, "F. D." referred to his own earlier March review:

> As we said just a while ago, the spiritual tendencies of this young composer full of gifts and rich in talent excuse us for defining the climate of his thought. Even more than *Le Tombeau resplendissant,* this *Hymne* demonstrates that

> the desire for eternal beatitude has been given to him from above and that he aspires to come out from the prison of the body in order to contemplate the divine light, just as it is said in *The Imitation* [*of Christ* by Thomas à Kempis]. Messiaen means for his music not only to speak to the soul but moreover to edify it. He leads the concert audience into "the sounds of truth and of life," along the flowery paths of poetry he learned to frequent from his infancy. The blood of the author of *L'âme en bourgeon* and *Souvent le cœur qu'on croyait mort* [*The Budding Soul* and *To Love After Death*, by Cécile Sauvage] flows in his veins.[48]

These were very personal and even obscure references that Messiaen must have provided "F. D.": references to his mother's writings and the *Imitation of Christ*, a copy of which "traveled everywhere" with Messiaen and which had likewise been one of his mother's favorite books (reread the winter before her death).[49]

"F. D." assisted Messiaen by exegeting the symbols embedded in the *Hymne au Saint-Sacrament*, which likely would not have been at all apparent to the listener. These details must have come from Messiaen himself. Consider, for example, the description of the communicant who has just received the Blessed Sacrament and feels "plunged into rapture," as well as Messiaen's affinity for fairy tales: The listener hears the sound of "small bells coming from distant places" and is "transported into the very middle of fairyland."[50] Then "F. D." juxtaposes the Eucharist with fairy tales a second time: After quoting Messiaen's final poetic lines in the piece—"The living bread that gives life, / eternal life!"—the reviewer adds that not only is this ending a bit too short, but also that it will not be replacing Dukas's ballet *The Peri* anytime soon.[51] Even this apparent aside likely came from knowing Messiaen's devotion to his conservatory master (who would pass away two years later).

These obscure details suggest that "F. D." was in conversation with Messiaen about his works. At least to some extent, then, "F. D." functioned as the budding composer's own frame for reception. If so, then Messiaen, in this crucial year of 1933, seems to have self-consciously associated himself with this wider cultural stage of the "new order," a spiritual revolution against the "primacy of reason" symbolized by Bergson, Maritain, Mauriac, Daniel-Rops, and, in the beginning, Huysmans. Just one month after the review of *Hymne au Saint-Sacrament* appeared, the first issue of *L'Ordre nouveau* (titled *Mission ou démission de la France* [*Mission or Resignation of France*], May 1933) published its manifesto calling for a *révolution spirituelle*, a nonconformist middle way between older solutions on both the right and the left:

> Against capitalist disorder
> and communist oppression,
>
> against homicidal nationalism
> and impotent internationalism,
>
> against parliamentarianism and fascism,
> *L'Ordre nouveau* puts institutions at the service of the personality and subordinates the State to Humanity.[52]
>
> *L'Ordre nouveau* aimed at nothing less than the "spiritual rebirth" of Europe.[53]

1935: Planting

France's 1930s continued to unfold. Almost exactly one year after this review, the Stavisky riots (of 6 February 1934) marked a crucial turning point for the nation. The right-wing coalition that tried to take over the National Assembly awakened the Left from its slumber. The seeds had been planted for the Popular Front victory of 1936. The year 1935 served as the decade's midpoint not only on the calendar but in political currents as well.

During the summer of that year, Messiaen composed the *Nativité* suite, an organ cycle of nine movements (symbolizing nine months of Mary's maternity). His titles and scriptural references were here again (as with the *Ascension* suite) inspired by Dom Marmion's classic collection of conference meditations, *Le Christ dans ses mystères*. However, in the *Ascension* suite, Marmion's meditations served as simple pointers to liturgical and scriptural texts. In *La nativité*, Messiaen drew more deeply on Marmion's theological content. This is that turning-point moment in which Messiaen leaves behind the vague "mystical" and embraces the "theological."

One element of Dom Marmion's work is essential to understanding his influence on Messiaen's *Nativité*—and that element is "theological," namely, Marmion's theological doctrine of "divine adoption" and, as a corollary, some version of "predestination."[54] The centrality of this doctrine to Marmion's theology can be seen in just three short passages occurring early in his book:

> But the main reason for keeping alive such feelings within us is our status as children of God. The Divine Sonship of the Father's only-begotten is of the essence and eternal. But, in an infinitely free act of love, the Father has willed to add a sonship, a childship, of *grace*. He adopts us as His children, to the extent that one day we shall share in the beatitude of His own inner life. This is an inexplicable mystery; but faith tells us that when a soul receives sanctifying grace at baptism, that soul participates in the divine nature: "that you may become partakers of the divine nature" [2 Peter 1:4]; the soul becomes truly a child of God: "You are gods, and all of you the sons of the Most High" [Ps. 81 (82):6; John 10:34] . . . In a very real, a very true sense, we are divinely begotten by grace.[55]

> The marvels of divine adoption are so great that human language can never sound their depths. It is a wonderful thing for God to adopt us as His children; but the means He has chosen for effecting and establishing that adoption within us is something more wonderful still. And what is this means? It is His own Son: "in His beloved Son." I have already expounded this truth

elsewhere [i.e., in *Christ, the Life of the Soul,* section 4], but so vital is it, that I cannot refrain from going back to it here.[56]

That is why contemplation of the mysteries of Christ is so fruitful for the soul. The life, the death, the glory of Jesus are the example for our life, our death, our glory. Never forget this truth: we are acceptable to the Eternal Father only *to the extent that we imitate His Son,* to the extent that He sees in us a resemblance to His Son. Why is that? Because this very resemblance is what, from all eternity, we have been destined [*prédestinés*] for. There is for us no other form of holiness than that which Christ has shown us; the measure of our perfection is fixed by *the degree of our imitation of Jesus.*[57]

The moral emphasis on the "imitation of Jesus" is thoroughly Catholic—and for Messiaen, for whom *The Imitation of Christ* was a key text (as it was for his mother), this emphasis would have great appeal.

However, the doctrines of "adoption" and "predestination" are somewhat unusual for a Roman Catholic voice—so much so that a recent English translator of Marmion's *Le Christ dans ses mystères* felt the need to append a long note addressing the monk's use of the word "*prédestiné*" at the beginning of the book. (In fact, he avoids the problem by translating "*prédestiné*" as "destined" instead of "predestined.")[58] Especially since its use by sixteenth-century Reformers to minimize the cooperation of human will in personal salvation, this Augustinian doctrine has tended to be sidelined in Catholicism, which instead embraced an Aristotelian-Thomistic emphasis on works done within a life of virtue.[59]

However, a particular aspect of this return to mysticism and metaphysics would have had special appeal for Messiaen: the emphasis on the *eternal.* In Marmion's scheme, God stands outside time and knows from all eternity not only his initial desires and designs for the universe but also the eventual outcomes. In other words (quoting Marmion's translator), "God, being outside time, knows which individuals will in the event achieve the eternal destiny planned for them."[60]

If we keep Marmion's own approach in view, the structure of *La nativité* (which can otherwise look somewhat haphazard) as composed in the summer of 1935 makes sense.[61] The nine movements (symbolizing maternity) are symmetrical in two ways. First, the center and fulcrum of the work is its meditation on the theological doctrine of divine adoption in the middle (fifth) movement: "The Children of God." The preceding four movements ascend to this climactic teaching, and the following four movements descend from it, not in the sense of decreased energy (for the most energetic movement is the finale), but rather in the sense of a dramatic denouement or unfolding.

The second symmetry is chiastic. The acts leading up to and then down from the climax are also parallel with one another:

Virgin and Child	1 ↔ 9	God Among Us
Shepherds	2 ↔ 8	Magi
Eternal Designs	3 ↔ 7	Jesus Suffering
Word	4 ↔ 6	Angels
	5 Divine Adoption	

The union of humanity and divinity is the point of movements 1 and 9. The departure of the shepherds and of the Magi are paralleled in movements 2 and 8. God's "Eternal Designs" of predestination (movement 3)[62]—"God, in his love, predestined us to be his adopted children, through Jesus Christ, to the praise of the glory of his grace"—are accomplished necessarily through the Incarnation—God's taking on flesh and hence assuming suffering (movement 7). The Word (movement 4) precedes all of creation—"At his side, before the stars existed, he engendered me"—and the Word is also the first of God's children—"The Lord said to me: You are my Son." Like the Word, the angels (movement 6) also preceded temporal creation and exist outside of time; yet they, too, like the Word, manifest themselves in time at the birth of Christ.

The symmetries may be seen more easily if the work is represented schematically:

1. The Virgin and Child
    2. The Shepherds
        3. Eternal Designs (i.e., predestination)
            4. The Word
                5. The Children of God (i.e., divine adoption)
            6. The Angels
        7. Jesus Accepts His Suffering
    8. The Magi
9. God Among Us

Messiaen's turn away from "the mystical" toward "the theological" can be located both conceptually and chronologically. Conceptually, the unexpected and definitive turn is the organizing principle of "divine adoption" (or "divinization" or "theosis") as God's predestined "eternal design."[63] Messiaen's Catholicism, somewhat out of the mainstream, was thus shaped by Marmion's highly idiosyncratic reading of the tradition. Chronologically, the shift occurred between summer 1932—the initial composition of the *Ascension* immediately following Messiaen's June wedding—and summer 1935—the composition of *La nativité* three years later.

The composition of *La nativité* was contemporaneous with the formation of the musical group La Spirale, a first attempt at defining a new generation of interwar musicians. Its members were all connected with the Schola Cantorum, including Messiaen, who had been appointed to his post teaching organ improvisation after the school's radical reorganization in December 1934.[64] Committee members of La Spirale included its leader, Georges Migot, Messiaen and Claire, Daniel-Lesur (who had also just acquired his post teaching counterpoint at the Schola), and André Jolivet (who, along with his wife Hilda, lived close to the Messiaens). La Spirale's first concert took place on 12 December 1935 with its manifesto printed on the program's front page: "to participate in the promotion of contemporary music, through concerts of French works, and through organizing exchange concerts with composers from other countries. It wishes to serve music and in order to do so, it will give fewer world premieres; instead, it will give repeat performances of significant works."[65]

1936: Flowering

The seeds of 1935 flowered in 1936. The Popular Front coalition of socialists and other leftist elements came to power and promised a progressive way out of the depths of the Depression. It was a moment of enormous hope, as passionate as it was to be short lived.

On 27 February Messiaen's *La nativité* was premiered on the organ of the Trinité—the nine movements were divided between three of his friends and fellow organists: Daniel-Lesur, Jean Langlais, and Jacques Grunenwald.[66] In the programs, Messiaen included a manifesto that solidified the 1933 review's critique of "the primacy of reason" and the redemptive value of emotion:

> Emotion, the sincerity of the musical work.
> Which will be at the service of the dogmas of Catholic theology . . .
> Theological subject matter? The best, since it contains all subjects.
> And the abundance of technical means allows the heart to overflow freely.[67]

A new agenda is encapsulated in just a few sentences: "Emotion" and the heart's "overflowing" counter the "primacy of reason" and the waning neoclassicism of the 1920s. And yet "emotion" will be held in check by the ordering principle of Catholic theological dogmas—in this *Nativité* suite, most specifically those found in Dom Marmion.

The vagaries of early century "mysticism" are gone; so, too, is the "mystical's" discursive use of leveling all religions to expressions of a single experience.

Meanwhile, 1936 continued to unfold. In early May, the left-wing coalition of the Popular Front won elections in both Spain and France. In June, Léon Blum's government took over, France's first socialist government. Reaction in Spain followed swiftly as General Franco staged a coup and set off the Spanish Civil War.

On 3 June, in the midst of world-historical events, the newly formed musical group La Jeune France—successor to the previous year's La Spirale—gave its first concert. The group's four members were Messiaen, Daniel-Lesur, Jolivet, and Yves Baudrier. The concert notes featured their nonconformist manifesto setting a middle-way course between the "revolutionary" left and the "academic" right: "As the conditions of life become more and more hard, mechanical and impersonal, music must always bring to those who love it, its spiritual violence and its courageous reactions. 'Young France' . . . a group of four young French composers who are friends . . . proposes the dissemination of works [that are] youthful, free, [and] as far removed from revolutionary formulas as from academic formulas."[68]

Once again a "nonconformist" vision of an *ordre nouveau* is written into the musical scene.[69] The influence of both Daniel-Rops and Emmanuel Mounier's "personalism" is evident in the attack on the "mechanical and impersonal"; the need for a "spiritual revolution" appears in the praise of a "spiritual violence" that is "courageous"; and a nonconformist third way is charted between merely "revolutionary formulas" on the left and "academic formulas" on the right. It is difficult not to wonder whether someone in this group—Messiaen himself?—had knowingly adapted this last phrase from Jacques Maritain's open "Letter to Jean Cocteau" published nearly a decade earlier. The order that Cocteau was seeking (in his postwar *retour à l'ordre* [return to order]), Maritain had written, was "*order* . . . obviously, not the academic kind of order which is a false one . . . That which scandalizes our contemporaries the most is order: I mean order in spirit and in truth which is just as much the enemy of a stuffed-shirt order as it is of disorder."[70]

Messiaen's thoughts turned toward the domestic during the hot days of summer 1936. Having successfully premiered *La nativité,* he now turned to composing the *Poèmes for Mi* (his pet name for Claire) for voice and piano.[71] The nine-movement structure, echoing *La nativité,* was perhaps intended as a votive offering to the Virgin Mary's maternity—and as the childless couple's prayer for intercession.

1. Thanksgiving (*Action de grâces*)
2. Landscape
3. The House
4. Terror
5. The Wife
6. Your Voice
7. The Two Warriors
8. The Necklace
9. Fulfilled Prayer

In the program for their premiere, Messiaen subtitled the work "Poems of O.M. on the Sacrament of marriage."[72] The marital theme is found in several of the movements, but nowhere so explicitly as in the seventh song, *Les deux guerriers* (*The Two Warriors*):

> Behold us two in one.
> Forward!
> Like warriors cased in iron! . . .
> Forward sacramental warriors!
> Strain joyfully your shields,
> shoot into the sky the arrows of devotion at dawn:
> You will arrive at the gates of the City.[73]

The text conveys a sense of mission and battle—perhaps melodramatic in retrospect, but understandable within the overall atmosphere of 1935–36: L'Ordre nouveau, La Spirale, and La Jeune France.

However, it can also be seen within the proliferation of discourse about marriage within Catholic circles in the 1930s. As late as the Code of Canon Law promulgated in 1917 (just as the Great War was ending), drawing on the tradition of both Augustine and Aquinas, Canon 1013 had defined two "ends" (or purposes) of marriage: a primary end of "procreation and nurture of children" and a secondary end of "mutual help and the remedying of concupiscence."[74] However, the war had drastically changed society and culture far more than anyone could have anticipated, and by the end of the 1920s such an archaic understanding of marriage was inadequate for the new modernity. By 1924 Abbé Jean Viollet had begun his ministry of answering couples' inquiries about sexuality (and especially contraception), and he published frequently on the topics of marriage, family, contraception, sterilization, and eugenics: *Éducation de la pureté et du sentiment* (*Education about Purity and Feeling* [1925]); *L'éducation par la famille* (*Education by the Family* [1926]); *Morale familiale* (*Familial Morality* [1927]); *Les devoirs du mariage* (*The Duties of Marriage* [several editions by 1928]); *Eugénisme, stérilisation, leur valeur morale* (*Eugenics, Sterilization, Their Moral Value* [1929]).[75] In Germany, the lay theologian Dietrich von Hildebrand published his books *Reinheit und Jungfräulichkeit* (*Purity and Virginity* [1928]) and *Die Ehe* (*Marriage* [1929]).[76] These latter works immediately preceded the publication of the papal encyclical *Casti connubii* (31 December 1930), an unbending condemnation of contraception responding to the 1930 Anglican Lambeth Conference's reversal of its long-standing position on the matter.

As an extension of the path opened by the pope, the 1930s would be filled with Catholic writings that attempted to reconcile tradition with modernity.[77] In France, Abbé Viollet published *Le mariage* (*Marriage* [1932]), *La psychologie du mariage* (*The Psychology of Marriage* [1935]), *La loi chrétienne du mariage* (*Christian Law and Marriage* [1936]).[78] Also in 1936, the same year Messiaen wrote the

Poems for Mi, Hildebrand's work on marriage (1929) appeared in French translation with the extended title *L'amour et le mystère du mariage sacramentel* (*Love and the Mystery of Sacramental Marriage*). The following year (in which Messiaen's *Poems* were premiered), a French translation of Herbert Doms's groundbreaking (although somewhat unorthodox) *Du sens et de la fin du mariage* (*On the Meaning and End of Marriage* [1935]) was published by Desclée de Brouwer.[79]

It is difficult not to wonder whether Messiaen's "warrior" conception of marriage was not an attempt to reimagine the Catholic marriage of a couple unable to procreate in such a newly intense environment—"marriage" now as "sacramental war." In any event, *Les deux guerriers* testifies to the kind of strict Catholicism that Messiaen and Claire seem to have shared and practiced in common. So does *L'épouse* (The Wife):

> Go where the Spirit leads you,
> nothing can separate that which God has joined,
> go where the Spirit leads you,
> the wife is the extension of the husband,
> go where the Spirit leads you,
> as the Church is the extension of Christ.[80]

There is also a suggestion in the *Poèmes* that Messiaen had already begun reading Thomas Aquinas on the "glorified bodies" of resurrected human beings—a topic he would treat systematically three years later in *Les corps glorieux* (summer 1939). For example, in the third movement (*The House*), Messiaen again meditates on terrestrial ephemerality:

> We shall be leaving this house:
> I see it in your eye . . .
> We shall leave our bodies too.

In the end, however, he concludes that all these "images of sorrow" will disappear

When we contemplate Truth,
in bodies that are pure, young and eternally luminous.[81]

Aquinas's technically precise term *clarté* (brilliance) is not yet used as one of the attributes of risen bodies, but *lumineux* suggests that Messiaen had begun meditating on their "lighted" aspect. And he now focused on risen bodies rather than the amorphous "souls" of *La mort du nombre* (1930)—yet another indication of the transition from the "mystical" to the "theological," made between 1932 and 1935.

1937–39: After the Apocalypse: Glorified Bodies

Characteristic of their epoch, the *Poèmes pour Mi* share with other works following the Spanish Civil War's outbreak a surrealism that has become apocalyptic—for example, Salvador Dalí, Joan Miró, and Pablo Picasso.[82] The premiere of the *Poèmes* is especially suggestive: They were first performed on 28 April 1937; two days earlier, German and Italian airplanes had bombed the Spanish city of Guernica. By mid-June, Picasso had completed his massive painting; it was exhibited that summer at the Exposition internationale des arts et techniques dans la vie moderne, 25 May–25 November 1937 (International Exposition of Art and Technology in Modern Life). Meanwhile, the Popular Front government collapsed during that summer, a victim of continuing and even worsening economic chaos. The passage from 1937 into 1938 opened in Paris with the Exposition internationale du surréalisme, 17 January–24 February 1938 (International Exposition of Surrealism), organized by André Breton and Paul Éluard. Three weeks after its closing came Hitler's Austrian *Anschluss*; the Munich appeasement followed later that September. These were apocalyptic times.

Messiaen's plans for yet another "theological" organ work to succeed *La nativité* (1935) seem to have been in the background of his article titled "Around an Organ Work," which appeared contemporaneously in April 1939 with the article just cited, "Around a Publication." Here

Messiaen argued against the notion that his organ works, "because of their titles and because they can and should be played during services," were "more religious than the rest of my catalogue." This was not the case, he asserted. He further complained "that the label of 'mystic'—which was so kindly pinned to my back at the first performance of my *Banquet céleste*—does not correspond to the truth." Rather, he simply sought to express his "Christian and Catholic faith," and this "act of faith" had been translated "most satisfactorily" in *La nativité*.[83] The organ work that he was about to compose in the coming summer months—*Les corps glorieux*—would take the "theological" even further beyond the vague "mystical."

As early as the preceding summer of 1938, Messiaen's turn to eschatological and even apocalyptic themes in composing *Chants de terre et de ciel* (*Songs of Earth and Sky*) had suggested tranquility's numbered days.[84] However, when Messiaen left Paris on 28 June 1939 for his summer vacation at Petichet in the Alps, he could hardly have known that these would be his last days as a civilian. As a sign of just how much he did not anticipate the outbreak of war on 1 September, Messiaen wrote a letter on 7 August to one of the organizers of an international festival of music in Venice, at which he expected to appear and perform in September. The letter communicated (1) his curriculum vitae, (2) a list of his published works, (3) "several words about the religious character of my music and the technical particularities of my musical language," (4) the titles and subtitles of the work (i.e., *Chants de terre et de ciel*) to be performed at the Venetian festival, and (5) "Finally, an *analysis of this work. I must insist that this analysis be included in the program*."[85] This letter makes clear that, as late as three weeks before the war's outbreak, Messiaen had no idea that traveling to Mussolini's Venice would be impossible in the month to follow.

Thus, Messiaen spent the final days of summer peacetime in composing an eschatological masterwork, *Les corps glorieux: Sept visions brèves de la vie des ressuscités* (*Seven Brief Visions of the Life of the Resurrected for Organ*):[86]

Vision 1: "Subtlety of Glorified Bodies"
Vision 2: "The Waters of Grace"
Vision 3: "The Angel of Perfumes (or Incense = *parfums*)"
Vision 4: "Combat Between Death and Life"
Vision 5: "Strength and Agility of Glorified Bodies"
Vision 6: "Joy and Clarity of Glorified Bodies"
Vision 7: "The Mystery of the Holy Trinity"

This is the first of Messiaen's works explicitly following Aquinas's own text and argument.[87] Three movements represent qualities that Aquinas and other medieval thinkers attributed to glorified (i.e., resurrected) bodies: subtlety (Vision 1), agility (Vision 5), and clarity (Vision 6). As we will see, Messiaen does not invoke the fourth attribute of "impassibility," but it is implicit in his use of "strength" (Vision 5).[88] Messiaen had definitely been preparing for the composition by a close reading of Aquinas's treatise at least a year and a half earlier, perhaps already in 1937. In his May 1938 review of Tournemire's *L'orgue mystique*, Messiaen used Aquinas's technical language to describe the works' rhythms, harmonies, modes, and melodies: they seemed "to penetrate matter with the subtlety of a glorified body."[89]

Aquinas, both following while yet departing from his predecessor, Hugh of Saint Victor, recalls moments in Christ's life where he demonstrated possessing these four gifts.[90] Christ demonstrated the gift of "agility" when he walked on water. His body demonstrated "subtlety" when he was born of the Virgin Mary and "came forth from the closed womb"; this is a reference to the traditional pious belief that Mary remained a virgin (i.e., her hymen was left intact) even after Christ's birth. He demonstrated "impassibility" when he escaped unhurt in situations where a crowd wanted to stone him or hurl him down a cliff. Finally, he demonstrated "clarity" (or "brilliance")—the only one of these gifts that "is a quality of the very person in himself"—when he was transfigured.

The first trait Aquinas considers in his discussion of "glorified bodies" is the one that Messiaen does not include: impassibility.[91] This is the quality of being immune from suffering or undergoing any other change (i.e., "passion"). On closer consideration, however, it would seem that Messiaen has indeed embraced this trait; however, he has substituted the word "strength" (force) for it. His epigraph to Vision 5 ("Strength and Agility of the Glorified Bodies") is taken from Saint Paul: "Their body, sown in weakness, shall rise in strength (1 Cor. 15:43)." This is the same passage Aquinas uses in his discussion of impassibility:

> *On the contrary,* everything passible is corruptible, because "increase of passion results in loss of substance." Now the bodies of the saints will be incorruptible after the resurrection, according to 1 Cor. 15:42, "It is sown in corruption, it shall rise in incorruption." Therefore they will be impassible.
>
> Further, the stronger is not passive to the weaker. But no body will be stronger than the bodies of the saints, of which it is written (1 Cor. 15:43): "It is sown in weakness, it shall rise in power." Therefore they will be impassible.[92]

Messiaen may have preferred the concept of "strength" (or power = *la force*) because it is a positive statement of the attribute and not a negative definition (i.e., what does not undergo passion).

But there is another more likely reason he chose "strength." "Impassibility" carries with it a corollary problem to which Aquinas devotes a great deal of argumentation, namely, whether impassibility means that glorified bodies have no sensation. Eventually, Aquinas concludes that resurrected bodies will have those modes of sensation in which the sense organ receives the external "species" without themselves being changed—for example, receiving the color species of whiteness without the eye becoming white. However, glorified bodies will not possess those modes in which the sense organ receives the external "species" and is thereby changed—for example, the hand, which itself becomes hot when touching (receiving the species of) a hot object.[93]

Based on these distinctions, Aquinas concludes that, although glorified bodies will experience neither touch nor taste, they will nevertheless possess the senses of smelling, hearing, and seeing (for all three the medium is the air). Messiaen had meditated on this question carefully. In Vision 3, "The Angel of Perfumes"—*parfum* translates as perfume, scent, fragrance, bouquet, or aroma—Messiaen quotes the book of the Apocalypse: "And with the prayers of the saints there went up before God from the angel's hand the smoke of the incense."[94] Messiaen thus follows Aquinas's example to explain why the risen life must include the active sense of smell: "Smell also which is the object of the sense of smell will be there," writes Aquinas, "since the Church sings that the bodies of the saints will be a most sweet smell."[95]

However, most important for Messiaen is that glorified bodies will see light and hear music. "There will also be vocal praise in heaven," writes Aquinas; "hence a gloss says on Psalm 149:6, 'The high praises of God shall be in their mouth' that 'hearts and tongues shall not cease to praise God.' The same is had on the authority of a gloss on Nehemiah 12:27, 'With singing and with cymbals.'" As for sight, Aquinas argues: "The intensity of light does not hinder the spiritual reception of the image of color, so long as the pupil retains its diaphanous nature . . . But the clarity of a glorified body does not destroy the diaphanous nature of the pupil since glory does not destroy nature; and consequently the greatness of clarity in the pupil renders the sight keen rather than defective."[96]

"Subtlety" is the second trait Aquinas considers and Messiaen represents in his first vision. Here again, Messiaen's epigraph is identical to the one Aquinas quotes, signaling his close "theological" adherence to this section: "It is sown a corruptible body, it shall rise a spiritual body (1 Cor. 15:44)."[97] It would seem that Messiaen embraced "subtlety" and used it for the first of his seven visions partly because it links risen human bodies with the first created elements (i.e., the planets). (Compare the second of the *Visions de l'amen* (1943): "Amen of the Stars, of the Planet with the Ring.") "Subtlety takes its name from the power to penetrate," writes Aquinas. This power may come either through "smallness of quantity" or else "through paucity of matter, wherefore rarity is synonymous with subtlety: and since in rare bodies the form is more predominant over the matter, the term 'subtlety' has been transferred to those bodies which are most perfectly subject to their form, and are most fully perfected thereby: thus we speak of subtlety in the sun and moon and like bodies."[98]

Aquinas notes repeatedly that this kind of planetary "rarity" led certain ancients to postulate that glorified bodies were perfected by a "fifth, or heavenly, essence." Aquinas vehemently denies that the fifth essence can "enter into the composition of a body," insisting instead that the glorified body is in fact a corporeal one. This is amplified when he considers "Whether one glorified body can be in the same place together with another glorified body?"[99] Predictably, his answer is negative: "If two bodies occupy the same place, one is penetrated by the other. But to be penetrated is a mark of imperfection which will be altogether absent from the glorified bodies. Therefore it will be impossible for two glorified bodies to be in the same place."

By putting "subtlety" as the first vision of *Les corps glorieux*, Messiaen followed Aquinas's own conclusion: "Consequently the first reason for spirituality in the body is subtlety, and after, that, agility and the other properties of a glorified body. Hence the Apostle, as the masters expound, in speaking of spirituality indicates subtlety: wherefore Gregory says (Moral. xiv, 56) that 'the glorified body is said to be subtle as a result of a spiritual power.' "[100]

Messiaen next turns to agility, again following Aquinas closely even in his epigraph's reproduction of Aquinas's own scriptural quotation: "It is sown in weakness, it shall rise in power." Here again Aquinas notes that some ancients attributed the gift of agility to the presence of "the fifth, i.e., the heavenly essence," and once again he disapproves: "But of this we have frequently observed that it does not seem probable. Wherefore it is better to ascribe it to the soul, whence glory flows to the body."[101] For Aquinas, agility comes from the body's being "prompt and apt to obey the spirit in all the movements and actions of the soul." By means of this gift, "the glorified body will be rendered apt not only for local movement but also for sensation, and for the execution of all the other operations of the soul."

Asking "Whether saints will never use their agility for the purpose of movement?" Aquinas must deal with an objection based on a fundamental principle of Aristotelian physics: "[M]ovement is the act of the imperfect" (Phys. iii, 2).[102] As his first countertexts, Aquinas appeals to two beautiful lines from scripture:

> "They shall run and not be weary, they shall walk and not faint." (Is. 40:31)
> "(The just) shall run to and fro like sparks among the reeds." (Wis. 3:7)

Aquinas concludes: "Therefore there will be some movement in glorified bodies." As can be seen in the seventh and final of Messiaen's *Visions de l'amen* (1943), the "Amen of the Consummation" is a brilliant pianistic tour de force, a toccata boiling over with thrilling perpetual motion. Its rapid and lightly touched runs musically portray the velocity of these "sparks among the reeds."

For Messiaen, undoubtedly, it is Aquinas's linkage of movement and vision that is vitally important. Even after the saints have climbed the heavens, writes Aquinas, they will sometimes move as it pleases them in order to get a better view: "so that by actually putting into practice that which is in their power, they may show forth the excellence of Divine wisdom, and that furthermore their vision may be refreshed by the beauty of the variety of creatures, in which God's wisdom will shine forth with great evidence: for sense can only perceive that which is present, although glorified bodies can perceive from a greater distance than non-glorified bodies."[103]

There is something wonderfully charming and fairytale-like in this medieval outlook. The afterlife will be a spatial world filled with beautiful creatures. However, in order to see them, the saints will have to change place by moving around so as to be able to perceive all these wonders through the eyes in their corporeal bodies.

But there is yet another problem embedded in the notion of movement: time. Aquinas asks "Whether the movement of the saints will be instantaneous?" and counters received opinions by reaffirming corporeal space and bodies: "*On the contrary,* in local movement space and time are equally divisible, as is demonstrated in [Aristotle's] Phys. vi, 4. Now the space traversed by a glorified body in motion is divisible. Therefore both the movement and the time are divisible. But an instant is indivisible. Therefore this movement will not be instantaneous."[104]

Aquinas further notes that there cannot be any comparison here with the "movement" of an angel because "movement" for a body is not at all the same as "movement" for a pure spirit. Again, the emphasis on the embodiedness of the saints is made by sharply distinguishing them from angels. He restates this even more firmly a while later:

> Now it is impossible to take away from a body its being in some place or position, except one deprive it of its corporeity, by reason of which it requires a place or position: wherefore so long as it retains the nature of a body, it can nowise be moved instantaneously, however greater be the motive power. Now the glorified body will never lose its corporeity, and therefore it will never be possible for it to be moved instantaneously.[105]

After much consideration, Aquinas finally agrees with those who "with greater probability hold that a glorified body moves in time, but that this time is so short as to be imperceptible." As for the problem of the "end of time," he simply concludes: "Although after the resurrection the time which is the measure of heaven's movement will be no more, there will nevertheless be time resulting from the before and after in any kind of movement."[106]

"Clarity" (or "brilliance"), the fourth and final attribute—first appearing the previous year in the *Chants de terre et de ciel* (1938)—is vitally important for Messiaen both here in 1939 as well as in the forthcoming *Visions de l'amen* (as will be indicated in a cryptic quotation mistakenly attributed to Proverbs: "from brilliance to brilliance" [*de clarté en clarté*]).[107] Once again Messiaen follows Aquinas closely as the sixth vision's epigraph quotes the same scriptural passage Aquinas does: "The just shall shine as the sun in the kingdom of their Father."[108] Aquinas insists once more that, although "the cause of this clarity is ascribed by some to the fifth or heavenly essence," this explanation "is absurd, as we have often remarked." Rather, the glorified body, brilliant in its radiance, will still be a body: "[C]larity which in the soul is spiritual is received into the body as corporeal."

Finally, if we want to know just how brilliant the body will be, we can look at the sun and compare—for the glorified body will be brighter than the sun. However, even a nonglorified eye will not be destroyed by the effect of heating (as happens when looking at the sun) while looking at the glorified body. Rather, "though the clarity of a glorified body surpasses the clarity of the sun, it does not by its nature disturb the sight but soothes it: wherefore this clarity is compared to the jasper-stone (Apocalypse 21:11)."[109] In the book of Apocalypse, jasper, green although translucent, is the first of twelve listed precious stones upon which the celestial city is built.[110]

By following Aquinas's argument so meticulously, Messiaen's *Les corps glorieux* takes his self-identity as a "theological" composer to new lengths. He has moved from the disembodied Neoplatonic "soul" to the hylomorphic Aristotelian-Thomistic "body-soul" composite. The influence of nineteenth-century romanticism and spiritualism—typical, for example, of his mother's affection for the poetry of Lamartine—has given way to the reading of more orthodox "theological" texts. As Dom Marmion himself explicitly observes: "God is so magnificently lavish in what He does for His Christ, that He wills that the mystery of the resurrection of His Son shall extend *not only to our souls but also to our bodies.* We shall rise again, we too. *That is a dogma of the Faith.* We shall rise again bodily, like Christ, with Christ. How could it be otherwise?"[111] Significantly, by becoming more theological, Messiaen had also become more eschatological—a fitting position as historical events turned apocalyptic.

Messiaen completed *Les corps glorieux* just several days before 1 September 1939, the day on which Hitler invaded Poland and sparked the Second World War. The work would lie untouched for the next two years as he was mobilized for the military, captured, and imprisoned in the POW camp. In that camp he would compose and premiere the "Quatuor pour la fin du temps."[112]

Conclusion

Why the turn from the "mystical" to the "theological"—to this *ordre nouveau*—in a time of cultural crisis? I suggest that, for members of the new generation attracted by figures like Daniel-Rops, the postwar innovations of the 1920s—including Jean Cocteau's "order considered as anarchy"—had lost their appeal. This was even more true of the legacy of the fin de siècle, which extended itself into work like Tournemire's, that of the symbolists, decadents, Rosicrucians, and other "mystical" movements. The three primary competing ideologies of the 1930s—democratic capitalism, Communism, and Fascism—seemed set on a crash course for yet another catastrophe. What was needed was not more chaos but less; not more vagueness but rather clarity.

Turning to the "theological" was a means of preserving the "poetics of the marvelous"—especially that espoused by the surrealists (of whose camp Messiaen considered himself a member)—while simultaneously embracing order.[113] Messiaen brought all of these themes together in a late-life interview:

> For the surrealists, it was a hallucinatory domain; for Christians, it is the domain of faith . . . They haven't seen, but they have a secret intuition about what they don't see. Now, I think music, even more than literature and painting, is capable of expressing this dreamlike, fairy-tale aspect of the beyond, this "surreal" aspect of the truths of the faith . . . By means of this language, I achieve possibilities for giving expression to everything superterrestrial, everything that's supernatural.[114]

Yet in the final analysis, Messiaen needed this "surreal" to be true: This is the necessity of the turn from the "mystical" to the "theological."[115] And so we have Messiaen's own words in 1967, on the eve of turning sixty: "[T]he Truths of the Faith *are* startling; they are fairy-tales, in turn mysterious, harrowing, glorious and sometimes terrifying, always based on a luminous, unchanging Reality . . . It's certain that in the truths of the Catholic faith I found this attraction of the marvelous multiplied a hundredfold, a thousandfold, and it's no longer a matter of theatrical fiction but of something real. *I chose what was true.*"[116]

7 Rethinking the Modernity of Bernanos: A Girardian Perspective

Brian Sudlow

Since the 1990s there has been a broad critical consensus that the polemical writings of Georges Bernanos are paradoxically modern in substance and style. In his essay on *Les grands cimetières sous la lune* (*A Diary of My Times*, 1938), Bernanos's tract about the Spanish Civil War, Michel Estève underlines how Bernanos's dissent from the textbook Catholic response to the war was evidence of his affirming the primacy of conscience over ideology.[1] Pierrette Renard has mounted the most complex and detailed argument in the secondary literature to demonstrate how Bernanos, in his polemical writings, was a modern in spite of himself.[2] Most recently, Claire Daudin has sustained this critical tradition, arguing in *Dieu a-t-il besoin de l'écrivain?* (*Does God Need the Writer?*) that Bernanos's personal faith bespeaks no corporate allegiance to the church.[3] In keeping with the view that resistance to modernity is another manifestation of modernity, Bernanos has also been classed as one of the right-wing anarchists alongside the likes of Léon Bloy or Louis-Ferdinand Céline.[4] This approach depicts Bernanos as a child of the Belle Époque who shared the violent skepticism of the anti-Enlightenment about the republican political project but plowed his own furrow in reacting against it. The work of all these critics is serious, profound, and extensive. Moreover, a rapid survey of Bernanos's polemical writings, particularly from 1936 on, appears to corroborate their conclusions, especially when we consider how much Bernanos speaks about the "free man," or the extent to which he distances himself from the torchbearers of the anti-Enlightenment in the interwar period, with the persistent exception of Édouard Drumont.

Still, even if the concept of Bernanos's modernity allows us to account for certain aspects of his writing, its counterintuitive nature gives rise to the suspicion that its motives are far from disinterested. In spite of what critics have asserted about his pertinence to the young, there is no particular proclivity among French youth for the works or the views of Bernanos. Indeed, since French youth has shown itself persistently deaf to Bernanos's repeated appeals to its untainted idealism, and since many of the disputes in which Bernanos was involved are now long dead, one may legitimately wonder whether the critical framing of Bernanos as *moderne* is an attempt to proof his work against its creeping irrelevance. Otherwise, such rebranding smacks of a kind of well-intentioned but ideologically inspired gerrymandering to ensure clear ground appears between him and the accursed torchbearers of the anti-Enlightenment. Bernanos is one of us; he could not be one of them.

The starting point of this present investigation is that such an agenda of ideological sanitization, combined with critical overdependence on the discourses of hegemonic social theory, has occluded important dynamics within Bernanos's political writings. Both have, for example, tended to obscure the fact that Bernanos's attacks on Franco's Spain or on the French Right of the late 1930s, are rooted in an aversion to violently imposed social unity, which also lies, paradoxically, at the root of Bernanos's contempt for contractual or democratic politics. They have likewise narrowed criticism's account of the paradoxes of Bernanos's *Les grands cimetières sous la lune*, in which Bernanos, the right-wing Catholic and monarchist, embraces an Enlightenment conceptualization of freedom—a position that I have hitherto argued—by taking sides against the nationalists during the Spanish Civil War.[5]

Now, it is also counterintuitive to qualify contractual models of society as *violent*. Nevertheless, there are two reasons that it is pertinent to a discussion of Bernanos's polemical writings. First, as one who deprecates Enlightenment individualism, Bernanos deplores the radical autonomy of subjects who, from a contractual perspective, form a unity that can be coerced by the will of the majority. Bernanos's resistance to the democratic will cannot thus simply be reduced to the effects of extreme individualism. It is this paradox that descriptions of Bernanos as anarchist fail to account for. Second, as a moralist, Bernanos constantly eschews the appeal to abstract notions such as freedom of conscience and engages instead in a process of myth deconstruction by attacking the coercive agendas, which political discourses of all shades seek to veil. Corralling Bernanos's analyses within the vocabulary of abstract moral discourse thus proves an obstacle to understanding the imaginative sensibilities and iconoclastic insights that underpin his frequent jeremiads. Those who plead in favor of a Bernanos *moderne* do so, therefore, at the cost of these distinctions.

Given these reservations about existing interpretations of Bernanos's political writings, the aim of this chapter is to challenge and enrich critical approaches to Bernanos's polemical work. To this end, it first explores and assesses in greater detail the widely accepted arguments in favor of the modernity of Bernanos's political writings. Then it addresses Sven Storelv's analysis of Bernanos's polemical writings, which breaks with the consensus that tries to define them in relation to modernity. Finally, this chapter considers the extent to which René Girard's mimetic theory provides a more useful tool than these other methods for understanding Bernanos's many complexities as an observer of French political life between the wars. For the purposes of this chapter, with its exploratory aims and its limited space, soundings of Bernanos's political writings are restricted to *Scandale de la vérité* (*The Scandal of Truth* [1939]), *Nous autres Français* (*We French* [1939]), and *Les enfants humiliés* (*The Humiliated Children* [1949]), three tracts written after the Spanish Civil War but before the blitzkrieg that the Germans launched against France in spring 1940. Forming a loose trilogy—"three works that hang together," as Jacques Chabot has observed—these texts represent the state of Bernanos's political *témoignage* (witness) on the eve of France's crushing defeat.[6]

Prima facie, Girard's mimetic theory, which focuses on the relationship between desire, deceit, and violence in literary, cultural, political, and religious contexts, appears eminently suitable to rereading the writings of Bernanos, a figure often characterized as temperamentally violent and who was preoccupied with violence throughout his writing career. This chapter argues, however, that rather than being a pure agent of violence, Bernanos belongs to that tradition of writers who, according to Girard, expose the illusions and myths that veil mimetic desire and the violence it can unleash on the individual and societal levels.[7] Thus this chapter aims to resituate Bernanos's apparent anarchism and his belated disdain for counter-Enlightenment figures in the context of his engagement with moral and cultural dynamics, which would later become central to Girard's mimetic theory. In corroboration of our findings, I also consider in the course of the analysis how Girard's last work, *Achever Clausewitz* (translated in the English as *Battling to the End*, 2007) strangely echoes some of the predictions of uncontrollable violence to be found in Bernanos's tracts. For it seems that what Girard has identified as an apocalyptic escalation of violence—*la montée aux extrêmes*—was heralded by Bernanos, caught between the horrors he witnessed in Majorca and the coming world war.

Renard's *Bernanos moderne* and Storelv's *Bernanos prophète*

The analysis and assessment of two key approaches to Bernanos's polemics serves as a launching point for developing a new critical framework. The first approach is found in Renard's essay on Bernanos's modernity, which stands as an exemplar of the critical consensus noted at the beginning of this chapter. The second is found in two essays by Sven Storelv, who, by using the imagery of the *Book of Revelation* (*Apocalypse*) as a basis for his commentary on Bernanos's

Essais et écrits de combat I (*Essays and Militant Writings*, vol. 1) foreshadows the Girardian analysis of Bernanos's polemical writings, which this chapter aims to elaborate further on.

Renard

Renard's essay in *Études bernanosiennes 21* puts before us three principal arguments to sustain the critical depiction of Bernanos's modernity. First, Renard argues that his sense of the liquidation of the past and the disorientation this induces are signs that he feels the modern impossibility of integrating experience and knowledge;[8] second, she asserts that since Bernanos sees this disintegration as a negative thing, he assumes a constant attitude of combat against it, whence the habitual violence of his rhetoric or his call to youth for a chivalrous *ralliement* (alignment, in this case with the forces of order) or his definition of prayer as revolt;[9] and third, she observes that Bernanos's modernity is further confirmed by his *témoignage*, the literary form that his combat assumes.[10] This is manifested, for Renard, in the freedom of criticism he exercises against the church and then in the blending of fiction and history in his last polemical works, which, again according to Renard, show him retreating into a kind of subjective enclave to comment on events.[11] Renard's Bernanos finally embraces a kind of autonomy and interiority, and thus incoherently—though Renard would no doubt prefer *paradoxically*—Bernanos launches his attacks on modernity from the vantage point that modern subjectivity provides him with.

Despite the textual evidence that Renard marshals in favor of these arguments, they are problematic on several levels. The first argument alludes to the view that treats nostalgia as a manifestation of modern sensibility in flight from present incomprehension, a view also articulated by David Lowenthal.[12] Yet this is unconvincing in the case of Bernanos, who finds experience and knowledge difficult to reconcile but not impossible. Indeed, since he is firmly convinced that their reconciliation can be found at the highpoint of Christianity in the Middle Ages, his analysis of modernity does not plunge itself into the past by way of analgesic nostalgia but rather by way of preparing the past's retrieval. In this respect a second problem with Renard's analysis concerns its assumption that the retrieval of the past can be only an exercise in nostalgia pitched against the exorable linearity of time. It can be argued, however, that writers whose imaginative formation has been liturgical and sacramental[13]—and this was indeed the case for Bernanos not only as a Catholic but also as a pupil in a minor seminary during the early years of the liturgical movement in France—envisage the past in ways that are metachronological because ultimately eschatological. Renard's implication that Bernanos's call for a renewal of the *chevalerie de la chrétienté* (chivalry, order of knighthood, of Christendom) is a nostalgic and pantomimic performance, undertaken to counter his disorientation, thus fails to consider how the liturgy, a central process in the formation of Catholic sensibility and imagination, could provide a model for the imaginative reactualization in the present of something that happened in the past.

Renard's second argument about Bernanos's combat as the response to his modern disorientation also poses problems. Renard claims that Bernanos forms part of the tradition whose fulminating heralds include Baudelaire and Nietzsche and which condemns the world—Renard recapitulates Nietzsche's words—as "impious, immoral, inhuman."[14] Yet we would be mistaken if we failed to appreciate in Bernanos's rhetoric against his enemies the wounding of a more fundamental desire for reconciliation. Bernanos's well-known inclination to fall out with his contemporaries was countered by an instinctive readiness to bury the hatchet, as he did with Jacques Maritain (though not successfully with Charles Maurras). Given Bernanos's literary filiation to Léon Bloy, in both theme and language,[15] Bernanos's fulminations against his enemies can arguably be read in the light of Bloy's conclusion to his own *Exégèse des lieux communs* (*Exegesis of Commonplaces*), which, after excoriating all the axioms of bourgeois sensibility, concludes with this disarming appeal: "You should think of this, poor imbecile, and in thinking of it, step back from being stupid and making the wretched suffer. For this is what we are, you and I, and nothing but this: great depths" ("great waters" in the standard English translations of Psalm 79 [78], which Bloy is quoting here).[16] The combat of Bernanos and Bloy is not a revolt against perpetual incomprehension or a statement of never-ending hostility but most often a corollary of their belief in the possibility of eventual reconciliation. "[I confide you] to the sweet mercy of God," Bernanos writes to Maurras in his last letter to him on 21 May 1932 since for Bernanos there is reconciliation in no other locus.[17] To return to the theme of combat, although it is also true that Bernanos defines prayer as revolt—"the only revolt that stands upright"[18]—we would be mistaken to assume that this is simply an affirmation of raw human agency or a spiritual variation on what was fundamentally a political agenda. Bernanosian prayer stands upright because it is a theocentric movement. Indeed, it is only when the prayer of Bernanos's fictional saints renounces anthropocentrism and the maximalization of human agency that it can avoid being disintegrating; as the last page of the *Journal d'un curé de campagne* (*Diary of a Country Priest* [1938]) notes, "hating yourself is easier than you think; grace means forgetting yourself."[19]

Renard's view that the increasing interiority of Bernanos's works is a sign of modernity is much better founded, though lacking in certain essential nuances. In the polemical works, especially the late ones, Bernanos's *témoignage* is certainly marked by the predominance of the "gaze, the role of experience, the importance of the present and of reason, the use, in fact, of the method of the Enlightenment."[20] Yet here, Renard arrives at her conclusion—the method of the Enlightenment—with undue haste. The tendencies that she identifies in Bernanos's writings might equally be clarified by drawing on Charles Taylor's distinction between the "porous" and the "buffered individual." In his monumental opus *A Secular Age*, Taylor posits a distinction between the premodern individual, who is porous with respect to the meaning and purpose of the world insofar as they are exogenous to the individual's consciousness, and the buffered individual, who constructs that meaning and purpose from the inside out or endogenously.[21] Still, Taylor maintains, there is a porous or open version of buffered individuality—an *open immanence*—which, although conscious of its own psychological egocentricity, is open to an exogenously located meaning and purpose in a world created by a divine subject. This latter kind of interiority, if it is buffered in its internal dynamics, is nevertheless porous in its fundamental assumptions.

Even though Bernanos, therefore, retreats further and further inside himself in his polemical works, mixing historical commentary with fictional or even fable-like representations of moral questions, why should we conclude that he is embracing the Enlightenment given that he remains nevertheless convinced of, and attached to, a world of universally valid meanings and purposes that only porosity to the divine make available to him? After all, in spite of his great rage at injustice and weakness among the clergy, Bernanos does not become a religious skeptic. Neither does he adopt an anthropocentric view of the problems that beset the public arena; on the contrary, Bernanos constantly answers the question of humanity by posing again and again the question of God. It is in fact only his belief in some universally valid reality beyond the material world that makes it possible for Bernanos to forget himself. Now, this is of critical importance since it demonstrates that Bernanos's coordinates are not simply those required by the need to contest the modernity that surrounds him. There is all the difference in the world—and not simply a difference in reverse—between ineluctable immanence and an immanence open to that which is without. If this is the method of the Enlightenment, then it is—*pace* Renard—strangely hostile to the skepticism and unbelief that the Enlightenment intended to herald.

Renard's view of Bernanos's modernity appears to be influenced by an overdependence on hegemonic social and cultural theories, as do the views of other like-minded critics. For her, it is necessary to locate Bernanos on this terrain of the Enlightenment even when such conclusions run counter to what we know to have been Bernanos's most enduring tendencies. Even if, to the extent that his thinking displays the characteristics of Taylorian open immanence, we recognize Bernanos's stylistic tendencies as *modern*, we can still ask whether Renard coherently frames Bernanos's work by making it so utterly dependent on the very ideological hegemony that he deplored. Although such an analysis could account for the reactionary characteristics of Bernanos's polemical work, it appears to end in a paradox that is itself more stylistic than substantive.

Storelv

A more convincing account of Bernanos's political works, and one that dissents from the consensus about his modernity, can be found in the work of Norwegian critic Sven Storelv. In his essays "Remarques sur le mythe du déclin du monde" (Remarks on the Myth of the Decline of the World) and "Bernanos, Discours pamphlétaire et discours apocalyptique" (Bernanos, Polemical Discourse and Apocalyptic Discourse), Storelv argues that analysis of the *Essais et écrits de combat I*, the first volume of the Pléiade edition of Bernanos's political writings, could usefully begin by considering Bernanos's imaginative preoccupation with the powers of evil.[22] This preoccupation, which is sometimes advanced as a reason to classify Bernanos's view of evil as Manichean, is attributed by Storelv to the influence of the *Book of Revelation* on Bernanos's thought. In the first of these essays Storelv criticizes Magdalena Padberg's 1963 thesis, *Das Romanwerk von Georges Bernanos als Vision des Untergangs* (*The Novels of Bernanos as a Vision of Decline*), which, he says, obscures the prophetic character of Bernanos's fictional work by restricting the meaning of myth to pure fable. By way of developing a prophetic reading of Bernanos's fictional work, Storelv then develops the parallels between it and the *Book of Revelation*, notably with regard to its imagery of the natural world, the signs of coming destruction, and the demonic.[23]

His conclusion that Bernanos appropriates the language and themes of the biblical prophetical tradition is furthered in his second essay, "Bernanos, Discours pamphlétaire et discours apocalyptique," in which he develops two pieces of evidence to corroborate the parallels between Bernanos's writings and the *Book of Revelation*. The first is Bernanos's favored depiction of the devil as the ape of God, the imitator or mimic, whose mimesis of the divine is an invitation to idolatry and an explanation of the devil's hostility to God. The second is the subsequent impostures by which this hostility is concealed. These two beasts—idolatry and imposture—are, according to Storelv, the very powers of Evil, which Bernanos never ceases to denounce. For Storelv, therefore, it is not modernity or the Enlightenment that allows us to account for the paradoxes and power of Bernanos's polemical writings. Rather, it is the nexus of idolatry and imposture, derived from the *Book of Revelation*, which is "the basic kernel whose influence regulates the play of meanings in all of Bernanos's polemical writings."[24]

Although Storelv's analysis is stimulating and certainly not dependent on a counterintuitive classification of Bernanos as *moderne*, textual evidence for Bernanos's reliance on the *Book of Revelation* is not abundant. In the first of these essays, Storelv provides only one substantial textual reference from the *Book of Revelation* (referring to chapter 13 and the two beasts), and in the second essay there are none. Storelv also appears to depict the biblical prophetic tradition as unproblematic even though the *Book of Revelation* is a notoriously dense and multilayered text that has posed many problems for biblical hermeneutics.[25] The centrality Storelv accords to the *Book of Revelation* in Bernanos's imagination also leads to its own hermeneutic problems. In one instance he associates the image of the dragon, mentioned once in *Nouvelle histoire de Mouchette* (1937),[26] with the dragon of *Revelation*, but ignores the fact that, for example, there are potentially far more classical than biblical sources for Jambe-de-Laine's wild, snorting horse in *Monsieur Ouine* (1946).[27]

In spite of these issues, Storelv's analysis provides fruitful categories in which to approach Bernanos's work, especially given the recurrence of the problems of truth, deceit, masquerade, and imitation in

Bernanos's polemical writings. Most important, Storelv's analysis foregrounds not the thematic preoccupations of Bernanos's writing—unlike much Bernanosian criticism, which has focused relentlessly on themes such as holiness, priesthood, childhood, or evil—but rather the discursive mechanisms that drive it forward. Now, if Storelv fails to root these dimensions of Bernanos's writings convincingly in the *Book of Revelation*, they can in fact be found linked systemically in the later work of cultural anthropologist René Girard, who conceptualizes the processes of mimetic behavior (with which we can associate idolatry and the *monde à rebours* [world in reverse]) and myth (with which we can associate imposture) as key drivers of human conduct and human cohesion.

The usefulness of a Girardian reading of Bernanos suggests itself immediately with respect to Renard's claim that Bernanos's attack on the Spanish nationalists and on the church in Majorca was effectively a paradoxical statement of Bernanos's belief in freedom of conscience. From a Girardian perspective we need reach no such conclusion. In Girardian anthropology, the cohesion of a community, regardless of culture, is always the result of a process in which the buildup of violence, induced by dueling desires, is relieved through the persecution of a scapegoat who is both innocent (because it has done nothing wrong) and guilty (because its persecution can somehow forge cohesion anew). The contribution of Christianity to this process, says Girard, has been to declare the total innocence of the scapegoat and to posit renunciation or love as the cure for dueling desires.[28] Reread in this light, Bernanos's preoccupation in *Les grands cimetières sous la lune* (which then hangs over *Scandale de la vérité*, *Nous autres Français*, and *Les enfants humiliés*) is not freedom of conscience or the emancipation of the individual—ethical principles of a worldview that Bernanos found abhorrent in any case—so much as the relentless declaration of the innocence of those who were murdered by the Spanish nationalists in Majorca. *Saving the honour of honour*, Bernanos's stated aim in *Scandale de la vérité*, is tied implicitly to his repeated attempts to save the innocence of the Majorcan innocents and, more tangibly, to denounce their persecutors and all the myths invented to disguise the latter's guilt.

A Girardian Reading of Bernanos

There is no immediate reason to label the declaration of innocence as a particularly Girardian instinct *avant la lettre*. After all, Bernanos's concern with innocence made little difference to his obstinate lifelong anti-Dreyfusardism. Moreover, the stylistically violent polemics for which Bernanos would become well known, notably through *Les grands cimetières sous la lune* and his radio speeches during the Second World War, might from a Girardian perspective be thought to make him insensitive to the processes that generate and disguise violence.

Quite the contrary is true, however. The Girardian resonances of Bernanos's polemical writings are seen in his growing sensitivity, from the mid-1930s on, first, to the escalation of violence (a violence induced by imitation) and, second, to the power of myth. In Girardian theory violence emerges from the rivalry created by desire. For Girard, desire is always something imitative.[29] The desire of the subject is not a binary relationship with an object (as it was for the romantic tradition) but arises by a kind of triangulation when the subject learns the desirability of the object from the desire of another subject (called by Girard the model) for the same object. In primitive societies the rivalry and violence that grew out of these competing desires—and which would reach its crisis when the rivalry and not the object had become thematic—had to be controlled by various social mechanisms (such as taboos), but, argues Girard, when these were no longer sufficient, primitive societies always chose some scapegoat as a kind of safety valve to purge themselves of the accrual of violent tension.[30] To retain the advantages achieved by the persecution of the scapegoat, the community needed to be protected from the truth of its actions by the generation of myths, traces of which Girard finds across all the cultures that he studies. Myth thus completes the violent cycle of desire, rivalry, and mimetic crisis and at the same time perpetuates it by declaring falsely the guilt of the scapegoat and hiding the crimes of those guilty of violence.

The possibility of a Girardian reading of Bernanos's polemical works in this chapter is made plausible by the correlations between the major elements of Girardian theory and the two poles of idolatry (denoting mimetism, rivalry, and violence) and imposture, which Storelv identifies but does not ground adequately in his analysis. It is also rendered plausible by the critical work of Paul Delvaux, who has long since pointed to tangible Girardian patterns in Bernanos's fictional writings.[31] The correlations between dynamics in Bernanos's polemical writings and Girardian theory are made clear in the analysis of *Nous autres Français* and *Scandale de la vérité,* which follows. They are corroborated but also brought into question by the subsequent analysis of *Les enfants humiliés,* a text that contains all the elements Girard has identified as integral to the system of religious violence. Throughout, our findings are illuminated by reference to Bernanos's perception of the escalation of violence and Girard's view, set out in *Achever Clausewitz,* that in the period of Western secularization, when pagan and Christian mechanisms to control violence (respectively, scapegoating, and renunciation and forgiveness) are much less readily available, there is bound to be an escalation toward extremism in humanity's performance of violent rivalry. Indeed, this was one of Bernanos's greatest preoccupations on the eve of the Second World War; knowing the capacity of humanity for violent rivalry, he feared the kind of war that modern humans would wage on each other. The implications of this *montée* are, however, apparent first in Bernanos's treatment of violence and of myth.

Violence and the Escalation toward Extremes

The composition of *Nous autres Français* was interrupted by that of *Scandale de la vérité,* which was subsequently published first. *Nous autres Français,* like *Scandale de la vérité* and *Les enfants humiliés,* is a series of reflections following no grand schema. A vague plan, nevertheless, emerges, which sees the first four sections largely devoted to revisiting the errors of Charles Maurras and Action française and the last two sections describing and rehearsing the providential prince whom the royalist Bernanos believed France needed in its hour of crisis. Within this tract, therefore, we are constantly confronted by the contrast between the values of honor and truth, which such a prince represents to Bernanos's mind, and the violence and myth which he believes characterize the modern world and which are modeled by the Nazis and the Spanish nationalists and epitomized by Maurrassian nostalgia.

To this end, for example, Bernanos distinguishes the violence of the Spanish nationalists or of the Nazis from his own arguably violent ideal of chivalry by noting their rage for conquest: "the Beasts unleashed, roaring, march upon men."[32] Their taste for conflict is, he says, the sign of a fratricidal fury whose aims are in fact proprietary.[33] In other words, they conquer in order to possess. Here Bernanos anticipates a key Girardian theme: that violence results from the unsatisfied desire of the subject for an object possessed by another.

It is significant, therefore, in this regard that at the same time Bernanos denounces the unarmed ruse of the usurer against the poor as "the most effective form of force."[34] Bernanos thus makes the link between the concupiscent pursuit of wealth (a key theme in his earlier tract *La grande peur des bien-pensants*, 1931 [*The Great Fear of the Conformist Thinkers*]) and the violence that it very often precipitates. While criticizing the violence of totalitarianism, Bernanos maintains his contempt for the more subtle violence to be found under the conditions of political and economic liberalism. By corollary, Bernanos's concern for the poor can be read as a plea for the scapegoats of capitalism and as an indictment of materialist, democratic society, which he denounces at length in the conclusion to *La grande peur des bien-pensants*.[35]

If such violence goes out in pursuit of the desirable, it emerges, for Bernanos, from the power of imitation. In the period before the

Second World War, Bernanos's fear was that the French nationalists would rehearse against their compatriots or against the Germans the same insuperable pattern of hostility seen in Spain and which led to the themacity of violence in the crisis he witnessed in Majorca. Having once shared the anti-German discourse of the Right, he sees it now (without necessarily shedding it entirely) in relation to the violent ends that it serves: "Well before the racism of Mr. Goebbels, an anti-German mysticism had surreptitiously fostered in us the concept of a German race, a damned race, able to be subjected to any form of degrading imposition, unworthy of forgiveness."[36] Bernanos found in the rhetoric of the Right in 1939 a desire to see the Germans not merely defeated but made subject and even excluded from reconciliation—unworthy of forgiveness. In this respect Bernanos identifies the kind of oppressive rivalry that Girard will later class as that of "monstrous doubles." For Bernanos, at least in this case, the concept of race functions as a kind of mask that accords to one's adversary a monstrous character and justifies hostility against it.[37]

If we pursue this Girardian line, it is striking that Girard's last book, *Achever Clausewitz,* sets out insights into violence that Bernanos again anticipates in *Nous autres Français*. The central thesis of *Achever Clausewitz* is that without a scapegoat or without Christian renunciation (i.e., without the mechanisms that promise to solve violent tension), violence is likely to escalate inexorably in what Girard calls an escalation to extremes.[38] Now Bernanos's appreciation of the scapegoat mechanism is implicit rather than explicit—though it could be fruitful to look at figures like the two Mouchettes in that light—but in *Nous autres Français* he predicts this very escalation of violence in the context of the approaching war, especially in the minds of his erstwhile fellow militants from Action française. The problem of Charles Maurras, says Bernanos, is that since he does not believe in the reign of God's grace, he prefers what Bernanos calls the precept of realism: "When your enemy is prostrate with his face to the ground, unconscious, do not miss the opportunity to smash the back of his head with a truncheon."[39] Bernanos also notes Maurras's inconsistency in criticizing the violence of others while quite unconsciously advocating violence to achieve his own ends. Thus, while Maurras excoriated the Germans for their policy of total war, he also applauded the bombings of Madrid and Barcelona.[40]

I return to this process of self-deception later since it is intrinsic to the myths that disguise violence. What is crucial here, however, is that, for Bernanos, the Maurrassian Right had lost the ability to draw a line in the sand between mercy and the iron law of justice and thus had no means to oppose the mounting violence. From this perspective, the ironic rule of Action française's strategy for restoring the monarchy "by every means, including legal ones," finds its logical outcome in a violent hostility that is no longer a *means* but now an *end* in itself.

How did Bernanos come to perceive this danger of exponentially mounting violence? Precisely through his experience of the Spanish Civil War, where he felt its logic had been played out perfectly. If we note that Maurras was ultimately in favor of Munich—surely evidence against the argument that Bernanos is pursuing—it is only right to point out his eagerness for rearmament against Germany before that time. We might label this *opportunism* rather than *realism*, but that aside, it is clear that Bernanos expected the very worst from the coming conflict, including the logical apogee of unbridled hostility in the kinds of extermination campaigns he had witnessed in Spain. There would be no easy limit on the coming violence; Bernanos thus foreshadows the Girardian escalation to extremes.

Storelv's first beast of *idolatry* is redolent of the mimesis and possessiveness that Bernanos describes but fails to capture fully the links that Bernanos perceives between desire, possessiveness, and violent hostility to the adversary. For Bernanos, as for Girard, however, the driving force behind so many events is unregulated, imitative desire that always threatens to explode into uncontrollable violence. That Bernanos is opposed to the violence of liberal capitalism and political totalitarianism shows that his position is better accounted for not in relation to Left and Right or to modernity but rather in relation to his perception of the moral links between desire, possession, and violence.

Myth

Nous autres Français also foreshadows the link that Girard will later establish between violence and myth. As Bernanos observes, "Myths spring up under the feet of the realist, and this imbecile is wrong to be surprised, for they come from him . . . To each new obscene trick of the realists corresponds a myth which is nothing other than obscene trickery itself."[41] For Girard the purpose of myth is especially to mask the real sources of violence when exercised to create or recreate communal unity.[42] Still, by extension, myth is found everywhere in Girard's system; *Mensonge romantique et vérité romanesque* (*Deceit, Desire and the Novel: Self and Other in Literary Structures*) explores how the myth of romantic desire (insofar as it depends on a binary system of desiring subject and desired object) had been exposed by a canon of writers who perceived the triangulation of desire.[43] What is key for Girard, however, is that where there is violence, there will always be a myth to disguise its root in mimetic desire.

For Bernanos likewise the perpetrators or advocates of violence show signs of constantly needing the blanket of myth to conceal the sources of their action. Bernanos is so convinced of this that he concludes: "The world will tomorrow belong to myths."[44] Bernanos had always denounced lies, but here he perceives an escalation of myths corresponding to the escalation of extremes of violence. The application of this principle to Action française, with all its characteristic violence, was also inevitable. In *Nous autres Français* Bernanos remarks quite crushingly that what Maurras supposes to be the "real France" is not in the least "real."[45]

In thus denouncing one of Maurras's favored depictions of France—*le pays réel* (France as she ought to be—the France of the monarchy) as opposed to the *pays légal* (France as defined by Republican constitutions and legislation)—Bernanos was only recapitulating the theme of his earlier tract *Scandale de la vérité*. This tract was originally conceived as a preface to an anthology of texts by Édouard Drumont compiled by Fr. Raymond Bruckberger, OP. When the anthology's publication fell through, however, the tract was reworked into publishable form for the *Nouvelle revue française*, where it appeared in April 1939. It was Bernanos's first opportunity to speak at length about the 1938 Munich pact, about France's part in it, and above all about the actions of Charles Maurras in welcoming the appeasement of Nazi Germany. For Bernanos, in contrast, the betrayal of France's duty to Czechoslovakia represented a grave dishonor. Indeed, the denunciation of this crime was, according to Bernanos, the only truth that could pose a scandal to the post-Munich mood of political pragmatism and narrow self-interest.

The word *scandal* again has Girardian overtones since what is scandalous breaks the illusions created by the myths that are needed to hide the violence of the community.[46] *Scandale de la vérité* itself is an exercise in the relentless deconstruction of the myths that, Bernanos believed, were essential to the cause of the Maurrassian Right, as to the members of Action catholique and the French hierarchy. In a series of accusations Bernanos fingers their mythic impostures. They treat the temporal domain as if it were the spiritual and vice versa; justice, truth, and honor have been used as a veil for self-interest such that their *politique* too often assumes the just garb of *mystique*; moreover, he denounces Action française as an impostor of the true monarchical tradition.[47] For Bernanos, myth seems as omnipresent as incipiently violent desire.

From a Girardian perspective, it is again significant that Bernanos connects his deconstruction of these myths to the redemptive action of Christ, who, for Girard, exposes the great myth of the persecution of the scapegoat.[48] As for Catholics who would mythologize Christianity to serve political ends—arguably, the stock-in-trade of the counterrevolution—Bernanos demands that they stop using Christian revelation possessively as a tool to achieve their own purely human ends: "As for me, I shall never tire of repeating to those people that the truth does not belong to them at all, that the humblest of truths was redeemed by Christ, that just as much as any of us Christians it shares in the divinity of Him who deigned to assume our nature—*consortes ejus divinitatis*—Do you hear that, you liars?"[49]

Bernanos here condemns the kind of possessive proprietorship that Girard claims to be the root of all violent conduct, only in this case—and this is crucial—it is Christianity that is doubly sacrificed: first as an object deformed by ideological control and then by the myth that disguises its manipulation.

Arguably in this instance we see the convergence of Bernanos's concerns with escalating violence and escalating myth. The burden of Bernanos's witness is to challenge his coreligionists and fellow travelers on the right to embrace truth and renounce the manipulative and violent use of myth. As lies are to power, so truth is to honor, or so Bernanos instinctively felt. From this perspective, his attacks on the church over Spain are less an expression of freedom of conscience—*pace* Estève—and more an allegation that Spanish churchmen have not been faithful to their charge. Thus, Bernanos seems to stand before the spectacle of France on the eve of the Second World War, saying—like Steeny glaring at his manipulative mother, Michelle, and Mademoiselle, her intrusive sidekick—"Liar, liar."[50]

Sacrificial Dynamics in *Les enfants humiliés*

As I argued earlier, *Nous autres Français* and *Scandale de la vérité* can be read in the light of mimetic theory. Among its various themes *Nous autres Français* clearly rehearses the unfolding of violence inspired by desire, while *Scandale de la vérité* analyses how the violent generate myths in their defense. I have also argued that the correlations between Bernanos's thought and mimetic theory point to the advantages of a Girardian reading of Bernanos's polemical works when compared to the critical consensus represented by Renard.[51]

Now, these elements in Bernanos's polemical writings, which anticipate so many of Girard's reflections on the origins of violence and the use of myths, find an even more intense realization in *Les enfants humiliés*. Therein, Bernanos's analysis of interwar France, its relations with it military veterans, and its conduct toward Germany depict a cultural situation that has many correlations with Girard's understanding of the sacrificial mechanisms within human culture. Yet, at the same time, *Les enfants humiliés* points to a significant dissonance between Girard's and Bernanos's thinking.

Les enfants humiliés, like its immediate predecessors, is a short tract with little formal organization. It is essentially a reflective diary—it is given the subtitle of *Journal 1939–1940*—and brings to a head Bernanos's thoughts about France's situation after Munich and before the defeat of June 1940. The text was completed by April 1940 and dedicated to Bernanos's Brazilian friends Mr. and Mrs. Virgilio de Melo Franco, but it was first published in 1949, a year after Bernanos's death from cancer. Stylistically speaking, it corresponds to the immanent pattern that Renard rightly detects in the late Bernanos. And yet it sees a dialogue unfold between Bernanos and his own childhood—"the little child that I was," to use his oft-repeated expression—which in the contrast it draws between holy "childhood" and "the humiliated children" is a rigorous exercise in the supernatural realism by which light Bernanos analyzed all of life, fictive or real.

The Girardian elements that emerge from *Les enfants humiliés* are very distinct. First, Bernanos's conviction was that France had been stolen from the French, principally by *les clercs*, the jurists and intellectuals, who had replaced the sentiment of "the homeland" with the concept of "the State."[52] The French people were, therefore, the victims of a violent privation before they even had a chance to realize the danger of the rivalry posed by this dangerous elite. Second, those responsible for this theft, alongside the powerful, governing class, appear to Bernanos as the constant aggressors of the French people. The context of the world wars—the memory of the first and the arrival of the second—leads Bernanos to label this group as *l'Arrière* (the Homefront) and himself and his fellow veterans of World War I as *l'Avant* (the Front). Crucially, those who belong to *l'Avant* are destined to become the scapegoats of the incipient violence that *l'Arrière* has fomented in the first place. The Girardian overtones here are remarkable: "For they know well that they have in their bones *the oldest of human religious traditions*, they are not unaware that every purification supposes a prior expiation, and the Rearguard, without daring to say so, is waiting for the Vanguard to perform that expiation."[53]

This sacrificial understanding of the role of the veterans (and indeed of *la jeunesse* since Bernanos sees the veterans as the young generation who fought between 1914 and 1918) recurs throughout the text; whatever happens, it is they who are made to be the scapegoats for the violent crimes committed by *les clercs* against France, and it is their deaths that help restore order, just as the death of the Girardian scapegoat restores harmony: "Over this gigantic killing machine which is the War, they have hoisted the national flag, and everything mediocre that it churns out from now on will be billed to the homeland, put down as war materials."[54]

Clearly, Bernanos's understanding of the Front and the Homefront and of the exploitation of the one by the other foreshadows Girard's explanation of how primitive societies cope with the buildup of internal violence. Instead of seeing in Bernanos's division of the French people from the clerical elite a religiously inspired inflection of class war theory, we would do better to appreciate how his description of France during this period adumbrates the various agents and processes that characterize Girard's description of the persecution of the scapegoat.[55]

The foreshadowing of the Girardian model of sacrifice is completed by Bernanos through his criticism of the false peace to which this process of expiation leads. In an extended passage on the nature of peace, Bernanos describes the false peace after the expiation of the scapegoat as a kind of lassitude, a state into which people are drawn when they are exhausted by their self-indulgence.[56] Yet here also—it must clearly be recognized—the Girardian model is not as securely anticipated. The death of Girard's scapegoat refounds societal harmony—even if the death is disguised in myth. For Bernanos, in contrast, this false peace after the expiation of the scapegoat is tangibly an act of imposture and compromise: it is more a "truce" than "peace."[57] If we were to explain this dissonance simply by attributing Bernanos's perception of false peace to his sensitivity to myth, we would still fail to explain the almost miraculous power that Girard identifies in the scapegoating process to reestablish societal order. Ultimately, of course, Girard is an anthropologist, while Bernanos in his polemical writing is acting principally as a moralist.

Two further objections should be raised here to the correlations between Bernanos's writing and mimetic theory in *Les enfants humiliés*. First, surely Bernanos's celebration of the veterans and his nostalgia for war run clearly contrary to Girard's aversion for violence and for the condemnation of violence in mimetic theory. Second, Girard's thesis in *Achever Clausewitz* is that violence is bound to escalate in societies that have jettisoned ancient religious practices for controlling mimetic violence as well as the Christian solution thereto. In reply, one could argue that Bernanos's celebration of the veterans' honor paradoxically tries to establish at least one value in society that cannot be instrumentalized or reified; one value that, in other words, cannot suffer the violation that mimetic desire would subject it to. *Saving the honor of honor*, especially perhaps when that honor has been sealed in self-sacrifice, remains Bernanos's agenda. Thereby, Bernanos declares invalid all attempts at illicit mimetic appropriation.

In answer to the second objection just noted, it is curious that while *Nous autres Français* anticipated the violent escalation to extremes as described in Girard's *Achever Clausewitz*, *Les enfants humiliés* portrays dynamics that Girard would associate with earlier cultural moments. Even though Bernanos sometimes uses the language of Clausewitz—he describes the wars of the modern state with the Clausewitzian (and Hobbesian) expression "the war of all against all"[58]—*Les enfants humiliés* evokes what he himself terms "the oldest of human religious traditions."[59] Whereas Girard has come to believe that the ancient religions, as well as the Christian one, no longer provide a barrier to the escalation of violence, Bernanos seems instead to have arrived at the curious conclusion that the process of war itself can provide for modern France a quasi-religious catharsis. If this points to an undeniable divergence in their appreciation of cultural dynamics within modern France, what cannot be denied is Bernanos's appreciation of the potential of violence in *Nous autres Français* or his understanding of the dynamics of imitation and their role in explaining the processes of human society and culture. It is these processes, rather than any supposed modernity or concession to liberal ideology, which best explain Bernanos's many paradoxes and his unquestionably complex polemical works. And it is indeed his very awareness of the power of mimesis that leads Bernanos (echoing Saint Jerome) to characterize Satan ultimately as "the ape of God."[60]

Reservations and Conclusions

One could make a range of other objections to rereading Bernanos's polemical works in a Girardian light. If we contest an analysis of his nostalgia for some far-removed idea of Christendom—if, for example, we ask whether his understanding of the retrieval of the past should not be viewed as a form of eschatology—we must still concede that on his image of the Middle Ages he allowed himself to stencil anachronistically and perhaps unconsciously a person-centered view of freedom that belongs properly to the twentieth century. Bernanos himself might have objected to a Girardian reading of his works, not least because he would have deprecated Girard's early aversion to sacrifice in a Christian context (corrected under the influence of Raymund Schwager)[61] and would surely have held in contempt Girard's modernist tendency to make scripture say what he says it means; bizarrely, in *Achever Clausewitz,* a book purporting to define the apocalypse, there is very little commentary on the *Book of Revelation.* One could argue, furthermore, that Bernanos is guilty of his own violence and myth making, especially in his hounding of the Maurrassian vision of the world and in the way he constructs much of his understanding of the monarchical ideal.

Still, his reason for this is rooted not in some paradoxical inflection of enlightened individual autonomy, as Renard and Estève believe, but in his commitment to the defense of innocence and in his sense that violence and myth sacrifice innocence and truth to power. The interrelatedness of these themes can serve as a corrective to narrower readings of Bernanos that, for example, would foreground emphatically his role as witness or his opposition to the modern world arguably at the expense of their relation to this central nexus of Bernanosian themes.[62] Most important, their interrelatedness challenges the portrayal of Bernanos as a *modern*, a portrayal too intent on plotting Bernanos's coordinates against hegemonic social and cultural categories. Bernanos's opposition to totalitarianism and his hatred of liberalism emerge from the same contempt he felt for the varying modes of their possessive aggression toward humanity and the means by which the powers-that-be of all political stripes sought to veil it in myth.

There is undoubtedly an interiority and a subjectivity in Bernanos's last political tracts, which sustain a reading of Bernanos as a stylistic modern. Still, such a paradox has little to say about Bernanos's substantive preoccupation with myth and violence and with his anticipation of the Girardian model of scapegoating in the context of modern France. When these preoccupations are considered, however, it is clear that in his polemical writings on the eve of the Second World War, Georges Bernanos discovers something that René Girard would later attempt to elucidate throughout his theoretical work: that the world can be more accurately interpreted not through its pretexts and justifications but through its envies and its desires.

8

"Into the Catacombs of the Past": Women and Wartime Trauma in the French Catholic *Ressourcement* Project (1939–45)

Brenna Moore

In her memoirs, *Traversée en solitaire* (*Solo Crossing*), French Catholic medievalist Marie-Madeleine Davy (1903–99; her name is also spelled Marie-Magdeleine) recalls a remarkable afternoon in Paris in December 1943. Trained under Étienne Gilson, Davy had been hired as a lecturer in religion at the École des hautes études, and she had prepared to teach on the likeness (*semblance*) between the soul and God among the Cistercian monks of the twelfth century. About ten minutes into her presentation, three German officers walked into the auditorium, stood by the door, and stared at her. "I felt pale. My jaw tightened. All my efforts were required to concentrate on keeping my voice steady."[1] For the past three years, Davy had been an active member of the underground Resistance, hosting clandestine meetings in the Fortelle château, just outside Paris.[2] "In those moments of fear," she wrote, "one's imagination takes over. I instantly saw myself shot."[3] Convinced that she would never again have an opportunity to speak, Davy abandoned her planned lecture topic and shifted to her most beloved: the idea of love in Bernard of Clairvaux. Davy plunged without introduction into "the sweetness of love described by the Cistercian Abbot." She claimed to have experienced Bernard's words in that moment as a sudden welcome but encroaching presence, a force before which she willingly surrendered: "[T]he tenderness of his words," she wrote, "invade me, and I forget, momentarily, the unusual presence [of the soldiers]." Bernard's words realigned her imagination from a panicked visualization to something that engendered sudden happiness as she quoted "by memory texts that delight me."[4] Davy finished the lecture and the students dispersed. The officers introduced themselves to Davy. By pure coincidence one had been a professor of medieval philosophy in Germany, and he—oddly—suggested they meet sometime to talk about medieval theology. Already too closely aligned with the Resistance to befriend a German soldier, Davy refused, walked quickly out of the lecture hall (not waiting for students at the bottom of the stairs as usual), and never saw them again. She arrived at her studio, breathless, with the texts of Bernard, she wrote, "still floating in me."[5]

For a generation of French Catholics like Davy, Christian medieval and patristic texts had the capacity to galvanize one's intuitive, affective capacities in the brutal present of the war. These materials contained regenerative power, provoked spiritual and personal rejuvenation, and could awaken the energies needed for the clandestine acts of resistance.[6] In wartime and postwar Roman Catholic theological circles, this widespread turn to the archives of Christian premodernity became known as *ressourcement*, or a "return to the sources." On the basics of ressourcement, scholars tend to be in broad agreement: Jesuit and Dominican theologians like Henri de Lubac (1896–1991), Marie-Dominique Chenu (1895–1990), and Jean Daniélou (1905–74) pioneered the movement known as *la nouvelle théologie* through the rediscovery of patristic and medieval theological writings. This retrieval prompted new ways to understand central doctrines (the relationship between nature and grace, theological anthropology, ecclesiology), and in the process they dismantled the older, more conservative neoscholastic paradigm and subsequently helped pave the way for the Second Vatican Council.[7]

But this story of change, narrating one of the most significant transformations in Catholic theology in the twentieth century, warrants closer scrutiny. We have become accustomed to thinking of this change as the clean and clear application of the method of ressourcement against the worn-out old categories of the neo-scholastics. However, this gives too smooth a surface to much more jagged, pluriform, even traumatic reality. It obscures the emotional context of ressourcement, the kind of affective invading force these twentieth-century critics felt in their encounters with medieval and patristic sources. And the affect and power of ressourcement, like Davy's sudden channeling of her beloved Bernard, was inextricable from the context of the traumas of war and holocaust. During the war, for this group of French Catholic intellectuals, the reading, teaching, internalizing, and discussing of premodern Christian sources were crucial practices of self-formation. Understanding the transformations that the premodern sources could allegedly enable provides a richer understanding of how the Catholic imagination and the political sphere intersect, one that takes seriously questions of practice and subject formation.[8]

However, if we ask questions about the affective power of these sources, we must do so in relationship to a wider cast of characters. The story of ressourcement tends, for understandable reasons, to veer almost invariably toward a handful of prominent theologians alone, figures like de Lubac, Chenu, and Daniélou. But this occludes the presence of nonclerical intellectuals, women like Davy, and a diverse range of male and female editors, writers, archivists, and theologians who pored over premodern Christian materials with avid and focused concentration. In addition to Davy, one could cite women medievalists such as Marie-Thérèse d'Alverny (1903–91), Régine Pernoud (1909–98), and Jeanne Ancelet-Hustache (1905–81) or the memoirist, contemplative, and theologian Raïssa Maritain (1883–1960). They offered critical, informed, and detailed analysis of Christian mysticism, the medieval period, and Christian history more generally, and yet their efforts are scarcely recognized.[9] We should begin to attend to these contributions if only to enable a fuller, richer understanding of the ressourcement impulse, which energized and transformed modern Catholicism.

By looking at a new cast of characters like Davy, d'Alverny, and Maritain, who are only rarely, if ever, incorporated into the story of ressourcement, we see that these women put old texts to new uses. The sources that some of these women resurrected not only enabled affective transformations, as the example of Davy demonstrates, but, as I will show, introduced into the process of ressourcement an interpretation of Christianity that stressed its complex, heterodox nature. In the war and postwar period, these women pulled up different kinds of sources that brought an encounter with *difference* into the story of the Christian past. The Latin medieval West is animated by an encounter with Islam, Christian apophatic sources complement meditative traditions in Buddhism, and the tradition of French Catholicism becomes inseparable from its Jewish roots. They did not do this from any privileged vantage point as "women," but their borderland position in relation to professional theology and history inevitably brought in a perspective that was new.[10]

"To Plunge into These Old Books": Premodern Sources, Affective Transformation, and the Context of Occupation

Whether male or female, lay or ordained, amateur or professional, few French Catholics involved in ressourcement fit the alleged measure and restraint of historical writing. They all can be counted among those who rebelled against the approach to history modeled in Germany, which had defined itself through training more aligned with science than philosophy and literature.[11] When the members of this community of French Catholics reflected on their approach to the Christian past, they did so not with scientific paradigms but with metaphors of life and death. Étienne Gilson urged his students to have the prophet Ezekiel in their mind's eye as they pored over their ancient manuscripts: "Prophesy! Make these dry bones live!"[12]

Marie-Madeleine Davy recalled her days as a student at the Institut catholique in Paris until 1941, where the atmosphere of magisterial positivism and neo-scholasticism still reigned. In learning about the church fathers at this Catholic university, she recalled having the distinct impression of assisting at an autopsy of a cadaver.[13] Instead of poking at a lifeless body, she wanted to summon the church fathers back to life and reinscribe them in the present.

Henri de Lubac also relied on metaphors of corpses, mortality, and regeneration. He claimed that modern neo-scholasticism had turned the living tradition of Christianity into something dead, and so the new historian of Christianity must "rediscover" Christianity by "going back to its sources, trying to recapture it in its periods of explosive vitality," with the confidence that the sources from the archive could be "interiorized and lived."[14] De Lubac's ideal historian of Christianity could generate a faith more expansive and alive and also rooted, even rock solid: "The litheness of the living," he wrote, "is more solid than the rigidness of a corpse."[15]

But it was Raïssa Maritain who, in 1943, marshaled the most vivid metaphors of life and death for the historian. "Historical books," she wrote, "can be truly holy because if done well, the writers make miracles. It is absolutely necessary that they raise the dead and cause the dead to walk before them and before us. They must light the catacombs of the past into which they lead us." She continued: "To accomplish such a task the intuition of the mind does not suffice—what is needed is the intuitive heart. It is necessary to love what you are telling and to love it madly . . . Like the prophet one must lie down against the dead child, breast against breast, mouth against mouth, and infuse into him one's own life."[16]

Historical work of the sort Maritain described involved a set of emotions—an intuitive heart—and bodily practices typically not associated with the quest for disinterested historical knowledge. Accordingly, Maritain argued that all work describing the past—both memory and history—would entail the affections of the scholar. "History must ever take into account—contrary to the conviction of the critical school—*feeling* and *emotion*, which is to say the human soul," she wrote in one postwar essay.[17] Feeling and emotion were the proper posture *and* the proper subject for the historian. In this deliberately *inner* encounter with the sources from the past, affectively and even erotically charged, we see that the wartime ressourcement work of both Catholic men and women scholars echoed long-standing practices in Christian mysticism in which the goal is to summon into existence the Christ of the past and render him interior to the life of the living.[18] These modern Catholics equally aimed to revitalize the authors from the archive as vividly as possible.

The yearning to attend to the relationship with the dead makes emotional sense in the context of the period. During the occupation, from 1940 to 1944, Marie-Madeleine Davy's life was a constant combination of the preoccupation with the medieval period and the morally charged, perilous activity of the Resistance.[19] She lectured on medieval theology at the École des hautes études throughout the war and produced translations and commentaries on the twelfth-century affective mystics William of St. Thierry and Bernard of Clairvaux both during and after the war.[20] In some cases, the medieval discussion topics provided innocent cover for the clandestine efforts of the Resistance. Davy had been loaned a large estate, the Fortelle château, located outside of Paris in Rozay-en-Brie, which she transformed into a sanctuary for Jews and Resistance fighters and where she simultaneously hosted discussions on medieval history and theology (the famous "*rencontres de la Fortelle*"), activities for which she won a national medal for heroism.[21]

But the fascination with premodern mysticism was often more than merely a superficial cover for the "real" work of resistance. As Davy saw it, the interiorization of Christian medieval mystical texts galvanized the inner strength needed to sustain underground efforts, as we saw with Bernard's sermons in the presence of the German soldiers. After another brush with danger in 1943, Davy turned to Meister Eckhart's treatise on divine consolation as soon as she was safe at home: "Do I need to be consoled? No. But I feel the need to focus my thoughts on the essential."[22] For Davy, Eckhart's words were powerful enough to corral her thoughts "toward the essential." They were an animating, directive force. Such work enabled constant vigilance around the psyche during the occupation (de Lubac would agree that "the psychic pollutants are more potent than the physical ones"[23]). As they saw it, sources like Eckhart were interventionist: they could fortify one's attention and guard it against the constant threat of occupation propaganda. The rallying cry of the Resistance journal *Témoignage chrétien*, "France, take care not to lose your soul!" had a similar goal in mind, that the mind, soul, and psyche required surveillance, and these mystical texts were powerful tools that could do this deliberately self-disciplinary work.[24]

For this reason Davy admired her colleague Simone Weil's "deliberately and consistently maintained effort at attention." According to Davy, "Weil felt that she was excessively easily influenced . . . With the greatest frankness Weil writes, 'If there were twenty or so young Germans in front of me at this minute, singing Nazi songs in a chorus, part of me would immediately become Nazi.' "[25] Davy admired Weil's admission. In the midst of the occupation, Davy put the verb *occuper* (to occupy) to new uses. She spoke of seeing in mystical premodern sources the claims that "God [rather than fascism] occupies every part of the soul."[26] In these moments of *occupation divine*, the soul becomes, as she put it, "possessed, hence the language which reminds us of St. Teresa, St. John of the Cross, or Angela of Foligno. The soul is a prey to that *sobria ebrietas* of which such lovers of God as Bernard of Clairvaux or St. Thierry have spoken."[27] Many of the mystical sources she and her colleagues read were not typically doctrinal in genre but were practical books containing specific exercises one had to read, to reread, to meditate upon, and to learn so as to bring about an abiding, deeply desired transformation of one's self; they became inner tools of self-protection.

Davy held this in common with some of the clerical theologians who were also involved in resistance work in the midst of ressourcement. Recalling the war years in Lyons, where he was a seminary professor (and the "undisputed master" of the wartime and postwar Catholic intellectual scene)[28] and active in the community of Christian resisters against Nazism, de Lubac wrote: "The tension was constant. We lived in a fever increased by hunger, by the daily horror of the news, by the next day's uncertainty. And yet," he added, "work was carried on, became even more intense. It was at this time that the series *Sources chrétiennes* began, that the *Revue du moyen âge latin* was founded."[29] Along with Jean Daniélou, de Lubac helped launch these journals to make these primary sources—mainly devotional and theological treatises—available in French translation. On the one hand, to immerse oneself in ancient material during the war was to create a counterspace: "There was nothing more pleasurable," de Lubac recalled, "to forget as much as possible the daily increasing threat of Hitler, than to plunge into these old books."[30] But there was more to it than this. In 1941 de Lubac had claimed that Europeans found Nazi symbols and myths so alluring because modern Christianity had failed to speak to people's desire for transcendence, to their "sense of the Sacred." Clerics treated theology too rationally, and Nazi symbols tapped into this desire to encounter something infinite and intense, which had for far too long lain dormant. These rediscovered medieval and patristic texts could, for de Lubac, redirect the sense of the sacred back to its proper channels.[31]

Cut Off at the Roots: The Christian Past in the Context of Exile

As we have seen, for Catholics like de Lubac and Davy, who were in France during the occupation, premodern texts contained a disciplining power for one's attention and could generate a kind of psychic counterspace, guarding one's imagination from the onslaught of occupation propaganda.

But by those who spent the war in exile, the texts were put to completely different emotional uses. Across the Atlantic, Davy's colleague and acquaintance Raïssa Maritain lived the war years in New York with her husband, Jacques Maritain, and her sister. Although a convert to Catholicism, Raïssa Maritain was a Jew under Nazi law. Rather than having anything to do with the occupying forces, Christian premodern texts in this setting spoke instead to the isolation of the exile, the devastation of hearing the news as it came from Europe, and the sudden abandonment of home and friends.

Raïssa Maritain was a lifelong intellectual, a writer, poet, philosopher, and contemplative. But unlike Davy, for reasons vaguely related to her struggles with health and her 1904 marriage to Jacques Maritain, she abandoned her university plans and never obtained the degree in philosophy she had started studying for at the Sorbonne.[32] Maritain was twenty years older than Davy and had immersed herself in Christian medieval sources decades earlier, reading Jean-Joseph Surin and Angela of Foligno in her friend Charles Péguy's bookshop as early as 1903. There she joined a whole generation of young thinkers who mined the writings of the Christian mystics and saints for alternatives to the secular republican ideology they repudiated.[33] In 1921 Maritain published a translation of *Des mœurs divines* (*The Divine Ways*), attributed to Thomas Aquinas, and in 1925 she embarked on the translation of the seventeenth-century disciple of Thomas, John of St. Thomas, titled *Les dons du Saint-Esprit de Jean de Saint-Thomas* (*The Gifts of the Holy Spirit of John of St. Thomas*). She published the latter as a series of articles in 1926 and as a book in 1929.[34] In 1925 Maritain selected and presented portions of Teresa of Avila's texts for *La vie spirituelle*, the new Dominican journal dedicated to mysticism and asceticism, and wrote commentary and analysis of Thomas Aquinas on the intellect and the affections in 1939, 1943, and 1945.[35]

But during the 1939–44 period in particular, Maritain came to see these Christian texts, long familiar to her, as harbingers of experiential, affective transformation directly related to the war. In the context of exile, Raïssa did not have the work, friendships, and intellectual projects in the United States that Jacques had. She spoke almost no English. From her exile she confessed to her friend Cardinal Charles Journet, the Swiss theologian, "here we're breathing depleted air, insufficient for us to really live. I see myself as if in a dream; I cannot even think about the house I left, our little empty chapel, it gives me a vertigo of pain. But in this way at least I share in the suffering of all who had to abandon their homes."[36] Even Jacques confessed to Journet a few weeks later, "Never have I seen her suffering like this as she is in exile; one would say all the roots of her life are cut off."[37]

After a few months in New York, Maritain began writing her most famous book, *Les grandes amitiés* (translated into English as *We Have Been Friends Together*), which is a two-volume meditation on the past.[38] Just as de Lubac "plunged into his old books" and Davy immersed herself in the Resistance, Bernard, and Eckhart, Raïssa Maritain looked backward in time. She said explicitly that the unbearable nature of the present compelled her to think about the past. On 6 July 1940, just weeks after France had surrendered and established the Vichy collaborationist government, Maritain wrote the following in the preface to her new book: "Life for me draws to a close, ended by the catastrophe that has plunged France into mourning and, with France, the world." She continued: "For the afflicted are not—cannot be consoled, the persecuted are not succored, God's truth is not spoken . . . In the present, I do not feel that I am present. I turn my thoughts toward the past and toward the future; toward the future hidden in God."[39] Maritain's wartime scholarship in *Les grandes amitiés* represents a different kind of retrospection. Hers was less a tool of spiritual competition with Nazi myth making and more an affectively charged and imaginative entry into French Catholicism's—and her own—history in Paris in the 1920s and '30s. In *Les grandes amitiés* Maritain's historical depictions eulogized her friends and mentors, people like Henri Bergson (1859–1941), Charles Péguy (1873–1914), and Léon Bloy (1846–1917), all of whom had been instrumental figures in the intellectual florescence of the French Catholic revival of the early twentieth century. As the culture that had sustained these intellectuals withered in Europe, Maritain brought it back to life (mouth against mouth, breast against breast, to draw on her own imagery) in the pages of her American writings. Maritain had taken the advice of Charles Journet, who suggested seeing her new writing project as a series of letters to her now dead friends and to new friends in the future.[40] Maritain began to overcome, if only partially, this afflicted sense of being "cut off at the roots" by plunging into the archives.

Maritain's retrospection works on an uneven, complex temporal grid. As she resurrects her friends and mentors from the *renouveau catholique*, she sets them alongside the medieval sources central to the ressourcement project, premodern mystical writers she had long studied. She places Thomas Aquinas, Gertrude, Pascal, Plotinus, and Jean-Joseph Surin alongside twentieth-century friends like Péguy and Bloy. Her *grandes amitiés* with Thomas, Bergson, Bloy, and Plotinus did not, in 1940, involve mastering abstract theory or the exegesis of texts but entailed a set of bodily, emotional dispositions. Each of these figures she eulogized and revitalized, whether from 1210 or 1910, so that they "bathed our souls," Maritain explained in her book, "with their spiritual influence. They did not know one another, but we brought them together in ourselves by loving them."[41] The primary hermeneutics of the past *grandes amitiés* is one of affectively, even erotically animated friendships that spanned the centuries. She explains her first encounter with Plotinus: "A wave of enthusiasm flooded my heart," she recalls reading the *Enneads*. "The next moment I was on my knees before the book, covering the page I had just read with passionate kisses, and my heart burning with love."[42] And of Thomas she wrote, "We therefore became attached to Saint Thomas as to a real friend, by sympathy, by admiration, and by gratitude. It is very certain that no one could know him without loving him."[43] Through her memorial/historical writing, Maritain immersed herself in the world of intense emotive bonds with authors, friends, and texts—bonds that were absent in the barren experience of exile. We know that throughout this experience of intense writing about these friendships she secluded herself in their New York apartment, going through letters, diaries, and the writings of her medieval and modern friends. If de Lubac thought an encounter with Christian historical texts (Nyssa, Origen) could redirect emotional life back into the proper channels, and if Davy saw the Christian medieval sources (Bernard, Eckhart) as galvanizing forces for one's psychic attention in the midst of the propagandizing present, then for Maritain the closer source of autobiographical memory fused with the premodern figures released her from a sense of isolation and kindled a new trust in the future. They gave her hope: "[Their] abundant seed will later bear fruit in a form which we ourselves cannot imagine . . . All these men [Aquinas, Péguy, Bloy] will have been in France the first workmen in the reconstruction which will perhaps be known to a world of the future."[44] Picturing Maritain's temporally chaotic retrievals of the past brings to mind Paul Klee's famous painting *Angelus novus*, so movingly described by Walter Benjamin as having its face turned to the past, wishing to "pause for a moment, to awaken the dead and to piece together what has been smashed," but blown by a wind from paradise "irresistibly into the future."[45]

Both Davy and Maritain suggest that the sources were crucial affective tools in the midst of the crises of occupation and exile, but, curiously, both were also relatively reticent to speak directly and at length about their experiences during the war. In her study of women historians in the French revolutionary context, Bonnie Smith has argued that women "amateur historians" who lived in the late eighteenth and early nineteenth centuries had a "relationship to the past that was filtered through trauma."[46] She sees women historians reaching for narratives of others as a way to handle unacknowledged wartime trauma without confronting it directly. "The historian," in the revolutionary context, according to Smith, "did not search for knowledge of facts but rather undertook to bridge the gap to tend a painful wound that came from suffering and death."[47] This is helpful to think about in this mid-twentieth-century context: Perhaps the mystical texts themselves were a way to move through the traumas of the war without having to name it and articulate it directly. These Christian texts that people like Davy, de Lubac, and Maritain were reading, rereading, remembering, and discussing during the war often concern life boundaries and their ruptures and dissolutions, the recognition of mortality, and the dynamics through which individuals lose their limited sense of self. As religious texts often do, these materials describe ways in which human beings come to terms with their own finitude in the face of forces they cannot control.

Furthermore, in the intellectual circuits in which Davy and Maritain traveled, there was a widespread sense that the medieval period was the occasion of intense emotional experience, especially grief, melancholy, sadness. To encounter medieval texts was to encounter a world putatively flooded with emotion, fueled by an abiding confidence that to read these texts could incite similar experiences in the present. For example, the works of novelist Léon Bloy (Maritain's godfather), although he had died in 1917, occupied a prominent presence in the wartime French Catholic fascination with premodernity. In his most famous novel, he describes a memory he had as a young man in a French town during a flood, where people were running screaming into a church to "implore a saint whose bones were there to deliver them from evil. The volume of lamentation was enormous . . . I began crying and praying, and then I knew . . . what the Middle Ages must have been . . . The thousand years of the Middle Ages were the great Christian period of mourning."[48] For many in this community, this perception of the medieval enabled one to encounter these modes of affective experience in the present: enormous lamentation, screaming, crying, praying. In her own memoirs, Maritain's frenzied fusion of the medieval and the modern similarly seeks to tap into and garner the emotions from former times. "How often," Maritain wrote, "Bloy's face streaming tears, did he not read us pages from Saint Angela of Foligno, in Ernest Hello's beautiful translation! We felt that Léon Bloy had experienced the words of God to Saint Angela."[49] Although Maritain said very little about the Holocaust in her memoirs (in her wartime poem she had assigned it to the anomalous category of "What cannot be told/What the mind refuses to bear"), the groans of the Hebrew Bible, the suffering of the medieval saints, and the tears of the Virgin and Léon Bloy are on every page.

Expanding the Reach of Ressourcement

After the war, Marie-Madeleine Davy's first publication was a tiny 1946 volume titled *Aimer toutes les mains* (*Loving Every Hand*), with only six hundred copies produced. Dedicated to "one who has died and one who is still alive," it is a remarkable meditation on "those who were present at the scandal."[50] Those who "saw what happened" in between 1939 and 1944 have an "arrow," as Davy put it, "embedded in the flesh." The whole text is a cautious plea against retribution. "From what I have witnessed," she wrote, "there is no point of revenge." As tempting and common as vengeance is (simply a human urge, she explains, like the Romans who marked transgressors by branding their foreheads), it is meaningless and enslaving. "Only love," she writes, "is totally free," a love that could "love the hands" that planted food, fed men and women, healed and tended wounds during the war but that could also love even the hands that sowed ignorance and violence.[51] In another context, this postwar call against vengeance might be banal, but Tony Judt describes how common extrajudicial acts of violent retribution were in continental Europe in the immediate postwar years.[52] Those who were suspected of collaboration with the Nazis were routinely rounded up and subjected to anarchic acts of violence. In the context of 1946, Davy's words were prescient.

For the purpose of understanding Davy's role in ressourcement, what stands out in this text is a visible expansion of the kinds of sources she used to ground her claims. Her regenerative program for the shattered present was increasingly vast in scope, stretching out beyond the sources from the Latin West to include texts from the Far East and India, pulling in Hindu, Buddhist, and Islamic sources (the latter certainly owed to her friendship with Louis Massignon). "Indeed," Davy explained after the war, "the mystics of the Middle Ages remained dear to me, I never abandoned them. However, the home of my soul proved to be eastern. This brought me an expansion of my whole being. Something heavenly, paradisiacal, hot."[53] Eventually

Davy understood herself less and less exclusively as a medievalist. She was drawn to scholarly pioneers from Europe who had immersed themselves in Eastern culture, and she eventually wrote a book on Henri Le Saux (1910–73), the French Benedictine monk who moved to India, plunged into Hindu asceticism, changed his name to Swami Abhishiktananda, and became a theologian of Hindu-Christian relations. Davy's book, *H. Le Saux, Swami Abhishiktananda, le passeur entre deux rives* (*Ferryman between Two Shores*) captures these newly emerging interests. From 1949 on, she directed the series Sources et feux (Sources and Light) for Griffon d'Or.[54] This publication shared some of the original impulses of de Lubac's and Daniélou's *Sources chrétiennes* series, reprinting translations of the church fathers and other medieval and patristic Christian texts. But Sources et feux typically set these materials alongside sources from Eastern traditions, as Davy would later explain. The goal was not, as she put it, "to confuse Christian apophatism with Buddhist emptiness. One cannot mix the paths, but understand that the traditions overlap and complement one another."[55]

For the remaining decades of Davy's publishing career, she highlighted connections between the mystical impulses of various traditions, for example, her 1976 publication, *Le thème de la lumière dans le judaïsme, le christianisme, et l'islam* (*The Theme of Light in Judaism, Christianity, and Islam*), and at the end of her life she served as lead director of the four-volume series on comparative mysticism.[56] Her lectures and publications blended the medieval Christian sources that proved such able psychic tools in the midst of the war with these new materials from outside the confines of Western Christendom.

The broadening of the ressourcement impulse beyond the sources exclusive to Latin, Western Christendom draws deeply from interwar traditions of primitivism and exoticism, which had been circulating freely in Paris's vibrant Catholic salons.[57] But it accelerated in the wake of the war, when suddenly the Western European heritage, including Christianity, was no longer the unchallenged standard setter for the rest of the world.[58] Appalled by the horrors of the war, scholars like Davy yearned to locate sources of truth outside the confines of the West.[59] In the 1940s and beyond, the collapse of the great colonial empires, the emergence of the third world, non-European, non-Christian nations seemed worthy of serious attention. The speeding up of travel and communication made for a new awareness of difference and otherness. The classic "Catholic" response to these transformations was often an appeal to "tradition," to "Christianity," to "Latin culture"—all associated with a mythically "pure" past, recoverable only by downgrading the new voices. But in the case of Davy, we see something new: a Catholic appeal to a tradition now understood as connected with and complementary to precisely the difference that was beginning to gain recognition.

For similar reasons, Davy's ressourcement efforts began to show that much of Christian history includes a dark undertow, reminding us of the human capacity for violence and cruelty. One of Davy's most widely cited articles, "Le thème de la vengeance au moyen âge" (The Theme of Vengeance in the Middle Ages), deals with justifications of violence as retribution during the Crusades.[60] Finding recoverable theologies of nonviolence and forgiveness in the patristic and monastic writers, Davy cited Thomas Aquinas as the source of theological justification for anger and retribution. She published widely on the symbols of the clown, the dog, and the acrobat in medieval sermons and how they served as vehicles to communicate anxieties about religious and cultural difference. For all of the affective transformations enabled by beloved premoderns, the whole of Christian premodernity was not simply a monolithic site of uncritical nostalgic yearning.

Davy was not alone. In the career of one of her contemporaries, Marie-Thérèse d'Alverny, we see a similar reaching out to incorporate the presence of difference into the sources of Christianity. D'Alverny was born in the same year as Davy, 1903, and operated with an equally expansive theory of ressourcement. As a young student at the University of Strasbourg, d'Alverny had also come under the spell of Étienne Gilson, studying medieval philosophy and specializing in the *mentalité* of the twelfth and thirteenth centuries.[61] For most of her life, d'Alverny worked as an archivist and curator at the Bibliothèque nationale's Department of Manuscripts. She was also a published scholar, codirector (along with M. D. Chenu) of the journal Gilson had launched in 1926, *Archives d'histoire doctrinale et littéraire du moyen âge,* and "master philologist and historian of ideas," according to Gilles Constable.[62] The central theme energizing all of d'Alverny's work was the Christian understanding of Islam in the medieval period.[63] She published extensively on the interactions between Islam and Christendom in the twelfth and thirteenth centuries and wrote several articles dedicated to the prominent role of the Persian Muslim philosopher and scientist Avicenna in medieval Christian thought. In 1948 d'Alverny published her most widely cited academic article, a detailed comparison of two different twelfth-century Latin translations of the Qur'an.[64] Here she examined one translation by the Englishman Robert of Ketton that she considered to be "governed by a spirit of systematic degradation"—full of mistakes and quotations out of context. She set it alongside an analysis of a translation by another twelfth-century scholar, Mark of Toledo, which she considered far superior though less well known. D'Alverny preferred the latter for its close allegiance to Arabic syntax and its more literal and therefore trustworthy translation.[65] D'Alverny's scholarship steered often to the Christian scholars in the medieval period who showed genuine curiosity about the texts and traditions of Islam. For example, she admired medievalists who learned Arabic and spent years on their translations of Islamic texts (even if the purpose was to support the supremacy of Christian revelation). As she said, "The desire to obtain reliable documents rather than indulge in foolish legends concerning Mohammed, in order to obtain a firm basis for study and discussion, is a good sign of renaissance in learning."[66]

Moreover, for d'Alverny, as for Davy, the sources of Christianity had as much to reject as to resurrect. In 1962 she published an article on the uniform, widely held misogyny among medieval Christian writers, stating plainly that her exposition is "harsh," but the texts are boring: They all say the same derogatory things about women and "lack variety and original ideas."[67] But d'Alverny's attention was drawn primarily to those medievalists who were curious, patient, and open to genuine learning about the other. The "spirit of a discoverer" is one that "befits a good historian" even today.[68]

We see a similar move in the wartime works of Raïssa Maritain. Like Davy and d'Alverny, during the war, Raïssa Maritain's retrospective gaze to the past and its sources came to include non-Christian materials. She presented herself in her two-volume memoirs, *Les grandes amitiés*, as a leading figure in the *renouveau catholique* but here for the first time in her life she really presents herself as a Jew. Although she converted to Catholicism as a young adult, it is to her Jewish roots that her attention is drawn in the context of the war. The first chapter of *Les grandes amitiés* begins with Maritain's childhood in Russia and includes a vivid depiction of her grandfather's Hasidism and the celebration of Jewish holidays in their home. If the hegemonic narrative of Jews between 1940 and 1944 was one of Jewish inassimilability and pollution, she countered this through a carefully crafted depiction of the Russian Jewish culture she knew as a child. Her childhood memories come in richly detailed flashes, shrouded in an aura of nostalgia. The Jewish holidays feature prominently in this story, radiating with religious and sensory detail. Her memory of Passover is the most vivid: "But the most impressive feast was that of the Passover. Night was falling, and the bitter herbs were eaten; then prayer began. Filled with the mystery of this Passover, I was charged with asking, in Hebrew, questions to which my grandfather replied by the recitation of the biblical narrative and the explanation of the rites of the Passover night. Then came the climax of the sacred night: the passage of the Angel."[69] Catholic readers in France and the United States, Maritain surely hoped, would be able to relate easily to these stories of ascetic sainthood and a rich liturgical sensorium. In addition to her own Jewish upbringing, her perspective on Catholic history in the interwar years evoked Bergson's Judaism, Bloy's bizarre theology of the Jews, and his love of Jewish poets.

Maritain's efforts at Judaizing her memories and thus the French Catholic revival deepen her earlier work on Jewish and Christian unity, which was focused primarily on biblical exegesis and scriptural retrieval, another cornerstone of the ressourcement project in twentieth-century France. In 1935 she published *Histoire d'Abraham ou la sainteté dans l'état de nature* (*The Story of Abraham or Sanctity in the State of Nature*) largely an analysis of the book of Genesis highlighting the "living bond" between the Old and New Testaments.[70] In *Histoire d'Abraham* Maritain subverted traditional Christian readings of Judaism as legalistic, arguing that legalism is "not a temptation of Jews qua Jews." "Any community," she insisted, "which holds in honor the law of God risks falling victim to it."[71] Maritain's retrieval and analysis of the sources of scripture aimed to subvert the anti-Semitic narrative, which saw Judaism as constraining rather than generating genuine spiritual interiority. Thus we see in the scholarship of Davy, d'Alverny, and Maritain a reaching out to new sources beyond medieval Christianity—as urgent and interventionist as these texts were in the wartime context—and pull into the story the presence of difference *internal* to Christianity's own story. Their ressourcement efforts were governed by a sense that affective transformation could be gained through an encounter with the Christian past, and it was possible to include otherness and difference in the reading of it.

The emerging perspective we see from people like Davy, d'Alverny, and Maritain, as I argued earlier, was occasioned by the war, but it may also have something to do with their being women, not because their sex grants them any essential privileged vantage point but because their experiences in the archive, in the salons, in the seminaries were so vastly different from those of their male counterparts that they would inevitably have generated a different view. Consider, for example, Davy's story: She was born in 1903 in Paris and never quite fit in with the ideals of the young French Catholic *mademoiselle*. She recalls preferring to wear pants instead of dresses and was constantly chastised by her mother for not using the feminine pronoun for herself. Like her contemporary Simone de Beauvoir, she associated the masculine with life and freedom. "If I was given the choice," Davy wrote, "I might have opted for the male. I'm not sure I accommodate myself well to my femininity. The bottom line for me was to be able to live my life in a way men did—that is to say independent and free—at a time when women were mostly under the authority of men."[72] Refusing the conventional destiny allotted to the second sex, Davy enrolled at the Sorbonne as an undergraduate. Her mentor Étienne Gilson encouraged her to pursue graduate work in Catholic theology at the Institut catholique in Paris, and she enrolled in 1936.

Davy was the first female to enroll there and, at the time, the only one. She recalls her time there as "the most painful period of my youth, without a doubt." The professors, Jesuits, she wrote, "were excellent, but the teaching given seemed to me sad, pathetic, and in any case of little interest."[73] She describes having to sit in the far back of the auditorium during lectures, "the place furthest from the professorial chair near the door. Apart from those who shared my bench, nobody saw me. Apart from two or three students, I was ignored."[74] She had enrolled at the Institut catholique only on a trial basis, but in 1941, after five years of successfully completing courses, she made an appointment with the institute's director, a bishop, to inquire about earning credit toward a degree for her work done so far. She recalls the meeting: "No. There's no question, he said. You are a woman!" Davy added that he "pronounced the word 'woman' as if it was 'plague' or 'cholera.'" She left the meeting without saying good-bye and "forgot about theology, and only focused on the painful occupation and resistance."[75] Later she would earn her PhD in philosophy from the Sorbonne but never obtained the *agrégation de philosophie*, the golden key to France's top teaching positions.[76]

Some of Raïssa Maritain's experiences were similar ones of marginalization. In 1922, as she was making arrangements for the Thomist retreats she and Jacques coordinated at their home in Meudon, one of their mentors, the Dominican theologian Réginald Garrigou-Lagrange (1877–1964) confessed to her that he did not want to include women in Thomist retreats even though these gatherings were her idea. Afterward she reflected on this episode in her journal. "A great theologian preaches Love to women, but teaches Intelligence to his disciples. The two ought to be preached and taught simultaneously." "These poor intellectual women!" she added, "How people mistrust them!"[77] Fifteen years later Garrigou-Lagrange would point not to Maritain's sex but to her Judaism as the dangerous pollutant threatening the community of French Thomists. She painfully described this betrayal in a letter a few months later to her friends Pierre and Christine Van der Meer de Walcheren: "We have been insulted before . . . But now racism is at the bottom of the hatred, it is impossible for me not to see that this insult is aimed at *my* blood! It is intolerable . . . If we left France today, those who would miss us would not add up to more than ten."[78] Marie-Thérèse d'Alverny, too, had her share of similar experiences. She finally left the Department of Manuscripts at the Bibliothèque nationale in 1962 after she was not made head of the department when Jean Porcher retired. She confessed to a friend that she was the "victim of a plot" under circumstances "so scandalous" that she had to realize the "humorous side of the situation."[79] One wonders whether such incidents inoculated these women against the many forms of seductive, uncritical attachment to the tradition of the Christian past that we see more commonly in ecclesial apologetic approaches to history.[80] Situated on the edges of the professional Catholic historical, theological, and philosophical disciplines themselves, these women "prowled the borderlands of Christianity," to use Michel Foucault's provocative phrase.[81] They engaged with the Jewish roots of the French Catholic revival's protagonists, medieval theologians curious about Islam, and the "complementarity" of Eckhart's apophatic mysticism and the goals of Buddhist meditation traditions. In their position of outsider-insider in relation to Catholic theology and history, their minds flourished. Although their contributions are not always easy to detect (many of these women published furtively, under initials, anonymously, especially early in their careers), these three women published hundreds of books, essays, articles, and translation projects and oversaw the publication of probably thousands more. They revamped what could have been merely the piling on of more details onto Christian history in order to lay claim to a refurbished sense of the religious past, one much more dynamic and bracing.

Yves Congar once said that "tradition" is alive and never stagnates because people come to the tradition and read it from new perspectives, noticing aspects of it that had been there all along but had never been recognized. This is what happened here. Congar was also the one to have noted that it was Charles Péguy who coined the phrase "ressourcement." Revolution and reform, Péguy argued, happens only by the "appeal made by a shallower tradition to one more profound; by a less perfect one to a more perfect, to reach a new level of depth, a return to the source, a ressourcement in a literal sense."[82] The more perfect, profound tradition rediscovered here was one thoroughly proximate to the non-Christian sources that were just beginning to gain recognition. This did not entail an abandonment of the medieval materials of Christendom—Bernard, Thomas, and William of St. Thierry "remained dear" to them, in Davy's words, and were crucial mental tools in wartime. Texts like the medieval sources—in Maritain's case fused with the modern—could enable focus, heighten one's attention, or immerse one in a world of affective, erotic friendships in the midst of isolation and exile. But in each of these cases, they eventually reached outward from Latin Christendom to pull in something new.

Conclusion

So what can we learn from the wide-ranging efforts of these ressourcement thinkers, women like Davy, d'Alverny, and Maritain, who labored alongside more familiar figures like de Lubac? For one, their stories help us reassess how the cultural and theological sources of Catholicism energized politics in the French context in the war years. Scholars such as Mark Antliff have persuasively shown how the mythic power of Catholicism, particularly in the interwar period, had served a right-wing political agenda and reinvigorated the antidemocratic right. Catholic aesthetic and devotional texts were used to underwrite an extreme, anti-Enlightenment and anti-Semitic agenda whose aim was to purge France of difference and restore contact with its putatively uncorrupted Latin roots.[83] This is undoubtedly part of the complex story of Catholicism and politics in the French context. Yet if we move forward to 1940–45 and the postwar period and look at a different set of scholars—women, who are only very rarely if ever incorporated into French Catholic intellectual history—another story comes into view. These women put Christian sources to different use. When they descended into the archives of the Christian sources, they did not emerge equipped to undermine modern republican ideals or reinvigorate anti-Semitism and right-wing monarchism. When they "walked backwards into the future," to use Jay Winter's language,[84] it was to recover roots of Christendom that were more heterodox than typically acknowledged and to make room for difference. The newly resurrected sources could be tools to imagine the tradition differently: The French Catholic revival was energized by Judaism, medieval theology was influenced by the Islamic philosopher Avicenna, and Eckhart and Bernard complemented Buddhist texts on egolessness. Moreover, for each of them, the practices of reading, discussing, remembering, meditating, and internalizing these texts were crucial tools of subjective transformation in wartime, whether offering focus for resistance or the endurance for a long exile.

To be sure, if the writings of Raïssa Maritain, Davy, d'Alverny and de Lubac demonstrate a recurrent fascination with the past, it is no surprise. Roman Catholicism's ongoing preoccupation with the past is well known. Although there has always been a spectrum of approaches and attitudes toward the old, the ancient, and the dead, it is perhaps the illiberal tendencies for which it is most famous. Nostalgia for the "Latin" medieval shored up Catholic authoritarian discourses throughout the modern period. Fidelity to an "unchanging tradition" animates the defenses for a male-only clergy. Indeed, one could imagine that Nietzsche had Catholics in mind when he claimed that those obsessed with what is no longer can only be today's "grave-diggers."[85] For Nietzsche, one must be tethered neither to the past nor to the future; one must be committed exclusively to the present. These French Catholics who ventured "into the catacombs of Christianity's past" during the descent into violence and chaos of 1939–45 did so not as a refusal of the present but as a creative way to engage their tumultuous world as scholars, citizens, and human beings.

9

La Relève and Its Afterlife: A Current of Catholic Renewal in Twentieth-Century Quebec

Joseph Dunlop

Though a preeminent example of French intellectual culture, the influence of the *renouveau catholique*—the early twentieth-century revival of French Catholic literature and thought—stretched out beyond metropolitan France and even francophone Europe to touch an island of European intellectual life in North America: Quebec. Perceiving themselves as part of a larger European intellectual milieu, young French Canadians seized upon the new ideas emerging from Catholic France to refashion their understanding of faith and its relationship to politics, culture, and society. One of the most important vehicles for this Catholic revival in Quebec was the Montreal-based periodical *La Relève,* founded in 1934 by a group of young francophone Canadian intellectuals.[1] *La Relève* enjoyed a unique role in Quebec as a propagator of the "new Christian humanism" of the 1930s due to the ties of friendship that bound these young Catholic intellectuals to the French philosopher Jacques Maritain and his wife, Raïssa. The Maritains were key figures in the *renouveau catholique,* influencing a variety of Catholic artists, intellectuals, novelists, politicians, and social reformers in the Americas and Europe. It is unsurprising, then, that *La Relève*'s trajectory should be similar to that of many other Catholic writers and activists of the era. Initially strongly influenced by ideas of a more militant Catholicism, *La Relève* subsequently followed Maritain in his critique of the Catholic authoritarianism exemplified by Franco's Spain and Pétain's France. The post-1945 period witnessed an even greater openness among the *Relèvistes* as they moved away from the relatively cautious Maritain toward a less defined Catholic progressivism, an ethos shared by many of the other Catholic intellectuals who would play a prominent role in the fast-paced modernization of Quebec during the 1960s and '70s.[2] And in the years following the Second Vatican Council, as Maritain became increasingly critical of radical shifts in Catholic theology and practice, the sympathy of a number of *Relèvistes* lay with more experimental Catholic thinkers rather than with Maritain's calls for a return to orthodoxy. The evolution of the *Relève* group—from 1930s' Catholic militancy to the eclectic pluralism of the postwar period—therefore mirrors the dual legacy of the interwar Catholic revival: rejuvenating the faith among many Catholics, while ultimately calling into question more traditional understandings of Catholic belief and identity.

La Relève has often been portrayed as a departure from the conservative-minded Catholic nationalism of early to mid-twentieth-century Quebec. Retrospective writings and interviews by a number of former *Relèvistes* stress the review's nonconformity and its divergence from the religious and political norms of Quebec in the 1930s and '40s.[3] Historians and other commentators have also emphasized *La Relève*'s role in challenging the predominant conceptions of Catholicism and nationalism during this period, foreshadowing the years of turbulent change that accompanied the rapid socioeconomic modernization of Quebec society during the 1960s and '70s. The literary critic and novelist Gilles Marcotte—a friend to many former *Relèvistes* during the postwar years—saw the review as "the wolf in the fold," its vision of Catholicism offering a subtle but critical alternative to the period's "official Catholicism" and ideological conservatism.[4] Elsewhere, *La Relève* has been singled out for its "neo-Catholicism" and for offering "a new way to be Catholic."[5] In many respects these characterizations capture something of the flavor of *La Relève* in the later 1930s and '40s. At the beginning, though, the review was a product of the Catholic and nationalist mainstream in Quebec. Indeed, the origins of *La Relève* were representative of the period's middle-class French Canadian Catholicism, with its rich web of distinctively Catholic institutions, social and youth organizations, and schools. The small circle of young men who founded *La Relève* were all graduates of the Collège Sainte-Marie, a prestigious Jesuit institution well known in Quebec for its role in furnishing the next generation of the French Canadian elite. At Sainte-Marie, the education of the *Relèvistes* would have been suffused with a traditionalist French Canadian nationalism, combined with the militant social Catholicism of the 1920s and '30s.[6] This combative and proselytizing Catholic activism was strongly evident in the student review *Nous*, to which a number of the future *Relèvistes* contributed.[7] In particular, the articles of *Relève* cofounder Paul Beaulieu conveyed the missionary zeal and the desire to defend Catholic values that were so characteristic of the mentalities of interwar Catholicism. The Catholicism evoked in the pages of *Nous* was sharply defined, opposed to Communism, Protestantism, atheism, and free thinking and was confident in its own values and solutions to social ills.

This conception of Catholicism was also evident in the youth movements which played such a key role in the intellectual and social formation of *La Relève*'s cofounders, Paul Beaulieu and Robert Charbonneau. Beaulieu was deeply committed to the Catholic scout movement throughout the 1930s, and his writings on scouting convey the strong sense of ideological superiority that often defined Catholic social activism during this period.[8] According to Beaulieu, the values of Catholic scouting served as antidotes to the anxiousness, "pagan" values, and moral dissolution that he saw as characteristic of so much of modern, urban life. The task of scouting, in his eyes, was the restoration of "Christian public life" and the rechristianization of modern society.[9] A similar sense of Catholic mission informed Robert Charbonneau's involvement with Jeune-Canada, the most prominent of the various nationalist youth groups that appeared in Quebec during the 1930s.[10] Charbonneau was actively involved with the group from its founding in 1932 to around 1936. Although Jeune-Canada's aims were principally nationalist, its politics and social ideology were resolutely Catholic. Antiliberal, opposed to the monopolistic excesses of laissez-faire capitalism, and disgusted by the partisanship of parliamentary democracy, Jeune-Canada's social ideology drew heavily on a conservative reading of Catholic social teaching. Anti-Semitic attitudes were also prevalent at Jeune-Canada, though there is no evidence to suggest that Charbonneau shared these views.[11] In fact, Charbonneau would later criticize groups like Jeune-Canada for promoting the ideal of "an exclusively Christian society," whereas he emphasized the need for a common citizenship open to people of all faiths and ideological persuasions.[12] Nevertheless, Jeune-Canada's anti-Semitism did not initially impel him to resign from the group, nor did it prevent *La Relève*'s editor in chief, Claude Hurtubise, from attempting to join it twice.[13] Indeed, during the early to mid-1930s, it is unlikely that either Charbonneau or Hurtubise would have seen the anti-Semitism present at Jeune-Canada as a sufficient reason for breaking ties with the group. Founded by many of their former classmates from the Collège Sainte-Marie, Jeune-Canada represented a familiar social and ideological milieu, and anti-Semitism itself would have been considered largely acceptable within many nationalist circles in Quebec during this period.[14]

La Relève's origins, then, were in a social and intellectual context defined by a strident Catholic nationalism with its own mentalities, institutions, and structures. Even the *Relèvistes*' fascination with the French *renouveau catholique*, a movement that has usually been portrayed as a "progressive" influence upon francophone Catholicism, initially emerged from the widespread popularity of France's Catholic avant-garde among Quebec's conservative-minded clergy and Catholic bourgeoisie.[15] Though by the later 1930s Jacques Maritain had become a controversial, even unwelcome, figure for some Quebec Catholics, in the early part of the decade his credentials were considered impeccably orthodox.[16] As his biographer Jean-Luc Barré observes, Maritain's reputation in the 1910s and '20s had been that of "a Catholic of the right, indeed of the extreme right," and he was regarded in France as "the leader of a neo-Thomism that was regularly confused with Maurrasism."[17] It was this reputation that accounted for his popularity among French Canadian Catholic nationalists.[18] Even after Maritain broke with Maurras following the papal condemnation of Action française in late 1926, he was likely still viewed in Quebec as an author of the Catholic right and remembered for his earlier writings, which had championed intellectual and political order against the liberalism of the Third Republic. When Maritain made his first trip to Quebec in 1934, he was received as an intellectual celebrity, as the preeminent representative of contemporary Thomist thought rather than as a pioneer of liberal or Left Catholicism.[19] And when the *Relèvistes* first met Maritain in October of that year, the French philosopher was just beginning his initial, tentative engagements with democratic thought.[20]

La Relève was thus born at a moment of transition, when Maritain and his circle were still disentangling themselves from the longstanding alliance between French Catholicism and the politics of the counterrevolutionary right.[21] The early years of *La Relève* reflected this time of change, a period when Saint-Denys Garneau, one of the review's contributors, could praise both Maritain and the right-wing Catholic nationalist Henri Massis in the same letter.[22] During the mid-1930s, the review's articles contained a mixture of social Catholicism, French Canadian nationalism, and frequent references to the authors of the *renouveau catholique*. Holding it all together was *La Relève*'s commitment to an integral Catholicism, one that rejected Communism and socialism, as well as the fascistic experiments of the new European right. Claude Hurtubise, the review's editor in chief, summed up *La Relève*'s position in an early article on the plight of Catholic youth in a world of competing and often anti-Catholic ideologies. He quickly discarded the doctrines of Canada's new socialist party, the Canadian Commonwealth Federation (CCF), and dismissed the CCF's Christian socialist leader, the Rev. J. S. Woodsworth. Catholic youth, wrote Hurtubise, "does not want people like Woodsworth, Protestants of English stock, bringing about this necessary restoration, to the benefit of their false doctrines. It would be imperfect, it would be against us."[23] In contrast, the writers at *La Relève* had a little more sympathy for the Far Right in their early issues, reflecting the admiration among many Quebec nationalists for the European right's dynamic and dictatorial leadership, its nationalism, and its call to order.[24] But in the view of the young writers at *La Relève*, the non-Catholic foundations of Fascist and Nazi ideology undermined even these purportedly positive characteristics. *La Relève* contributor Roger Duhamel acknowledged a number of Italian Fascism's accomplishments, notably its supposed achievement of class harmony, as well as its salvation of the principle of private property, both key tenets of social Catholicism. Ultimately, though, Duhamel came down against the regime on account of its self-declared totalitarianism, which conflicted with the Catholic ideal of an organic, decentralized society.[25] Similarly, Claude Hurtubise admitted that Nazism should not be completely rejected: it had reestablished authority and social order in a chaotic postwar Germany and had served to awaken the energies of the German people. Nazism, though, was compromised by the fact that it was not "guided by Catholic thinking": "It can never be said enough, the truth is found only in Catholicism, and any work that sets out to be humane must have that foundation. Other doctrines are true only insofar as they agree with it. It is therefore up to Catholics to establish this new order. Otherwise it will be done without us, against us."[26]

This combination of robust self-assurance and anxiety at the rise of non-Catholic ideological competitors was characteristic of Catholic lay movements during the interwar years. With the strong encouragement of Pius XI, lay Catholic militants sought to mobilize the faithful in opposition to the materialism and spiritual vacuity of modern societies.[27] Youth played an important role in this effort, particularly in Europe, where religious and political movements competed to recruit young students and workers.[28] In Quebec, *La Relève* was one of a number of Catholic youth movements that emerged during the interwar years, all of which aimed to reinforce the presence of Catholicism in the lives of French Canadian youth.[29] Preventing Catholics from moving toward dangerous and non-Catholic ideologies and organizations was a priority for such movements, with the editors of *La Relève* lamenting the fact that "the worst enemies of order and intelligence" had been the first to seize upon the potential of youth as a social force. According to the review's manifesto: "The role of youth, so cruelly inaugurated during the war, can only continue to grow. It is therefore necessary to rally the young people, give meaning to their efforts, rather than leave them to turn, through a need for action which is natural to their youthful vigor, towards socialism or the pettiness of political party clubs."[30]

In addition to their integrally Catholic social doctrine, the *Relèvistes* also subscribed to a vision of Western cultural degeneration, a narrative shared by many French Catholic intellectuals and which was also popular among other antiliberal writers during the early twentieth century, such as the Russian philosopher Nicolas Berdyaev (whom the *Relèvistes* admired), as well as T. S. Eliot and Oswald Spengler.[31] This narrative portrayed the history of the West in terms of a long decline following the cultural and spiritual highpoint of the Middle Ages, which was idealized as a period of political and religious unity, one subsequently disrupted by the individualism of the Renaissance and the schisms of the Reformation. The disintegration of Western society had only been exacerbated with the coming of the modern age, and under the shadow of the Depression, many of *La Relève*'s writers showed a distinct antipathy to the parliamentary democracy and capitalism of the liberal West. In their view, Western fragmentation was not simply evident on a political and economic level but had also compromised society's understanding of the human person, whose integrity and wholeness had been "mutilated by the different systems since the Renaissance and the Reformation," in the words of Robert Charbonneau.[32] Moving away from a liberal conception of the individual as an "isolated atom," *La Relève* looked to the more communitarian notion of the person espoused by European

Christian thinkers such as Berdyaev, who aimed to restore an image of humankind associated with "a concrete spirituality, where everything is organically bound together."[33] This, in part, was what a rechristianization of society meant for *La Relève*: the reconstruction of society around a Christian and communitarian understanding of the person.

In terms of politics, *La Relève* showed a marked lack of interest in Quebec's domestic political scene, though the private correspondence of Claude Hurtubise reveals that he, at least, held the same contempt for the provincial Liberal party that was so evident among his friends at Jeune-Canada and in many other social Catholic circles throughout the province.[34] For many militants within this Catholic and nationalist milieu, the Liberals were perceived as bourgeois, beholden to U.S. and English Canadian big business, and insufficiently committed to the nationalist cause. Captivated by the clash of ideologies in Europe—and anxious about the future of Catholicism in the face of Fascism, Communism, and liberalism—*La Relève* tended to pay far more attention to politics at the international level. As I have noted, the review's early political sympathies leaned toward the Right, though both Italian Fascism and German Nazism were measured against the standard of Catholic social teaching and ultimately found wanting. More appealing, initially, was the Catholic authoritarianism typified by the Portuguese Estado Novo of Antonio Oliveira de Salazar and by the Austrian Catholic dictator Englebert Dollfuss, who had been assassinated in July of 1934 by Austrian Nazis. Both men were praised in *La Relève* by Roger Duhamel, who described them as great men, able to "take the destinies of their countries in hand, and apply a policy of equity and moderation, postulated by Christian morality."[35] Of all of *La Relève*'s contributors, Duhamel was probably the closest adherent to the conservative brand of social Catholicism favored by so many Quebec nationalists; later, according to Hurtubise, Duhamel would drift even farther to the Right.[36] In 1934, however, his views were widely representative of Quebec's Catholic intelligentsia and of many activist Catholic youth.[37] Robert Charbonneau, for instance, had also admired Dollfuss's qualities as a Catholic leader and had gone so far as to express envy for Dollfuss's death as a martyr for his faith.[38]

The *Relèvistes'* encounter with Jacques Maritain in October 1934 set the review's intellectual and political trajectory on a new course.[39] Meeting with members of *La Relève* and Jeune-Canada, Maritain troubled a number of these young French Canadians by criticizing their nationalist preoccupations.[40] Although some members of Jeune-Canada seem to have rejected Maritain's critique, the *Relèvistes* began to cultivate a fruitful and long-lasting intellectual collaboration with the French philosopher.[41] Maritain's influence was evident in the review's evolving stance on nationalism, which the *Relèvistes* began to reconceptualize in cultural and communitarian—rather than ethnic—terms and which they situated within a hierarchy of values, where the importance of the "national" was placed below the Christian notion of the person.[42] As the friendship between the *Relèvistes* and Maritain strengthened, the review's tone as a whole began to reflect the tenets of his "new Christian humanism": a concern for social justice and the working class; an acceptance of religious and ideological pluralism; and an openness to cooperation with non-Catholics on social and political issues of common concern. By March 1936 Charbonneau could mark the beginning of *La Relève*'s third year by writing that Catholicism need not be linked to capitalism nor to the politics of order "and that in our day the truth, as Maritain says, is very much on the left."[43] This new orientation toward the Left, however, was strictly contained within the boundaries of social Catholicism. The review remained resolutely anti-Communist, and even during the later 1930s *Relèviste* Robert Élie would write that the communist "mystique invites the world to suicide."[44] Élie saw Catholic working-class organizations, such as the Jeunesse ouvrière chrétienne, as a more beneficial and ideologically sound solution to "the worker question."[45] This was a position that was broadly shared by the *Relèvistes.* In 1939, for instance, Claude Hurtubise could applaud the call of American writer Paul Hanley Furfey for a Catholicism of "extremism," one opposed to the immorality of unbridled capitalism and social inequality but still attached to the principles of the social encyclicals of the papacy.[46]

Despite a continued adherence to a core of Catholic social ideas, the engagements of the *Relèvistes* during the later 1930s reflected growing divisions within the Catholic intellectual community. Since the late 1920s, the French Catholic intellectual milieu had begun to splinter, first over the pope's condemnation of Action française, followed by differences of opinion over the political riots of February 1934 in Paris and the Italian invasion of Ethiopia in 1935.[47] It was the Spanish Civil War, however, that led to the most obvious divisions among Catholic intellectuals. Seeing Franco's uprising against the republic as a "crusade" against Communism and anticlericalism, much of Catholic international opinion lined up behind the Nationalist revolution. Maritain, however, dissented from this Catholic consensus, along with a number of other prominent French Catholic writers, such as François Mauriac and Georges Bernanos, all of whom were literary heroes to the *Relèvistes*.[48] Maritain was openly critical of Franco's Catholic credentials, calling into question his claims to be fighting a latter-day "holy war." Maritain could point to the brutal war of retribution that the Nationalists waged against the Basques, who were both Catholic and Republican, and to the military support Franco received from the anti-Christian forces of Nazism and Italian Fascism. The Christianity represented by Franco—one of Christian symbols, institutions, and rhetoric but without charity, mercy, or justice—became a growing concern for Maritain during the later 1930s and into the 1940s, when he opposed a similar Catholic authoritarianism manifested in the Vichy regime. His opinions, however, remained squarely in the minority among many Catholics, and he was attacked in the Catholic press as a "red Christian."[49]

If Spain was an important turning point for Maritain, it was also a key moment for the *équipe* at *La Relève*, who began to find itself more and more at odds with the prevailing conservatism of French Canadian Catholicism.[50] With the tenor of French Canadian public opinion overwhelmingly supportive of Franco, Maritain felt that he was no longer welcome in Quebec, and he deliberately chose to stop visiting the province during the later 1930s.[51] These circumstances angered the *Relèvistes,* and Jean Le Moyne always held that it was a major scandal that so many French intellectuals—many of whom were prominent Catholics—should have found a much greater welcome in English Canada and the United States than in Quebec, the self-proclaimed bastion of French culture and Catholicism in North America.[52] Le Moyne contended that Maritain and other proponents of the "new Christian humanism," such as Yves Simon and Étienne Gilson, were kept out of Quebec by a concerted effort of "the Vatican, our sanctimonious hierarchy, our devoted clergy, our pious laity and our equally pious press."[53] And Maritain was attacked by clerics in Quebec, both for his views on Spain and later for his opposition to Pétain and Vichy.[54] His popularity among the Catholic establishment in Quebec, so evident in the early 1930s, had waned as a consequence of his supposedly heterodox political opinions and the progressive tenor of his "new Christian humanism."

The story of *La Relève*'s own response to the Spanish Civil War is important because it displays the limits of acceptable opinion in Quebec during the 1930s. As such, it was primarily a history of things unsaid. From 1937 on, the *Relèvistes* made a number of attempts to speak out against Franco. They proposed a lecture at Montreal's Cercle universitaire so that Maritain could respond to his critics, but he declined.[55] André Laurendeau, a close friend of the review, suggested publishing an interview with the French Catholic poet Robert Honnert, a critic of Franco, but while Charbonneau was enthusiastic, Paul Beaulieu and Claude Hurtubise seem to have been more cautious.[56] In a later interview Laurendeau recalled that *La Relève* eventually vetoed the publication of his article on Honnert for fear of the review being placed on the Index.[57] In March 1937, *La Relève* published what turned out to be the review's sole public statement on the Spanish Civil War, "Méditation sur la guerre d'Espagne" (Meditations on the War in Spain) by Émile Baas, an Alsatian writer sympathetic to Maritain and his ideas. The article was cautiously neutral, observing that there might be compelling reasons to fight for either the Nationalists or the Republicans.[58] However, it was precisely this neutrality that was objectionable to many readers in Quebec: staunch Catholics who identified the Spanish Republic with the forces of international Communism. Consequently, *La Relève* was chided by the Quebec Jesuit review, *L'Ordre nouveau*, for taking an insufficiently anti-Communist stance.[59] Despite this public criticism and their fears of ecclesiastical censorship, the *Relèvistes* persisted in their hopes of making a public comment on the Spanish conflict. As late as February 1939, Maritain advised Beaulieu that it was best for *La Relève* to refrain from publishing on the subject.[60]

By the eve of the war, *La Relève*'s anti-Fascist sentiments had strengthened, and both Charbonneau and Hurtubise voiced concern at the rise of Far-Right sympathies in Quebec.[61] But despite their opposition to Fascism at home, the *Relèvistes* were initially opposed to Canadian participation in the impending European war. This isolationist position was informed by their French Canadian nationalism—which rendered many Quebeckers reluctant to involve Canada in what was widely perceived as a British imperial struggle—by their pacifism, and by their ambivalence to the liberal democracies of Europe and North America, which they saw as compromised by capitalist greed and class division.[62] Nevertheless, there were also compelling factors that might have pushed them toward the war effort: their love for France, their friendships with prominent French writers, as well as their Christian humanist values, values that were unquestioningly threatened by the Nazis.[63] It was ultimately their connection with Maritain that drew them into playing a role in the conflict. In 1940 Charbonneau and Hurtubise founded *Les Éditions de L'Arbre*, a new publishing wing of *La Relève*.[64] The purpose of *L'Arbre*, as Hurtubise explained it to Maritain, was to develop "Christian culture in Canada" and to maintain "the French presence among us."[65] *La Relève*'s connection to Maritain also added a political edge to the religious and literary goals of *L'Arbre*. With publishing in France under the control of the Vichy and German authorities, independent publishing houses in Quebec offered an important venue for dissident French writers in exile. Through Maritain, then living in exile in New York, *L'Arbre* published a broad array of anti-Fascist Christian writing and also established ties with partisans of de Gaulle active in North America.

L'Arbre's work as a "resistance" publisher displays the internationalism of the European and North American Catholic intellectual community during the war years. *La Nouvelle Relève* and *L'Arbre* published French Catholic writers alongside Italian Catholic politicians such as Don Luigi Sturzo and Count Carlo Sforza, as well as German and Russian exiles such as H. A. Reinhold and Waldemar Gurian. This exchange of ideas between francophone and non-francophone Catholics was furthered by a new collaboration between *La Nouvelle Relève* and *Commonweal*, an American Catholic review that also had links to Maritain. Writing in 1939, Hurtubise drew the attention of readers in Quebec to the new intellectual vitality and social activism of American Catholicism, and from 1940 on, *La Relève* and its successor, *La Nouvelle Relève*, featured articles from *Commonweal* in French translation.[66] But perhaps even more significant than the emergence of this wartime Catholic internationalism was the new intellectual and political pluralism of the *Relèvistes*' engagements during the 1940s. Like many other Christian democrats and anti-Fascist Catholics, the war pushed the *Relève* group into working with non-Catholics in the shared struggle against the extreme Right. For *L'Arbre*, the key figure in this regard was Henri Laugier, a scientist and prominent French socialist and Gaullist living in exile in Montreal and New York. Laugier directed *L'Arbre*'s series "France Forever," a collection of political and scientific texts funded by de Gaulle's Free France, as well as by the U.S. Office of War Information (OWI). Laugier's connections with Free France also ensured that *L'Arbre* was well placed to provide the French provisional government and its institutions—particularly the Université d'Alger, the first "Free France" university—with books.[67]

We should not underestimate the extent to which these alliances with even the non-Communist Left were a major, and sometimes uneasy, departure for the young Catholics at *L'Arbre* and *La Nouvelle Relève.* Despite a common commitment to the struggle against Fascism, Laugier's republican and socialist background was foreign to even relatively progressive Catholics such as Charbonneau and Hurtubise. The culture clash between *la France laïque* and Catholic Quebec was neatly illustrated in 1942, when Laugier suggested that *L'Arbre* publish a collection of the "sacred texts of liberty," such as the 1789 and 1793 Declarations of the Rights of Man, the American Bill of Rights, and the British Magna Carta. Unnerved by this idea, Charbonneau and Hurtubise wrote to Maritain and asked whether "such a work of rather rationalist inspiration" was not likely to damage rather than further "the cause we are defending." "Do you believe," they asked, "that Catholic publishers could publish such a work?"[68] Maritain, who was then in the process of developing a Catholic argument for human rights, reassured them that the concept had a Christian foundation and was not simply drawn from rationalist philosophy.[69]

This exchange exemplifies many of the anxieties, as well as the sense of new possibilities, experienced by francophone Catholics during the "democratic turn" of the late 1930s and '40s. Maritain's attempt to reconcile what he described as "the France of religious faithfulness and spirituality and the France of human emancipation" set the tone for a new European Catholic engagement with democratic structures and ideals.[70] In Quebec, Maritain's benediction of democratic values allowed young Catholics such as Charbonneau and Hurtubise to combine their religious faith with a new commitment to human rights. Not long after Maritain had written to *L'Arbre* about the Christian basis of personal rights, Charbonneau joined Quebec's *Association des libertés civiques,* an organization that was perceived by traditionalist nationalists to be alien, if not hostile, to French Canadian values.[71] Similarly, in 1942 Hurtubise became a founding member of *La Ligue des droits civiques,* a non-Catholic organization that challenged the civil-rights abuses of the Duplessis government in Quebec.[72]

By the close of the war, *L'Arbre* had begun publishing works by other prominent figures of the Left, including Léon Blum and the Russian socialist Victor Serge. In many respects, this collaboration with the Left was the fulfillment of Maritain's social and political writings during the 1930s, an example of Christian and non-Christian cooperation toward the common good. Such cooperation, however, could result in unintended consequences. As Jacques Michon has observed, Charbonneau and Hurtubise's introduction to a network of intellectuals and activists drawn from the liberal and socialist Left would result in an increased independence from Maritain's direction.[73] In March 1942 Maritain advised Charbonneau against publishing *La marche du fascisme* by Italian writer Giuseppe Antonio Borgese. "Do you know that Borgese is the most fanatical anti-Catholic in the United States?" wrote Maritain. "He is a man of great talent, but he has brought here all the passion of the old Italian free-thinkers."[74] Despite Maritain's objections, *L'Arbre*'s edition of Borgese eventually appeared in 1945.[75] By this point, Maritain's personal involvement with *L'Arbre* and *La Nouvelle Relève* had begun to wane. In November 1944 he left New York to return to a recently liberated France. Shortly thereafter, he reluctantly accepted an appointment as the French ambassador to the Holy See. Although he would return to North America in the spring of 1948 to take up an appointment at Princeton, the period of his closest friendship and collaboration with the *Relève* group had come to a close.[76] Shortly after Maritain took up his new post at Princeton, *L'Arbre* and *La Nouvelle Relève* were both forced to close due to financial problems.[77] The review's final issue would appear in September 1948.

The new pluralism of *L'Arbre*'s later years signaled the end of a particular type of Catholic engagement. While Maritain had espoused pluralism and cooperation with non-Catholics, he had also defended the integrity of an identifiably Catholic political and social position.[78] But the intellectual milieu of the postwar "New Catholic

Left" would be primarily defined by a more fluid approach to Christian social engagement, stressing subjectivity and dialogue with the Marxist and existential avant-garde.[79] Consequently, the 1950s and '60s would witness the gradual disintegration of a distinctively Catholic intellectual pillar, the boundaries of which had been defined by Maritain's neo-Thomism and the traditional principles of social Catholicism: class harmony, natural communities, subsidiarity, and antistatism. An undated text by Robert Charbonneau, evidently written in the years following the war, indicates Charbonneau's disillusionment with the neo-Thomism he had once embraced under Maritain's influence.[80] Charbonneau came to believe that his youthful adherence to Thomism had prevented him from thinking for himself, and he decried the intellectual uniformity that he felt Thomist philosophy had instilled within Catholicism. "It is because they found their own St Thomas Aquinas that the Chinese have degenerated," he wrote, presumably referring to Mao.[81] His friend Robert Élie would draw a similar parallel between totalitarianism and the nearly hegemonic role that Thomism played in the pre–Vatican II church: "What was Stalin if not an orthodox thinker, just as we were orthodox Thomists?"[82] Looking back on the postwar years, Jean Le Moyne, too, would write of "the impossibility of accounting for every aspect of our modernity within the framework of Thomism and using nothing but the methods of neo-Thomism."[83]

This rebellion against Thomism, which had enjoyed a privileged position within Catholic philosophy since the pontificate of Leo XIII, was a widespread phenomenon in postwar Catholic intellectual circles.[84] More broadly, it reflected not only the decline of a particular school of philosophy but also the fading of a specific type of Catholic mentality. The decline of Thomism on the intellectual plane was accompanied by the end of distinctly pillarized Catholic social and political institutions, such as the Christian democratic parties in Europe, as well as Catholic trade unions, which phased out their confessional identity in Quebec and France during the early 1960s.[85] Moreover, with the coming of the Second Vatican Council and the experimental postconciliar period, many of the fundamental tenets of the Catholic faith itself would seem suddenly open for debate. Thus, the landscape of postwar Catholicism took on a much less clear-cut shape than the church of the 1920s, '30s, and early '40s. This new complexity was reflected in the intellectual engagements of the new Catholic avant-garde. Compared to the concerns of younger Catholic philosophers, theologians, and political activists, the neo-Thomism of Maritain's generation seemed to take on a more conservative character. Catholic thinkers such as Teilhard de Chardin, whose mélange of evolutionary theory and Christianity was seen by Maritain as a "poetic intuition" rather than a coherent intellectual position, gained widespread popularity among many younger Catholic writers, including former *Relèviste* Jean Le Moyne.[86]

Eventually the new intellectual horizons of the *Relève* group would lead to a break from their mentor, though the *Relèvistes* would continue to warmly remember the friendship they had enjoyed with Jacques and Raïssa Maritain during the 1930s and '40s. In 1954 Le Moyne, Hurtubise, Robert Élie, and Marcel Raymond, another former *Relève* contributor, planned to visit the Maritains at Princeton, but they were ultimately persuaded not to go by Albert Béguin, editor of the Left Catholic review *Esprit*. According to Le Moyne, Béguin warned the former *Relèvistes*: "You have changed too much . . . he would no longer recognize you . . . You would cause him too much pain. You know, Teilhard is the Devil for him . . ."[87] For Le Moyne, the publication of Maritain's book *Le paysan de la Garonne* (*The Peasant of the Garonne*, 1966) confirmed Béguin's warnings. In *Le paysan*, Maritain attacked many of the new developments in the post–Vatican II church and accused reformist theologians of abandoning traditional Catholic beliefs in favor of a vacuous and ill-conceived notion of progress and change. Teilhard de Chardin—or rather, the appropriation of his work by a younger generation of Catholic theologians—was particularly criticized.[88] The negative controversy that ensued after the publication of *Le paysan* was evidently sufficient to prevent Le Moyne from even reading the book when it first appeared: "It took me several years before I had the courage to look through this book. I picked it up again—with great difficulty—after reading Fr. de Lubac's *necessary* book, *Teilhard posthume* . . . What sadness! What a lesson!"[89]

The religious and intellectual itinerary of the surviving *Relèvistes* became increasingly radicalized during the closing decades of the twentieth century. In Quebec, the coming of the Second Vatican Council (1962–65) coincided with a period of rapid social and political change known as the "Quiet Revolution." Over the course of the decade, the boundaries of acceptable discourse and criticism—both within Quebec and in the larger Catholic community—shifted fundamentally, and the council itself heightened expectations and accelerated calls for change. In the wake of Vatican II, many Catholics continued to hope for ongoing reform within the church and felt free to voice their criticisms of church governance and teaching. Robert Charbonneau, for instance, saw the council as "a good start," but he and a number of his former colleagues at *La Relève* believed that much more work was required in order to renew the church.[90] During the 1980s and '90s Le Moyne and Hurtubise would continue to discuss the state of the church in their correspondence with one another. These letters reveal Hurtubise's disappointment with the papacy of John Paul II, whom many critics saw as initiating a restoration of preconciliar norms and practices. Hurtubise's correspondence also shows his preoccupation with the work of controversial Catholic theologians such as Hans Küng, whose work questioning papal infallibility had been censured by the Holy See. He wrote approvingly of Küng's attempts to reconceive "the whole of theology, the Church, ways of approaching God, faith, Christ."[91] Far from the integral Catholicism of his youth, based around a carefully articulated set of theological and social beliefs, the Hurtubise of the 1980s and 1990s hoped to boldly reimagine the totality of the Catholic faith itself: "Vatican II must become, or better, after the disastrous interlude of J. P. II, must 're-become' the source of a new conception of faith."[92]

This call for a far-reaching transformation of the church indicates the extent to which Hurtubise's understanding of Catholicism had changed over the course of the twentieth century, an experience paralleled in the lives of many other members of this generation of former Catholic militants. The Catholicism he envisaged in 1990 was a far more nebulous and open-ended entity than the highly structured, cohesive church of the middle decades of the twentieth century. It is something of an historical irony that this radically revised Catholicism should be one of the end points of *La Relève*'s spiritual itinerary. The review had been one of many lay groups founded during the interwar period that sought to strengthen Catholicism's place in the modern world. Such groups played an important role in laying the foundation for the Second Vatican Council. The emergence of this widespread population of activist lay Catholics, seeking to live out their faith in accordance with the realities of modern, religiously and ideologically pluralistic societies, were key in shaping the reformist concerns of Vatican II and in preparing for the reception of the council's teachings.[93] However, though the impetus of such lay organizations may have eventually led toward a reform of the church, their original goals centered around a Catholic reformation of wider society. Youth groups such as *La Relève* were initially outward-looking, evangelical movements that aimed to mobilize students around Catholic values and to prevent youth from drifting toward ideologies hostile to the church. They sought to revitalize Catholicism by reaffirming the commitment of the church's members rather than through a reform of the church itself. It was an unexpected consequence that such movements would ultimately produce currents of renewal that significantly altered the character of modern Catholicism.

This transformation from Catholic militancy to internal renewal can be attributed to a wide array of factors, and it is beyond the scope of this chapter to tell that story fully. Broad social forces were at play, but we should not discount the personal contribution of intellectual figures such as Jacques Maritain. His work informed a number of the documents of Vatican II, and within Quebec his ideas shaped an entire generation of lay Catholics, including prominent Canadian public figures such as Prime Minister Pierre Elliott Trudeau.[94] Indeed, it was a shared appreciation for Maritain and the *renouveau catholique* that helped cement the friendship between Trudeau and Jean Le Moyne, who worked in the prime minister's office during the 1960s and '70s.[95] And it was during his tenure as a speechwriter for Trudeau that Le Moyne arranged for a final message to be sent to Maritain from the surviving members of *La Relève*. After the death of his wife in 1960, Maritain spent his final years living among the religious community of the Little Brothers of Jesus in Toulouse, formally joining the monastic order in 1971. With the aid of the Canadian ambassador to France—another admirer of Maritain—Le Moyne sent a telegram from the Canadian embassy to Maritain, congratulating him upon his entrance into holy orders.[96] Le Moyne hoped that a diplomatic cable would not only express the good wishes of *La Relève* but would also reflect Maritain's wider intellectual legacy in Canada.[97] This message, testifying to Maritain's influence upon the *Relèvistes* and many of their contemporaries, offers a fitting conclusion to this chapter:

> Deeply moved to hear you have joined Foucauld's brothers. Accept my fervent and respectful wishes, and those of the La Relève group which, though dispersed, has stayed faithful to the spirit you communicated and is still sustained by the essence of your message. We are in communion with you in the humility which, following your example, we have dared to desire.[98]

10 Louis Massignon: A Catholic Encounter with Islam and the Middle East

Anthony O'Mahony

Louis Massignon (1883–1962) was a singular figure in the French Catholic intellectual world between the First and Second World Wars up until Vatican II.[1] His place in the French Catholic milieu defies easy categorization: soldier-diplomat, leading scholar of Islam and the Muslim World, politically engaged, a religious activist, and latterly ordained a Catholic priest in the Melkite Catholic Church in 1950.[2] Massignon was considered by some of his contemporaries to be a unique mediating voice in France's relations with the Arab world.[3]

Two poles defined his life and work. The first was the world of French Catholicism, with its rich and complex range of religious thought, which had wide influence across Europe and in overseas Catholic missions.[4] In this world Massignon held a special empathy for those converts, like himself, who had discovered or rediscovered the Christian faith.[5] He also guarded the legacy of Charles de Foucauld as a source for the revival of Catholic thought in France, especially within the context of France's encounter with Islam in North Africa and the Levant.[6] Massignon is identified by Étienne Fouilloux as one of those "theologians in lounge suits" (*théologiens en veston*) who, during the interwar years, sought a renewal of ideas in the Catholic Church in its engagement with modernity: "located between, on the one hand, the excesses of the modernist-progressivists, and on the other hand a response of Roman theologians based on a neo-Thomist scholasticism. This *third party* was in fact a nebulous grouping stretching from Blondel to Chenu, passing through Gilson, Maritain, and Congar."[7]

The second pole was the Arabic world and Islam; Massignon was deeply involved in the politics of the relationship between the Muslim world and France. Albert Hourani observed: "By the originality of his ideas and the force of his personality, Massignon had a deep influence on Islamic studies in France, and indeed on French views of Islam; he was perhaps the only Islamic scholar who was a central figure in the intellectual life of his time."[8]

It is difficult to imagine Massignon outside of the French context. The honor of France was to him something of an absolute, and he felt deeply the drama and contradictions in France's Arab policy.[9] These commitments brought about lasting personal tensions in France and with his Muslim friends.[10] His fidelity to the Catholic Church and Islam made for a distinct religious encounter in the world of politics.[11] In his seeking to overcome these difficult loyalties his position has been described as "religiously heroic."[12] Massignon understood that the French colonial empire was entering its twilight. In 1952 he published an article titled "The West Facing the East: The Primacy of a Cultural Solution,"[13] in which he asserted that in the clash between Europe and the Muslim world the priority should be given to a cultural solution, "a solution of justice possible by means of *exemplary* names and maxims of *wisdom*; which the instincts of the masses understood."[14] Massignon held a view of history that sees the handing on of knowledge of God from one individual to another as the only significant process and therefore most deserving of study.[15]

Massignon's influence in framing the encounter between Christianity and Islam has grown significantly since his death. His ideas are today often deployed in the intellectual defense of the dialogue of civilization "by *challenging* the idea that 'civilization-based thinking' is necessarily a conflict-generating factor and arguing that, contrary to fashionable assumptions, a civilizational dialogue that wants to contribute to a more peaceful world order requires, in a qualified way, 'stronger' civilizational identities."[16]

Massignon held a deeply personal vision of Islam and of the relations between Muslims and Christians. Throughout his life and work he sought to create new thought within Christian theology on Islam. He often commented that he did not consider himself a theologian[17] but rather someone who had experienced a deep mystical encounter with the "other" in such a manner that it reordered his understanding of the Christian presence within Islam: "[I]dentifying himself as a Christian who was converted in a Muslim context, Massignon then dedicated himself as a Christian to Muslims."[18] Massignon understood that his views were controversial to many in the church, but, ever loyal to the fidelity of the Catholic faith, he always sought clarification from theologians and church authorities. In many ways this is what made his contribution to Christian thought on Islam so integral and influential. He held that it was only by remaining close to the authority of the church and authentically within the tradition that truth could be sustained. In 1937 Massignon relayed the "work" of his conversion experience, illuminating a commitment to the deeply personal and a respect for orthodoxy:

> Trying to live, among my Christian brethren, just as I live among the others, my faith, hope and love, pregnant of the full dogma [*sic*]. My only way to love my friends is to love them personally, with all that may seem to them, in their R.C. friend, "queer, obsolete, or borrowed," with all that I recognize as the living structural personality of the Roman Catholic Church: ecclesiastic hierarchy, sacramental realism, vows perpetual, all that warrants my irrevocable love.[19]

Political Spirituality: Massignon and Ali Shariati

Massignon's influence was not limited to fellow Catholics. Several Muslim students studied with him, including Ali Shariati (1933–77), a highly influential Shiite who played a critical role in the revival of religious thought in Iran just prior to the Islamic revolution in 1979. Ali Shariati was referred to as the Péguy of Iran.[20] Whilst working for a doctorate in Iranian philology between 1959 and 1964 he came into contact with Massignon. Shariati himself translated two works by Massignon into Persian: *Étude sur une courbe personnelle de vie, le cas de Hallâj, martyr mystique de l'Islam* (*A Study on the Personal Contour of Life: The Case of Hallâj, Mystic Martyr of Islam*) and *Salmân Pâk et les prémisses spirituelles de l'Islam iranien* (*Salmân Pâk and the Spiritual Premises of Iranian Islam*).[21] Shariati was profoundly moved by his encounter with Massignon, which he described in his *Kavir* (Desert—subtitled "Those that I venerate" [*Ma'bud-ha-ye-man*]):[22]

> I have never in my life seen anything more sublime than this old Frenchman aged 69; I refer not only to his moral and intellectual superiority but also to his physical charm, making all the faces which I observed in Paris appear insipid. His white hair was cut short, with two slight tufts growing behind his ears, casting reflections of light and giving the whole of his physiognomy a divine and extraordinary purity from which I found it very difficult to detach my gaze.[23]

Turning to Shariati's observations on Massignon, the importance of persons such as Salmân Pâk and, further, Fatima to Shariati's thought was undoubtedly directly due to Massignon's influence. It is also certain that the very "committed" attitude of Massignon regarding Islam and the Muslims provided for Shariati a specially practical concept of Islamology, which he did not conceive as an academic study but rather as an *ideology* transforming mentalities and society. What Shariati adopted from his master, Massignon, was thus not simply his theoretical ideas on Islam but also his ideas or attitudes leading to action: Salmân and Fatima were examples of committed lives that should be followed, and Islamology was to carry a revolutionary message. Michel Cuypers has reflected that Massignon to Shariati was more than a professor or a teacher of ideas; he was a master of life. Shariati was not so much seduced by Massignon's ideas strictly speaking but rather by his intellectual asceticism; his attitude as that of a scientist with total integrity when facing reality, his concern for the only truth in the presence of facts. Reflecting on his years in Paris, Shariati concludes: "More than anything else, the merit for what I have learnt and above all, *for what has become of me* belongs entirely to Louis Massignon, who united within himself the Orient and the Occident."[24] In a long autobiographical letter to his son in early 1977 (only a few months before his death), Shariati recounts how he renounced his personal preferences, which inclined more toward philosophy, mysticism, and poetry (and which could have made him into a brilliant intellectual academic).[25] Instead, he studied sociology and history, which he considered to be more useful for the Islamic society of his time, a society that needed to abandon its metaphysical idealism and discover concrete social realism. Shariati deliberately wanted to be, and effectively was, a socially committed intellectual. Massignon placed his gifts at the service of the Catholic Church and France. For Shariati, it was a prime moral obligation to put his intellectual work to the service of society. This theme runs through all of his works, but this choice was certainly made at a great cost: "The *highest degree of martyrdom*, the giving of oneself and the generosity, [he writes to his son] does not consist in renouncing just one's goods and one's life, but also one's own growth and own total fulfilling in respect of existence, spirituality and science. It means making yourself available to the others, talking to them, responding to the elementary and ordinary needs of their lives."[26]

We can also see the impact that Massignon's Marian thinking had upon Shariati, who reflected: "It is Mary, who made that dry and haughty Yahweh descend from his throne . . . it was she who made him come to earth, made him tender and tame on Earth."[27]

Massignon was not the only Catholic influence upon Shariati. Ervand Abrahamian, one of the foremost historians of Iran and political scientist of the Islamic revolution and its thinkers, writes as follows:

> Through Massignon, Shariati was exposed to a radical Catholic journal named *Esprit*. Founded by Emmanuel Mounier, a socially committed Catho-

lic, *Esprit* in the early 1960s supported a number of left-wing causes, particularly national liberation struggles in the Third World. It carried articles on Cuba, Algeria, Arab nationalism, economics, underdevelopment, and contemporary Communism—especially the different varieties of Marxist thought. Its authors included Massignon, Michel Foucault, Corbin, Fanon, radical Catholics, and Marxists such as Lukács, Jacques Berque and Henri Lefebvre. Moreover, *Esprit* in these years ran frequent articles on Christian-Marxist dialogue, on left Catholicism, on Jaurès's religious socialism, and on Christ's "revolutionary, egalitarian teachings." Despite the influence of Massignon and *Esprit*, Shariati later scrupulously avoided any mention of radical Catholicism. To have done so would have weakened his claim that Shiism was the only world religion that espoused social justice, economic reality and political revolution.[28]

Massignon's Vision of Islam and Christian-Muslim Relations

Massignon understood the relationship between Christianity and Islam through the lens of the tragic figure of the mystic al-Hallâj (857–922).[29] Al-Hallâj, who was "martyred" in Baghdad for heresy, represented for Massignon a direct parallel to the suffering of Jesus on the Cross.[30] As Christianity had suffering and compassion as its foundation, so, too, according to Massignon, did Islam. Indeed, he regarded suffering as fundamental to Semitic and Jewish tradition: "This brings us to a fundamental problem of Semitic, and particularly Jewish psychology, in its most 'Kierkegaardian' aspect: there is a hidden but divine good in suffering, and this is the mystery of anguish, the foundation of human nature."[31]

Massignon's mystical Catholicism informed his entire engagement with Islam. It was "commitment" to the "other" outside his own Christian faith that made Massignon such a powerful witness. The Dominican scholar Jean-Pierre de Menasce, OP, states, "If the attitude of Christians toward Muslims and Islam (and consequentially toward all the great religions) has changed in the last forty years, through objective understanding, through gripping the highest and most central values, through a complete respect for people and institutions, and all this as a result of Christian intensity and not despite it, this is a great extent owed to Louis Massignon."[32] Indeed, the explicit recasting of the Western missionary effort by the French theologian and cardinal of the church, Jean Daniélou, SJ, after the Second World War as one finding Christ even more than preaching him can be traced directly to Daniélou's association with Massignon.[33]

Abbé Harpigny in his study *Islam et Christianisme selon Louis Massignon*, divides Louis Massignon's life into three episodes: *le cycle hallagien*—which ended with the submission of his doctoral dissertation, *La passion d'al-Hosayn-ibn Mansour al-Hallâj, martyr mystique de l'Islam* in 1922; *le cycle abrahamique*—up until his ordination as a priest in the Melkite Greek Catholic Church in Cairo in 1950; and *un cycle gandhien*—a period of political activism that ended with his death in 1962.[34]

In his study *Étude sur une courbe personnelle de vie*, Massignon wrote, "one must choose for each individual their personal axis which is particular to them."[35] Undoubtedly it would conform to his personal spiritual journey to choose an axis, meaning in his case his Christian vocation to witness, his relation to the divine, and even more precisely the Cross, which was the guiding theme in his life. Tracing Massignon's "courbe de vie" (lit. the curve of one's life), we can see how his research, teaching, political and spiritual engagement, his life as seeker, professor, grammarian, linguist, and sociologist, as well as the public man commissioned to the service of the state or the man of action, the religious man and even the priest, constantly offering himself to Muslim souls, all met in one pivotal theme: Islam. As the axial point, Islam also provided the link between his vocation and Arab Christianity as expressed in the religious culture and ecclesiology of the Melkite Catholic Church.

Examination of the thought, or rather the vision, of Louis Massignon concerning Islam demands a particular approach in order to grasp his own way into the subject: concern with the texts (and the Arabic language) certainly, but also a constant awareness of a guiding thread, which was a dialogue of life with Muslims.[36] Massignon willingly differed from those who dissected with a lancet, and he himself was not without contradictions. Where his disciples or his detractors denounced these contradictions, he preferred synthesis. For him the important thing was to approach Islam and its people with the grace he received from it and his personal engagement with it. As one of his disciples, an Arab Christian, Brother E. S. Sabanegh, put it: "The value judgments made by Massignon on al-Hallâj or Islam are the outpouring of a burning faith and a passionate temperament for whom effective and affective engagement is never far from intellectual convictions."[37] Massignon investigated a number of vocations in Islam, of which he judged that of al-Hallâj to be above all others. One scholar has observed that "the very exploratory character of his writings, and indeed of his often enigmatic prose, continues to draw from us something which mere scholarship can never do: a glimpse of the *spirit* which animated these classical works."[38]

Massignon understood his reconversion to Catholic Christianity in Iraq in 1908 as "an interreligious moment of grace."[39] For a strong spirit such as his, the turnaround was a complete one. Henceforth his whole life was to be devoted to God and to mystical, spiritual causes (in fact, his life as a scholar was already committed to the study of Islam, his thesis on al-Hallâj having been conceived as early as 1907).[40] In the course of a public lecture that he gave in Paris in 1959, at seventy-six years of age and at the end of a long life devoted to Islamic studies and Christian Islamic dialogue, Massignon described the point of conversion, or what he referred to as the "visitation of the stranger":[41]

> Baghdad: there, leader of an official archaeological mission, but ascetic life, disguised, under protection (amân) of an Arab family of Muslim nobles; dressed vaguely like a Turkish officer on leave, desert crossing in search of a ruin between Karbala and Najaf (al-Okhaydir); caught in a trap (preparations for Turkish Revolution, 1908), arrested as a spy, struck, threatened

> with execution, attempt at suicide through holy horror of myself, sudden self-recollection, eyes shut before an inner fire that judged me and burnt my heart, certainty of a pure, ineffable, creative Presence, suspending my sentence at the prayer of invisible beings, visitors to my prison, whose names struck my thoughts: the first name, my mother (then praying in Lourdes), the fifth, the name of Charles de Foucauld. Saved by my hosts, at their risks: Dakhâla, Ijâla, Diyâfa. Return, amid a thousand obstacles, to France.[42]

The irruption of grace in 1908, which occurred in the Middle Eastern world of Islam, connected with Muslim hospitality and the Muslim respect for the "given word" (*la parole donnée*), was not only to transform his life as a Christian but also to transfigure his vision of Islam. "Converted to Christianity by the Witness of God which the Muslim faith implies," he was to consider Islam, the mediator of his personal grace, as the mediator of universal grace.[43] The providential role of Islam is thus to "gather all the excluded" against all those who are "religiously privileged," the "exclusivists of salvation" who want to keep God for themselves alone.[44] It is

> a flaming sword, a holy lance raised against God's privileged people, a reminder and a threat to Christianity, provoking not only the heroism of the Crusades which will unite it, and of the Franciscan proto-martyrs of Morocco, but the institution of liturgical feasts and the foundation of religious orders . . . an evangelical lance stigmatizing Christianity for thirteen centuries . . . the providential guardian of the Holy Places.[45]

Massignon was haunted by the desire to communicate this vision of Islam, through his scholarly work, through the sodality of prayer (*badaliya*), which he established,[46] through his apostolate of the word among Christians, and through his intercessions with the hierarchy. All the circles in which he lived or which he touched were to be influenced by his vision. His Orientalist colleagues would give no currency to his "mystical" views; theologians would frown at this reversal in perspective. But nothing would stop him; he was faithful unto death to the mission assigned to him. He was to devote himself to his thesis with unremitting effort. With the publication of his two major works in 1922, the *Passion d'al-Hallâj* and the *Essai sur les origines du lexique technique de la mystique musulmane* (*Essays on the Origins of the Technical Language of Islamic Mysticism*), the culture of Muslim life in the first three centuries was opened up. Through erudition and technical skill, the potential of the Muslim faith in revealing what is truly spiritual was highlighted. For many, this was a discovery.[47]

As Robert Caspar reminds us, a danger of distortion always exists when the work of an Orientalist who is not necessarily a theologian is taken up and used by a theologian who is not an Orientalist. In the case of Louis Massignon, the difficulty is enhanced by the extremely technical nature of the vocabulary of Muslim mystics and also, it has to be said, by the use of French words in Massignon's translations, which therefore have a Christian resonance and are apt to mislead non-Arabic speakers. Even the best ones are no exception to this.[48] Massignon's work on al-Hallâj and Muslim mysticism is at the heart of his scholarly work. However, it is not confined to these subjects but extends to varied fields, sometimes very unexpected ones, such as his studies of the Shiite tradition. There is, though, one recurrent theme: the study of the issues raised by the relationship between Islam and Christianity—his course of studies at the Collège de France on Muslim and Christian apologetics; his study of the encounter between Muhammad and the delegation of Christians from Najran (*mubahala*); and the series of articles on the Seven Sleepers, a tradition that was common to both religions.[49]

In the latter case, that of the Seven Sleepers, the apostolate of the pen was taken up and prolonged by that of the word and of action. Massignon undertook to revive pilgrimages to the places where these saints are venerated, particularly to the cave (Stiffel) at Vieux-Marché in Brittany, where Christians and Muslims pray side by side even today. But his favorite work in the most profound of domains—that of prayers of intercession—was undoubtedly the sodality of the Badaliya ("substitution" in Arabic).[50] It has united, and still unites, small groups of believers who offer their supplications, and sometimes their life, in "substitution" for their Muslim brothers before God.[51] Prefigured from January 1913 in Cairo and in 1934 in Damietta, when Massignon and his cofounder, the Melkite Catholic Mary Kahil, prayed together to consecrate the work, it was to develop especially after 1947 in Cairo, Damascus, Paris, Algiers, and Dakar.[52]

Massignon's particular conversion narrative might be considered a novelty in French Catholic thought in the early twentieth century. Indeed, Griffiths observes that those converts to Catholicism under the influence of Islam relinquished, as their Christian faith grew, any strong attachment that they had had to Islam, with the exception of Massignon.[53] Based on his experience of a "visitation of a stranger," Massignon developed a theologoumenon (theological statement that is of individual opinion and not of doctrine) in which he sought a new framework for understanding Islam, placing it at the level of affinity with Jews and Christians, as an Abrahamic religion.[54] In fact, Massignon sought to articulate a Catholic theology of Islam rooted in doctrine and expressed in action.[55] He was always extremely conscious that as a committed and believing Catholic Christian he wished the church to enter into a dialogue with his fundamental intuition, thus finding a space for Muslim belief within Catholic Christianity. Massignon's religious vocation can be traced through his conversion in 1908 to the formation of the Badaliya with Mary Kahil in 1934 and his ordination as a priest in the Melkite Catholic Church.[56] Leading scholars today affirm as a matter of fact that Massignon made a decisive contribution to the Vatican II document *Nostra aetate,* thus confirming the influence of Massignon as a key figure in creating new Christian thinking on Islam.[57] Christian Troll, an influential Jesuit scholar on Islam, evaluates Massignon's influence in these terms: "Whereas, on the one hand, Vatican II's positive description of central aspects of the Muslims' faith and practice and its new outlook on Islam would be unthinkable without Massignon's insights and commitment, on the other hand, the Council, as has been shown, refrained from adopting key elements of Massignon's idiosyncratic theologico-prophetic vision of Islam and its prophet."[58]

Massignon and France's Policy toward North Africa and the Middle East

Not only was Massignon a seminal voice in French Catholic thought leading up to the Second Vatican Council, but he also had a long-term relationship with the French diplomatic and political establishment from the First World War onward regarding North Africa and the Middle East. In 1917 he was attached to the delegation of Georges Picot in his negotiations with Mark Sykes, the British representative who drafted the secret treaty of 1916, which oversaw the establishment of the French and British mandate system in the Arab provinces of the Ottoman Empire.[59] In 1919 he was part of George Clemenceau's team which negotiated with Faisal on the future of Syria,[60] and in the 1930s he played an important role in the French colonial establishment's centennial celebrations of the capture of Algiers in 1830.[61] In the postwar period, Massignon found himself in a position of opposition against French colonial policy. He was opposed to the Madagascar massacres in 1947; French policy toward the Palestinian question and the establishment of the state of Israel from 1947 to 1948; the dispatch of the Moroccan monarch, Mohammad V, into exile in 1953; repression of the nationalist movements in Morocco and Tunisia; and the high drama over civil conflict in French Algeria.

With the conquest of Algeria, France became the ruler of a significant Muslim population. Henri Laurens has reminded us that French policy toward the region was made largely by administrators, military men, missionaries, and diplomats but that the universities were absent from this debate on engagement with, and rule over, Muslim peoples. In fact, the French university system (understood as including the secondary schools or lycées) had a weak institutional base for most of the nineteenth century, and it was only during the

Third Republic, in the context of war with Germany, that a new model for the university was developed as a constitutive part of the regime, which is sometimes spoken of as a "republic of professors."[62] In the area of Islamic studies the republic restored the École des langues in 1873, and Massignon in due course would become a pupil at this institution. It was during this period that the Third Republic sought greater knowledge of the Muslim world. In fact, this geographical-cultural nomenclature gained wider usage at the turn of the century, against the background of the emergence of pan-Islamism within the Ottoman Empire and across Asia.[63]

Massignon's political and university career under the Third Republic unfolded as France's Muslim policy developed. His work on the sociology of the Muslim world, especially in the period up to 1940, was closely linked to the concerns of France's Muslim policy. Laurens has identified whole passages by him included in published articles and administrative reports.[64] This aspect of Massignon's work bears witness to the way in which the Third Republic was able to integrate a range of academics specializing in the Muslim world into the defining of its policy. The Fourth and Fifth Republics did not follow suit.

Another essential aspect of Massignon's career involved his interventions at a senior level in the determination of long-term policy, which reflected a constant desire to integrate his religious and political ideas, often based on his sociological work. The character of this long-term policy might be seen as an attempt at mitigating the shock of colonialism within the Muslim world through a desire to demonstrate respect for Arab civilization and culture. Massignon often pleaded for a greater role of the Arabic language against what he saw as the dominant administrative presence of French imposed in an often authoritarian manner. Massignon had a distinct appreciation of and vision for Arabic culture, demonstrated by his work in the Academy in Cairo, which sought to accommodate the Arabic language and modernity. Massignon's vision of the relationship between France and the Arab world emerged in juxtaposition to his constantly evolving understanding of Islam. He seems to have been influenced prior to 1914 by modernist views as articulated by Salafist circles and these encouraged in his own mind a progressive rapprochement between the juridical customs of metropolitan France and its Muslim dependencies.

Massignon's basic desire was to see Muslim emancipation take place within modernity as mediated by the French colonial context, which itself should be based upon tolerance and an open spirit.[65] However, Massignon's voice, although listened to by a wide circle of political administrators within the French elite, was only one among many. In fact, it was Robert Montagne (1893–1954) who, from the second half of the 1930s, would replace him as "prince counselor" and who, it should be said, had more acquaintances among the military than in the diplomatic corps.[66] Massignon's early attachment to a modernist vision of Islam can be understood only if one considers the Islam in question not as an eternal, fixed Islam but as a society-based religion that was constantly evolving. In the 1930s he became more aware of the doctrinal hardening, together with what he considered a certain intellectual closure, then taking place in Salafist circles, hand in hand with its direct entry into politics with the birth of modern Islamism, especially with the Muslim Brotherhood in Egypt.[67] It is interesting that the term "semi-Wahabite" makes an appearance in Massignon's thinking, as he seems to make a distinction between modernists and more Islamist currents. His contribution to Muslim policy in the Third Republic was characterized by efforts toward reconciliation between the French and the Muslim world.

In this context, the official policy of *laïcité* (secular constitutionalism) in France expressed itself in a manner that would find little space for the kind of mystical religiosity that Massignon studied, and for the values of which he would often publicly testify.[68] His orientation might even be considered as a protest against the state of affairs that promoted *laïcité* as a norm: According to him it had significant detrimental consequences for Muslims, whose religion he valued, under French rule.

Massignon's academic and public life were particularly affected by the great changes that were coming into play in France after the liberation in 1944. He witnessed a decline of those values that had been uppermost in his life since his conversion in 1908. The French Empire experienced the shock of decolonization; the influence of the church in French society was on the wane; French political society had been deeply wounded by military defeat; and the self-confidence of French culture, even though not overwhelmed, was diminished. It is within this context that the growing tensions and conflicts in relations between France and its Muslims could often take on an apocalyptic character when viewed from Massignon's perspective. As Jacques Wardenberg well describes, "he resorted to a view and practice of life in which suffering and sacrifice, but also resurrection and sainthood were leading terms."[69] Louis Massignon developed this theme of history in a series of letters to Paul Claudel in 1908 and 1909, in which the meaning of history is to be found not in the impersonality of social evolution but in the divine word in the individual seed.[70]

Massignon and Jerusalem: Theology and Politics in the Holy Land

The character of Louis Massignon and how it was manifested in his life and his influence needs to be considered. Not only was the Badaliya at the heart of his spiritual life and of his sometimes heroic zeal; not only are the texts that he edited for the Badaliya and his verbal communications to the Badaliya in which he poured out his heart most revealing as regards his intimate spiritual life;[71] but this work, which was dearer to him than any other, led him to develop relationships with the highest levels of the Catholic hierarchy. Massignon might have appeared sometimes to be one of the less reassuring sons of the church. He was scathing in his comments about theologians and the ecclesiastical race in general, including certain members of the hierarchy, and he possessed a particular distaste for ultramontanism.[72] But this was only a superficial aspect of his personality, one that had multiple facets. Deep down he was not only an obedient son of the church, but he also had a heartfelt desire to receive the church's blessing on his work and his apostolate. Many bishops and religious leaders were visited by him and were at times very surprised at his humble attitude.

It was to the pontiffs that he turned to receive a blessing for the work of the Badaliya—to Pius XI, Pius XII, and John XXIII. Massignon seems to have had an open relationship with Pius XII and was often granted a private audience, for example, in 1949, 1953, and 1955. His intermediary, apart from the Melkite patriarch, was Méhémet-Ali Mulla-Zadé (1881–1959), also known as Father Paul Mulla, a Muslim convert to Catholicism.[73] It must be added that Massignon sometimes had to defend this work before the hierarchy as a result of some more or less well-intentioned denunciations. One fact should be noted immediately: One name that reappears in his relations with the Vatican is that of Giovanni Battista Montini, at the time pro-secretary of state (1952–54) before becoming archbishop of Milan. This was not, as one might suppose, a formality; rather, there are very clear signs that the relationship between Louis Massignon and the future pope Paul VI had gone far beyond the stage of formalities.[74]

Massignon's first private meetings took place with Pius XI, who demonstrated some encouragement for the various activities undertaken by him, all directed toward an attitude of openness and desire for knowledge of "our Muslim brother."[75] Massignon's apostolate appears to be totally in accord with Pius XI's intentions, as expressed in the pontiff's statement to a bishop in 1931: "Until now, we have done very little for Islam. The language, religion, practices, and the way of thinking of Islam must be studied in depth: and then, through acts of benevolence, we must address it directly, attempting to gain its esteem, and finally its love."[76] During his first meeting with Pius XI on 18 July 1934, the account of which is preserved in the Massignon family archives, researched by Agathe Mayeres, Massignon asked the pope to bless his creation of the Badaliya. The profound intention of this Badaliya, a term that in Arabic means "to put oneself in the place of," implies substituting oneself—in and through prayer, fasting, and sacrifice—and, for Muslims, to offer oneself in their place.[77] In addition, during the same audience, Massignon emphasized the importance of Abraham and "sought to extend to the whole Latin Church the special office said for this 'saint' in the Latin patriarchate of Jerusalem."[78]

Massignon based his religious thought on the idea of Abrahamic religions, which articulated in his mind a relationship between Jews, Christians, and Muslims. The Second Vatican council responded to this idea of Massignons when it posited in *Lumen gentium* that Muslims "profess to hold the faith of Abraham," although the council fathers did not endorse a genealogical link between Islam and the Jewish-Christian tradition.[79] In making Abraham the first expatriate who assumes the exclusion of the children of Ishmael, who, in his intercession for the condemned of Sodom substituted himself for them, and who, by the accepted sacrifice of Isaac, founded the sacerdotal vocation of his people, Massignon delivered his "spiritual testament." All his prayers and all his actions began from Abraham in order to find their full expression in configuration to the crucified Christ. According to Massignon, then, it is with Abraham—the Abraham who left Ur and reached Palestine—that everything begins. The spiritual power of the remarkable prayers that the patriarch offered to God for Ishmael, the exiled son; for Isaac, the sacrificed son; and for Sodom, the condemned city, fix for all time the destiny of all believers, especially in that Holy Land, which was given to him forever, for himself and his spiritual descendants: "since spiritually one possesses only what one has renounced here below. The problem of the true meaning of the possession of the Holy Land begins with the offering of Isaac. It is given to Abraham only because he offered him up, and because Isaac agreed to his being sacrificed."[80]

For Massignon, Abraham is also the first exemplar of hospitality, of the right of asylum. The problems of the beginning of humanity are also those of its end, especially that of the sacred character of the right of asylum and that of respect for the stranger. This representation inevitably leads us to the question of Palestine and its Holy Places, the equitable resolution of which is the indispensable prelude to the reconciliation of the Abrahamic religions.[81] During the second private audience granted him by Pius XI in September 1935, Massignon offered the Holy Father the first copy of his work *Les trois prières d'Abraham*, distributed, as Monseigneur Mulla explained to Secretary of State Pacelli, "to educated persons praying for the conversion of Islam in order to clarify their intentions and re-ignite their zeal."[82] This "proselytism" is in accordance with the wish of Pius XI, who, in his encyclical *Rerum ecclesiae* (1926), confirmed mission as a priority of his pontificate.

On the question of Palestine, the Holy Places, Zionism, and the State of Israel, Massignon stood against the prevailing majority of French intellectuals, albeit on different accounts at different times, during the interwar period and after the Second World War: He began with enthusiasm for the Zionist cause, but this underwent a reversal, evolving eventually into acute anti-Zionism. Massignon supported the Zionist movement beginning in 1917, when he met Chaim Weizmann, who was raising awareness for the claim of the "right of return to Israel."[83] After 1936 he spoke out against what he considered to be the colonization of Palestine, the partition of the Holy Land, and the establishment of the State of Israel.[84]

Jerusalem had a special meaning for Massignon as a place of eschatological significance where the political and the religious joined in a reordering of human history to the divine. In 1948 he stated the following:

> One must admit that, if there is one country where the temporal bows before the spiritual to recognize our need for global unity, it is Palestine; the one point of insertion where the spiritual enters the temporal and geography; there is only one place that history predestined to be the Holy Land, Jerusalem, from the time of Abraham; not that it consists as a purely federal district of the UN or, which would be better, an international centre for UNESCO, but as a magnetization of the desire for peace and prayer for

> justice toward the high place of Jerusalem. For Christians the Holy Land is not an archeological site but the fatherland [*la patrie*] of their souls even before death; and one day the bishops, even the bishop of bishops, must return to Jerusalem.[85]

Massignon recognized that the history of the Jewish people was characterized by suffering and that this suffering might be of an atoning nature. However, he also perceived that Jewish spirituality, which he admired—the age-old vocation of the Jewish people to exile, accompanied by the immortal hope of returning to Palestine—had been appropriated, demessianized, and secularized in the nineteenth century and had essentially become an economic vocation.[86] Further, in Massignon's eyes the Holocaust did not give the people of Israel any special rights; in any case, he saw no analogy whatsoever between the Passion of Christ and that of the Jewish people. The Holocaust had been apprehended in the continuity of the pogroms before the war and was in fact its result, a result made even more terrible by a godless society and its belief in technology, which were the true culprits. Thus the question of the settlement of Jews in Palestine, Massignon believed, did not have to be considered in a fundamentally new way after the Holocaust. Although such settlement might be partly legitimate, it should certainly not be implemented at the expense of other legitimate claims: those of Christianity, of Islam, and of the Palestinian Arab people. The greatest priority remained the strengthening of relations between Christianity (especially France) and the Arab Muslim world.[87]

Such opinions earned Massignon serious enemies at a time when the argument that anti-Semitism was more or less the same as anti-Zionism was beginning to gain ground in Europe. Massignon's attacks against the colonization and the forced industrialization of Palestine, supported by foreign capital, were clearly very little understood by a public that, on the contrary, saw only the positive aspects of Jewish colonization, its dynamism, and its capacity to exploit arid land. Added to this was Massignon's virulent Anglophobia; at times

Britain and its city bankers seemed to him to be the great culprits behind the conflict. At the same time Jewish activists fought the very same British people, whom they saw as colonialists and as taking a rather pro-Arab stance. By wanting to strongly curb Jewish immigration into Palestine, as it had done in 1939, Britain appeared, in the eyes of the Zionists, to betray yet again the promise made in the Balfour Declaration.[88] In French popular opinion, the Israeli problem was often seen not in terms of the Israeli-Arab conflict but rather in terms of decolonization; de Gaulle, to take an example, was not at all unhappy to see the influence of Great Britain diminish in the region.[89] Massignon combined his anti-Zionist arguments with religious considerations, which no doubt had still less chance of being understood. For example, he inserted the Virgin Mary into his political consideration of the modern State of Israel and the fate of the Palestinians. Highlighting Muslim veneration of the figure of Miriam in Sura 19 of the Quran in comparison to the "negative position" of Judaism on Mary, Massignon reflected on the importance of recognizing the religious history of the Holy Land and tied this to the legitimacy of the State of Israel.[90]

The breakthrough that the work of Louis Massignon achieved in the somewhat restricted field of the Christian vision of Islam was bound to challenge some views: not so much on the value of Muslim mysticism, which most theologians of spirituality were quite happy to admit, but more on the place of Islam in the history of salvation.[91] Now, Islam suddenly seemed to be reemerging, six hundred years after Christ, from a line that traced itself back to Abraham, with its own prophet, revelation, scripture, and mission. Did all of this not question such doctrines as well established and indeed defined, with respect to salvation, as the Christian notion of time, the closing of the apostolic revelation at the death of the last apostle, and the uniqueness of the path of salvation (if not of salvation itself) as traced out by the Bible and by Christ? Louis Massignon had broken through walls and opened new windows in a vision and a style that were his own. It was only natural that these "transtheological" breakthroughs, as

Robert Caspar has called them, should be borrowed to make an attempt at a new formulation of the history of salvation on a theological level, especially as parallel studies concerning the time of salvation, the theology of non-Christian religions, and the notion of prophecy contributed to widen the horizons. As far as the place of Islam in the divine plan of salvation was concerned, several Catholic thinkers took up the views of Massignon.[92]

Conclusion

Massignon, albeit in a distinct manner, belonged to a wide milieu of Catholic thought in the French world, which, by its creative originality, resourced theological tradition, deep ecclesial culture, a Christian dialogical mission to the religions, and an engagement with politics that still grasps the imagination. This extraordinary outpouring was not an act of an individual but of a deep cultural desire to participate in the world. His conversion in Iraq in 1908 with the "visitation of the stranger" worked itself out over the following decades in scholarship, theological thought, and political activism. Massignon is the most influential figure in the Christian encounter with Islam in the modern world. Although much of his thought is disputed today, it nevertheless continues to provoke religious questions with power to disturb. Through his influence he created a new language for the Catholic Church to engage with Muslims and Islam at the Second Vatican Council. He was also someone who provoked other vocations. Jean de Menasce, who converted from Judaism to Christianity and who became himself a leading Catholic thinker on mission, Israel, and religious traditions of Persia, provides a fitting summary of the character of Massignon's thought and work:

> His influence has extended far beyond the world of Islam, and one can say that his work has been decisive in the new orientations given to missionary work in the Catholic Church, not only in France. The spirit which he inherited from de Foucauld is characterized by contemplation and a life that is

humble and poor like that of Nazareth; a life in which the missionary puts himself on the same level as the most unsophisticated and abandoned, those whom he wishes to teach, above all, that God loves them. It was this attitude which allowed Massignon to penetrate into every search for God, without syncretism but with an understanding proceeding from within which aimed at the heights. This he did as a scholar and a Christian.[93]

Notes

Introduction

Katherine Davies and Toby Garfitt

1. Hans Urs von Balthasar, *The Glory of the Lord: A Theological Aesthetics*, vol. 1, *Seeing the Form* (1968; Edinburgh: T. & T. Clark, 1982), 18.

2. Phillip A. Ballinger, *The Poem as Sacrament: The Theological Aesthetic of Gerard Manley Hopkins* (Leuven: Peeters, 2000), 162.

3. Balthasar, *Seeing the Form*, 157.

4. Graham Ward, *Christ and Culture* (Malden, Mass.: Blackwell, 2005), 205–6.

5. Jean Wahl, *Vers le concret* (Paris: Vrin, 1932), 4, note.

6. Alan D. Schrift, *Twentieth-Century French Philosophy: Key Themes and Thinkers* (Oxford: Blackwell, 2006), 18.

7. Wahl, *Vers le concret*, 24. "There is a necessary dialectic precisely because there is a realism. The real is the limit of the dialectic, it is its origin, it is its end, its explanation and its destruction" (23).

8. See Stefanos Geroulanos, *An Atheism That Is Not Humanist Emerges in French Thought* (Stanford, Calif.: Stanford University Press, 2008), for a critical analysis and contextualization of *Vers le concret*, 72–80.

9. See Wahl, *Vers le concret*, 14, and John Milbank, Catherine Pickstock, Graham Ward, eds., *Radical Orthodoxy: A New Theology* (London: Routledge, 1999), 15.

10. See, for example, Étienne Fouilloux, *Une église en quête de liberté: La pensée catholique française entre modernisme et Vatican II 1914–1962* (Paris: Desclée de Brouwer, 1998); Émile Poulat, *La question religieuse et ses turbulences au xxe siècle* (Paris: Berg International, 2005); Bruno Duriez et al., *Les catholiques dans la République 1905–2005* (Paris: Éditions de l'Atelier, 2005); Michel Alain-René, *Catholiques en démocratie* (Paris:

Éditions du Cerf, 2006). Examples of studies on the development of a self-consciously modern Catholic identity are the following: Stephen Schloesser, *Jazz Age Catholicism: Mystic Modernism in Postwar Paris, 1919–1933* (Toronto: University of Toronto Press, 2005); Jean-Dominique Durand, *Les Semaines sociales de France 1904–2004* (Paris: Éditions Parole et Silence, 2006). See also the collection of postwar "avant-garde" Catholic texts by Jean-Marie Domenach and Robert de Montvalen, eds., *The Catholic Avant-Garde: French Catholicism Since World War II* (New York: Holt, Rinehart and Winston, 1967).

11. For an investigation of the tensions that were experienced in the reconciliation between Catholicism and modernity during the interwar period in Paris, with a specific focus on the difficult relationship between the "lived" Catholic life and the world of intellectual discourse, see Katherine Jane Davies, "Three 'Voices' of the Interwar French Catholic Revival: Jacques Maritain, Charles Du Bos, and Gabriel Marcel and the Tensions of Reconciliation with the World" (PhD diss., University of Manchester, 2008).

12. Fouilloux, *Une église en quête de liberté*, 70–73; Étienne Fouilloux, "La culture de l'Église catholique," in *Histoire du christianisme*, vol. 12: *Guerres mondiales et totalitarismes (1914–1958)*, ed. Jean-Marie Mayeur (Paris: Desclée, 1990), 167. For the late nineteenth-century neoscholastic revival see, for example, James Hennessey, "Leo XIII's Thomistic Revival: A Political and Philosophical Event," in *Celebrating the Medieval Heritage: A Colloquy on Aquinas and Bonaventure*, ed. David Tracy, *Journal of Religion* 58 Supplement (1978): 185–97. For the Catholic modernist crisis in France, see Pierre Colin, *L'audace et le soupçon: La crise du modernisme dans le catholicisme français, 1893–1914* (Paris: Desclée de Brouwer, 1997), and David Schultenover, SJ, ed., *The Reception of Pragmatism in France and the Rise of Roman Catholic Modernism, 1890–1914* (Washington, D.C.: Catholic University of America Press, 2009); for a broader treatment of Roman Catholic modernism, see Darrell Jodock, ed., *Catholicism Contending with Modernity* (Cambridge: Cambridge University Press, 2000).

13. See, for example, Jacques Prévotat, *Les catholiques et l'Action française: Histoire d'une condamnation, 1899–1939* (Paris: Fayard, 2001), and Eugen Weber, *L'Action française* (Paris: Stock, 1962).

14. John F. X. Knasas, "Whither the Neo-Thomist Revival," *Logos: A Journal of Catholic Thought and Culture* 3, no. 4 (2000): 129; Jürgen Mettepenningen, *Nouvelle Théologie–New Theology: Inheritor of Modernism, Precursor of Vatican II* (London: T & T Clark, 2010), 25. See also Gerald A. McCool, *From Unity to Pluralism: The Internal Evolution of Thomism* (New York: Fordham University Press, 1989).

15. Hervé Serry, *Naissance de l'intellectuel catholique* (Paris: La Découverte, 2004); Philippe Chenaux, *Entre Maurras et Maritain: Une génération intellectuelle catholique (1920–1930)* (Paris: Les Éditions du Cerf, 1999); Frédéric Gugelot, *La conversion des intellectuels au catholicisme en France (1885–1935)* (Paris: CNRS Éditions, 1998); Pierre Colin, *Intellectuels chrétiens et esprit des années 1920* (Paris: Les Éditions du Cerf, 1997); Claire Toupin-Guyot, *Le Centre catholique des intellectuels français (1941–1976)* (Rennes: PU de Rennes, 2002); Guy Zelis, ed., *Les intellectuels catholiques en Belgique francophone aux XIXe et XXe siècles* (Louvain-la-Neuve: Presses Universitaires de Louvain, 2009), and "Les intellectuels catholiques: Histoire et débats," special issue, *Mil Neuf Cent. Revue d'histoire intellectuelle* 13 (1995).

16. Toupin-Guyot has traced the collective itinerary of the intelligentsia of this institution and its work for dialogue between Christianity and modernity.

17. See Emmanuel Godin and Christopher Flood, "French Catholic Intellectuals and the Nation in Post-War France," *South Central Review* 17, no. 4 (2000): 45–60, for the citation of a discussion of the "golden age" of Catholicism with specific reference to Gérard Cholvy and Yves-Marie Hilaire, *Histoire religieuse de la France contemporaine* (Toulouse: Privat, 1988), and Étienne Fouilloux, *Les chrétiens français entre crise et libération: 1937–1947* (Paris: Seuil, 1997).

18. Florian Michel, *La pensée catholique en Amérique du Nord: Réseaux intellectuels et échanges culturels entre l'Europe, le Canada, et les États-Unis (années 1920–1960)* (Paris: Desclée de Brouwer, 2010).

19. See Julian Jackson, *The Politics of Depression in France, 1932–1936* (Cambridge: Cambridge University Press, 2002).

20. See, for instance, Jean-Claude Delbreil, *La revue "La vie intellectuelle": Marc Sangnier, le thomisme, et le personnalisme* (Paris: Cerf, 2008).

21. The phrase "opening to the Left" is borrowed from John Hellman, "The Opening to the Left in French Catholicism: The Role of the Personalists,"

Journal of the History of Ideas 34, no. 3 (1973): 381–90. For the left-leaning Catholic democratic press see, for example, Aline Coutrot, *Un courant de la pensée catholique: L'hebdomadaire Sept (mars 1934–août 1937)* (Paris: Éditions du Cerf, 1961); for the party political inroads into Christian democracy in France, see Jean-Claude Delbreil, "Christian Democracy and Centrism: The Popular Democratic Party in France," in *Political Catholicism in Europe 1918–45*, ed. Wolfram Kaiser and Helmut Wohnout (London: Routledge, 2004), vol. 1, 116–35; and on Catholicism and Communism see Oscar L. Arnal, "The Brief Pilgrimage of *Terre nouvelle*," *Journal of Religious History* 11, no. 4 (1981): 578–94. For accounts of Mounier, see John Hellman, *Emmanuel Mounier and the New Catholic Left 1930–1950* (Toronto: University of Toronto Press, 1981); for nonconformism, see Jean-Louis Loubet del Bayle, *Les non-conformistes des années 30* (Paris: Seuil, 1969), and Steve Bastow, "Third-Way Discourse in Interwar France," *Journal of Political Ideologies* 6, no. 2 (2001): 169–89. For other critical surveys of Catholic political engagement during this period in France see René Rémond and Aline Coutrot, *Les catholiques dans la France des années 30* (Paris: Éditions Cana, 1979), and, more broadly situating France among other European manifestations of Catholic politics, see Martin Conway, *Catholic Politics in Europe 1918–1945* (London: Routledge, 1997); Tom Buchanan and Martin Conway, eds., *Political Catholicism in Europe: 1918–1965* (Oxford: Oxford University Press, 1996); and David Handley, ed., *Christian Democracy in Europe: A Comparative Perspective* (London: Pinter, 1994).

22. Henry Rousso, *Le syndrome de Vichy: De 1944 à nos jours*, 2nd ed. (Paris: Seuil, 1990); Eric Cionan and Henry Rousso, *Vichy, un passé qui ne passe pas*, 2nd ed. (Paris: Seuil, 1996).

23. For a general summary of historiography on Vichy see, for example, Omer Bartov, "The Proof of Ignominy: Vichy France's Past and Presence," *Contemporary European History* 7, no. 1 (1998): 107–31; Bertram M. Gordon, "The 'Vichy Syndrome' Problem in History," *French Historical Studies* 19, no. 2 (Autumn 1995): 495–518.

24. James F. McMillan, "France," in *Political Catholicism in Europe*, 58–60.

25. Peter Van Kemseke, "The Societal Position of Catholic Democracy in France," in *Christian Democracy in the European Union, 1945/1995*, Kadoc

Studies 21, ed. Emiel Lamberts (Leuven, Belgium: Leuven University Press, 1997), 176–77.

26. Michael Kelly, "French Catholic Intellectuals During the Occupation," *Journal of European Studies* 23 (1993): 179–91, 189–90.

27. Étienne Fouilloux, *Les chrétiens français entre crise et libération, 1937–1947* (Paris: Seuil, 1997), 165–90.

28. Jean-Luc Barré, *Jacques and Raïssa Maritain, Beggars for Heaven*, trans. Bernard E. Doering (Notre Dame, Ind.: University of Notre Dame Press, 2005), 341–85. Relations between Maritain and Garrigou-Lagrange initially soured over the Spanish Civil War; see Fouilloux, *Une église en quête de liberté*, 113.

29. See Toupin-Guyot, *Le Centre catholique des intellectuels français.*

30. Jürgen Habermas, "Modernity's Consciousness of Time and Its Need for Self-Reassurance," in *The Philosophical Discourse of Modernity: Twelve Lectures* (Cambridge: Polity/Basil Blackwell, 1987), 6–7.

31. Ibid., 7.

32. Louis Dupré, "The Modern Idea of Culture: Its Opposition to Its Classical and Christian Roots," in *Modernity and Religion*, ed. Ralph McInerny (Notre Dame, Ind.: University of Notre Dame Press, 1994), 4–9.

33. See Julia Kristeva, *Time and Sense*, trans. Ross Guberman (New York: Columbia University Press, 1996), 252, for her use of the term "uncivilized" signs.

34. The text of this communication is printed in *Cahiers François Mauriac* 9 (Paris: Grasset, 1982), 9–12, cited in François Chaubet, *Paul Desjardins et les décades de Pontigny* (Villeneuve-d'Ascq [Nord]: Presses universitaires du Septentrion, 2000), 175.

35. Joseph W. Evans, "Jacques Maritain's Personalism," *Review of Politics* 14, no. 2 (1952): 168–69.

36. Jacques Maritain, *Religion and Culture*, trans. J. F. Scanlan (London: Sheed and Ward, 1931), 26; and Jacques Maritain, *The Things That Are Not Caesar's*, trans. J. F. Scanlan (London: Sheed and Ward, 1932), 102.

37. Evans, "Jacques Maritain's Personalism," 175.

38. Jacques Maritain, *Sept leçons sur l'être*, in Maritain, *Œuvres 1912–1939* (Brussels: Desclée de Brouwer, 1975), 772.

39. Jacques Maritain, *The Degrees of Knowledge*, trans. Gerald B. Phelan (London: Geoffrey Bles, 1959), 79.

40. Max Weber, "Politics as a Vocation," in *The Vocation Lectures: "Science as a Vocation," "Politics as a Vocation,"* ed. David Owen and Tracy B. Strong, trans. Rodney Livingstone (Indianapolis, Ind.: Hackett, 2004), 83–84. For an examination of how Catholic intellectual engagement could involve an "ethics of responsibility" see Katherine Jane Davies, "A 'Third-Way' Catholic Intellectual: Charles Du Bos, Tragedy, and Ethics in Interwar Paris," *Journal of the History of Ideas* 71, no. 4 (2010): 637–59.

41. Marcel, "An Outline of a Concrete Philosophy," in *Creative Fidelity*, trans. Robert Rosthal (New York: Noonday Press, 1964), 66.

42. Gabriel Marcel, "Incarnate Being as the Central Datum of Metaphysical Reflection," in *Creative Fidelity*, 21.

43. Bastow, "Third-Way Discourse," 172.

44. Mettepenningen, *Nouvelle Théologie*, 37.

45. Ibid., 32.

46. See, for instance, "La notion de philosophie chrétienne," session of 21 March 1931, *Bulletin de la Société française de philosophie* 31 (1931): 37–93; and Philibert Secrétan, ed., *La philosophie chrétienne d'inspiration catholique* (Fribourg: Academic Press, 2006).

1. "Catholicisme ondoyant": Catholic Intellectual Engagement and the Crisis of Civilization in the 1930s

Michael Kelly

1. Bernard-Henri Lévy, *Le siècle de Sartre* (Paris: Gallimard, 2000); Régis Debray, *I.F. suite et fin* (Paris: Gallimard, 2000).

2. G. W. F. Hegel, *Hegel's Philosophy of Right*, trans. T. M. Knox (Oxford: Oxford University Press, 1967), 13.

3. Michael Kelly, "French Intellectuals: The Legendary Exception," in *The French Exception*, ed. E. Godin and T. Chafer (New York: Berghahn, 2005).

4. Denis Pelletier, "Le 'silence' des intellectuels catholiques français," *Revue d'histoire ecclésiastique* 95, no. 3 (2000): 289–304.

5. Hervé Serry, *Naissance de l'intellectuel catholique* (Paris: Éditions La Découverte, 2004); Bruno Duriez et al., eds., *Les catholiques dans la République (1905–2005)* (Paris: Éditions de l'Atelier, 2005).

6. Jacques Julliard, "Naissance et mort de l'intellectuel catholique," *Mil neuf cent. Revue d'histoire intellectuelle* 13 (1995): 5–13; Étienne Fouilloux, "'Intellectuels catholiques?' Réflexions sur une naissance différée," *Vingtième siècle* 53 (1997): 13–24.

7. Clive Castaldo, "Socialism and Catholicism in France: Jaurès, Guesde, and the Dreyfus Affair," in *Religion, Society, and Politics in France Since 1789*, ed. F. Tallett and N. Atkin (London: Hambledon, 1991), 138.

8. Frédéric Gugelot, *La conversion des intellectuels au catholicisme en France, 1885–1935* (Paris: CNRS Éditions, 1998).

9. Eugen Weber, *Action française: Royalism and Reaction in Twentieth-Century France* (Stanford, Calif.: Stanford University Press, 1962).

10. Jacques Maritain, *Primauté du spirituel: Pourquoi Rome a parlé* (Paris: Plon, 1927); Jacques Maritain, *The Things That Are Not Caesar's*, trans. J. F. Scanlan (New York: Scribner's, 1931).

11. René Rémond, *Les catholiques, le communisme, et les crises 1929–1939*, Collection kiosque (Paris: Colin, 1960); Dominique Borne and Henri Dubief, *La crise des années 30, 1929–1938: Nouvelle histoire de la France contemporaine* (Paris: Seuil, 1989); Robert W. D. Boyce, *The Great Interwar Crisis and the Collapse of Globalization* (Basingstoke: Palgrave Macmillan, 2009).

12. Borne and Dubief, *La crise des années 30*, 20–41.

13. Boyce, *Great Interwar Crisis.*

14. Otto Spengler, *The Decline of the West* (Oxford: Oxford University Press, 1991).

15. Paul Valéry, "La crise de l'esprit," in *Europes: De l'antiquité au XXe siècle: Anthologie critique et commentée*, ed. Y. Hersant and F. Durand-Bogaert (Paris: Laffont, 2000), 405.

16. George Lichtheim, *Marxism in Modern France* (New York: Columbia University Press, 1966); Tony Judt, *Marxism and the French Left* (Oxford: Clarendon, 1986).

17. Robert Soucy, *French Fascism: The First Wave, 1924–1933* (New Haven, Conn.: Yale University Press, 1985); Robert Soucy, *French Fascism: The Second Wave, 1933–1939* (New Haven, Conn.: Yale University Press, 1995).

18. Kay Chadwick, ed., *Catholicism, Politics and Society in Twentieth-Century France* (Liverpool: Liverpool University Press, 2000).

19. Denis de Rougemont, "Cahier de revendications," *La Nouvelle revue française* 231 (1932): 801–45.

20. Michel Trebitsch, "Le front commun de la jeunesse intellectuelle: Le 'Cahier de revendications' de décembre 1932," in *Ni gauche ni droite: Les chassés-croisés idéologiques des intellectuels français et allemands dans l'entre-deux-guerres*, ed. G. Merlio (Paris: Maison des sciences de l'homme d'Aquitaine, 1995).

21. Jean-Louis Loubet del Bayle, *Les non-conformistes des années 30* (Paris: Seuil, 1969).

22. William J. Gibbons, ed., *Seven Great Encyclicals* (New York: Paulist Press, 1963), 20.

23. Ibid., 161.

24. Ibid., 125.

25. Jacques Maritain, *True Humanism*, trans. M. R. Adamson (London: Bles, 1938).

26. Jacques Maritain, *Humanisme intégral: Problèmes temporels et spirituels d'une nouvelle chrétienté*, nouvelle éd. (Paris: Aubier, 1968), 106.

27. Ibid., 118.

28. Anne Freemantle, ed., *The Social Teachings of the Church* (New York: Mentor-Omega, 1963).

29. Maritain, *Humanisme intégral*, 10.

30. Ibid., 265.

31. Ibid., 298.

32. Patrick Troude-Chastenet, "La critique de la démocratie dans les écrits personnalistes des années 30: Esprit et Ordre nouveau," *Cités* 16 (2003–04): 161–76.

33. Zeev Sternhell, *Ni droite ni gauche: L'idéologie fasciste en France*, 2nd ed. (Paris: Éditions de Seuil, 1987).

34. Emmanuel Mounier, *Œuvres*, t. 1, *1931–1939* (Paris: Éditions de Seuil, 1961), 137–74.

35. Ibid., 139.

36. Tony Judt, *Past Imperfect: French Intellectuals 1944–1956* (Berkeley: California University Press, 1992), 172.

37. Mounier, *Œuvres*, t. 1, 140.

38. Ibid., 137.

39. Ibid., 340.

40. Ibid., 314.

41. Emmanuel Mounier, *Œuvres*, t. 3, *1944–1950* (Paris: Éditions de Seuil, 1962), 543.

42. Ibid., 568.

43. Maurice Blondel, "L'action: Essai d'une critique de la vie et d'une science de la pratique," in *Œuvres complètes*, vol. 1 (Paris: Presses Universitaires de France, 1995).

44. Gabriel Marcel, *Être et avoir* (Paris: Aubier Montaigne, 1935).

45. Ibid., 220–21; Gabriel Marcel, *Being and Having*, trans. K. Farrer (London: Collins Fontana, 1965), 165.

46. Gabriel Marcel, "Remarques sur les notions d'acte et de personne," in *Essai de philosophie concrète* (Paris: Gallimard, 1967), 163.

47. Charles Péguy, *Notre jeunesse* (Paris: Gallimard, 1933), 27.

48. Michel Winock, *Le siècle des intellectuels* (Paris: Seuil, 1999), 485.

2. Paul Valéry and French Catholicism: Recognizing the Context of Renewal

Paul Gifford

The edition of Valéry's *Cahiers* referred to is the facsimile edition published by the Centre National de la Recherche Scientifique: *Paul Valéry, Cahiers*, 29 vols. (Paris: CNRS, 1957–61). References in the text and notes follow the style *C* IX, 911.

1. This was the submitted title of my review of Michel Jarrety, *Paul Valéry* (Paris: Fayard, 2008). The review appeared in the *Times Literary Supplement* under the edited title "Myths of France," 13 March 2009.

2. See, for example, Valéry on Maurice Barrès in *Cahiers* XVI, 688; *C* XIV, 642; *C* XVI, 447; on Bourget, *C* XV, 513; on Maurras, *C* IX, 911.

3. The abbreviation RP in French designates a Reverend Father or priest; RR.PP. is the plural form.

4. Writing to Gide in 1901, Valéry comments as follows: "Curiously enough: this isn't the first time this weird sort of thing has happened to me . . . So what manner of odd apostle do I come over as? I must say: I do have a real passion for the Church. I haven't found in it one screw that isn't marvelously well positioned, nor any missing. All the qualities of an ideal mechanism, and top of the list, the independent validity of the mechanism,

discounting the worth of its agents, etc. But these top ratings of mine are pretty suspect, more damning, actually, than lack of orthodoxy or free-thinking. But anyway, there's the result for you. So what are we to make of it?" *André Gide–Paul Valéry Correspondance, 1890–1942*, preface and notes by Robert Mallet (Paris: Gallimard, NRF, 1955), 385–86.

5. On Valéry's early "liturgism," see "L'âme veuve et son jeune prêtre," in Paul Gifford, *Paul Valéry: Le dialogue des choses divines* (Paris: Corti, 1989), 225–53.

6. Valéry gives an account of his visit in *C* XII, 320–22. See also Gifford, *Paul Valéry*, 38–39.

7. On the meeting with Bernanos in 1929, see Jarrety, *Paul Valéry*, 737.

8. Jarrety's biography gives a good account of his interactions with de Gaulle via Claude Mauriac; ibid., 1165–71. De Gaulle personally ensured Valéry's supply of penicillin in his final illness and decreed that Valéry was to have a state funeral, the first since Victor Hugo.

9. Valéry had been on familiar terms with Pétain since 1930, when the Académie française had entrusted him with a delicate and much-acclaimed "discours de réception" for the newly elected member, subsequently published in Paul Valéry, *Variétés*, in *Œuvres*, t.1, ed. J. Hytier (Paris: Gallimard, Bibliothèque de la Pléaide, 1957), 1098–1127. See also Jarrety, *Paul Valéry*, 754–57.

10. Jarrety, *Paul Valéry*, 1097–98.

11. This theme is treated in "From Animal to Human: René Girard and Charles Darwin," an interview with René Girard by Pierpaolo Antonello and Paul Gifford, Girard-Darwin conference, Cambridge, 2009, video available at the "Imitatio" website, http://www.imitatio.org/mimetic-theory/video-audio-selections/girard-darwin-conference-cambridge-fall-2009.html.

12. Paul Valéry, *Lettres à quelques-uns* (Paris: Gallimard, NRF, 1952), 136.

13. Quoted by Robert Mallet, in *André Gide–Paul Valéry Correspondance 1890–1942*, introduction, 31.

14. "The closed house" is the title of the fifth of Claudel's *Cinq grandes odes* (1910): It refers both to exclusive monogamy (as opposed to adulterous romantic passion) and to the belief system of the post–Vatican I Catholic Church. Valéry refers to his intellectual method, as practiced in the *Cahiers*, as a self-enclosed and finite system, enabling human subjectivity to be represented and elucidated objectively (see, for example, *C* VII, 244).

"The non-communicating vessels" is a play on the title of a surrealist work by André Breton, *Les vases communicants* (1932), an expression that has since passed into the French language.

15. On this vexing question see Gifford, *Paul Valéry,* 400–406, and Jarrety, *Paul Valéry,* 1199–1209.

16. See Valéry, "Cantiques spirituels," *Œuvres,* t. 1, ed. J.Hytier, (Paris: Gallimard 'Bibliothèque de la Pléiade', 1957) 445–57.

17. Valéry, "Sinistre," *Œuvres,* t. 2, 301.

18. BNF, Fonds Valéry, Proses anciennes ms., 115–16.

19. Ibid.

20. Valéry, *La Jeune Parque, Œuvres,* t. 1, 96.

21. Valéry, *Œuvres,* t. 1, 988–1013.

22. Valéry, *Lettres à quelques-uns,* 203.

23. BNF, Fonds Valéry, Histoires brisées ms. III, 22.

24. Ibid., carnet "Agar, Rachel, Sophie," f. 8.

25. Histoires brisées ms. III f. 6. v.

26. Christopher Lash, "The Variety of Forces Shaping Contemporary Catholicism," BBC Radio 4, 12 May 1979.

3. A Strange Christian: Simone Weil

Florence de Lussy

Translated and adapted by Toby Garfitt

1. Simone Weil, *Oppression and Liberty* (London: Routledge and Kegan Paul, 1958), 1–23.

2. Simone Pétrement, *La vie de Simone Weil,* vol. 1 (Paris: Fayard, 1973), 401.

3. Weil, *Oppression and Liberty,* 37–124.

4. Simone Weil, "Factory Journal," in Simone Weil, *Formative Writings, 1929–1941* (New York: Taylor and Francis, 1987), 149–226.

5. It is of course possible to construct a less simplistic typology with intermediate levels, such as *moral* participation in events having to do with society or exchanges of letters in which Weil's arguments in favor of a marginalized class can be seen in terms of parapolitical action (for instance, her correspondence with Victor Bernard, the technical director of the Rosières factory near Bourges).

6. Simone Weil, *Waiting for God* (New York: Putnam, 1951), 66 (hereafter cited as *WG*).

7. Simone Pétrement, *Le dieu séparé* (*A Separate God*) (Paris: Cerf, 1984).

8. André Boulanger, *Orphée: Rapports de l'orphisme et du christianisme* (*Orphism and Christianity*) (Paris: Rieder, 1925). This well-informed and unbiased (if now rather old) work was too generous in its assessment of the links between these cults and early Christianity. More recent studies such as Walter Burkert's *Ancient Mystery Cults* (Cambridge, Mass.: Harvard University Press, 1987) play down such links and correct popular misconceptions. Mystery religions are not salvation religions.

9. Boulanger, *Orphée*, 27.

10. Weil, *Sur la science* (Paris: Gallimard, 1966), 232; also Simone Weil, *Œuvres complètes*, ed. Florence de Lussy (Paris: Gallimard, 1988–), VII.1: 475. There will eventually be seven volumes, and each may include up to four separate parts. Hereafter cited as *OC*.

11. *OC* IV.1: 152. See Benedict Spinoza, *Ethics*, V, 23, note: "*et nihilominus sentimus experimurque, nos aeternos esse*" (But, notwithstanding, we feel and know that we are eternal).

12. Weil, *Oppression and Liberty*, 140–46, 146.

13. See what Levinas says about Hegel in Emmanuel Levinas, *Difficult Freedom: Essays on Judaism*, trans. Sean Hand (London: Athlone, 1990), 235.

14. Edgar Morin, *Le monde moderne et la question juive* (Paris: Seuil, 2006), 62.

15. Simone Weil, *Letter to a Priest* (London: Routledge and Kegan Paul, 1953); hereafter cited as *LP*). Couturier was a leading figure in the art world and had posed for Matisse.

16. George Steiner gives an illuminating and convincing account of Jewish self-hatred, comparing Simone Weil to Ludwig Wittgenstein in this respect. Steiner uses the term "autoflagellation" and suggests that a pathological element may be involved. George Steiner, "Bad Friday," review of *Simone Weil: Portrait of a Self-Exiled Jew* by Thomas R. Nevin, *New Yorker*, 2 May 1992, 86–91.

17. See the allusion to Plato's *Philebus* in Weil's *Intuitions pré-chrétiennes*, at the beginning of the section "A propos de la doctrine pythagoricienne." Plato refers to "a very ancient revelation, which may even be the original revelation," *OC* IV.2: 244.

18. See Stanislas Breton, "Simone Weil, l'admirable," *Esprit* 211, no. 5 (May 1995): 31–46. George Steiner, in his review of Nevin's book on Weil (see note 16, this chapter), makes a similar point, suggesting that she kept knocking at the door, but as soon as Perrin opened it affectionately, she always pulled away.

19. "Until the very end of the pontificate of Pius XII, the intellectual atmosphere in French Catholicism remained heavy, and almost unbearable": Étienne Fouilloux, *Une église en quête de liberté: La pensée catholique française entre modernisme et Vatican II, 1914–1962* (Paris: Desclée de Brouwer, 1998), 301. Fouilloux also refers to "a series of interventions by Rome [which] consistently and inexorably destroyed a number of initiatives, generous movements, and even simple acts of kindness" (302). He claims that "the Rome of 1958 was closer to that of 1907 than to that of 1962" (ibid.).

20. See letter from Gabriel Marcel to Charles Du Bos, and Du Bos, *Journal*, cited by Étienne Fouilloux, *Au cœur du XXe siècle religieux* (Paris: Éditions ouvrières, 1993), 239.

21. See Jürgen Mettepenningen, *Nouvelle Théologie–New Theology: Inheritor of Modernism, Precursor of Vatican II* (London: T & T Clark, 2010).

22. See Anne Mercedes Maloney, "Gabriel Marcel's Critique of the Thomist Proofs for God's Existence" (PhD diss., Marquette University, 1988). *Dissertations (1962–2010) Access via Proquest Digital Dissertations.* Paper AAI8904274. http://epublications.marquette.edu/dissertations/AAI8904274.

23. Jacques Maritain's *À travers le désastre* was published in 1941 by the Éditions de la Maison française in New York, in its Voix de la France series, and subsequently smuggled via Switzerland into France, where it had four printings between 1941 and 1942.

24. Simone Weil, "On Personality," in *Selected Essays 1934–1943*, trans. Richard Rees (London: Oxford University Press, 1962), 20. This whole essay can be seen as a refutation of Maritain's argument concerning the question of human rights.

25. Weil to Gustave Thibon, late 1941, in *Cahiers Simone Weil* 4, no. 3 (September 1981), 130.

26. Weil confided this at the time to her friend Hélène Honnorat, who later mentioned it in an interview with Simone Pétrement; unclassified papers of Simone Pétrement, Bibliothèque Nationale de France.

27. "Neque enim quaero intelligere ut credam, sed credo ut intelligam" (The believer does not seek to understand that he may believe, but he believes that he may understand) (Anselm, *Proslogion*, chapter 1).

28. Maurice de Gandillac, *La philosophie de Nicolas de Cues* (Paris: Aubier/Montaigne, 1941).

29. See the conclusion to Florence de Lussy, "Simone Weil et Nicolas de Cues (1401–1464): Un usage de l'infini mathématique," *Cahiers Simone Weil* 32 no. 3 (September 2009): 329–50.

30. Stanislas Fumet, *Histoire de Dieu dans ma vie* (1978; new ed., Paris: Cerf, 2002), 450.

31. "The Thomist conception of faith [i.e., 'firm belief in all that the Church teaches'] implies a 'totalitarianism' as stifling as that of Hitler, or more so" (*LP*, 40).

32. For Weil, the official adoption of Christianity by the Roman Empire was one of the two great catastrophes in the history of Christianity (the other was the Albigensian crusade and the Inquisition that accompanied it). On these two questions, see the complementary but contrasting positions of two contemporary historiographers: Paul Veyne, *Quand notre monde est devenu chrétien (312–394)* (Paris: Albin Michel, 2007), and Marie-Françoise Baslez, *Comment notre monde est devenu chrétien* (Tours: CLD, 2008).

33. Alain, *Entretiens au bord de la mer* (Paris: Gallimard, 1931), 275, 276, 273.

34. "Everything proceeds as though, under the same name of Christianity and within the same social organism, there were two separate religions—that of the mystics and the other one" (*LP*, 39). In her essay "Forms of the Implicit Love of God" (in *Waiting for God*), Weil makes a dozen references to a "direct contact with God" (using this or an equivalent expression), which clearly reflects her own experience. The implication is that one can become an authentic believer only if one has *already* had a personal encounter with the Lord.

35. Hans Urs von Balthasar, *The God Question and Modern Man* (New York: Seabury, 1967). Originally published as *Die Gottesfrage des heutigen Menschen* (Vienna: Herold, 1956).

36. In *Waiting for God.*

37. Balthasar, *God Question and Modern Man*, 64.

38. Aeschylus, *Agamemnon*, l. 179. See *OC* VI.3, 69, where Simone Weil quotes this in relation to Saint John of the Cross ("by the Cross in the wisdom of God"). Her genius lies in her profound, intuitive grasp of the link between suffering and truth, as expressed most memorably in "The Love of God and Affliction," in *The Simone Weil Reader*, ed. George A Panichas (New York: McKay, 1977), 439–91.

39. Hans Urs von Balthasar, *Theo-Drama: Theological Dramatic Theory*, vol. 3, *Dramatis Personae: Persons in Christ* (San Francisco: Ignatius Press, 1992), 42.

40. *OC* VI.3, 69.

41. Balthasar, *God Question and Modern Man*, 63.

42. Augusto del Noce, *L'epoca della secolarizzazione* (Milan: Giuffrè, 1970); see his introductory essay on Simone Weil and the love of God.

43. It was only in September 1943, with the encyclical of Pius XII, *Divino afflante spiritu*, that official approval was given to biblical studies and patristics. "Sources chrétiennes" then came into its own. See Étienne Fouilloux, *La collection "Sources chrétiennes": Éditer les pères de l'église au XXe siècle* (Paris: Cerf, 1995). Fouilloux refers to the "champions of the neo-scholastic revival," who "reigned, not only in Rome, but in the majority of seminaries and teaching institutions of the Catholic world" (41). Later in the same volume he evokes the criticisms voiced by the founders of "Sources chrétiennes," regretting the "narrowing and hardening of the great scholastic tradition into a textbook theology that is little more than a caricature" (131).

44. See *OC* VI.3: 393.

45. Alexander Roberts and James Donaldson, eds. and trans., *Ante-Nicene Christian Library*, 25 vols. (Edinburgh: T & T Clark, 1867–73). See *OC* VI.4: 424.

46. The term "worker-priest" was not widely known until 1954, when the movement was condemned by Pius XII, but it came into use at least as early as 1943. See Pierre Vallin, "Prêtres et ouvriers," *Esprit et vie* 110 (2004): 3–9; Émile Poulat, *Naissance des prêtres-ouvriers* (Paris: Casterman, 1965), 334.

47. *OC* II.2: 289–307.

48. Simone Weil returned to this theme the following year in London, using almost the same terms: "It is not a new Franciscan order that is needed. A coarse robe and a monastery are a separation. These people

must be in the world, touching it, with nothing in between," in Weil, *Écrits de Londres et dernières letters* (Paris: Gallimard, 1957), 105.

49. "The missionaries—even the martyrs amongst them—are too closely accompanied by guns and battleships for them to be true witnesses of the Lamb," in Simone Weil, *Letter to a Priest* (New York: Taylor and Francis, 2013), 33.

50. The word is Joseph Ratzinger's. Interestingly, in the debate between Jürgen Habermas and Ratzinger, the latter suggests that it is probably necessary to question both the tradition of Western rationality and the claim of the Christian revelation to be universal. He adds: "It is important . . . to *listen* and to accept some form of genuine relatedness to these other cultures, too. It is important to include the other cultures in the attempt at a polyphonic relatedness, in which they themselves are receptive to the essential complementarity of reason and faith" (Habermas and Ratzinger, *The Dialectics of Secularization: On Reason and Religion* [San Francisco: Ignatius Press, 2006], 79).

51. This expression is found in the 1992 Catechism of the Catholic Church and has been used by theologians such as the Dominican Claude Geffré.

52. "In any case, what is needed is a new religion. Or a Christianity modified to the point of becoming different; or something else" (*OC* VI.4: 348).

53. Breton, "Simone Weil, l'admirable," 46.

54. See J. P. Little, "Simone Weil's Concept of Decreation," in *Simone Weil's Philosophy of Culture: Readings toward a Divine Humanity*, ed. Richard H. Bell (Cambridge: Cambridge University Press, 1993), 25–51.

55. Hans Urs von Balthasar, *My Work: In Retrospect* (orig. German 1990; San Francisco: Ignatius Press, 1993), 38.

4. Jean Grenier and the "Spirit of Orthodoxy"

Toby Garfitt

1. Martyn Cornick, "Jean Paulhan and the *Nouvelle revue française*: Literature, Politics, and the Power of Creative Editorship," *Yale French Studies* 106 (2004): 53.

2. Martyn Cornick, *The Nouvelle revue française under Jean Paulhan 1925–1940* (Amsterdam: Rodopi, 1995), 5, 37. See also Toby Garfitt, "'La plus profonde exigence': Jean Grenier, la *NRF*, et l'*Essai sur l'esprit*

d'orthodoxie," in *Les chemins de l'absolu,* Actes du Colloque de Saint-Brieuc, novembre 1998 (Ville de Saint-Brieuc: Editions Folle Avoine, 1999), 11–28.

3. See letters: Grenier to Jean Paulhan, 23 November 1929, *Correspondance Paulhan-Grenier 1925–1968* (Quimper: Calligrammes, 1984), 23, and Grenier to Paulhan, 9 April 1935, Institut Mémoires de l'édition contemporaine.

4. Grenier, "Sur l'Inde," *La Nouvelle revue française* 202 (July 1930): 55–69; 203 (August 1930): 170–85; 204 (September 1930): 338–55.

5. Letter from Daniel Halévy to Grenier, 18 June 1936, Bibliothèque Nationale.

6. Grenier, "L'âge des orthodoxies," *Nouvelle revue française* 271 (April 1936): 481–93, 482. Reprinted in *Essai sur l'esprit d'orthodoxie* (Paris: Gallimard, new edition 1967 [1938]), 27–40, 29.

7. Grenier, "L'âge des orthodoxies," 30–31 (484).

8. Ibid., 35 (488).

9. Raymond Christoflour, "Le mouvement des idées," *Mercure de France,* 1 September 1938, 421–25.

10. Grenier, "L'âge des orthodoxies," 492.

11. Grenier, *Le choix* (Paris: Presses Universitaires, 1941), 54.

12. Grenier, *L'esprit du Tao* (Paris: Flammarion, 1957).

13. Georges Sadoul, "Un pourfendeur du marxisme," *Commune* 33 (May 1936): 1131–38.

14. See Jeannine Kohn-Étiemble, *226 Lettres inédites de Jean Paulhan* (Paris: Klincksieck, 1975), 103–10, 429–35.

15. Letters from Paulhan to Grenier, 18 April and 13 May 1936, IMEC, quoted in Cornick, *Nouvelle revue française,* 89.

16. Georges Friedmann, "Autour d'un manifeste," *Europe* 162, 15 June 1936.

17. Grenier, "Thibaudet politique et moraliste," *Nouvelle revue française* 274 (July 1936): 37–43, 42.

18. See Toby Garfitt, *Jean Grenier: Un écrivain et un maître* (Rennes: La Part Commune, 2010).

19. Letters from Mounier to Grenier, 9 October 1934 and 12 November 1934, BN.

20. Letters from Lambert to Grenier, 15 January and 10 February 1935, BN. See also "Lettres d'Edmond Lambert à Louis Guilloux," *Europe* 960 (2009): 181–84.

21. Quoted in a letter from Grenier to Paulhan, 25 February 1935, IMEC.

22. Grenier, "Sagesse de Lourmarin," *Cahiers du Sud* 183 (May 1936): 390–97. Reprinted under the title "L'herbe des champs," in *Inspirations méditerranéennes* (Paris: Gallimard, 1941), 98–111.

23. Albert Camus to Jean Grenier, 18 June 1938, *Albert Camus and Jean Grenier Correspondence 1932–1960*, ed. Marguerite Dobrenn, trans. and introduction by Jan F. Rigaud (Lincoln: University of Nebraska Press, 2003), 18.

24. Jean Guéhenno to Grenier, 22 September 1942, *Grenier–Guéhenno Correspondance 1927–1969*, ed. Toby Garfitt (Rennes: La Part Commune, 2011), 171.

25. Grenier to Camus, 12 February 1947, *Correspondance 1932–1960*, 97.

26. Grenier to Guéhenno, 30 June 1929, *Grenier–Guéhenno Correspondance*, 39.

27. Ibid., 10 March 1931 and 24 September 1935, 70, 124.

28. Grenier, *Essais sur la peinture contemporaine* (Paris: Gallimard, 1959), 157.

29. Grenier, *À propos de l'humain* (Paris: Gallimard, 1955), 184–92.

30. Friedmann, "Autour d'un manifeste," 237.

31. Grenier, "L'orthodoxie contre l'intelligence," *Nouvelle revue française* 275 (August 1936): 298–314, at 313. Reprinted in *Essai sur l'esprit d'orthodoxie*, 43–59, at 58–59.

32. Ibid., 59 (313).

33. Guéhenno to Grenier, 1 August 1936, *Grenier–Guéhenno Correspondance*, 133.

34. Émile Burnouf, *La science des religions* (Paris: Maisonneuve et Larose, 1876), 313.

35. Grenier, *Essai sur l'esprit d'orthodoxie*, 13–16.

36. Ibid., 37.

37. Ibid., 16.

38. Ibid., 19.

39. Max-Pol Fouchet, "L'intellectuel et les orthodoxies," *Esprit* 77 (February 1939): 693–703.

40. Raymond Christoflour, "L'intelligence devant les partis," *Mercure de France*, 1 September 1938, 421–25.

41. N. A. Berdyaev, review of *Essai sur l'esprit d'orthodoxie*, by Jean Grenier, *Put'* 57 (August–October 1938): 84–86, trans. Fr. S. Janos (2005), in Berdyaev Online Bibliotek Library (database online), http://www.berdyaev.com/berdiaev/berd_lib/1938_435.html, accessed 30 January 2012.

42. Jean Rimaud in *Études* 237 (October 1938): 701–2.

43. Susan Rubin Suleiman, "Between the Street and the Salon: The Dilemma of Surrealist Politics in the 1930s," *Visual Anthropology Review* 7, no. 1 (1991): 50n28.

44. Michel Onfray, *La pensée de midi: Archéologie d'une gauche libertaire* (Paris: Galilée, 2007), 39. See also Michel Onfray, *L'ordre libertaire: La vie philosophique d'Albert Camus* (Paris: Flammarion, 2011).

45. Grenier, *Essai sur l'esprit d'orthodoxie*, 62.

46. Grenier, "Ils ont faim," *Nouvelle revue française* 291 (December 1937): 1040.

47. Fouchet, "L'intellectuel et les orthodoxies," 703.

48. Grenier, *Essai sur l'esprit d'orthodoxie*, 9.

49. See Michel Bergès, *Vichy contre Mounier: Les non-conformistes face aux années 40* (Paris: Economica, 1997), 100, quoted in Véronique Anzépy-Chavagnac, *Jean de Fabrègues et la jeune droite catholique: Aux sources de la révolution nationale* (Paris: Presses universitaires du Septentrion, 2002), 328.

50. Max-Pol Fouchet, *Un jour je m'en souviens: Mémoire parlée* (Paris: Mercure de France, 1968), 54.

51. Grenier, *La dernière page* (Paris: Ramsay, 1988), 68, 70–71.

52. Grenier, *Sur la mort d'un chien* (Paris: Gallimard, 1957), 55.

53. Grenier, *Essai sur l'esprit d'orthodoxie*, 9.

54. Ibid., 42.

5. Charles Du Bos's Catholicism and His Politics of Sincerity in Interwar France

Katherine Davies

1. Quoted in Albert Thibaudet, "La sincérité," *Nouvelle revue française* 193 (1929): 545.

2. See, for example, Jacques Rivière, "Sincérité envers soi-même," *Nouvelle revue française* 37 (1912): 5–18; Benjamin Cremieux, "Sincérité

et imagination," *Nouvelle revue française* 134 (1924): 538–48; Albert Thibaudet, "Sincérité et vérité," *Nouvelle revue française* 178 (1928): 91–93.

3. See Henri Massis, "L'influence de M. André Gide," *Jugements II* (Paris: Plon, 1924), 13.

4. François Mauriac, *Cahiers André Gide 2: Correspondance André Gide–François Mauriac 1912–1950*, ed. Jacqueline Morton (Paris: Gallimard, 1971), 129.

5. Ibid.

6. Charles Du Bos, 11 May 1929, *Journal 1926–1929* (Paris: Buchet-Chastel, 2004), 788.

7. Angelo Philip Bertocci, *Charles Du Bos and English Literature: A Critic and His Orientation* (New York: King's Crown, 1949); Angelo P. Bertocci, "Comparing Literatures: The Experience of Charles Du Bos," *Comparative Literature* 24, no. 1 (1972): 1–31; Charles Dédéyan, *Le cosmopolitisme littéraire de Charles Du Bos*, 6 vols. (Paris: Société d'édition d'enseignement supérieur, 1965–71). For other works on Du Bos's criticism, his intellectual and spiritual journey, and biographical accounts see Jacques Bossière, *Perception critique et sentiment de vivre chez Charles Du Bos* (Paris: Nizet, 1969); Michel Crépu, *Charles Du Bos, ou, la tentation de l'irréprochable* (Paris: Éditions du Félin, 1990); Anne-Marie Gouhier, *Charles Du Bos* (Paris: Vrin, 1951); Michèle Leleu, *Approximation et certitude: Charles Du Bos* (Paris: Desclée de Brouwer, 1976); Georges Poulet et al., eds., *Permanence de Charles Du Bos* (Paris: Desclée de Brouwer, 1976). See also the series *Cahiers Charles Du Bos* (Neuilly-sur-Seine: Société des Amis de Charles Du Bos).

8. Paul Claudel, quoted by Charles Du Bos, 25 April 1927, *Journal 1926–1929*, 260.

9. Bossière, *Perception critique et sentiment de vivre*, 11; Bertocci, *Charles Du Bos and English Literature*, 23; Maurice Nédoncelle, "La phénoménologie d'une conversion," in *Permanence de Charles Du Bos*, ed. Poulet et al., 279–81.

10. Frédéric Gugelot, *La conversion des intellectuels au catholicisme en France (1885–1935)* (Paris: CNRS Éditions, 1998).

11. Lionel Trilling, *Sincerity and Authenticity* (Cambridge, Mass.: Harvard University Press, 1972), 2.

12. Alessandro Ferrara and Fred J. Evans, *Modernity and Authenticity: A Study in the Social and Ethical Thought of Jean-Jacques Rousseau* (Albany: State University of New York Press, 1993), 86–87.

13. Thibaudet, "La sincérité," 548.

14. Ibid., 549.

15. See, for example, Stephen Schloesser's reference to multiple realisms in his *Jazz Age Catholicism: Mystic Modernism in Postwar Paris 1919–1933* (Toronto: University of Toronto Press, 2005).

16. Jürgen Mettepenningen, *Nouvelle Théologie–New Theology: Inheritor of Modernism, Precursor of Vatican II* (London: T & T Clark), 25–31. The author notes an increasing emphasis on the mysteries of the church, the historical Christ, and the church as a community of believers (28).

17. Du Bos to Maritain, 1 March 1929, Fonds Charles Du Bos, Ms 38187: 16–20; hereafter cited as Fonds CDB. Du Bos declared to Maritain his pleasure that spiritual enlightenment could be reached in multiple ways. My thanks go to Louis Mouton and Claire Mouton for permission to cite the correspondence of Du Bos and to the Bibliothèque littéraire Jacques Doucet, Paris, at which Du Bos's archive is held.

18. Du Bos, 19 February 1929, *Journal 1926–1929*, 719.

19. For the relationship of Du Bos and orthodoxy see André Blanchet, "Charles Du Bos entre Bremond et les néo-thomistes," in *Permanence de Charles Du Bos*, ed. Poulet et al., 259–66. For an alternative theological evaluation of Du Bos's concerns see Étienne Gilson, "Charles Du Bos et les théologiens," *Cahiers Charles Du Bos* 18 (1974): 3–16.

20. Mettepenningen, *Nouvelle Théologie*, 22.

21. Du Bos, 27 October 1928, *Journal 1926–1929*, 640.

22. Du Bos to Henri Bremond, 24 November 1926, Fonds CDB, Ms 37854: 23–25.

23. Du Bos, 23 April 1927, *Journal 1926–1929*, 251.

24. Ibid., 14 May 1929, 797.

25. Ibid., 28 October 1928, 645.

26. Ibid., 11 May 1929, 792. "Saint Thomas Aquinas has never converted anyone . . . once conversion is fully accomplished, the hour of Saint Thomas Aquinas . . . sounds or at least should sound." See also Du Bos to Maritain, 16 February 1929, Fonds CDB, Ms 38187: 14–15.

27. Du Bos, 23 April 1927, *Journal 1926–1929*, 251.

28. Maurice Blondel, "Le procès de l'intelligence," in Paul Archambault et al., *Le procès de l'intelligence* (Paris: Bloud et Gay, 1922), 236–37.

29. Du Bos, 10 April 1927, *Journal 1926–1929*, 229. Blondel, "Le procès de l'intelligence," 264–65, at 237. Paul Archambault made a strikingly similar diagnosis about scholastic philosophy in the context of his critique of Maurrasian intellectualism: "According to the scholastics, every definition consists . . . in reducing its sense to another more simple, more essential sense." Archambault, "L'Intelligence et l'intellectualisme," in *Le procès de l'intelligence*, 10.

30. Blondel, "Le procès de l'intelligence," 264–65.

31. Blanchet, "Charles Du Bos entre Bremond et les néo-thomistes," 261.

32. In his autobiography Gabriel Marcel wrote: "Charles Du Bos and I had weekly meetings with Jacques Maritain, who took great pains to help us understand Thomist thought better and to appreciate it more. All three of us showed good will, but the result was meager indeed." Gabriel Marcel, "Autobiographical Essay," in *The Philosophy of Gabriel Marcel*, ed. P. A. Schilpp and L. E. Hahn (La Salle, Ill.: Open Court, 1984), 30.

33. Du Bos, 14 May 1929, *Journal 1926–1929*, 800–1.

34. Ibid., 26 November 1929, 927.

35. Du Bos, 29 June 1931, *Journal 1930–1939* (Paris: Buchet-Chastel, 2005), 252.

36. Du Bos, 26 November 1929, *Journal 1926–1929*, 926–27.

37. Du Bos to François Mauriac, 9 February 1929, *Cahiers Charles Du Bos* 15 (1971): 20.

38. *Vigile* 1 (1930), quoted in Gugelot, *La conversion des intellectuels*, 309; and Du Bos, 17 October 1931, *Journal 1930–1939*, 346.

39. Du Bos, 18 May 1931, *Journal 1930–1939*, 180.

40. See Altermann to Du Bos, 5 October 1930, Fonds CDB, Ms 33821: 16–20.

41. Ibid.

42. Du Bos to Altermann, 2 October 1930, Fonds CDB, Ms 37776: 36–38.

43. Du Bos, 17 October 1931, *Journal 1930–1939*, 344–46.

44. See Du Bos, 14 December 1927, *Journal 1926–1929*, 403.

45. Du Bos, 17 October 1931, *Journal 1930–1939*, 346.

46. Gouhier, *Charles Du Bos*, 43.

47. Du Bos, 27 March 1926, *Journal 1926–1929*, 50.

48. Ibid.

49. Du Bos, 12 April 1933, *Journal 1930–1939*, 524–25.

50. Ibid., 524.

51. Charles Du Bos, *Grandeur et misère de Benjamin Constant* (Paris: Corrêa, 1946), 29.

52. Subtitle to *Grandeur et misère.*

53. Jacques-Bénigne Bossuet's phrase applied to Constant by Du Bos, *Grandeur et misère*, 27.

54. Paul Bourget, quoted by Du Bos, *Grandeur et misère*, 27.

55. Du Bos, *Grandeur et misère*, 238.

56. Ibid., 37–41.

57. Ibid., 37–38.

58. Ibid., 38.

59. Paul Desjardins was responsible for the inauguration of the famous meetings at the Cistercian abbey at Pontigny. Every year from 1922 to 1939 the abbey played host for ten days to an international network of intellectuals, organized invariably around three broad themes: politics, philosophy, and literature. Du Bos especially, by virtue of his European educational and familial heritage, was an active participant. See François Chaubet, *Paul Desjardins et les décades de Pontigny* (Villeneuve-d'Ascq Nord: Presses universitaires du Septentrion, 2000).

60. Stephen Geroulanos, *An Atheism That Is Not Humanism Emerges in French Thought* (Stanford, Calif.: Stanford University Press, 2010), 21. For a discussion of humanism in the early twentieth century see, for example, Micheline Tison-Braun, *La crise de l'humanisme: Le conflit de l'individu et de la société dans la littérature française moderne*, t. II, *1914–1939* (Paris: Librairie Nizet, 1967).

61. Geroulanos, *Atheism*, 5.

62. Ibid., 100–30.

63. Emmanuel Berl, quoted in a letter from Du Bos to Marcel, 10 July 1929, Fonds CDB, Ms 33186: 11–15.

64. Ibid.

65. Charles Du Bos, *Dialogue avec André Gide* (Paris: Au Sans Pareil, 1929), 316–17.

66. Béatrice Didier, "Charles Du Bos et Ramon Fernandez: 'Déspiritualisation' ou respiritualisation' chez André Gide?" *Cahiers Charles Du Bos* 24 (1980): 41–48.

67. Fernandez to Du Bos, 21 March 1931, *Cahiers Charles Du Bos* 24 (1980): 65.

68. Ibid., 62–63.

69. Du Bos to Fernandez, 11–14 July 1931, *Cahiers Charles Du Bos* 24: 55, and see Du Bos, *Dialogue*, 327: "[B]etween my return to the Catholic faith and not only the substance but also the tone . . . of the Labyrinthe à claire-voie, if there is a concordance, there is no relation of cause and effect."

70. Du Bos to Fernandez, 11–14 July 1931, *Cahiers Charles Du Bos* 24: 59.

71. Ibid., 57. See Alan Sheridan, *André Gide: A Life in the Present* (Cambridge, Mass.: Harvard University Press, 1999), 119.

72. Du Bos to Fernandez, 11–14 July 1931, *Cahiers Charles Du Bos* 24: 57.

73. Ibid., 58.

74. Du Bos to Marcel, 9 March 1935, *Cahiers Charles Du Bos* 18 (1974): 53.

75. F. H. Bradley, quoted by Du Bos, 10 November 1933, *Journal 1930–1939*, 637.

76. The phrase "generation of 1933" is borrowed from Ethan Kleinberg, *Generation Existential: Heidegger's Philosophy in France, 1927–1961* (Ithaca, N.Y.: Cornell University Press, 2005), 54.

77. Du Bos, 10 November 1933, *Journal 1930–1939*, 637.

78. Jean Wahl, *Vers le concret* (Paris: Vrin, 1932). See Geroulanos, *Atheism*, for a critical analysis and contextualization of *Vers le concret*, 72–80.

79. Martin Heidegger, *Sein und Zeit* (1927), quoted in Wahl, *Vers le concret*, 5n2.

80. Wahl, *Vers le concret*, 14.

81. Du Bos, "Le temps et l'éternité," in *La conscience du temps: Correspondance de l'Union pour la vérité* (Paris: Union pour la vérité, Mars–Avril 1929), 25.

82. Ibid., 27.

83. For histories of the reception and the humanist "misreading" of Heidegger in France see Geroulanos, *Atheism*, and Tom Rockmore, *Heidegger and French Philosophy: Humanism, Antihumanism, and Being* (London: Routledge, 1995).

84. Kleinberg, *Generation Existential*, 70–71. On the history of the French translation of Heidegger's "Was ist Metaphysik?" see Denis Hollier, "Plenty of Nothing," in *A New History of French Literature*, ed. Denis Hollier (Cambridge, Mass.: Harvard University Press, 1989), 894–900. Because the French reception of Heidegger was dependent on Corbin's translations, it prefigured the conflation of the views of Heidegger and Sartre that the latter cultivated. For Corbin's "human reality" see Kleinberg, 111–12, 131–32.

85. Kleinberg, *Generation Existential*, 68. See Alexandre Kojève, *Introduction to the Reading of Hegel*, ed. Allan Bloom, trans. James H. Nichols Jr. (London: Basic Books, 1969).

86. Jean Wahl, "Heidegger et Kierkegaard," *Recherches philosophiques* 2 (1932–33): 349–70, 355.

87. Du Bos, 10 November 1933, *Journal 1930–1939*, 638–39.

88. For a discussion of the meaning of "aesthetics and ethics" see Kathrin Stengel, "Ethics as Style: Wittgenstein's Aesthetic Ethics and Ethical Aesthetics," *Poetics Today* 25, no. 4 (Winter 2004): 615.

89. Du Bos, 10 November 1933, *Journal 1930–1939*, 639.

90. Ibid., 640.

91. Ibid.

92. Du Bos, 1 May 1930, *Journal 1930–1939*, 40–41.

93. Katherine Jane Davies, "A 'Third Way' Catholic Intellectual: Charles Du Bos, Tragedy, and Ethics in Interwar Paris," *Journal of the History of Ideas* 71, no. 4 (2010): 637–59.

94. Jean-François Sirinelli, *Intellectuels et passions françaises: Manifestes et pétitions au XXe siècle* (Paris: Fayard, 1990).

95. Charles Du Bos, *Commentaires* (Paris: Desclée de Brouwer, 1946), xxvi.

96. Du Bos, 26 August 1934, *Journal 1930–1939*, 676.

97. Jacques Maritain, *Religion and Culture*, trans. J. F. Scanlan (London: Sheed and Ward, 1931), 54. Original French, *Religion et culture: Premier numéro de la collection des questions disputées* (Paris: Desclée de Brouwer, 1930).

98. Du Bos, 26 August 1934, *Journal 1930–1939*, 676.

99. Ibid., 676, 684.

100. Du Bos, 22 September 1938, *Journal 1930–1939*, 903.

101. Ibid., 26 August 1934, 685.

102. Gabriel Marcel, "En marge de la trahison des clercs," *Nouvelle revue française* 29 (1927): 832.

103. Du Bos, 26 August 1934, *Journal 1930–1939*, 677–78.

104. Elizabeth Markovits, *The Politics of Sincerity: Plato, Frank Speech, and Democratic Judgment* (University Park: Pennsylvania State University Press, 2008), 27.

105. Du Bos, 26 August 1934, *Journal 1930–1939*, 677.

106. Ibid., 12 March 1935, 697.

107. Du Bos to Marcel, 24 March 1936, *Cahiers Charles Du Bos* 18: 55. See also Jean-Pierre Caussade, *Abandonment to Divine Providence*, trans. John Beevers (London: Doubleday Image Books, 1975).

108. Lamennais, quoted by Du Bos to Marcel, 24 March 1936, *Cahiers Charles Du Bos* 18: 56.

109. Ibid., Du Bos to Marcel, 24 March 1936, 56.

110. Jean Daniélou, "Les orientations présentes de la pensée religieuse," *Études* 79 (1946): 7, quoted in Brian Daley, "The Nouvelle Théologie and the Patristic Revival: Sources, Symbols, and the Science of the Theology," *International Journal of Systematic Theology* 7 (2005): 363.

111. Henri de Lubac, "Causes internes de l'atténuation et de la disparition du sens du Sacré" (1942), quoted in J. A. Komonchak, "Theology and Culture at Mid-Century: The Example of Henri de Lubac," *Theological Studies* 51 (1990): 583.

112. Thanks go to Professor Richard Parish for his comments on Thomism as "the said" in contrast to those on the road to "saying."

113. Crépu, *Charles Du Bos*, 11.

114. Du Bos, 6 November 1928, *Journal 1926–1929*, 654.

6. From *Mystique* to *Théologique*: Messiaen's "*ordre nouveau*," 1935–39

Stephen Schloesser

Material in this essay has been taken from Stephen Schloesser, *Visions of Amen: The Early Life and Music of Olivier Messiaen* (Grand Rapids, Mich.: William B. Eerdmans, 2014). Reprinted by permission of the publisher; all rights reserved.

1. Nicholas Thistlethwaite, review of *Messiaen the Theologian*, ed. Andrew Shenton (Burlington, Vt.: Ashgate, 2010), in *Journal of the British Institute of Organ Studies* (Winter 2010): 192–94, at 192.

2. For an overview see Andrew Shenton, *Olivier Messiaen's System of Signs: Notes Towards Understanding His Music* (Aldershot, UK: Ashgate, 2008), 22–25.

3. Wilfred Mellers, *Celestial Music? Some Masterpieces of European Religious Music* (Woodbridge, Suffolk, UK: Boydell, 2002), 231; see also Mellers, "Mysticism and Theology," in *The Messiaen Companion*, ed. Peter Hill (Portland, Ore.: Amadeus, 1995), 220–33.

4. Olivier Messiaen, 23 April 1979, in Almut Rößler, *Contributions to the Spiritual World of Olivier Messiaen*, trans. Barbara Dagg and Nancy Poland (Duisberg: Gilles und Francke, 1986), 89; see Stephen Schloesser, "The Charm of Impossibilities: Mystic Surrealism as Contemplative Voluptuousness," in *Messiaen the Theologian*, 163–82, at 168n26.

5. Michel de Certeau identified a distinctively late nineteenth- and early twentieth-century strain of talking about "mysticism"; see Certeau, "Mysticism," trans. Marsanne Brammer, *Diacritics* 22, no. 2 (Summer 1992): 11–25, originally in *Encyclopaedia universalis* (1968); Certeau, "History and Mysticism," in *Histories: French Constructions of the Past*, ed. Jacques Revel and Lynn Hunt, trans. Arthur Goldhammer et al. (New York: New Press, 1995), 437–47 (originally "Histoire et mystique," *Revue d'histoire de la spiritualité* 89 [1972]: 69–82). For a more recent study surveying the British example, see Jane Shaw, "The Mystical Turn: Religious Experience in the Modern World," http://static.westminster-abbey.org/assets/pdf_file/0003/51195/ESA-lecture-2008.pdf.

6. Jane F. Fulcher, "The Politics of Transcendence: Ideology in the Music of Messiaen in the 1930s," *Musical Quarterly* 86, no. 3 (2002): 449–71; Fulcher, *The Composer as Intellectual: Music and Ideology in France, 1914–1940* (New York: Oxford University Press, 2005), 285–310; Philip Nord, *France's New Deal: From the Thirties to the Postwar Era* (Princeton, N.J.: Princeton University Press, 2010). For the *ordre nouveau* and nonconformism, see Jean-Louis Loubet del Bayle, *Les non-conformistes des années 30: Une tentative de renouvellement de la pensée politique française* (Paris: Éditions du Seuil, 1969); John Hellman, *Emmanuel Mounier and the New Catholic Left, 1930–1950* (Toronto: University of Toronto Press, 1981); Hellman, *The*

Communitarian Third Way: Alexandre Marc's Ordre Nouveau, 1930–2000 (Montreal: McGill-Queen's University Press, 2002); Mark Antliff, *Avant-Garde Fascism: The Mobilization of Myth, Art, and Culture in France, 1909–1939* (Durham, N.C.: Duke University Press, 2007), 155–201.

7. Deborah Mawer, "'Dancing on the Edge of the Volcano': French Music in the 1930s," in *French Music Since Berlioz*, ed. Richard Langham Smith and Caroline Potter (Aldershot, UK: Ashgate, 2006), 249–80.

8. For a classic study, see Louis Bouyer, "Mysticism: An Essay on the History of the Word," in *Understanding Mysticism*, ed. Richard Woods (New York: Image, 1980), 45–58. For the unabbreviated French original, see Bouyer, "Mystique: Essai sur l'histoire d'un mot," *La Vie spirituelle* 9 supp. (1949): 3–23. Michel de Certeau identified a distinctively late nineteenth- and early twentieth-century strain of talking about "mysticism"; see Certeau, "Mysticism," trans. Marsanne Brammer, *Diacritics* 22, no. 2 (Summer 1992): 11–25, originally in *Encyclopaedia universalis* (1968); see Certeau, "History and Mysticism." For more recent overviews, see Rajesh Heynickx and Evert Peeters, "The Muse of Mysticism: Transforming and Recycling Catholicism, 1900–1950," *Revue belge de philologie et de histoire* 88, no. 4 (2010): 1161–70, and Jane Shaw, "The Mystical Turn: Religious Experience in the Modern World," http://static.westminster-abbey.org/assets/pdf_file/0003/51195/ESA-lecture-2008.pdf.

9. "So far back as 1732 the word *misticité* was invented or adopted as a term of reproach and derision to characterize the so-called Quietism of Madame Guyon." Arthur Edward Waite, *The Way of Divine Union: Being a Doctrine of Experience in the Life of Sanctity, Considered on the Faith of Its Testimonies and Interpreted After a New Manner* (London: Rider, 1915), 16n2.

10. Joseph von Görres, *La mystique divine, naturelle, et diabolique*, trans. Charles Sainte-Foi (Paris: Mme Vve Poussielgue-Rusand [libraire], 1854–55); Prosper-Louis-Pascal Guéranger, *L'année liturgique*, 15 vols. (Le Mans: Fleuriot, 1841–1901); Jacques-Albin-Simon Collin de Plancy, ed., *Dictionnaire des sciences occultes*, vols. 48–49 of *Encyclopédie théologique*, ed. Jacques-Paul Migne (Paris: Ateliers catholiques du Petit-Montrouge, 1846–48); Jean Claude Gainet and Clovis Poussin, eds., *Dictionnaire d'ascétisme*, vols. 45–46 of *Encyclopédie théologique*, 2nd series, ed. Jacques-Paul Migne (1853–54); Jacques-Paul Migne, *Dictionnaire de mystique*

chrétienne ou Essai d'encyclopédisation historique et méthodique de tous les phénomènes merveilleux de l'âme, parvenue à l'état surnaturel et unie à Dieu par l'exercice et la pratique de la vie spirituelle, dans toute sa perfection . . . (Petit-Montrouge: Migne, 1858).

11. Paul Richer and Jean-Martin Charcot, *Les démoniaques dans l'art* (Paris: Delahaye et Lecrosnier, 1887); Max Nordau, *Dégénérescence*, trans. Auguste Dietrich, 2 vols. (Paris: Alcan, 1894); Jules-Désiré-Gabriel Cloitre, *Dégénérescence et mysticisme* (Bordeaux: Cassignol, 1902); Lucien Lévy-Bruhl, *La mentalité primitive* (Paris: Alcan, 1922); see also Lévy-Bruhl, *Les fonctions mentales dans les sociétés inférieures* (Paris: Alcan, 1910). For background, see Georges Didi-Huberman, *Invention of Hysteria: Charcot and the Photographic Iconography of the Salpêtrière*, trans. Alisa Hartz (Cambridge, Mass.: MIT Press, 2003), orig. *Invention de l'hystérie: Charcot et l'iconographie photographique de la Salpêtrière* (Paris: Éditions Macula, 1982); Ruth Harris, *Lourdes: Body and Spirit in the Secular Age* (New York: Viking, 1999); Cristina Mazzoni, *Saint Hysteria: Neurosis, Mysticism, and Gender in European Culture* (Ithaca, N.Y.: Cornell University Press, 1996); Jan Goldstein, "The Uses of Male Hysteria: Medical and Literary Discourse in Nineteenth-Century France," *Representations* 34 (Spring 1991): 134–65; Jan Goldstein, *Console and Classify: The Psychiatric Profession in the Nineteenth Century* (New York: Cambridge University Press, 1987); and Jan Goldstein, "The Hysteria Diagnosis and the Politics of Anticlericalism in Later Nineteenth-Century France," *Journal of Modern History* 54 (1982): 209–39.

12. William James, *The Varieties of Religious Experience; a Study in Human Nature; Being the Gifford Lectures on Natural Religion Delivered at Edinburgh in 1901–1902* (New York: Modern Library, 1902); Baron Friedrich von Hügel, *The Mystical Element of Religion as Studied in Saint Catherine of Genova and Her Friends* (London: Dent, 1908); Evelyn Underhill, *Mysticism: A Study in the Nature and Development of Man's Spiritual Consciousness* (London: Methuen, 1911); Waite, *Way of Divine Union* (1915).

13. Stephen Schloesser, *Jazz Age Catholicism: Mystic Modernism in Postwar Paris, 1919–1933* (Toronto: University of Toronto Press, 2005), 107–37.

14. A sampling of publications includes the following (ordered by date): Henri Bremond and Charles Grolleau, *Histoire littéraire du sentiment*

religieux en France depuis la fin des guerres de religion jusqu'à nos jours, 11 vols. (Paris: Bloud et Gay, 1916–33); Rudolf Otto, *Das Heilige: Über das Irrationale in der Idee des Göttlichen und sein Verhältnis zum Rationalen* (Breslau: Trewendt und Granier, 1917); Friedrich Heiler, *Das Gebet in der Mystik: Eine religionspsychologische Untersuchung* (Munich: Reinhardt, 1918); Friedrich Heiler, *Die Bedeutung der Mystik für die Weltreligionen* (Munich: Reinhardt, 1919); Reynold Alleyne Nicholson, *Studies in Islamic Mysticism* (Cambridge: Cambridge University Press, 1921); René Guénon, *Introduction générale à l'étude des doctrines hindoues* (Paris: Rivière, 1921); Rabindranath Tagore, *Art et anatomie hindous* (Paris: Éditions Bossard, 1921); Maurice de La Taille, *L'oraison contemplative* (Paris: Beauchesne, 1921); Rabindranath Tagore and André Gide, *L'offrande lyrique*, 18th ed. (Paris: Éditions de la Nouvelle revue française, 1921); Louis Massignon, *Al-Hallâj: Martyr mystique de l'Islam*, 4 vols. (Paris: Geuthner, 1922); Friedrich Heiler, *Die buddhistische Versenkung: Eine religionsgeschichtliche Untersuchung* (Munich: Reinhardt, 1922); Lucien Lévy-Bruhl, *La mentalité primitive* (Paris: Alcan, 1922); Emil Brunner, *Die Mystik und das Wort: Der Gegensatz zwischen moderner Religionsauffassung und christlichem Glauben dargestellt an der Theologie Schleiermachers* (Tübingen: Mohr, 1924); René Guénon, *Orient et Occident* (Paris: Payot, 1924); Rabindranath Tagore, *La religion du poète*, trans. A. Tougard de Boismilon (Paris: Payot, 1924); *Les appels de l'Orient* (*Les Cahiers du Mois* 9/10) (Paris: Émile-Paul, Frères, 1925); Louis Renou, *La valeur du parfait dans les hymnes védiques* (Paris: Champion, 1925); René Guénon, *L'homme et son devenir selon le Vêdânta* (Paris: Bossard, 1925); Émile Baumann, *L'anneau d'or des grands mystiques de Saint-Augustin à Catherine Emmerich* (Paris: Grasset, 1924); Jean Baruzi, *Saint Jean de la Croix et le problème de l'expérience mystique* (Paris: Alcan, 1924); Joseph Maréchal, *Études sur la psychologie des mystiques* (Bruges: Beyaert, 1924); Louis Renou, *La valeur du parfait dans les hymnes védiques* (Paris: Champion, 1925); Rudolf Otto, *West-östliche Mystik: Vergleich und Unterscheidung zur Wesensdeutung* (Gotha: Klotz, 1926); Nicholas Arseniev, *L'église d'Orient* (Amay-sur-Meuse [Belgium]: Prieuré d'Amay, 1928), orig. *Die Ostkirche* (Stuttgart: Frommann, 1927); Edmond Bruggemann, *Les mystiques flamands et le renouveau catholique français* (Lille: Mercure de Flandre, 1928); Romain Rolland, *Essai sur la mystique et l'action de l'Inde vivante: La vie de Ramakrishna* (Paris: Stock, 1929); Rudolf Otto, *Le sacré:*

L'élément non-rationnel dans l'idée du divin et sa relation avec le rationnel, trans. André Jundt (Paris: Payot, 1929, orig. *Das Heilige* [1917], cited).

15. This postwar trend away from "transcendence" toward "immanence" had already been at the heart of the prewar Roman Catholic modernist crisis, whose high-water mark occurred in 1907. See Stephen Schloesser, "*Vivo ergo cogito*: Modernism as Temporalization and Its Discontents: A Propaedeutic to This Collection," in *The Reception of Pragmatism in France and the Rise of Catholic Modernism, 1890–1914*, ed. David Schultenover (Washington, D.C.: Catholic University of America Press, 2009), 21–58.

16. Charles Tournemire, *L'orgue mystique: 51 offices de l'année liturgique inspirés du chant grégorien et librement paraphrasés*, 51 vols. (Paris: Heugel, 1928–36). See Schloesser, *Jazz Age Catholicism*, 282–322, and "Charm of Impossibilities."

17. A. Febvre-Longeray, review of performance of *Les offrandes oubliées* on 19 February 1931, *Le courrier musical*, 5 March 1931, 186, quoted in Nigel Simeone, *Olivier Messiaen: A Bibliographical Catalogue of Messiaen's Works*, Musikbibliographische Arbeiten series, vol. 14 (Tutzing: Schneider, 1998), 208.

18. Olivier Messiaen, *Diptyque: Pour orgue: Essai sur la vie terrestre et l'éternité bienheureuse* (Paris: Durand, 1930); Messiaen, *Les offrandes oubliées* (Paris: Durand, 1931); Messiaen, *La mort du nombre* (Paris: Durand, 1931); Messiaen, *Apparition de l'église éternelle: Pour orgue* (Paris: Lemoine, 1934); Messiaen, *Le tombeau resplendissant: Pour orchestre (1931)* (Paris: Durand, 1997).

19. Messiaen's use of the "soul" during this early period seems most likely to have derived from his mother's poetry. She had written *L'âme en bourgeon* while pregnant with Messiaen, an internal conversation with her unborn son. For a French-English bilingual version of the poem see Cécile Sauvage, *L'âme en bourgeon / The Budding Soul*, trans. and afterword by Philip Weller, in *Olivier Messiaen: Music, Art, and Literature*, ed. Christopher Dingle and Nigel Simeone (Burlington, Vt.: Ashgate, 2007), 191–278. See also a fully annotated version in Cécile Sauvage and Béatrice Marchal-Vincent, *L'œuvre poétique de Cécile Sauvage (1883–1927)*, 2 vols. (vol. 1, *Cécile Sauvage: Essai sur la mélancolie dans l'écriture poétique*; vol. 2, *L'œuvre poétique de Cécile Sauvage (1883–1927)*, ed. and annotated by

Béatrice Marchal-Vincent), PhD diss., Paris IV–Sorbonne, 1995 (Lille: Atelier National de Reproduction des Thèses, 1995), text 2:34–53; notes 2:308–23. This genre of internal dialogue may have been influenced in turn by one of Sauvage's favorite poets, Alphonse de Lamartine. One scholar discusses the "poetics of maternal echo" in Lamartine:

> The poet, in fact, internalizes the dialogue between self and other. Talking to himself is indeed the logical means of having a self-same interlocutor. In [Lamartine's] *Méditations* and *Harmonies,* the internalized dialogue remains embryonic, as the poet appeals to "my soul" in "Le Vallon" [The Valley] and in "Pourquoi mon âme est-elle triste?" [Why Is My Soul Sad?]. Embryonic dialogue reaches full maturity in "La Vigne et la maison" [The Vine and the House], where the subject is split in two . . . "moi" [me] and "mon âme" [my soul]. But these two are one and the same. As Lamartine writes in *Nouvelles Confidences,* the poet is among those who have "silently questioned their soul and who have answered themselves out loud."
>
> Aimée Boutin, *Maternal Echoes: The Poetry of Marceline Desbordes-Valmore and Alphonse de Lamartine* (Newark: University of Delaware Press, 2001), 25, 79

20. Diane Luchese, "Olivier Messiaen's Slow Music: A Reflection of Eternity in Time," and Benedict Taylor, "On Time and Eternity in Messiaen," both in *Olivier Messiaen: The Centenary Papers,* ed. Judith Crispin (Newcastle upon Tyne: Cambridge Scholars Publishing, 2010), 179–92 and 256–80; Jeremy S. Begbie, *Theology, Music, and Time* (New York: Cambridge University Press, 2000), 139–44; see also Paul Griffiths, *Olivier Messiaen and the Music of Time* (Ithaca, N.Y.: Cornell University Press, 1985).

21. Charles Tournemire to curate of La Trinité, July 1931, quoted in Nigel Simeone, "'Chez Messiaen, tout est prière': Messiaen's Appointment at the Trinité," *Musical Times* 145, no. 1889 (Winter 2004): 36–53, at 40. Emphasis added.

22. Olivier Messiaen, interview by José Bruyr, October 1931, "Olivier Messiaen," *L'écran des musiciens, seconde série* (Paris: Corti, 1933), 124–31, quoted in Peter Hill and Nigel Simeone, *Messiaen* (New Haven, Conn.: Yale University Press, 2005): 37–39. On 25 April 1932, Messiaen assisted Tournemire by playing pieces from *L'orgue mystique* the following spring (along with Daniel-Lesur and several other young star organists) at a grand

concert at Sainte-Clotilde, an evening aimed at making the massive work familiar to a wider audience. Tournemire's handwritten program is reproduced in Brigitte de Leersnyder, ed., *Charles Tournemire* (1870–1939), Cahiers et mémoires de l'orgue 41 (Paris: Les Amis de l'Orgue, 1989), 28–29. See Schloesser, *Jazz Age Catholicism*, 320.

23. Charles Tournemire, review of the second performance of Messiaen's *Les offrandes oubliées*, 6 December 1931, *Le courrier musical*, 15 December 1931, 594, quoted in Simeone, *Bibliographical Catalogue*, 208. Emphasis added.

24. *L'ascension*: orchestral version: composed summer 1932; orchestrated summer 1933; premiered in February 1935; published in June 1948. Organ version: composed summers of 1933–34; premiered in 28 May 1935; published in November 1934. Simeone, *Bibliographical Catalogue*, 38–39.

25. Dom [Abbot] Columba Marmion, *Le Christ dans ses mystères: Conférences spirituelles* (Namur [Belgium]: Abbaye de Maredsous, 1919). It is difficult to overstate the popularity of this work. First published in 1919, successive editions followed in 1921, 1922, 1923, 1925, 1926, 1928, 1929, 1930, and 1932; by 1930 the work had sold forty-five thousand copies (the latest edition as Messiaen assumed his new position as organist). Over the next three years—by which time the work had been translated into at least Flemish, English, German, Polish, Spanish, and Italian—another twenty-five thousand copies had been sold. As the work's subtitle ("spiritual conferences") suggests, its chapters consist of the kinds of edifying lectures or retreat conferences (*conférences*) delivered to fellow monks as preparation for their personal meditation. (It forms part of a trilogy, the first and last works of which are *Christ, the Life of the Soul* [1914], and *Christ, the Ideal of the Monk* [1923].) One indication of this is that the scriptural passages saturating Marmion's text—both as the starting point for commentaries as well as glosses on those meditations—are always quoted from the Vulgate edition of the Bible without translation, presuming that the reader (and original listeners) could read Latin. It should be added, however, that lay readers who had attended Catholic schools (and even many who had attended state schools) would be able to read Latin in the early twentieth century. "A survey was made among Belgian Catholics during the [First World] War which asked, 'Do you read religious books? Which titles and authors?' The name most frequently mentioned was that

of Marmion." J. Cardolle, *Aux jeunes: Et toi, connais-tu le Christ vie de ton âme? D'après l'œuvre de Dom Marmion* (Paris/Bruges: Desclée de Brouwer, 1949); quoted in Yves Balmer, "Religious Literature in Messiaen's Personal Library," in *Messiaen the Theologian,* 20. For a new translation see Abbot Columba Marmion, *Christ in His Mysteries,* trans. Alan Bancroft (Bethesda, Md.: Zaccheus, 2008).

26. Olivier Messiaen, *L'ascension: Quatre méditations symphoniques pour orgue* (*Ascension Day: Four Symphonic Meditations for Organ*) (Paris: Leduc, 1934). Emphasis added.

27. Review by "F. D." of the first performance of *Le tombeau resplendissant,* 12 February 1933; in *Le courrier musical,* 1 March 1933, 113; reprinted in Simeone, *Bibliographical Catalogue,* 213–14.

28. "F. D." might refer to Fernand Drogoul, a pupil of Vincent d'Indy who was already writing for the *Courrier musical* before the war. He was a great inspiration to the Catholic poet Pierre-Jean Jouve, who later dedicated his book on Mozart's *Don Juan* to him (a book that Messiaen was to use); his wife was Thérèse Aubray, a poet who was close to Paul Éluard and other surrealists and who corresponded with the Catholic critic Charles Du Bos. My thanks to Toby Garfitt for assistance.

29. Daniel-Rops, *Notre inquiétude* (1927). Note that 1927 is the same year in which Martin Heidegger published his landmark book, in which anxiety (*Angst*) plays a defining role in human existence: Heidegger, *Sein und Zeit* (Halle: Niemeyer, 1927). See Ethan Kleinberg, *Generation Existential: Heidegger's Philosophy in France, 1927–1961* (Ithaca, N.Y.: Cornell University Press, 2005). For this generation's self-understanding, see Schloesser, *Jazz Age Catholicism,* 108–10.

30. The topic of "inquiétude"—which can also be translated as agitation, concern, or simply inquietude—had been launched in the postwar era by Benjamin Crémieux's "Le bilan d'une enquête," *Nouvelle revue française* 120 (1923): 287–94. Crémieux, a Great War veteran who had been wounded three times, proposed that his generation was afflicted by a "new malady of the century" (*nouveau mal du siècle*), just as François-René de Chateaubriand's postrevolutionary romantic generation had been in the early nineteenth century. In 1924 Marcel Arland took up the theme and described postwar literature: "It is possible that one day such torments will appear naïve and that people will be surprised by that taste for moral

suffering, for this masochism, for this 'inquietude' which leads us to rather peculiar attempts." See Arland, "Sur un nouveau mal du siècle," *Nouvelle revue française* 125 (1924): 156; in Frédéric J. Grover, *Drieu La Rochelle and the Fiction of Testimony* (Berkeley: University of California Press, 1958), 101; compare Jean Grenier, "Les directions présentes de la littérature," *La vie des lettres et des arts* 12 (1924): 75–79; 13: 63–69. My thanks to Toby Garfitt for assistance. See also note 38 to this chapter below.

31. See Pascal: "Let us, therefore, not seek certainty and stability. Our reason is always deceived by inconstant appearances; nothing can affix the finite between the two infinites [of being and nothingness] that both enclose and escape it" (Pascal, *Pensées* [Pléiade]), 185; (Lafuma), 199; (Sellier), 230; see Schloesser, "Notes on the *Miserere* Plates," in *Mystic Masque: Semblance and Reality in Georges Rouault, 1871–1958* (Chestnut Hill, Mass.: McMullen Museum of Art, Boston College, 2008), 176; Schloesser, "1871–1901: Realism, Symbolism, Mystic Modernism," in Schloesser, *Mystic Masque*, 23–43, at 37.

32. Daniel-Rops, *Notre inquiétude*, 20–22, 31, 18, 27.

33. Ibid., 31.

34. "Even though we do not share the Catholic faith of Fr. Sanson," wrote Daniel-Rops, "we would like to render him this homage. In a striking way, he has summarized, in one of his lecture series (published under the title *L'inquiétude humaine* [*Human Anxiety*]) the facts of this problem." In another passage, he judged that "the Rev. Fr. Sanson, Oratorian priest, was correct in affirming the universality of the fact of human anxiety." Daniel-Rops, *Notre inquiétude*, 34n1, 29. The 1925 Lenten conferences given by the Rev. Pierre Sanson at the Cathedral of Notre-Dame of Paris were titled and later published as *L'inquiétude humaine: Le message de Jésus-Christ (Conférences de Notre-Dame de Paris)* (Paris: Éd. Spes, 1925). The volume's cover quoted a famous phrase from Saint Augustine's *Confessions* (I, 1) in both Latin and French: "inquietum est cor nostrum . . ."; "Notre cœur est inquiet . . ." [Our heart is restless . . .].

35. Daniel-Rops, *Notre inquiétude*, 285. Quotations from Sanson are in italics.

36. H. Stuart Hughes, *Between Commitment and Disillusion: The Obstructed Path and The Sea Change, 1930–1965* (1966, 1975; repr., with a new introduction, Middletown, Conn.: Wesleyan University Press, 1987), 65–67.

37. See Fulcher, *Composer as Intellectual*, 285–87; Hellman, *Communitarian Third Way*, 30–33; see Jean-Louis Loubet del Bayle, *Les non-conformistes des années 30: Une tentative de renouvellement de la pensée politique française* (Paris: Seuil, [1969] 2001). In May 1933, two months after the review by "F. D." the first issue of *Ordre nouveau* appeared.

38. Henri Daniel-Rops, *Le monde sans âme* (Paris: Plon, 1932). The book was at least partly written in response to Crémieux, *Inquiétude et reconstruction: Essai sur la littérature d'après guerre* (Paris: Éditions Corrêa, 1931). For the ongoing "inquiétude" debates, see François Hertel, "Essai sur l'inquiétude des jeunes," *L'action nationale* 6, no. 12 (December 1935): 219–37, and François Hertel, "Essai sur l'inquiétude des jeunes . . . II: Notes pour une histoire de l'inquiétude," *L'action nationale* 7, no. 1 (January 1936): 6–37; see André Laurendeau, "Lettre de Paris: Le chrétien et le monde moderne (entretien avec Daniel-Rops)," *L'action nationale* 8, no. 2 (October 1936): 111–17.

39. Daniel-Rops, *Le monde sans âme*, 12, 13, 195. By 1935 Daniel-Rops was arguing that "the French had not completely succumbed to 'materialist productivism' because their peasants were the repository of '*ancestral*' values. A romantic Péguyist notion that peasants were not materialistic but *instinctive* communitarians was common among Catholics in this period.' " See Hellman, *Communitarian Third Way*, 115. Emphasis added.

40. "F. D." (1 March 1933), 213–14. Daniel-Rops's *Le monde sans âme* had been published on 18 March 1932.

41. Henri Bergson, *Les deux sources de la morale et de la religion* (Paris: Alcan, 1932); Charles Gillouin, *Journal d'un chrétien philosophe: 1915–1921* (Paris: Nouvelle Librairie française, 1932).

42. These remarks are from Delbos's introductory lecture to his wartime series on French philosophy, posthumously reproduced from his notes and published as "Caractères généraux de la philosophie française," *Revue de métaphysique et de morale* 24, no. 1 (January 1917): 1–13, at 4–5. Reprinted as the first chapter in Delbos, *La philosophie française* (Paris: Plon, 1919), 1–15, at 4. Translated in Ralph Barton Perry, *The Present Conflict of Ideals: A Study of the Philosophical Background of the World War* (New York: Longmans, Green, 1922), 455.

43. Jacques Maritain, *Primauté du spirituel*, Le roseau d'or: Œuvres et chroniques no. 19 (Paris: Plon, 1927). For Maritain's "Roseau d'or" series see

Schloesser, *Jazz Age Catholicism*, 181–85. For an English translation see Maritain, *The Things That Are Not Caesar's*, trans. J. F. Scanlan (New York: Scribner, 1931).

44. Textual similarities in *Le tombeau resplendissant* (composed in 1931) demonstrate that Messiaen was a close reader of Paul Éluard, perhaps as early as *Capitale de la douleur* (*Capital of Pain*) (Paris: Gallimard/Éditions de la Nouvelle revue française, 1926). See Stephen Schloesser, *Visions of Amen: The Early Life and Music of Olivier Messiaen* (Grand Rapids, Mich.: William B. Eerdmans, 2014), 122.

45. "F. D." (1 March 1933), 214. The reviewer misquotes the title as *Un monde sans âme* (*A World Without Soul*).

46. See Schloesser, *Jazz Age Catholicism*, esp. 39–45.

47. Review by "F. D." of the first performance of *Hymne au Saint-Sacrement* (23 March 1933) in *Le courrier musical*, 15 April 1933, 196, in Simeone, *Bibliographical Catalogue*, 215–16, at 215. Composed in 1932, the work was lost during the war around 1944 and had to be reconstituted from memory. See Simeone, *Bibliographical Catalogue*, 28–31.

48. "F. D." (15 April 1933), 215–16.

49. Hill and Simeone, *Messiaen*, 374. See Pierre Messiaen, *Images* (Paris: Desclée de Brouwer, 1944), 153–54; Brigitte Massin and Olivier Messiaen, *Olivier Messiaen: Une poétique du merveilleux* (Aix-en-Provence: Alinéa, 1989), 52, 147; Jon Gillock, *Performing Messiaen's Organ Music: 66 Masterclasses* (Bloomington: Indiana University Press, 2010), 22, 327.

50. Messiaen himself self-consciously connected Catholicism and fairy tales in a discussion of the "Marvelous," a key concept in surrealism: "I very much believe that it is because of fairy tales that I became a believer . . . You could say that I passed over without thinking from the surreal of fairy tales to the supernatural of faith" (Massin and Messiaen, *Olivier Messiaen*, 27–28).

51. *La Péri, or The Flower of Immortality* (1912) is a ballet by Paul Dukas, Messiaen's composition teacher. In it, a young man's search for immortality involves interactions with a Peri (i.e., the descendant of a fallen angel in Persian mythology). (Compare the subtitle of *Iolanthe* [1882, Gilbert and Sullivan's "fairy opera"]: *or The Peer and the Peri*.) For *La Péri*'s influence on Messiaen's compositional technique, see Stuart Waumsley, *The Organ Music of Olivier Messiaen* (Paris: Leduc, 1968) 16, 18.

52. "Contre le désordre capitaliste et l'oppression communiste, contre le nationalisme homicide et l'internationalisme impuissant, contre le parlementarisme et le fascisme, *L'Ordre nouveau* met les institutions au service de la personnalité et subordonne l'État à l'homme." *L'Ordre nouveau,* no. 1, May 1933; in Véronique Auzépy-Chavagnac, *Jean de Fabrègues et la jeune droite catholique: Aux sources de la révolution nationale* (Villeneuve-d'Ascq (Nord): Presses universitaires du Septentrion, 2002), 201. Formatting altered to emphasize the character of "neither right nor left."

53. Historian Julian Jackson observes the following: "The most striking phenomenon of the 1930s is that all these various themes of republican renewal no longer exerted any claim on the imagination of the younger generations." The two most significant strands of the "spirit of the 1930s" were "first, an assertion of the 'primacy of the spiritual' (Mounier's *Esprit,* Aron and Dandieu's *Ordre nouveau*) . . . ; secondly, a technocratic disillusion with the ineffectiveness and squalidness of republican government (X-Crise, Coutrot)" (Jackson, "The Long Road to Vichy" [review article], *French History* 12, no. 2 [1998]: 213–24, at 221).

54. Marmion had already made this doctrine the cornerstone of the first book in his trilogy, published in 1919. The first chapter is titled "The Divine Plan of Our Adoptive Predestination in Jesus Christ." See Marmion, *Christ, the Life of the Soul,* trans. Alan Bancroft (Bethesda, Md.: Zaccheus, 2005), 3–36. For theology of the doctrine see *Theōsis: Deification in Christian Theology,* ed. Stephen Finlan and Vladimir Kharlamov (Eugene, Ore.: Pickwick, 2006).

55. Marmion, *Christ in His Mysteries,* 54.

56. Ibid., 57.

57. Ibid., 16. Emphasis added.

58. See translator's note in Marmion, *Christ in His Mysteries,* 16n65: "Marmion's word is *prédestinés,* 'predestined,' but it is important to keep in mind throughout the book that this word, and 'predestination' as Marmion uses it, does not in any way involve a denial of our wills being free to win heaven; not the slightest suggestion that God offers the eternal inheritance to some and not all." For "divinization" and the problem of grace and freedom in Western Christianity, see Karl Rahner, "Grace. III. Structure of

De Gratia," in Karl Rahner, ed., *Encyclopedia of Theology: A Concise Sacramentum Mundi* (New York: Seabury, 1975), 595–98, at 597.

59. Although Marmion does not put this at the center of his work, he nevertheless does not neglect it: "Sanctifying grace is the first and fundamental element of our assimilation to God, of the divine likeness within us. But we must also be the image of our Father by our virtues. Christ Jesus told us this Himself: 'You, therefore, must be perfect, as your heavenly Father is perfect.' [Matt. 5:48] Imitate His goodness, His forbearance, His mercy: it is thus that you will reproduce His features in you. 'Be you,' repeats St. Paul after Jesus, 'imitators of God,' as is fitting for 'very dear children' [Eph. 5:1]" (Marmion, *Christ in His Mysteries*, 56).

60. Translator's note, Marmion, *Christ in His Mysteries*, 16n65.

61. For an alternative comparison of Marmion and Messiaen see the helpful schematic table in Massin and Messiaen, *Olivier Messiaen*, 72. For *Nativité* see Olivier Latry and Loïc Mallié, *L'œuvre d'orgue d'Olivier Messiaen: Œuvres d'avant guerre* (Stuttgart: Carus, 2008), 119–85; Gillock, *Performing*, 49–98.

62. Messiaen's source for "Eternal Designs" (or "Plans"—*Desseins*) is clear: "[The apostle St. Paul was] the one chosen by God to bring to light the 'dispensation of the mystery which has been hidden from eternity in God'; it is in those terms that Paul indicates *the Divine plan* concerning us. We see the great apostle labor without respite to make known *this eternal plan*... Why do all the Apostle's efforts (as Paul takes care to say) aim at enlightening all men about the dispensation of *the Divine designs*?' Opening page of the first chapter in Marmion, *Christ, the Life of the Soul* (2005), 3. Emphases added.

63. Messiaen returned to the doctrine of adoptive filiation in an explicit way in his oratorio, *La transfiguration de notre seigneur Jésus-Christ* (*The Transfiguration*) (1969). See Olivier Messiaen and Claude Samuel, *Music and Color: Conversations with Claude Samuel*, trans. E. Thomas Glasow (Portland, Ore.: Amadeus, 1994), 145.

64. Nigel Simeone, "La Spirale and La Jeune France: Group Identities," *Musical Times* 143, no. 1880 (Autumn 2002): 10–36; Christopher Dingle, *The Life of Messiaen* (New York: Cambridge University Press, 2007), 45.

65. Quoted in Simeone, "Group Identities," 11.

66. Simeone, *Bibliographical Catalogue*, 45, 47.

67. For facsimile see ibid., 46; for another translation see Hill and Simeone, *Messiaen*, 59.

68. La Jeune France manifesto reproduced in Hill and Simeone, *Messiaen*, 63. Program for inaugural concert of La Jeune France, 3 June 1936, reproduced in Simeone, *Bibliographical Catalogue*, 16–17.

69. For this recontextualization of La Jeune France as a musical "nonconformism" within a broader "revolutionary spiritualism" of French youth and musicians, see Jane F. Fulcher, *Composer as Intellectual*, 285–310. Following Fulcher's lead and referring to her work, Philip Nord writes that Jeune France "imagined a France gripped by a 'crisis of civilization.' What the nation needed was a new, spiritual art that, hovering above the earthbound musical partisanship of the day, would uplift and regenerate. From this angle, the Jeune France of 1936 looks much like a musical homologue to the neither-right-nor-left nonconformism espoused by the likes of Emmanuel Mounier, and so it has been argued by the best-informed scholar in the field" (Nord, *France's New Deal: From the Thirties to the Postwar Era* [Princeton, N.J.: Princeton University Press, 2010], 265). See Sylvain Caron and Michel Duchesneau, "La musique et la foi entre les deux guerres: Vers un nouvel humanisme?" in *Musique, art, et religion dans l'entre-deux-guerres*, ed. Sylvain Caron and Michel Duchesneau (Lyon: Symétrie, 2009), 1–11.

70. Maritain, quoted in *Jazz Age Catholicism*, 188.

71. "Mi," the solfège syllable for E, is the highest note reached by a violin. "The top notes, however, are often produced by natural or artificial harmonics. Thus the E two octaves above the open E-string may be considered a practical limit for orchestral violin parts" (Walter Piston, *Orchestration* [New York: Norton, 1955], 45). I am grateful to Peter Bannister for directing me to the significance of this name. Note also that the French word *mie* is an address of love. In his translation of *Romeo and Juliet*, Pierre Messiaen translated Romeo's address to Juliet: "And trust me, love"—as "Ma mie, crois-moi." See Shakespeare, *Romeo and Juliet*, act 3, scene 5, line 58 (Pierre Messiaen, *Oeuvres III*).

72. Simeone, *Bibliographical Catalogue*, 52–55.

73. Olivier Messiaen, "Les deux guerriers" (The Two Warriors), *Poems for Mi*, trans. Felix Aprahamian, in Olivier Messiaen, *Complete Edition*, 32 compact discs, Deutsche Grammophon, 2008, 304–8.

74. *Codex iuris canonici* (1917), 1013, quoted in Robert E. Obach, *The Catholic Church on Marital Intercourse: From St. Paul to Pope John Paul II* (Lanham, Md.: Lexington Books, 2009), 121.

75. See works by Abbé Jean Viollet: *Éducation de la pureté et du sentiment* (Paris: Association du mariage chrétien, 1925); *L'éducation par la famille* (Paris: Association du mariage chrétien, 1926); *Morale familiale* (Paris: Association du mariage chrétien, 1927); *Les devoirs du mariage*, 4th ed. (Paris: Association du mariage chrétien, 1928). See also Viollet et al., *Pour restaurer la famille* (Paris: Éditions de la S.A.P.E., 1927); Viollet and André Lorulot, *L'église et l'amour: Controverse publique entre MM. l'abbé Viollet et André Lorulot* (Herblay [Seine et Oise]: Aux Éditions de "l'idée libre," 1929); Viollet et al., *Eugénisme, stérilisation, leur valeur morale* (Paris: SPES, 1929). For background see Martine Sevegrand, "Limiter les naissances: Le cas de conscience des catholiques français (1880–1939)," *Vingtième siècle: Revue d'histoire* 30 (April–June 1991): 40–54; Sevegrand, *Les enfants du bon Dieu: Les catholiques français et la procréation au XXe siècle* (Paris: Albin Michel, 1995); Martine Sevegrand and Jean Viollet, *L'amour en toutes lettres: Questions à l'abbé Viollet sur la sexualité, 1924–1943* (Paris: Albin Michel, 1996).

76. Dietrich von Hildebrand, *Reinheit und Jungfräulichkeit* (Munich: Kösel und Pustet, 1927); Hildebrand, *Die Ehe* (Munich: Müller, 1929).

77. Shaji George Kochuthara, *The Concept of Sexual Pleasure in the Catholic Moral Tradition* (Rome: Editrice Pontificia Università Gregoriana, 2007), 246–50.

78. See Abbé Jean Viollet: *Le mariage* (Tours: Mame, 1932); *La psychologie du mariage* (Paris: Association du mariage chrétien, 1935); *La loi chrétienne du mariage: Prescriptions et défenses* (Paris: Éditions Mariage et Famille, 1936). See also Viollet et al., *Où en sommes-nous? La doctrine familiale de l'église catholique et le problème du mariage dans les deux mondes* (Paris: Éditions Mariage et Famille, 1932).

79. Dietrich von Hildebrand, *L'amour et le mystère du mariage sacramentel*, trans. Benoît Lavaud (Fribourg, Switzerland: Fragnière Frères, 1936); Hildebrand, *Le mariage* (Paris: Cerf, 1936); Herbert Doms, *Du sens et de la fin du mariage*, 2nd ed., trans. Marie-Simone Thisse and Paul Thisse (Paris: Desclée de Brouwer, 1937); orig. *Vom Sinn und Zweck der Ehe* (1935).

80. Messiaen, "L'épouse" (The Wife), *Poèmes pour Mi*, in *Complete Edition*, 306.

81. Messiaen, "La maison" (The House), *Poèmes pour Mi*, in *Complete Edition*, 305; translation altered.

82. See Suzanne Pagé, *Années 30 en Europe: Le temps menaçant 1929–1939: Exposition du 20 février au 25 mai 1997, Musée d'art moderne de la ville de Paris* (Paris: Paris musées; Flammarion, 1997); Elena Filipovic, "Surrealism in 1938: The Exhibition at War," in *Surrealism, Politics and Culture*, ed. Raymond Spiteri and Donald LaCoss (Burlington, Vt.: Ashgate, 2003), 179–203; Steven Harris, *Surrealist Art and Thought in the 1930s: Art, Politics, and the Psyche* (New York: Cambridge University Press, 2004); Johanna Malt, *Obscure Objects of Desire: Surrealism, Fetishism, and Politics* (New York: Oxford University Press, 2004); Anne Umland et al., *Joan Miró: Painting and Anti-Painting 1927–1937* (New York: Museum of Modern Art; Distributed Art Publishers, 2008).

83. Messiaen, "Autour d'une œuvre d'orgue" (Around an Organ Work) (April 1939), in Stephen Broad, *Olivier Messiaen: Journalism 1935–1939* (Surrey, UK: Ashgate, 2012), French 73–74; English 134–35.

84. Olivier Messiaen, *Chants de terre et de ciel: Soprano et piano* (Paris: Durand, 1939). Composed in the summer of 1938. Simeone, *Bibliographical Catalogue*, 62–63. As Peter Manchester observes, "Christianity is a religion *about* time." See Manchester, "Time in Christianity," in *Religion and Time*, ed. Anindita Niyogi Balslev and Jitendranath Mohanty (Leiden: Brill, 1993), 109–37, at 109; see Begbie, *Theology, Music and Time*. For general overviews, see Eugen Weber, *Apocalypses: Prophecies, Cults, and Millennial Beliefs Through the Ages* (Cambridge, Mass.: Harvard University Press, 1999); Ulrich H. J. Körtner, *The End of the World: A Theological Interpretation* (Louisville, Ky.: Westminster/John Knox Press, 1995); Stephen D. O'Leary, *Arguing the Apocalypse: A Theory of Millennial Rhetoric* (New York: Oxford University Press, 1994). For Catholic apocalypticism in modern times, see Giovanni Filoramo, "Memory and the Metamorphosis of Apocalyptic Time in an Italian Millenarian Movement: The Case of Davide Lazzaretti and His Followers," in *Apocalyptic Time*, ed. Albert I. Baumgarten (Boston: Brill, 2000), 363–72. Messiaen's most direct statement about his firm beliefs in prophecies are found in his preface to Albert Roustit, *La prophétie musicale dans l'histoire de l'humanité* (Roanne: Horvath, 1970), translated as Messiaen,

preface to Roustit, *Prophecy in Music: Prophetic Parallels in Musical History*, trans. Dr. John A. Green (Paris: Imprimerie D. K., 1975).

85. Olivier Messiaen (from Petichet) letter to unidentified recipient, 7 August 1939, Carlton Lake Collection of French Manuscripts, Harry Ransom Center, The University of Texas at Austin, 186.1. I am grateful to the Harry Ransom Center for its kind permission to consult these documents. About the fifth point, Messiaen added: "This work, being long and complex, absolutely must have this commentary, especially if you take into account the fact that it will be sung in French for an audience that is international and *Italian* in particular." The *Chants de terre et de ciel* were to be sung by Marcelle Bunlet, with Messiaen accompanying at the piano. See also Hill and Simeone, *Messiaen*, 85.

86. Simeone, *Bibliographical Catalogue*, 64–67; Gillock, *Performing*, 99–142; Latry and Mallié, *L'œuvre d'orgue*, 187–230. In translating "glorieux" as "glorified" and not "glorious" I am following the common translation of Thomas Aquinas's discussions of "glorified bodies."

87. Massin and Messiaen, *Olivier Messiaen*, 31.

88. The discussion of "glorified bodies" in the *Summa theologica*, found in questions 82–85 of the "Supplement to the Third Part," was probably not written by Aquinas himself. The editor of the English translation notes: "The remainder of the Summa Theologica, known as the Supplement, was compiled probably by his companion and friend Fra Rainaldo da Piperno, and was gathered from St. Thomas's commentary on the Fourth Book of the Sentences of Peter Lombard." All of the quotations here were taken from *The "Summa Theologica" of St. Thomas Aquinas* [*ST*], translated by Dominicans of the English Province, 22 vols., 2d rev. ed. (London: Burns, Oates and Washbourne, 1920–42). For Aquinas's parallel writings on this topic, see also Saint Thomas Aquinas and Sandra Edwards, *Quodlibetal Questions 1 and 2* (Toronto: Pontifical Institute of Mediaeval Studies, 1983).

89. Messiaen, review of Tournemire in *La syrinx* (May 1938): 26–27, at 27.

90. What Aquinas says is:

> Of those four gifts, *clarity* alone is a quality of the very person in himself; whereas the other three are not perceptible, save in some action or movement, or in some passion. Christ, then, did show in Himself certain indications of those three gifts—of *agility*, for instance, when He walked on the waves of the sea; of *subtlety*, when He came forth from the closed womb

> of the Virgin; of *impassibility*, when He escaped unhurt from the hands of the Jews who wished to hurl Him down or to stone Him. And yet He is not said, on account of this, to be transfigured, but only on account of *clarity*, which pertains to the aspect of His Person. (Aquinas, *ST*, IIIa, q. 45, a. 1, reply to the third objection; emphases added)

91. Thomas Aquinas, *ST*, Suppl., q. 82: "The impassibility of the bodies of the blessed after their resurrection."

92. Ibid., a. 1: "Whether the bodies of the saints will be impassible after the resurrection?"

93. Ibid., a. 4: "Whether in the blessed, after the resurrection, all the senses will be in act?" For background, see Robert Edward Brennan, *Thomistic Psychology: A Philosophic Analysis of the Nature of Man* (New York: Macmillan, 1941).

94. Apocalypse (Revelation) 8:4 (Douay-CCD); compare *La Bible Fillion*: "Et la fumée des parfums monta, avec les prières des saints, de la main de l'Ange devant Dieu."

95. Aquinas, *ST*, Suppl., q. 82, a. 4. Aquinas is presumably referring to 2 Corinthians 2:14–16 and Ephesians 5:2.

96. Ibid.

97. Ibid, q. 83, a. 1: "Whether subtlety is a property of the glorified body?"

98. Ibid.

99. Ibid., a. 4: "Whether one glorified body can be in the same place together with another glorified body?"

100. Ibid., a. 1.

101. Ibid., q. 84, a. 1: "Whether the glorified bodies will be agile?"

102. Ibid., a. 2: "Whether the saints will never use their agility for the purpose of movement?"

103. Ibid.

104. Ibid., a. 3: "Whether the movement of the saints will be instantaneous?"

105. Ibid.

106. Ibid., reply to objection 5.

107. See Messiaen's "Author's Notes" for Vision 7 ("Amen of the Consummation"), *Visions de l'amen*, n.p. Messiaen's mistaken attribution comes from following Dom Marmion's commentary; see discussion in Schloesser, *Visions of Amen*, 435–39.

108. Aquinas, *ST*, Suppl., q. 85, a. 1: "Whether clarity is becoming to the glorified body?"

109. Ibid., a. 2: "Whether the clarity of the glorified body is visible to the non-glorified eye?"

110. Apocalypse (Revelation) 21:18–19; cf. 4:3 and 21:11.

111. Marmion, chapter 15, *Christ in His Mysteries*, 328–46, at 344. Emphasis added.

112. The story lends itself to popular recollections. See Rebecca Rischin, *For the End of Time: The Story of the Messiaen Quartet* (Ithaca, N.Y.: Cornell University Press, 2003); John William McMullen, *The Miracle of Stalag 8A: Beauty Beyond the Horror: Olivier Messiaen and the Quartet for the End of Time* (Evansville, Ind.: Bird Brain, 2010); Jen Bryant, *Music for the End of Time*, illustrated by Beth Peck (Grand Rapids, Mich.: Eerdmans Books for Young Readers, 2005). For an accessible analysis see Anthony Pople, *Messiaen: Quatuor pour la fin du temps*, Cambridge Music Handbooks (New York: Cambridge University Press, 1998).

113. The verb *émerveiller* does not translate easily into English; it means that the eyes are altered or filled with "marvel" in the same way that they might be filled with brightness or light ("brightened" or "enlightened," hence, "emarveled"). Note the same root in *émerveiller* and *le merveilleux* ("the marvelous")—the key concept for the surrealists (see Pierre Mabille, *Mirror of the Marvelous: The Classic Surrealist Work on Myth*, trans. Jody Gladding [Rochester, Vt.: Inner Traditions, 1998]; originally Pierre Mabille, *Le miroir du merveilleux* [Paris: Sagittaire, 1940]) and for Messiaen himself. "The Marvelous is my natural climate, at the breast of which I feel good. I have experienced the need to live a Marvelous, *but a Marvelous that might be true*!" Messiaen, in Massin and Messiaen, *Oliver Messiaen*, 27, emphasis added; see Messiaen and Samuel, *Music and Color*, 26.

114. Messiaen and Samuel, *Music and Color*, 233.

115. Massin and Messiaen, *Olivier Messiaen*, 94.

116. Olivier Messiaen, in Messiaen and Claude Samuel, *Conversations with Messiaen*, trans. Felix Aprahamian (London: Stainer & Bell, 1976), 6, 7, emphasis original; orig. Olivier Messiaen and Claude Samuel, *Entretiens avec Olivier Messiaen* (Paris: Belfond, 1967). See Messiaen and Samuel, *Music and Color*, 26; Dingle, *Life of Messiaen*, 36.

7. Rethinking the Modernity of Bernanos: A Girardian Perspective

Brian Sudlow

1. Michel Estève, "Bernanos et la guerre d'Espagne: Le témoin de l'Evangile," in *Georges Bernanos, témoin*, ed. Pierrette Renard (Toulouse: Presses universitaires du Mirail, 1994), 75–86.

2. Pierrette Renard, "Les *Écrits de combat* et la controverse sur la modernité," in *Études bernanosiennes 21: Bernanos et la modernité*, ed. Michel Estève (Paris: Lettres modernes minard, 1998), 73–144.

3. Claire Daudin, *Dieu a-t-il besoin de l'écrivain? Péguy, Bernanos, Mauriac* (Paris: Cerf, 2009).

4. François Richard, *L'anarchisme de droite dans la littérature contemporaine* (Paris: Presses universitaires françaises, 1988).

5. Brian Sudlow, "Bernanos's Political Vision: Continuity or Rupture in *Les grands cimetières sous la lune*" (master's thesis, University of Nottingham, 2003).

6. Jacques Chabot, "Notice sur *Nous autres Français*," in *Essais et écrits de combat*, ed. Michel Estève et al. vol. 2 (Paris: Gallimard, 1971), 1536.

7. René Girard, *Mensonge romantique et vérité romanesque* (Paris: Grasset, 1961); *La violence et le sacré* (1972) (Paris: Hachette, 2008); *Le bouc émissaire* (Paris: Grasset, 1982).

8. Renard, "Les *Écrits de combat*," 82.

9. Ibid., 121.

10. Ibid., 123–28.

11. Ibid., 139.

12. David Lowenthal, *The Past Is a Foreign Country* (Cambridge: Cambridge University Press, 1985).

13. Andrew Greeley, *The Catholic Imagination* (Berkeley: University of California Press, 2001).

14. Renard, "Les *Écrits de combat*," 76.

15. Max Milner, *Georges Bernanos* (Paris: Desclée de Brouwer, 1967), 55.

16. Léon Bloy, *Exegèse des lieux communs*, in *Œuvres* VIII, ed. Jacques Petit (1902 and 1913; Paris: Mercure de France 1968), 306.

17. Bernanos to Charles Maurras, 21 May 1932, in *Essais et écrits de combat*, ed. Estève et al., 1258.

18. Bernanos, *Les grands cimetières sous la lune* (1938), in *Essais et écrits de combat*, ed. Estève et al., 364.

19. Bernanos, *Journal d'un curé de campagne* (1936), in *Œuvres romanesques*, ed. Albert Béguin et al. (Paris: Gallimard, 1961), 1258; Bernanos, *Diary of a Country Priest*, trans. Pamela Morris (New York: Image Books, 1974), 231.

20. Renard, "Les *Écrits de combat*," 139.

21. Charles Taylor, *A Secular Age* (Harvard, Mass.: Harvard University Press, 2007), 37–41.

22. Sven Storelv, "Remarques sur le mythe du déclin du monde," 125–38, and "Bernanos, Discours pamphlétaire et discours apocalyptique," 147–56, in Sven Storelv, *Péguy, Bernanos*, ed. Reidar Veland (Oslo: Solum Forag A/S, 1993).

23. Storelv, "Remarques sur le mythe," 128.

24. Storelv, "Bernanos, Discours pamphlétaire et discours apocalyptique," 151.

25. Julia Kovacs and Christopher Rowland, in collaboration with Rebekah Callow, *Revelation: The Apocalypse of Jesus Christ* (Malden, Mass.: Blackwell, 2004), 13–38.

26. Bernanos, *Nouvelle histoire de Mouchette* (1937), in *Œuvres romanesques*, ed. Béguin et al., 1276; Bernanos, *Mouchette*, trans. J. C. Whitehouse (New York: Holt, Rinehart and Winston, 1966), 23.

27. Bernanos, *Monsieur Ouine* (1946), in *Œuvres romanesques*, ed. Béguin et al., 1360–61; Bernanos, *Monsieur Ouine*, trans. William S. Bush (Lincoln: University of Nebraska Press, 2000), 14–15.

28. René Girard, *Achever Clausewitz: Entretiens avec Benoît Chantre* (Paris: Carnets Nord, [1968] 2007).

29. Girard, *Mensonge romantique et vérité romanesque* (Paris: Grasset, 1961), translated as *Deceit, Desire and the Novel: Self and Other in Literary Structures* by Yvonne Freccero (Baltimore: Johns Hopkins University Press, 1966).

30. Girard, *La violence et le sacré* (Paris: Hachette 1972).

31. Paul Delvaux, "Monsieur Ouine: While awaiting his return . . . ," *Renascence* 41, nos. 1 and 2 (Fall 1988–Winter 1989): 99–106.

32. Bernanos, *Nous autres Français* (1939), in *Essais et écrits de combat*, ed. Estève et al., 659–60.

33. Ibid., 632.

34. Ibid., 633.

35. Bernanos, *La grande peur des bien-pensants* (1931), in *Œuvres romanesques*, ed. Béguin et al., 314–50.

36. Bernanos, *Nous autres Français*, 713.

37. Girard, *La violence et le sacré*, 248.

38. Girard, *Des choses cachées depuis la fondation du monde* (Paris: Grasset, 2007), 62–64.

39. Bernanos, *Nous autres Français*, 713.

40. Ibid., 654.

41. Ibid., 713–14.

42. Girard, *Le bouc émissaire.*

43. Girard, *Mensonge romantique.*

44. Bernanos, *Nous autres Français*, 718.

45. Ibid., 675.

46. Girard, *Celui par qui le scandale arrive: Entretiens avec Maria Stella Barberi* (Paris: Desclée de Brouwer, 2001).

47. Bernanos, *Scandale de la vérité* (1939), in *Essais et écrits de combat*, ed. Estève et al., 595–96.

48. Girard, *Des choses cachées.*

49. Bernanos, *Scandale de la vérité*, 603.

50. Bernanos, *Monsieur Ouine*, 135; Eng. trans., 3.

51. Renard, "Les *Écrits de combat* et la controverse sur la modernité."

52. Bernanos, *Les enfants humiliés* (1949), in *Essais et écrits de combat*, ed. Estève et al., 811.

53. Ibid., 792. Emphasis added.

54. Ibid., 799.

55. Girard, *Le bouc emissaire.*

56. Ibid., 838.

57. Ibid., 837.

58. Ibid., 805.

59. Bernanos, *Les enfants humiliés*, 792.

60. Ibid., 855.

61. Raymund Schwager, *Must There Be Scapegoats? Violence and Redemption in the Bible* (London: Harper and Row [1978], 1987).

62. Renard, *Georges Bernanos, témoin*; Monique Gosselin and Max Milner, *Bernanos et le monde moderne* (Lille: Presses universitaires de Lille, 1989).

8. "Into the Catacombs of the Past": Women and Wartime Trauma in the French Catholic *Ressourcement* Project (1939–45)

Brenna Moore

1. Marie-Madeleine Davy, *Traversée en solitaire* (Paris: Albin Michel, 1989), 31.

2. For more on Davy's role in the Resistance see Margaret L. Rossiter, *Women in the Resistance* (New York: Praeger, 1985), 111; Marc-Alain Descamps and Jacques d'Ares, *Marie-Magdeleine Davy, ou la liberté du dépassement* (Paris: Le Miel de la Pierre, 2001).

3. Davy, *Traversée en solitaire*, 34.

4. Ibid., 82–83.

5. Ibid., 37.

6. For three other excellent analyses exploring the power that Christian premodernity exerted in twentieth-century France for a range of political and theological purposes, see Mark Antliff, *Avant-Garde Fascism: The Mobilization of Myth, Art, and Culture in France, 1909–1939* (Durham, N.C.: Duke University Press, 2007); Bruce Holsinger, *The Premodern Condition: Medievalism and the Making of Theory* (Chicago: University of Chicago Press, 2005); Amy Hollywood, *Sensible Ecstasy: Mysticism, Sexual Difference, and the Demands of History* (Chicago: University of Chicago, 2003); Romy Golan, *Modernity and Nostalgia: Art and Politics in France Between the Wars* (New Haven, Conn.: Yale University Press, 1995).

7. For a useful overview of the history of *la nouvelle théologie*, see Jürgen Mettepenningen, *Nouvelle Théologie–New Theology: Inheritor of Modernism, Precursor of Vatican II* (London: Continuum, 2010); Étienne Fouilloux, *Une église en quête de liberté: La pensée catholique française entre modernisme et Vatican II, 1914–1962* (Paris: Desclée de Brouwer, 1998); Brian Daly, "The *Nouvelle théologie* and the Patristic Revival: Sources, Symbols, and the Science of Theology," *International Journal of Systematic Theology* 7 (2005): 362–82.

8. On issues of politics, religion, and subjectivity that have influenced my own thinking see Saba Mahmood, *Politics of Piety: The Islamic Revival and the Feminist Subject* (Princeton, N.J.: Princeton University Press, 2004), 32–34, 192–99.

9. Recent, and otherwise excellent, books on ressourcement do not include the contributions of any women: Mettepenningen, *Nouvelle*

Théologie–New Theology, and Hans Boersma, *Nouvelle Théologie and Sacramental Ontology: A Return to Mystery* (Oxford: Oxford University Press, 2009). For information on Davy, see d'Ares, *Marie-Magdeleine Davy, ou la liberté du dépassement;* on d'Alverny, see Charles Burnett, "Marie-Thérèse d'Alverny," in *Women Medievalists and the Academy*, ed. Jane Chance (Madison: University of Wisconsin Press, 2005); for Raïssa Maritain, see Brenna Moore, *Sacred Dread: Raïssa Maritain, the Allure of Suffering, and the French Catholic Revival (1905–1945)* (South Bend, Ind.: University of Notre Dame Press, 2012).

10. For a parallel argument that has influenced my own on women's scholarship and the discipline of history, see Bonnie Smith, *The Gender of History: Men, Women, and Historical Practice* (Cambridge, Mass.: Harvard University Press, 1998).

11. Philip Daileader and Philip Whalen, eds., *French Historians 1900–2000: New Historical Writing in Twentieth-Century France* (London: Wiley, 2010), xix.

12. Quoted in Étienne Gilson, *The Mystical Theology of St. Bernard*, trans. A. H. C. Downes (Collegeville, Minn.: Cistercian Publications, 1990), xiv.

13. Davy, *Traversée en solitaire*, 99.

14. Henri de Lubac, *History and Spirit: The Understanding of Scripture According to Origen*, trans. Anne Nash (San Francisco: Ignatius Press, 2007), 446.

15. Henri de Lubac, *Paradoxes of Faith*, trans. Simon P. Kreilkamp (San Francisco: Ignatius Press, 1987), 104.

16. Raïssa Maritain, "Léon Bloy's Columbus," *Commonweal* 36, no. 26 (16 October 1942): 606, 610.

17. Raïssa Maritain, "Léon Bloy: Master of Paradox," *Commonweal* 55, no. 7 (25 May 1951): 161.

18. For an analysis of memory and inculcating the experience of Christ, see Mary Carruthers, *The Book of Memory: A Study of Memory in Medieval Culture* (New York: Cambridge University Press, 1990).

19. In addition to Davy's own account of events in *Traversée en solitaire*, see Descamps and d'Ares, *Marie-Magdeleine Davy*, 88.

20. Among the most significant of these volumes are Davy's *Guillaume de Saint-Thierry: Meditativae orationes* (Paris: Vrin, 1934); *Un traité de la vie solitaire: Epistola ad fratres de Monte-Dei. Guillaume de Saint-Thierry* (Paris:

Vrin, 1940); *Bernard de Clairvaux, Saint Bernard* (Paris: Aubier, 1945); *Guillaume de Saint-Thierry: Deux traités de l'amour de Dieu* (Paris: Vrin, 1953); and *Guillaume de Saint-Thierry: Commentaires sur le Cantique des Cantiques* (Paris: Vrin, 1958).

21. Descamps and d'Ares, *Marie-Magdeleine Davy*, 44.

22. Davy, *Traversée en solitaire*, 99.

23. Henri de Lubac, "Letter to My Superiors," in *Theology in History* (San Francisco: Ignatius Press, 1996), 433. See also his *Christian Resistance to Anti-Semitism: Memories from 1940–1944* (San Francisco: Ignatius Press, 1990), 112.

24. Renée Bédarida and François Bédarida, *La résistance spirituelle, 1941–1944: Les cahiers clandestins du "Témoignage chrétien"* (Paris: Albin Michel, 2001), 44.

25. Davy, *Simone Weil* (Paris: Éditions universitaires, 1956), 68.

26. Davy, *Traversée en solitaire*, 110.

27. Davy, *Simone Weil*, 55.

28. For a very useful exploration of de Lubac's postwar stature at Lyon see Étienne Fouilloux, Bernard Hours, and Dominique Avon, *Les Jésuites à Lyon, XVIe–XXe siècle* (Lyon: ENS Éditions, 2005), 124–46, 231–45.

29. Henri de Lubac, *At the Service of the Church: Henri de Lubac Reflects on the Circumstances That Occasioned His Writing* (San Francisco: Ignatius Press, 1993), 50.

30. Ibid., 29.

31. Henri de Lubac, "Internal Causes of the Weakening and Disappearance of the Sense of the Sacred," in *Theology in History*, trans. Anne Nash (San Francisco: Ignatius Press, 1996), 223–40.

32. For a fuller account of Raïssa Maritain in English, see Brenna Moore, *Sacred Dread: Raïssa Maritain, the Allure of Suffering, and the French Catholic Revival, 1905–1945* (Notre Dame, Ind.: University of Notre Dame Press, 2013).

33. Roger Aubert, *La théologie catholique au milieu du XXe siècle* (Tournai: Casterman, 1954); R. C. Grogin, *The Bergsonian Controversy in France, 1900–1914* (Calgary: University of Calgary Press, 1988).

34. Raïssa Maritain, *Des mœurs divines: Opuscule attribué à Saint Thomas d'Aquin* [a translation of Aquinas] (Paris: Pouart, 1921); Maritain, *Les dons du*

Saint-Esprit: Traité de Jean de Saint-Thomas, trans. from Latin to French, with a preface by Réginald Garrigou-Lagrange, OP (Juvisy: Cerf, 1920).

35. Raïssa Maritain, "Est-il pour nous 'De la plus grande utilité de connaître les grâces dont nous sommes favorisés'"? *La vie spirituelle* 65, XI (5 February 1925).

36. Raïssa Maritain to Charles Journet, 24 January 1940, *Correspondance Journet-Maritain,* ed. René Mougel (Paris: Éditions Saint-Augustin, 2006), 3:42.

37. Jacques Maritain to Charles Journet, 6 May 1940, ibid., 3:68.

38. Raïssa Maritain, *Les grandes amitiés,* in Jacques Maritain et Raïssa Maritain, *Œuvres completes* (Paris: Éditions Universitaires, 1982–2000), vol. 14.

39. Ibid., 625–26.

40. Journet to Raïssa Maritain, 10 September 1940, *Correspondance Journet-Maritain,* vol. 3:60. This advice was bolstered by Journet's characteristic encouragement of Raïssa's writing: "Oh, [writing] your memoirs is such a good idea! I have always thought that you should have a journal, Raïssa, so you are able to talk about things that are not known or that we forget. And it would bring a dear light on the past."

41. Maritain, *Les grandes amitiés,* 743.

42. Ibid., 710.

43. Ibid.

44. Ibid., 722.

45. Walter Benjamin, "Theses on the Philosophy of History," in *Illuminations,* trans. Harry Zohn, ed. and with an introduction by Hannah Arendt (New York: Shocken, 1968), 257–58.

46. Smith, *Gender of History,* 12.

47. Ibid.

48. Léon Bloy, *La femme pauvre* (Paris: Mercure de France, 1897), 33.

49. Maritain, *Les grandes amitiés,* 721.

50. Marie-Madeleine Davy, *Aimer toutes les mains* (Angers-Paris: Au Masque d'Or, 1947), 2.

51. Ibid.

52. See the chapter "Retribution" in Tony Judt, *Postwar: A History of Europe Since 1945* (New York: Penguin, 2005), 41–62.

53. Davy, quoted in Descamps and d'Ares, *Marie-Magdeleine Davy,* 33.

54. See M.-M. Davy, *Henri Le Saux, Swami Abhishiktananda, le passeur entre deux rives* (Paris: Cerf, 1981).

55. Eric Edelmann, "L'instant ultime: Entretien avec Marie-Madeleine Davy," *Revue question de* 36 (May–June 1980): 5.

56. *Encyclopédie des mystiques*, vol. 1, *Chamanisme, Grecs, Juifs, Gnose, Christianisme primitif*; vol. 2, *Christianisme occidental, ésotérisme, protestantisme, islam*; vol. 3, *Égypte, Mésopotamie, Iran, hindouisme*; vol. 4, *Bouddhismes tibétain, chinois, japonais, Yi-King, tch'an, zen* (Paris: Payot, 1996, Petite Bibliothèque Payot).

57. Elizabeth Ezra, *The Colonial Unconscious: Race and Culture in Interwar France* (Ithaca, N.Y.: Cornell University Press, 2000). Michel Bressolette also makes this point in his preface to *Correspondance Maurice Sachs/Jacques et Raïssa Maritain, 1925–1938* (Paris: Gallimard, 2004), 9–11.

58. Stephen Schloesser, "Against Forgetting: Memory, History, Vatican II," *Theological Studies* 67 (2006): 275–319.

59. Edward Said, *Representations of the Intellectual* (New York: Random House, 1994), 37–40.

60. Marie-Madeleine Davy, "Le thème de la vengeance au moyen âge," in *La vengeance*: *Études d'ethnologie, d'histoire et de philosophie*, ed. R. Verdier (Paris: Éditions Cujas, 1984).

61. Charles Burnett, "Marie-Thérèse d'Alverny," in *Women Medievalists and the Academy*, ed. Jane Chance (Madison: University of Wisconsin Press, 2005).

62. Gilles Constable, "Marie-Thérèse d'Alverny (25 January 1903–26 April 1991)," *Proceedings of the American Philosophical Society*, 136, no. 3 (September 1992): 418–42. See Laurence K. Shook, *Étienne Gilson* (Toronto: Pontifical Institute of Mediaeval Studies, 1984), 44. D'Alverny also held a serious of prestigious grants and visiting appointments, including several in the United States at Berkeley and Columbia, and was awarded an honorary doctorate at Smith College in 1984.

63. For her full bibliography, see *Archives d'histoire doctrinale et littéraire du moyen âge* 149 (1991): 279–89.

64. Marie-Thérèse d'Alverny, "Deux traductions latines du Coran au moyen âge,"*Archives d'histoire doctrinale et littéraire du moyen âge*, 22–23 (1947–48): 69–131.

65. Ibid., 111.

66. Marie-Thérèse d'Alverny, "Translations and Translators," in *Renaissance and Renewal in the Twelfth Century*, ed. Robert Pouis Benson et al. (Toronto: University of Toronto Press, 1991), 429.

67. Marie-Thérèse d'Alverny, "Comment les théologiens et les philosophes voient la femme," *Cahiers de civilisation médiévale* 20 (1977): 105–29. Raïssa Maritain was the least likely among them to critique the tradition—note her sense at her conversion that the church was the "most perfect, like an immense pyramid of light, that enlightens all those at its base—the small, the humble, the simple, children . . . it is perfect; it is beautiful, there is not a single dark spot." Raïssa Maritain, "Récit de ma conversion" [1909], *Œuvres complètes*, vol. 15:827–34.

68. Marie-Thérèse d'Alverny, "Translations and Translators," 430.

69. Maritain, *Les grandes amitiés*, 637.

70. Raïssa Maritain, *Histoire d'Abraham ou la sainteté dans l'état de nature*, in Jacques Maritain et Raïssa Maritain, *Œuvres complètes*, vol. 14:568–617.

71. Ibid., 583n8.

72. Davy, *Traversée en solitaire*, 111.

73. Ibid.

74. Ibid., 57.

75. Ibid., 111.

76. Descamps and d'Ares, *Marie-Magdeleine Davy*, 22. For a useful overview of gender and higher education in this context see Toril Moi, *Simone de Beauvoir: The Making of an Intellectual Woman* (Oxford: Oxford University Press, 2008), 23–27.

77. Raïssa Maritain, *Journal*, in *Œuvres complètes*, vol. 15:275.

78. Raïssa Maritain to Pierre and Christine van der Meer de Walcheren, 9 April 1938, in *Le repentir: Déclaration de l'église de France* (Paris: Desclée de Brouwer, 1997), 38–41.

79. Marie d'Alverny to Gilles Constable, quoted in Constable, "Marie-Thérèse d'Alverny."

80. To be sure, for each of these women there were more allies than obstacles. For Davy, even at the Institut catholique, she had a close friend and confidant in the priest and scholar Rémy Pasteau (she names him as the only one that spoke to her). Pasteau was tragically killed in 1940 carrying a wounded solider on his back. To Raïssa Maritain, Charles Journet offered continual encouragement on her writing ("Of course you

must keep going!" he urged her in the midst of one of her books), and his publishing house in Switzerland printed her first works. Jean Cocteau encouraged her poetry ("You are a great poet"), praising her even before she had published anything. Jacques was of course single-handedly responsible for establishing her posthumous legacy. D'Alverny could count Étienne Gilson, Henri de Lubac, and M.-D. Chenu as allies and friends.

81. Michel Foucault, "Maurice Blanchot: The Thought from Outside," in Maurice Blanchot and Michel Foucault, *Foucault/Blanchot* (New York: Zone Books, 1987), quoted in Michel de Certeau, *Heterologies: Discourse on the Other* (St. Paul: University of Minnesota Press, 1998), 182.

82. Charles Péguy, quoted in Yves Congar, *Tradition and Traditions* (San Francisco: Ignatius Press, 2001), 9. Péguy used the word in *Les cahiers de la quinzaine*, 9th cahier, 6th series (24 January 1905).

83. Mark Antliff, *Avant-Garde Fascism: The Mobilization of Myth, Art, and Culture in France, 1909–1939* (Durham, N.C.: Duke University Press, 2007); see also Romy Golan, *Modernity and Nostalgia* (New Haven, Conn.: Yale University Press, 1995).

84. Jay Winter, *Sites of Memory, Sites of Mourning: The Great War in European Cultural History* (Cambridge: Cambridge University Press, 1998), 222.

85. Friedrich Nietzsche, "On the Use and Abuse of History for Life," in *The Portable Nietzsche*, trans. Walter Kaufmann (New York: Penguin, 1977), 222.

9. *La Relève* and Its Afterlife: A Current of Catholic Renewal in Twentieth-Century Quebec

Joseph Dunlop

I am indebted to Dr. Katherine Davies and Dr. Toby Garfitt for kindly inviting me to participate in this project. I would also like to express my appreciation to Dr. Martin Conway and Dr. Davies for their helpful comments on earlier drafts of this chapter, as well as to the editorial staff at Fordham University Press, whose close reading of the text has resulted in a markedly improved final product. Dr. Garfitt meticulously and expertly translated the many French quotations into English, and Dr. Andrew Gann generously provided additional translation assistance. In addition, I am grateful to André Biron and Anne Hurtubise, who granted me permission to quote from the letters and other papers of Claude Hurtubise, as well as to the Charbonneau family, who allowed me to quote from the letters of Robert Charbonneau. Finally, I would like to thank André Charbonneau, who graciously agreed to be interviewed for this project.

This research was made possible by a Doctoral Fellowship from the Social Sciences and Humanities Research Council of Canada and by a William and Nona Heaslip Trinity-St. Antony's Scholarship from the Heaslip Foundation. I would also like to acknowledge the support of Emmanuel College in the University of Toronto, which provided me with a Visiting Research Fellowship in 2013–14.

1. There are a number of important studies of *La Relève*, including Stéphanie Angers and Gérard Fabre, *Échanges intellectuels entre la France et le Québec (1930–2000): Les réseaux de la revue* Esprit *avec* La Relève, Cité Libre, Parti Pris *et* Possibles (Quebec: Les Presses de l'Université Laval, 2004); André J. Bélanger, *Ruptures et constantes: Quatre idéologies du Québec en éclatement: La Relève, La JEC, Cité Libre, Parti Pris* (Montreal: Hurtubise HMH, 1977); Michel Biron, *L'Absence du maître: Saint-Denys Garneau, Ferron, Ducharme* (Montreal: Les Presses de l'Université de Montréal, 2000), chap. 2; Jean-Charles Falardeau, "La génération de *la Relève*," *Recherches sociographiques* 6, no. 2 (1965): 123–33; Yvan Lamonde, *La modernité au Québec*, vol. 1, *La crise de l'homme et de l'esprit* (Montreal: Fides, 2011); Yvan Lamonde, "*La Relève* (1934–1939), Maritain et la crise spirituelle des années 1930," *Les cahiers des dix* 62 (2008): 153–94; Jacques Pelletier, "*La Relève*: Une génération des années trente," *Voix et images du pays* 5, no. 1 (1972): 69–139; Hélène Poulin, "*La Relève*: Analyse et témoignages" (master's thesis, McGill University, 1968).

2. Studies of the role of Catholicism in Quebec's "Quiet Revolution" of the 1960s and '70s include the following: Gregory Baum, *The Church in Quebec* (Ottawa: Novalis, 1991); Michael D. Behiels, *Prelude to Quebec's Quiet Revolution: Liberalism Versus Neo-Nationalism, 1945–1960* (Kingston-Montreal: McGill-Queen's Press, 1985); Michael Gauvreau, *The Catholic Origins of Quebec's Quiet Revolution, 1931–1970* (Kingston-Montreal: McGill-Queen's Press, 2005); E. Martin Meunier and Jean-Philippe Warren, *Sortir de la "Grande noirceur": L'horizon "personnaliste" de la Révolution tranquille* (Sillery: Les Éditions du Septentrion, 2002).

3. Paul Beaulieu, "1930–1940: Sortir de l'ornière," *Écrits du Canada français* 52 (1984): 57–65 [hereafter cited as *ECF*]; Beaulieu, "Re-découvrir Robert Élie," in *Robert Élie: Œuvres*, ed. Beaulieu (Montreal: Hurtubise HMH, 1979), i–v; Robert Charbonneau, *Chronique de l'âge amer* (Ottawa: Éditions du Sablier, 1967); Gérard Godin, "Robert Élie: Vis d'abord, on verra après," *Le magazine Maclean* 4, no. 11 (November 1964): 102; Jean Le Moyne, "Saint-Denys Garneau's Testimony For His Times," in *Convergence*, trans. Philip Stratford (Toronto: Ryerson Press, 1966), 199–220.

4. Gilles Marcotte, "Les années trente: De Monseigneur Camille à *la Relève*," *Voix et images* 5, no. 3 (1980): 523–24. See also Gilles Marcotte, "Jean Le Moyne, le magnifique," and "En votre aimable règlement . . . (Claude Hurtubise)," in *La littérature est inutile* (Quebec: Éditions du Boréal, 2009), 169–73, 174–77.

5. Jean Louis-Gagnon, *Les apostasies*, vol. 1, *Les coqs de village* (Montreal: La Presse, 1985), 67; Paul-André Linteau et al., *Quebec Since 1930*, trans. Robert Chodos and Ellen Garmaise (Toronto: Lorimer, 1991), 82.

6. For a detailed study of the classical college curriculum, with a particular emphasis on the Collège Sainte-Marie, see Catherine Pomeyrols, *Les intellectuels québécois: Formation et engagements, 1919–1939* (Paris-Montreal: L'Harmattan, 1996), 70–130.

7. Stéphane Gauthier, "Trois petites revues des années 30: *Opinions, Nous, Vivre*," in *Le rébus des revues: Revues cachées et petites revues*, ed. Jacques Beaudry (Quebec: Presses de l'Université Laval, 1998), 35–41. Copies of *Nous* can be located in the fonds Georges d'Auteuil and the fonds Collège Sainte-Marie at the Archives of the Jesuits of Canada, Montreal.

8. Paul Beaulieu, "Notes sur le scoutisme catholique," *La Relève* 2, no. 3 (November 1935): 89–93; Beaulieu, *Aperçus d'un scout sur la Pologne et la France* (Montreal: Fédération des Scouts catholiques de la province de Québec, 1940).

9. Beaulieu, *Aperçus d'un scout sur la Pologne et la France*, 9–20.

10. For studies of Jeune-Canada, see Denis Chouinard, "Des contestaires pragmatiques: Les Jeunes-Canada, 1932–1938," *Revue d'histoire de l'Amérique française* 40, no. 1 (1986): 5–28; Lucienne Fortin, "Les Jeunes-Canada," in *Idéologies au Canada français, 1930–1939*, ed. Fernand Dumont et al. (Quebec: Les Presses de l'Université Laval, 1978), 215–33; Donald J. Horton, *André Laurendeau: French-Canadian Nationalist* (Toronto: Oxford University

Press, 1992), chap. 2; Yvan Lamonde, "Les Jeune-Canada ou les 'Jeune-Laurentie'?: La recherche d'un nationalisme (1932–1938)," *Les cahiers des dix* 63 (2009): 175–215; Pomeyrols, *Les intellectuels québécois*, 255–83.

11. For anti-Semitism at Jeune-Canada, see Chouinard "Des contestaires pragmatiques," 11–12; André Laurendeau, "Why Keep Reminding Us That He's a Jew?" in *André Laurendeau: Witness for Quebec*, ed. and trans. Philip Stratford (Toronto: Macmillan, 1973), 277–78; Lamonde, "Les Jeune-Canada," 188–92.

12. Robert Charbonneau, "Notre nationalisme," *La Relève* 2, no. 8 (April 1936): 234n1.

13. Chouinard, "Des contestaires pragmatiques," 22.

14. For the relationship between French Canadian nationalism and anti-Semitism during this period, see Pierre Anctil, "Interlude of Hostility: Judeo-Christian Relations in Quebec in the Interwar Period, 1919–1939," in *Antisemitism in Canada: History and Interpretation*, ed. Alan Davies (Waterloo: Wilfred Laurier University Press, 1992), 35–65; Michael Oliver, *The Passionate Debate: The Social and Political Ideas of Quebec Nationalism, 1920–1945* (Montreal: Véhicule Press, 1991), 138, 158–59, 180–95.

15. Prominent sociologist Guy Rocher, for instance, recalls being encouraged by a number of his priest-professors to read Claudel, Mauriac, Bernanos, and Péguy while at classical college during the 1940s. See Guy Rocher, *Entre les rêves et l'histoire: Entretiens avec Georges Khal* (Quebec: VLB Éditeur, 1989), 18–19. See also Pomeyrols, *Les intellectuels québécois*, 78, 82.

16. Yvan Cloutier, "De quelques usages québécois de Maritain: La génération de *La Relève*," in *Saint-Denys Garneau et La Relève*, ed. Benoît Melançon and Pierre Popovic (Montreal: Fides, 1995), 61–72, 78.

17. Jean-Luc Barré, *Jacques and Raïssa Maritain: Beggars for Heaven*, trans. Bernard Doering (Notre Dame, Ind.: Notre Dame University Press, 2005), 253–54. For more on the links between the French right and neo-Thomism, see Barré, *Jacques and Raïssa Maritain*, 154–59; Eugen Weber, *Action Française: Royalism and Reaction in Twentieth-Century France* (Stanford, Calif.: Stanford University Press, 1962), 220.

18. Cloutier, "De quelques usages québécois de Maritain," 61–72. Cloutier demonstrates Maritain's popularity among the Quebec clergy

during the 1920s, including the positive appraisal of Maritain's work by conservative nationalists such as the abbé Lionel Groulx. Cloutier also quotes the French Canadian *Revue dominicaine* of 1921, which associated Maritain with Maurras and with the *Revue universelle*, a periodical that had close links to Action française (Cloutier, "De quelques usages," 63; for the *Revue universelle* see Barré, *Jacques and Raïssa Maritain*, 157–58; Weber, *Action Française*, 502–4). For the influence of Maritain, Henri Massis, and the French Catholic right on Lionel Groulx, the leading French Canadian nationalist of this period, see Lionel Groulx, *Mes mémoires*, vol. 1 (Montreal: Fides, 1970), 188. For more on Maritain's popularity in Quebec during the 1920s and early '30s see Cloutier, "L'influence de Maritain: Un déterminant de la réception de Vatican II au Québec," in *L'Église canadienne et Vatican II*, ed. Gilles Routhier (Quebec: Fides, 1997), 401–3; Lamonde, *La modernité au Québec*, 18–23.

19. For Maritain's reception in Quebec during his 1934 lecture tour see Cloutier, "De quelques usages québécois de Maritain," 69–72; Cloutier, "L'influence de Maritain: Un déterminant de la réception de Vatican II au Québec," 403–5; Lamonde, "*La Relève*," 157–66.

20. Bernard Doering, *Jacques Maritain and the French Catholic Intellectuals* (Notre Dame, Ind.: Notre Dame University Press, 1983), 178.

21. For the oscillating politics of the early *La Relève*, see Oliver, *Passionate Debate*, 115–19; for the intellectual and political dilemmas facing Maritain and other French Catholic thinkers after the condemnation of Action française, see John Hellman, "The Opening to the Left in French Catholicism: The Role of the Personalists," *Journal of the History of Ideas* 34, no. 3 (July–September 1973): 381–90.

22. Saint-Denys Garneau to Jean Le Moyne, 31 July 1934, Saint-Denys Garneau, *Lettres à ses amis*, ed. Robert Élie et al. (Montreal: HMH, 1967), 145.

23. Claude Hurtubise, "Compassion pour une jeunesse catholique," *La Relève* 1, no. 2 (April 1934): 30.

24. John English, *The Life of Pierre Elliott Trudeau*, vol. 1, *Citizen of the World: 1919–1968* (Toronto: Knopf Canada, 2006), 74–75; Lamonde, *La modernité au Québec*, chap. 11; Yvan Lamonde, "La rage de *Vivre* et les 'Cahiers Noirs' (1934–1935)," *Mens* 9, no. 2 (Spring 2009): 187–206; Linteau et al., *Quebec Since 1930*, 79–82; Oliver, *Passionate Debate*, 82–89, 97–100, 137–45, 168–75.

25. Roger Duhamel, "L'ordre corporatif sous le signe du fascio," *La Relève* 1, no. 8 (March 1935): 196–202.

26. Hurtubise, "Compassion pour une jeunesse catholique," 30.

27. Martin Conway, *Catholic Politics in Europe* (London: Routledge, 1997), 39–44.

28. Susan B. Whitney, *Mobilizing Youth: Communists and Catholics in Interwar France* (Durham, N.C.: Duke University Press, 2009).

29. For other militant Catholic youth groups in Quebec see Indre Cuplinskas, "Guns and Rosaries: The Use of Military Imagery in the French-Canadian Catholic Student Newspaper *JEC*," *Canadian Catholic Historical Association Historical Studies* 71 (2005): 7–28.

30. La Direction, "Positions," *La Relève*, vol. 1, no. 1 (March 1934): 2.

31. "Un nouveau moyen âge," *La Relève* 1, no. 8 (March 1935): 210–14; Northrop Frye, *T. S. Eliot* (Edinburgh: Oliver and Boyd, 1963), 7–9; Charles Taylor, *A Secular Age* (Cambridge, Mass.: Belknap Press, 2007), 732–35.

32. Robert Charbonneau, "Jeunesse et révolution," *La Relève* 2, no. 1 (September 1935): 4–5.

33. Nicolas Berdyaev, quoted in *La Relève*, "Un nouveau moyen âge," 211.

34. Claude Hurtubise to André Laurendeau, 27 June 1936, fonds Laurendeau, Bibliothèque et Archives nationales du Québec, Montreal Archival Centre, box 4, file P2/A, 30 [hereafter cited as BAnQ].

35. Duhamel, "Pour un ordre nouveau," *La Relève* 1, no. 4 (September 1934): 82–83.

36. Claude Hurtubise to André Laurendeau, 14 January 1937, quoted in Pomeyrols, *Les intellectuels québécois*, 421–22.

37. See, for instance, Adrien Cazes, "Un bâtisseur: Dollfuss," *JEC: Journal jéciste mensuel* 2, no. 5 (May 1936): 4; Cuplinskas, "Guns and Rosaries," 27.

38. Robert Charbonneau to André Laurendeau, 30 July 1934, fonds Laurendeau, BAnQ, box 3, file P2/A, 18.

39. Robert Charbonneau, "Rencontre avec Jacques Maritain," *ECF*, no. 49 (1983): 41.

40. Lamonde, "Les Jeune-Canada," 194; Lamonde, *La modernité au Québec*, 91–92. Robert Charbonneau included a fictionalized account of this encounter in his novel *Chronique de l'âge amer*, 55–59.

41. Lamonde, “Les Jeune-Canada,” 194; Charbonneau, *Chronique*, 57–58.

42. Robert Charbonneau et al., “Préliminaires à un manifeste pour la patrie,” *La Relève* 3, no. 1 (September–October 1936): 6–31; Lamonde, “*La Relève*,” 178–81; Lamonde, *La modernité au Québec*, chap. 6; Oliver, *Passionate Debate*, 119–21.

43. Robert Charbonneau, “Troisième année,” *La Relève* 2, no. 7 (March 1936): 196.

44. Robert Élie, “Le Christ et l'ouvrier,” *La Relève* 3, nos. 5–6 (April–May 1937): 159.

45. Ibid., 159–60.

46. Claude Hurtubise, “Espoir en Amérique,” *La Relève* 4, no. 8 (March 1939): 244–45.

47. Doering, *Jacques Maritain*, chap. 3.

48. Ibid., chap. 4.

49. Ibid., 88–89.

50. For an account of *La Relève*'s response to the Spanish Civil War, see Caroline Désy, *Si loin, si proche: La guerre civile espagnole et le Québec des années trente* (Quebec: Les Presses de l'Université Laval, 2004), chap. 4.

51. Paul Beaulieu, “La chaleur de l'accueil chez Jacques et Raïssa Maritain,” *ECF* 49 (1983): 39n12; Jacques Maritain to Paul Beaulieu, 22 October 1938, *ECF* 49 (1983): 25–26.

52. Le Moyne, “Les Maritain—de loin, de près,” *ECF* 49 (1983): 61–62.

53. Ibid., 62.

54. Désy, *Si loin, si proche*, 33–34, 36–38, 66; Paul Beaulieu, “La chaleur de l'accueil chez Jacques et Raïssa Maritain,” 12–13; Jean Le Moyne, “Les Maritain,” 64–65; Dom Albert Jamet, “M. Maritain: Un penseur? Oui. Mais un chef?” *Le Devoir*, 15 May 1943.

55. Maritain to Beaulieu, 31 October 1938, *ECF* 49 (1983): 25–26, 39n13.

56. Robert Charbonneau to Paul Beaulieu, 23 April 1937, 24 April 1937, *ECF* 57 (1986): 179–81.

57. Poulin, “*La Relève*: Analyse et témoignages,” 62–63.

58. Émile Baas, “Méditation sur la guerre d'Espagne,” *La Relève* 3, no. 4 (March 1937): 104–6.

59. “Le conflit espagnol,” *L'Ordre nouveau* 1, no. 14 (20 April 1937), p. 2.

60. Maritain to Beaulieu, 14 February 1939, *ECF*, no. 49 (1983): 28, 39n17.

61. Hurtubise to Laurendeau, 14 January 1937, fonds Laurendeau, BAnQ, box 5, file P2/A, 36; Charbonneau to Laurendeau, 8 January 1938, 12 January 1938, fonds Laurendeau, BAnQ, box 5, file P2/A, 40.

62. La Relève, "Position sur la guerre," *La Relève* 4, no. 7 (November–December 1938): 193–96; La Relève, "Pour une démocratie vraie," *La Relève* 4, no. 9 (July 1939): 265–67; Claude Hurtubise, "Conditions de l'unité canadienne," *La Relève* 4, no. 10 (January 1940): 293–95; Claude Hurtubise, "La guerre et la justice," *La Relève* 5, no. 1 (April 1940): 23–25.

63. For the *Relèviste* response to the fall of France see La Relève, "Espoir en la France," *La Relève* 5, no. 3 (November 1940): 65–67.

64. The Quebec literary historian Jacques Michon has authored the key studies on Les Éditions de L'Arbre. See Jacques Michon, "Les Éditions de L'Arbre, 1941–1948," in *Éditeurs transatlantiques: Études sur les Éditions de l'Arbre, Lucien Parizeau, Fernand Pilon, Serge Brousseau, Mangin, B.D. Simpson*, ed. Michon (Sherbrooke: Ex Libris, 1991), 15–41; Michon, "Les Éditions de L'Arbre, 1941–1948," *Voix et images* 41 (Winter 1989): 194–210; Michon, *1940–1948: Les éditeurs québécois et l'effort de guerre* (Montreal-Quebec: Bibliothèque et Archives nationales du Québec-Presses de l'Université Laval, 2009).

65. Claude Hurtubise to Jacques Maritain, 26 October 1940, fonds Claude Hurtubise, Library and Archives Canada, Ottawa [hereafter cited as LAC], R644, container 2, file 13.

66. Hurtubise, "Espoir en Amérique," 244–50.

67. Michon, "Les Éditions de L'Arbre," *Voix et images*, 199–203; Michon, "Les Éditions de L'Arbre," in Michon, *Éditeurs transatlantiques*, 18–23; Michon, *Les éditeurs québécois et l'effort de guerre*, 33, 53n16.

68. Charbonneau and Hurtubise to Maritain, 26 January 1942, fonds Hurtubise, LAC, container 2, file 15.

69. Maritain to Charbonneau and Hurtubise, 3 February 1942, fonds Hurtubise, LAC, container 2, file 15.

70. Jacques Maritain, "Religion and Politics," *Foreign Affairs* 20, no. 2 (January 1942): 273, quoted in Richard Pirquet, "La grande tâche du Président Roosevelt," *La Nouvelle Relève* 3, no. 8 (November 1944): 499.

71. Madeleine Ducrocq-Poirier, *Robert Charbonneau* (Montreal: Fides, 1972), 60.

72. Draft curriculum vitae of Claude Hurtubise, 2, fonds Jean Le Moyne, LAC, MG 30 D358, vol. 6, file 18.

73. Michon, "Les Éditions de L'Arbre, 1941–1948," *Voix et images*, 199.

74. Maritain to Charbonneau, 15 March 1942, *ECF* 49 (1983): 44.

75. Michon, "Les Éditions de L'Arbre," *Voix et images*, 199.

76. For Maritain's tenure as French ambassador to the Holy See and his time at Princeton, see Doering, *Jacques Maritain*, 203, chap. 7.

77. Michon, "Les Éditions de L'Arbre," *Voix et images*, 209.

78. See Conway, *Catholic Politics*, 43.

79. Doering, *Jacques Maritain*, 230–32; John Hellman, *Emmanuel Mounier and the New Catholic Left, 1930–1950* (Toronto: University of Toronto Press, 1981), 190–201, chapters 10 and 11; R. William Rauch Jr., *Politics and Belief in Contemporary France: Emmanuel Mounier and Christian Democracy, 1932–1950* (The Hague: Martinus Nijhoff, 1972), chapters 6 and 7.

80. Charbonneau, "Rencontre avec Jacques Maritain," *ECF* 49 (1983): 41–42.

81. Ibid., 42.

82. Gérard Godin, "Robert Élie: Vis d'abord, on verra après," 102.

83. Jean Le Moyne, "Les Maritain," 68.

84. Doering, *Jacques Maritain*, 223–25, 231ff.

85. Simon Lapointe, "L'influence de la gauche catholique française sur l'idéologie politique de la CTCC-CSN de 1948 à 1964," *Revue de l'histoire de l'Amérique française* 9, no. 3 (1996): 331–56; Jean-Marie Mayeur, *Des partis catholiques à la démocratie chrétienne, XIXe–XXe siècles* (Paris: Colin, 1980), 233–39; Rauch, chap. 7, esp. 313–19, 327–34.

86. Jacques Maritain, *The Peasant of the Garonne*, trans. Michael Cuddihy and Elizabeth Hughes (London: Chapman, 1968), 118; Jean Le Moyne, "Teilhard, or the Reconciliation," *Convergence*, 161–68.

87. Le Moyne, "Les Maritain," 68.

88. Maritain, *Peasant of the Garonne*, 116–26.

89. Le Moyne, "Les Maritain," 68. For the controversy occasioned by *Le paysan* see Doering, *Jacques Maritain*, 227–36.

90. André Charbonneau, interview by Joseph Dunlop, 5 January 2012.

91. Draft letter from Claude Hurtubise to Jean Le Moyne [n.d., c. 1989], fonds Claude Hurtubise, LAC, R644, container 1, file 28.

92. Ibid. Jean Le Moyne also remained highly critical of what he saw as reactionary elements within Catholicism, and in 1987 he took advantage of his appointment to the Canadian Senate to deliver a long, polemical address against Opus Dei on the Senate floor. See Debates of the Canadian Senate, Second Session, Thirty-Third Parliament, vol. 1 (30 September 1986, to 11 June 1987), 2 June 1987, 1150–54.

93. For the emergence of an activist Catholic laity in the early to mid–twentieth century see Étienne Fouilloux, "The Antepreparatory Phase: The Slow Emergence from Inertia (January 1959–October 1962)," in *History of Vatican II*, ed. Giuseppe Alberigo and Joseph A. Komonchak (Maryknoll, N.Y.: Orbis, 1995), vol. 1:88.

94. For Maritain's influence on Hurtubise's generation, see Yvan Lamonde and Cécile Facal, "Jacques et Raïssa Maritain au Québec et au Canada français: Une bibliographie," *Mens* 8, no. 1 (Autumn 2007): 157; see also Cloutier, "De quelques usages québécois" and "L'influence de Maritain: Un déterminant de la réception de Vatican II au Québec." For Maritain's influence on Pierre Trudeau see Pierre Elliott Trudeau, *Memoirs* (Toronto: McClelland and Stewart, 1993), 40; Trudeau, *The Essential Trudeau*, ed. Ron Graham (Toronto: McClelland and Stewart, 1998), 5; English, *Citizen of the World*, 54, 110, 147–49; Max Nemni and Monique Nemni, *Young Trudeau, 1919–1944: Son of Quebec, Father of Canada*, vol. 1, trans. William Johnson (Toronto: McClelland and Stewart, 2006), 239–45; Max Nemni and Monique Nemni, *Trudeau Transformed: The Shaping of a Statesman, 1944–1965, Son of Quebec, Father of Canada*, vol. 2, trans. George Tombs (Toronto: McClelland and Stewart, 2011), 70, 93, 95, 223, 226–31, 277, 281–82.

95. Tom Axworthy, one of Trudeau's principal aides, recalls Trudeau and Le Moyne engrossed in a long discussion of French Catholic philosophers, including Maritain, Mounier, and Teilhard de Chardin. Axworthy, an English-speaking Canadian from a Methodist background, sat silently in the room, mystified. See Tom Axworthy, "Faith and Personal Experience," in John English et al., eds., *The Hidden Pierre Elliott Trudeau: The Faith Behind the Politics* (Ottawa: Novalis, 2004), 161.

96. Jean Le Moyne, "Les Maritain," 68–69.

97. Telegram from Jean Le Moyne to the Canadian ambassador to France and to Jacques Maritain, 22 December 1971, *ECF* 49, 81–82; Le Moyne, "Les Maritain," 69.

98. Telegram from Jean Le Moyne to the Canadian ambassador to France and to Jacques Maritain, 22 December 1971, *ECF* 49, 81–82.

10. Louis Massignon: A Catholic Encounter with Islam and the Middle East

Anthony O'Mahony

1. Mary Louise Gude, *Louis Massignon: The Crucible of Compassion* (Notre Dame, Ind.: Notre Dame University Press, 1996); Christian Destremau and Jean Moncelon, *Louis Massignon, "le cheikh admirable"* (Paris: Plon, 1993; repr. Le Capucin, 2005); A. O'Mahony: "The Influence of the Life and Thought of Louis Massignon on the Catholic Church's Relations with Islam," *Downside Review* 126, no. 444 (2008): 169–92.

2. A. O'Mahony, "Louis Massignon as Priest: Eastern Christianity and Islam," *Sobornost/Eastern Churches Review* 29, no. 1 (2007): 6–41.

3. Jacques Mercanton, "Louis Massignon: Un médiateur entre le génie français et l'Orient arabe," *Cahiers de l'Association internationale des études françaises* 13 (1961): 85–101.

4. Yannick Essertel, *L'aventure missionnaire lyonnaise 1815–1962: De Pauline Jaricot à Jules Monchanin* (Paris: Cerf, 2001); Françoise Jacquin, *Jules Monchanin prêtre 1895–1957* (Paris: Cerf, 1996); F. Jacquin, "Jules Monchanin (1895–1957): Regards croisés d'occident et d'orient," *Mémoire spiritaine* 7 (1998): 129–43; F. Jacquin, "L'immersion d'Henri de Saux dans l'hindouisme 1950–1973," in *L'altérité religieuse: un défi pour la mission chrétienne XVIII–XXe siècles*, ed. F. Jacquin and Jean-Françoise Zorn (Paris: Karthala, 2001), 191–205; and F. Jacquin, "Louis Massignon et l'abbé Monchanin," *La vie spirituelle* 694 (1991): 175–83.

5. Frédéric Gugelot, "Les convertis issus de l'islam," in Gugelot, *La conversion des intellectuels au catholicisme en France (1885–1935)* (Paris: CNRS Éditions, 2010), 211–24. Vincenzo Poggi, SJ (Pontifical Oriental Institute, Rome), suggests, in the following order, those who changed Catholic Church attitudes to Muslims and Christian-Muslim relations: Charles de Foucauld (1858–1916); Louis Massignon (1883–1962); and two

Muslim converts to Christianity—Franciscan priest Abd el-Jalil (1904–79) and Paul Mehmet Ali Mulla-Zadé (1881–1959), "Paul Ali Mehmet Mulla Zadé Islamologo di tre papi," *Orientalia Christiana Analecta* 292 (2012): 10–248, at 11. See also Maurice Borrmans, ed., *Mulla-Zadé et Abd-el-Jalil: Deux frères en conversion. Du Coran à Jesus. Correspondance 1927–1957* (Paris: Cerf, 2009).

6. Louis Massignon, "An Entire Life with a Brother Who Set Out on the Desert: Charles de Foucauld," in *Testimonies and Reflections: Essays of Louis Massignon*, ed. Herbert Mason (Notre Dame, Ind.: University of Notre Dame Press, 1989), 21–31. De Foucauld is often described as "Le 'marabout chrétien,'" see, Hugues Didier, *Petite vie de Charles de Foucauld* (Paris: Desclée de Brouwer, 2005), 97–140; H. Didier, "Louis Massignon et Charles de Foucauld," in *Louis Massignon et ses contemporains*, ed. Jacques Keryell (Paris: Karthala, 2004), 93–110; Jean-François Six, *Le Grand Rêve de Charles de Foucauld et Louis Massignon* (Paris: Albin Michel, 2008); J.-F. Six, *L'Aventure de l'amour de Dieu: 80 lettres inédites de Charles de Foucauld à Louis Massignon* (Paris: Éditions du Seuil, 1993).

7. Jean-Dominique Durand, "L'histoire religieuse en France: Entre œcuménisme et intelligence catholique. L'œuvre d'Étienne Fouilloux," in *Chrétiens et sociétés XVI°–XX° siècles*, no. 10 (2003): 13–22, at 20. These figures made a significant contribution to the development of the Holy See's policy regarding the dialogue of cultures: "a policy which in a quarter of a century moved from severe condemnation of the nascent ecumenical movement to its official recognition: from a determined anti-Semitism to the proscription of a 'teaching of contempt'; or from a centuries-old hostility to the 'infidels' to the beginnings of Islamo-Christian dialogue which anticipated *Nostra Aetate*"; Agathe Mayeres, "L'influence de Louis Massignon sur la politique du Saint-Siège en matière de dialogue des cultures: Une vision paradigmatique de coexistence des religions abrahamiques en Palestine," in *Pie XI et la France: L'apport des archives du pontificat de Pie XI à la connaissance des rapports entre le Saint-Siège et la France*, ed. Jacques Prévotat, collection de l'École française de Rome, 438 (Rome: École française de Rome, 2010), 75–85, at 76.

8. A. Hourani, *Islam in European Thought* (Cambridge: Cambridge University Press, 1990), 48; A. Hourani, "Obituary: Prof. Louis Massignon," *The London Times*, 21 November 1962. Albert Hourani (d. 1993) was a

former professor of Middle Eastern history at the University of Oxford and converted to Catholicism in the 1950s. What influence Massignon had on Hourani is difficult to say. Although Hourani recognized Massignon's influence on his work, he stopped short of subscribing to Massignon's view that Islam was divinely inspired. See Derek Hopwood, "Albert Hourani: Islam, Christianity and Orientalism," *British Journal of Middle Eastern Studies* 30, no. 1 (2003): 127–36.

9. Massignon, "Interprétation de la civilisation arabe dans la culture française" (1946), in *Opera minora*, ed. Abbé Y. Moubarac (Beirut: Dar al-Maaref, 1963; Paris: Presses Universitaires de France, 1969), 1:187–202. References to *Opera minora* are hereafter abbreviated in the style *OM* 1:187–202.

10. Guyot Claire, "Entre morale et politique: Le centre catholique des intellectuels français face à la décolonisation (1952–1966)," *Vingtième siècle: Revue d'histoire* 63 (1999): 75–86.

11. Robert Caspar, "La vision de l'islam chez Louis Massignon et son influence sur l'église," in *Louis Massignon*, ed. Jean-François Six (Paris: Édition de l'Herne, 1970), 126–47.

12. J. Waardenburg, "Massignon: Notes for Further Research," *Muslim World* 56, no. 3 (1966): 157–72, at 168.

13. Massignon, "L'Occident devant l'Orient: Primauté d'une solution culturelle," *Politique étrangère* 17, no. 2 (1952): 13–28. The dialogue of cultures was central to Massignon and Monchanin; see Françoise Jacquin, "Pour une compréhension spirituelle des cultures: Louis Massignon et l'abbé Monchanin," in *Louis Massignon et le dialogue des cultures* ed. Daniel Massignon (Paris: Cerf, 1996). 341–56 Benedict XVI rearticulated this as an aspect of Catholic engagement with Islam: see Barbara Wood and Andrew Unsworth, "Pope Benedict XVI, Interreligious Dialogue and Islam," in *Catholics and Shi'a Dialogue: Ethics in Today's Society*, ed. A. O'Mahony, Wulstan Peterburs, OSB, and Mohammad Ali Shomali (London: Melisende, 2008), 44–68; Rocco Viviano, "Benedict XVI and Interreligious Dialogue: The Case of Islam and Christian-Muslim Relations," *Landas: Journal of Loyola School of Theology* 24, no. 2 (2010): 21–59.

14. Quoted in Fabio Petito, "In Defence of Dialogue of Civilisations: With a Brief Illustration of the Diverging Agreement Between Edward Said and Louis Massignon," *Millennium* 39, no. 3 (2011): 759–79, at 777.

Massignon is often posited as a counterpoint to Edward Said's anticivilization discourse, which itself is based on a secular imperative in the context of the encounter between Christianity and Islam. See Said on Massignon, "Islam, the Philological Vocation and French Culture: Renan and Massignon," *Islamic Studies: A Tradition and Its Problems*, ed. Malcolm H. Kerr (Malibu, Calif.: Undena, 1980), 53–72; Said, *Orientalism: Western Conceptions of the Orient* (London: Routledge and Kegan Paul, 1978), 263–74.

15. Hourani, *Islam in European Thought*, 97.

16. Petito, "In Defence of Dialogue of Civilisations," 760.

17. Louis Massignon had sent his text examining Islamic apologetics—*Examen du "Présent de l'homme lettré" by Abdallah Ibn al-Torjoman* (following the French translation published in *Revue de l'histoire des religions* XII [1886]), with a preface by Daniel Massignon, an introduction by Père Henri Cazelles, and observations by Père Albert (M.-J.) Lagrange; Collection "Studi arabo-islamic del PISAI," no. 5, Rome, PISAI, 1992, vol. 13, 134 pages—to several Catholic thinkers for guidance and commentary as he did not consider himself to be a theologian; certainly, as a recent convert, he may have been hesitant to posit a view in relation to current Catholic "orthodoxy." Massignon's text had a long history. In the fifteenth century a Franciscan from Mallorca (the figure in the title) reached Tunis, where he became a Muslim. He wrote an apology of Islam directed against Christianity, which is still known and used in modern Islamic discourse today. By chance, a copy of this French translation reached Egypt, and a francophone Muslim used it in his discussions with Christians. See Jacques Jomier, "Louis Massignon en Égypte," in *Louis Massignon et le dialogue des cultures*, 281–92. During the First World War, a priest in Egypt became directly or indirectly involved in these discussions, and as Massignon was in Cairo in 1917, having been mobilized to work for the Sykes-Picot mission, he was consulted by this priest. Following their conversation Massignon edited a small work and had it typed out in October and November of that same year. This text was not published, but Massignon attached great importance to it and kept it within easy reach in his Paris office. In the preface to this text his son, Daniel Massignon, placed the work in the context of the whole of his father's life: "This essay took only a few weeks to write, and this shows clearly that it was an opportunity for him to expose thoughts which had developed and

matured over the years" (v–x). Louis Massignon would have liked to obtain the opinion of specialists of Christian exegesis and theology before distributing this text on a large scale and publishing it. He first approached Père Lagrange, director of l'École biblique et archéologique de Jérusalem, but was not very successful: The copy he had sent the director was returned to Massignon with only a few notes. He was not much more successful with Jacques Maritain. In 1923 Massignon sent Maritain the manuscript and requested a response, but Maritain replied that he was too busy and was "reluctant to try and understand the numerous theological schools in Islam," (quoted from a letter from Maritain to Massignon in the preface by Daniel Massignon to *Examen* [9n16]). The copy sent to Maritain remained in the latter's archives until about 1985, when it was returned to Daniel Massignon. However, Massignon's inquiry appears to have lingered for Maritain. In his *Le paysan de la Garonne: Un vieux laïc s'interroge à propos du temps présent* (*The Peasant of the Garonne: An Old Layman Questions Himself About the Present Time* [London: Chapman, 1968]), Maritain observes: "Massignon, who knew the mystics of Islam perfectly well, wished that some day the Church would canonize Hallâj," 277. For further discussion of Abdallah Ibn al-Torjoman (or Anselm Turmeda) and Massignon's *Examen du "Présent de l'homme lettré" by Abdallah Ibn al-Torjoman* see the detailed review by Jacques Jomier, OP, in *Islamochristiania* (Rome) 19 (1993): 333–38; Míkel de Epalza, "Actualidad de Turmeda en la polémica islamo-cristiana en Francia," *Awraq: Estudios sobre el mundo árabe e islamico contemporáneo* 13 (1992): 271–86; and Roger Boase, "Autobiography of a Muslim Convert: Anselm Turmeda (c. 1353–c. 1430)," *al-Masaq* 9 (1996–97): 45–98.

18. Jean Jacques Waardenburg, "Louis Massignon (1883–1962) as a Student of Islam," *Die Welt des Islams* 45, no. 3 (2005): 312–42, at 323.

19. "Tu Vertex et Apex," *OM* 3:789.

20. Yann Richard, "Shariati et le gouvernement islamique," *Le Monde*, 31 January (1979): 2. Mohamed Talbi, a leading Islamic thinker, found that Massignon was "a mystical visionary" who opened up his mind "to a spiritual and philosophical Sufism that he had not previously encountered." Massignon's mysticism was, however, challenging to Talbi's "dominating traditional Sunni Islam"; Ronald L. Nettler, "Mohamed Talbi: 'For Dialogue Between All Religions,'" in *Muslim-Jewish Encounters*

Intellectual Traditions and Modern Politics, ed. Ronald L. Nettler and Suha-Taji Farouki (Reading: Harwood, 1998), 171–99, at 175.

21. Massignon, "Étude sur une courbe personnelle de vie, le cas de Hallaj, martyr mystique de l'islam," *Dieu vivant*, cahier 4 (1945): 11–39; "Salmân Pâk et les prémisses spirituelles de l'islam iranien," *Société d'études iraniennes*, cahier 7 (1934). The French philosopher Michel Foucault, who was aware of the religious thought of Ali Shariati, commented on his relationship with Massignon, whom he had acknowledged as a source of his own understanding of Islamic mysticism: "Chariatti . . . knew at the time the work of Fanon and of Massignon," in "À quoi rêvent les Iraniens?" *Le nouvel observateur*, no. 726 (16–22 October 1978): 48–49, at 49. Foucault, who was in a reflective mood witnessing events in Iran in the autumn of 1978, said, "How sensible for men living there [Iran] to seek, even at the cost of their life, something of which we in the West have forgotten the very possibility since the time of the Renaissance and the great crisis of Christianity: a *political spirituality*. Already I can hear some Frenchmen laughing, but I know that they are wrong," quoted in Yann Richard, *Shi'ite Islam* (Oxford: Blackwell, 1995), 213. See also Pierre Rocalve, "Massignon et le shi'isme," *Luqmân* (Paris-Tehran), no. 2 (1991): 53–64; Pierre Rocalve, "Louis Massignon et l'Iran," in *Louis Massignon et le dialogue des cultures*, Actes du Colloque organisé par l'Organisation des Nations Unies pour l'éducation, la science, et la culture, l'Association des amis de Louis Massignon, et l'Institut international de recherches sur Louis Massignon (Maison de l'UNESCO, 17 et 18 December 1992), ed. D. Massignon (Paris: Éditions du Cerf, 1996), 307–39.

22. In Michel Cuypers, "Une rencontre mystique: Ali Shariati–Louis Massignon," *Mélanges de l'Institut dominicain d'études orientales* 21 (1993): 291–330.

23. Shariati, quoted by Pierre Rocalve, "Louis Massignon et l'Iran," in *Louis Massignon et le dialogue des cultures*, 324. "It is well known what role Al-Hallaj, the martyr mystic, played in the spiritual life of Massignon, but only a handful are aware of the role that the Christian mystic, Massignon, played in the spiritual life of Shariati, one of the most significant modern Muslim thinkers"; Yann Richard, "Ali Shariati et Massignon," *Se comprendre* 98 (1998): 1–7; reprinted in *Louis Massignon et l'Iran*, Travaux et mémoires de l'Institut d'études iraniennes 5, ed. Eve

Pierunek and Yann Richard (Paris: Peeters, 2000), 111–24. See also A. O'Mahony, "The Image of Jesus and Christianity in Shi'a Islam and Modern Iranian Thought," in *A Faithful Presence: Essays for Kenneth Cragg*, ed. David Thomas and Claire Amos (London: Melisende, 2003), 256–73. See also A. O'Mahony, "Cyprian Rice, OP, L'islam chiite et la mission dominicaine en Perse-Iran, 1933–1934," *Mémoire dominicaine: Les dominicains et les mondes musulmans* 15 (2001): 217–25. See the overview of existing scholarship on Massignon, Shiite Islam and Iran by A. O'Mahony, "Mysticism, Politics, Dialogue: Catholic Encounters with Shi'a Islam in the Life and Work of Louis Massignon," in *Catholics and Shi'a in Dialogue: Studies in Theology and Spirituality*, ed. Anthony O'Mahony, Wulstan Peterburs, OSB, and Mohammad Ali Shomali (London: Melisende, 2004), 134–84.

24. Quoted in Cuypers, "Une rencontre mystique," 312.

25. Ibid., 321.

26. Ibid., 322.

27. Shariati, *Œuvres complètes*, vol. 33, part 1: 49–50, and vol. 33, part 2: 718–19, quoted by Yann Richard, "Lettre à mes amis d'Iran sur Dibâtch et Shariati," *La croix-L'événement*, 3 August 1994, 13, quoted in Maurice Borrmans, *Jésus et les musulmans d'aujourd'hui* (Paris: Desclée, 2005), 244. See also Christopher Clohessy, "Mary and Fātima in the Catholic and Shīa Traditions" in *Catholics and Shi'a in Dialogue: Studies in Theology and Spirituality*, 121–33.

28. Ervand Abrahamian, *Radical Islam: The Iranian Mojahedin* (London: Tauris, 1989), 108. Martin McDermott, SJ, a Jesuit scholar of Shi'a Islam, has written a critique and comparison of Christian liberation theology and Khomeini's political-religious thought. Interestingly, both movements emerged in the late 1970s and sought political power and influence in the 1980s, and both experienced a decline in the decades that followed. See "Liberation Theology and Imam Khomeini's *Jihad*: A Comparison," in *Faith, Power, and Violence: Muslims and Christians in a Plural Society, Past and Present*, ed. John J. Donohue SJ and Christian W. Troll SJ (Rome: Orientalia Christiana Analecta, 1998), 75–83.

29. Herbert Mason, "Louis Massignon et al-Hallâj," *Présence de Louis Massignon: Hommages et témoignages*, ed. Daniel Massignon (Paris: Éditions Maisonneuve et Larose, 1987), 105–12.

30. Roger Arnaldez, "Hallâj et Jésus dans la pensée de Louis Massignon," *Horizons maghrébins: Louis Massignon: Homme de dialogue des cultures*, no. 14–15 (1989): 171–78.

31. Massignon, "Nature in Islamic Thought," in *Testimonies and Reflections*, 83. See also Joel L. Kraemer, "The Death of an Orientalist: Paul Kraus from Prague to Cairo," in *The Jewish Discovery of Islam*, ed. Martin Kramer (Tel Aviv: University Press of Tel Aviv, 1999), 181–223, 189–94. Kraemer states: "Even though Massignon's study of Islam was *engagé* and *mystique*, he respected the philological skills of Jewish scholars like Goldziher and Kraus. Goldziher had helped him with his *Kitâb al-tawâsîn*, and Kraus contributed to his *Akhbâr al-Hallâj*. Massignon was impressed by the appreciation that Goldziher, Kraus and others showed for al-Hallâj and tried to explain their attraction to Sufi texts" (192).

32. J.-P. de Menasce OP, "Reconnaissance à Louis Massignon," in *Mémorial Louis Massignon*, ed. Y. Moubarac (Cairo: Institut d'études de Dar el-Salam, 1963), 81. These views expressed by de Menasce are more surprising as he was deeply skeptical of Islam as a distinct religious tradition: "Islam, without doubt, is to be ranked among the heresies. The biblical revelation, although poorly known, is not unknown and is formally rejected with respect to the essential truths: the Incarnation and the Trinity"; Menasce, "La théologie de la mission selon Kraemer," *Neue Zeitschrift für Missionswissenschaft* 1 (1945): 251. See also Philippe Gignoux, "Louis Massignon et Jean de Menasce," in *Louis Massignon et ses contemporains*, ed. Jacques Keryell (Paris: Karthala, 1997), 155–62.

33. Fritz Frei, *Médiation unique et transfiguration universelle: thèmes christologiques et leurs perspectives missionnaires dans la pensée de J. Daniélou* (Bern: Peter Lang, 1981). For relations with Massignon see Marie-Thérèse Bessirard, "Louis Massignon et le Père Daniélou," in *Louis Massignon et ses contemporains*,163–80. For the important idea of "presence" in the life and spirituality of Charles de Foucauld see François Daguet, "Présence du Christ aux non-chrétiens: Jacques Maritain, héritier de Thomas d'Aquin et de Charles de Foucauld," *Revue thomiste* 106, nos. 1–2 (2006): 205–41.

34. Guy Harpigny, *Islam et christianisme selon Louis Massignon* (Louvain: Université Catholique de Louvain, 1981), 27–28. See also Harpigny, "Le sacerdoce selon Louis Massignon (1883–1962): Attitude chrétienne

devant l'islam" (PhD diss., Université catholique de Louvain, 3 vols., 1978). Harpigny gives us an overview of Massignon's place in Catholic theological reflection on Islam, "L'islam aux yeux de la théologie catholique," *Aspects de la foi de l'islam* (Brussels: Publications des Facultés universitaires Saint-Louis, 1985), 199–239.

35. Massignon, "Une courbe personnelle de vie."

36. Paul Nwyia, SJ, "Massignon ou une certaine vision de la langue arabe," *Studia islamica* 50 (1979): 125–49.

37. E. S. Sabanegh, "Le cheminement exemplaire d'un savant et d'un chrétien à la rencontre de l'islam," in *Présence de Louis Massignon*, 122. Brother Martin, Édouard S. Sabanegh (1916–85), closely followed Massignon's ideas for a life of engagement with Muslims in his native Egypt. E. S. Sabanegh, *Muhammad B. Abdallah, "Le Prophète": Portraits contemporains, Égypte, 1930–1950* (Paris: Vrin, 1981). Massignon's idea of sanctity in Muslim mysticism was widely debated in Catholic circles. For example, Christopher Dawson, an English Catholic, wrote the following: "The martyrdom of al-Hallaj is the culmination of the Christian tendencies which were already latent in the earlier Sufi movement. As M. Massignon has shown, al-Hallaj had founded his ideal of mystical sanctity on the Koranic tradition of Jesus, and this imitation of the Koranic Christ led him on to a literal conformity with the real Christ in His Passion and Death" (C. Dawson, "Islamic Mysticism," in *Enquiries into Religion and Culture* [London: Sheed and Ward, 1933], 173).

38. David E. Burrell, "Mind and Heart at the Service of Muslim-Christian Understanding: Louis Massignon as Trail Blazer," *Muslim World* 88, nos. 3–4 (1998): 268–78, at 268.

39. S. H. Griffiths, "Sharing the Faith of Abraham: The 'Credo' of Louis Massignon," *Islam and Christian-Muslim Relations* 8, no. 2 (1997): 193–210, at 194. Griffiths states that Massignon undertook theology toward Islam in a manner similar to that of the church fathers; for him, "as for many of the ancient fathers of the church, this was the way to read the Bible—as if it already contained, almost literally, the patterns one should use in putting a religious construction upon events of extra-biblical reality" (197). The importance and significance of this style of encounter is developed in Geneviève Gobillot, "Les pères de l'église et la pensée de l'islam," in *L'Orient chrétien dans l'empire musulman: Hommage au professeur Gérard*

Troupeau, ed. Geneviève Gobillot and Marie-Thérèse Urvoy (Paris: Éditions du Paris, 2005), 59–90.

40. Apart from his thesis, we have three volumes of *Opera minora*, containing some 207 of Massignon's articles.

41. Guy Harpigny, "Louis Massignon: L'hospitalité et la visitation de l'étranger ," *Recherches de science religieuse* 75, no. 1 (1987): 39–64.

42. Daniel Massignon, "Voyage en Mésopotamie et conversion de Louis Massignon en 1908," *Islamochristiana* (Rome) 14 (1988): 127–99, at 129, quoted in Ian Latham, "The Conversion of Louis Massignon in Mesopotamia in 1908," *Aram: Society for Syro-Mesopotamian Studies* 20 (2008): 245–67.

43. Massignon, "Foucauld au desert," *OM* 3:773. I am deeply indebted to the study by Caspar, "La vision de l'islam," 126–47. On the relationship with de Foucauld, see Hugues Didier, "Louis Massignon and Charles de Foucauld," *Aram: Society for Syro-Mesopotamian Studies* 20 (2008): 337–53.

44. Caspar, "La vision de l'islam." Ian Latham notes the close connection held in Massignon's mind between Joan of Arc and al-Hallaj:

> For the mysterious "Visitation of the Stranger" that he speaks of, while situated within the context of verifiable events, is by its nature an "inner," hidden reality, yet claiming to come from "outside." Massignon as a young man had shared his agnostic father's humanist admiration for Joan of Arc: they admired particularly the courage and fidelity of her "witness" to her "voices," in the face of her judges, and until her death by fire. In fact the young Massignon, together with his friend Henri Maspero, risked their careers by publicly protesting against an author who defamed her: both were refused their "agrégation" (right to teach in a Lycée), and both were sent away (by Henri's father, Gaston Maspero). Louis Massignon went to Egypt, where he discovered another "witness," Hallâj. For, Massignon discovered, Hallâj had, like Joan of Arc, witnessed until death. Tied and tortured on a gibbet in the centre of Baghdad, he had continued to proclaim his own "oneness" with the One God: "Ana 'l Haqq" (I [am] the Truth). While being carried on a stretcher from the boat to the Hospital, as they were passing the place of Ḥallâj's tomb, he felt the presence of Hallâj; and later, suffering intense fever, he muttered repeatedly "Haqq." (Daniel Massignon, "Voyage en Mésopotamie et conversion de Louis Massignon en 1908," *Islamochristiana* [Rome] 14 [1988]: 127–99, at 148n77, quoted in Ian Latham, "Conversion of Louis Massignon," 254).

45. Caspar, "La vision de l'islam," 132–33. Jerusalem had a particular place in Massignon's theological view of history; see Patrick Laude, "La Jerusalem axiale de Louis Massignon," in *Louis Massignon au cœur de notre temps*, ed. Jacques Keryell (Paris: Karthala, 1999): 331–42; Christian Destremeau, "La question sioniste: L'état d'Israël," in *Louis Massignon et ses contemporains*, 289–308; Andrew Unsworth, "Louis Massignon, the Holy See and the Ecclesial Transition from 'Immortale Dei' to 'Nostra Aetate': A Brief History of the Development of Catholic Church Teaching on Muslims and the Religion of Islam from 1833 to 1965," *Aram* 20 (2008): 299–316. Unsworth has suggested that Paul VI's pilgrimage to Jerusalem in January 1964 might be considered "Badaliya on a grand scale. It is interesting to speculate as to whether Montini had a sense of living out Massignon's 'prophetic' words of 1948": "[A]nd one day the bishops, even the bishop of bishops, must return to Jerusalem," in Massignon, "Dieu vivant," quoted by A. O'Mahony, "*Le pèlerin de Jérusalem*: Louis Massignon, Palestinian Christians, Islam, and the State of Israel," in *Palestinian Christians: Religion, Politics, and Society*, ed. A. O'Mahony (London: Melisende, 1999), 166–89.

46. Paolo Dall'Oglio SJ, "Louis Massignon and *Badaliya*," *Aram: Society for Syro-Mesopotamian Studies* 20 (2008): 329–36. Badaliya continues to inform Catholic thought on mission and dialogue. Dall'Oglio is the principal founder of the monastic community Dayr Mar Musa al-Habashi in Syria, which is dedicated to ecumenism and relations between Christians and Muslims. The monastery, which is mixed men and women, reflects the Eastern Catholic tradition based upon the life and eremitical endeavor of Charles de Foucauld and Massignon's ideas on Christian relations with Muslims and Islam; see Dall'Oglio, "La refondation du monastère syriaque de saint Moïse l'Abyssin à Nebek, Syrie, et la Badaliya massignonienne," in *Badaliya: Au nom de l'autre (1947–1962)—Louis Massignon*, ed. Maurice Borrmans and Françoise Jacquin (Paris: Cerf, 2011), 372–74. Dall'Oglio was kidnapped in April 2013 during the Civil War in Syria; his whereabouts are unknown.

47. Louis Massignon's bibliography as a scholar is impressive. For the complete bibliography see Youakim Moubarac, *Pentalogie islamo-chrétienne, I: L'œuvre de Louis Massignon*, Pentalogie islamo-chrétienne I (Beirut: Éditions du Cénacle Libanais, 1972–73). Among his studies, the first place must go to his two doctoral dissertations of 1922: *La passion d'al-Hosayn-ibn*

Mansour al-Hallâj, martyr mystique de l'islam (Paris: Geuthner, 1922), 2 vols. Massignon continued to work on a new edition of this work until his death in 1962. After his death, the new edition was completed by a group of scholars working together with the Massignon family and friends and was published as *La passion de Husayn ibn Mansur Hallâj, martyr mystique de l'islam* (Paris: Gallimard 1975), 4 vols. The second edition was translated into English by Herbert Mason as *The Passion of al-Hallâj: Mystic and Martyr of Islam*, Bollingen Series 98 (Princeton, N.J.: Princeton University Press, 1982), 4 vols. An abridged version appeared as *Hallâj: Mystic and Martyr*, ed. and trans. Herbert Mason (Princeton, N.J.: Princeton University Press, 1994). Also important is Massignon's second thesis, which accompanied his work on Hallâj: *Essai sur les origines du lexique technique de la mystique musulmane* (Paris: Geuthner, 1922; Paris: Vrin, 1954; Paris: Vrin, 1968); translated into English by Benjamin Clark as *Essays on the Origins of the Technical Language of Islamic Mysticism* (Notre Dame, Ind.: University of Notre Dame Press, 1997). One important addition to this bibliography is *Testimonies and Reflections: Essays of Louis Massignon*, selected and translated by Herbert Mason (Notre Dame, Ind.: University of Notre Dame Press, 1989).

48. Caspar, "La vision de l'islam," 134.

49. A. O'Mahony, "Louis Massignon, the Seven Sleepers of Ephesus and the Christian-Muslim Pilgrimage at Vieux-Marché, Brittany," in *Explorations in a Christian Theology of Pilgrimage*, ed. Craig Bartholomew and Fred Hughes (Aldershot, U.K.: Ashgate, 2004), 126–48.

50. M. Borrmans, "Aux origines de la Badaliya," *Badaliya: Au nom de l'autre* (1947–1962), *par Louis Massignon*, ed. Maurice Borrmans and Françoise Jacquin (Paris: Éditions du Cerf, 2011), 19–48.

51. Joseph Ratzinger (Benedict XVI) wrote the following: "The idea of substitution is one of the primitive facts of the biblical testimony, the rediscovery of which in today's world can help Christianity to renew and deepen in a decisive way the conception it has of itself," in "Substitution," *Encyclopédie de la foi* (Paris: Cerf, 1967), 273, quoted in J.-F. Six, *Light of the Night* (London: SCM Press, 1996), 207. See the study by M. Borrmans on Badaliya in the context of modern Catholic encounter with Islam, "Essai d'une 'Badaliya nouvelle,'" *Badaliya*, 329–47.

52. Agnes Wilkins, OSB, "Louis Massignon, Thomas Merton and Mary Kahil," *Aram: Society for Syro-Mesopotamian Studies* 20 (2008): 355–73.

53. Richard Griffiths, "The Influence of Islam," in Griffiths, *The Reactionary Revolution: The Catholic Revival in French Literature 1870-1914* (London: Constable, 1966), 244–55, at 255.

54. Unsworth, "Louis Massignon, the Holy See," 299–316.

55. Griffith, "Sharing the Faith," 194.

56. Wilkins, "Louis Massignon, Thomas Merton and Mary Kahil," 355–73.

57. Christian S. Krokus, "Louis Massignon's Influence on the Teaching of Vatican II on Muslims and Islam," *Islam and Christian–Muslim Relations* 23, no. 3 (2012): 329–45, at 329.

58. Christian Troll, "Changing Catholic Views on Islam," in *Islam and Christianity: Mutual Perceptions Since the Mid–Twentieth Century*, ed. Jacques Waardenburg (Leuven: Peeters, 1998), 19–77, at 28; Troll, "Catholicism and Islam," in *The Catholic Church and World Religions: A Theological and Phenomenological Account*, ed. Gavin D'Costa (London: T & T Clark, 2011), 71–10. In 1948 Massignon gave an interview titled "Le signe marial," in which he offered a theological account of Muhammad's prophethood: "To be 'false' it is necessary to prophesy falsely. 'Positive prophecy' is generally shocking for those who hear, preaching as it does a reversal of human values. But Muhammad, who believed in such total reversal in a terrifying manner, could not have been but a 'negative prophet' [prophète négatif], quite authentically. He never pretended to be an intercessor or saint . . . but affirmed that he was a witness, the Voice which cries in the desert the final separation of the good from the evil, the witness of separation," quoted by David Kerr, " 'He Walked in the Path of the Prophets': Toward Christian Theological Recognition of the Prophethood of Muhammad," in *Christian-Muslim Encounters*, ed. Yvonne Yazbeck Haddad and Wadi Zaidan Haddad (Florida: University of Florida Press, 1995), 426–44, at 439. For Massignon, negative prophecy was an eschatological category that bore witness to the Last Day; see John Flannery, "Christ in Islam and Muhammad, a Christian Evaluation," in *The Catholic Church in the Contemporary Middle East*, ed. A. O'Mahony and John Flannery (London: Melisende 2010), 331–52.

59. Massignon is often placed alongside T. E. Lawrence; see A. H. Hourani, "T. E. Lawrence and Louis Massignon," in *Présence de Louis Massignon*, 167–76, and Gérard Khoury, "Louis Massignon et Lawrence:

Deux visions de l'Orient arabe en avance sur leur temps," in *Louis Massignon au cœur de notre temps*, 87–110. Paul Nwyia, a Jesuit from a Chaldean Catholic family and a former student of Massignon, characterized the differences between Lawrence and Massignon in a very helpful reflection on the Arabic language in Islamic mysticism:

> Lawrence loved Arabia (hence his infatuation with the *Arabia deserta* of Doughty), while Massignon was interested in the Arabs through their language in order to better understand them. This comparison between the two men is not ours: it was made by Massignon himself when, speaking of his meetings with King Faisal I, he wrote, "The Arabic we spoke to each other was of freely 'chosen' terms; but I systematically avoided our abstract and little-known words; nor did I seek to compete with the dialectal Arabic which Lawrence, the man of the 'Seven Pillars' had forged, rich in terms of kindness and insult, antagonistic, distrustful and haughty, that of the leader of a gang discussing piratical action. That was not what I wanted with Faisal, but to penetrate the very meaning for him of his own tradition, in the form of ideas that I wanted to later transpose into mine." (*OM* I: 212)
>
> The different way in which they spoke Arabic arose from the different ways in which they approached the Arab world: different and yet extraordinarily alike, almost mystical in both cases. Where Massignon speaks of "not annexing the other to oneself" and of employing "a mental de-centering in order to enter the universe of the other," Lawrence evokes the "supreme detachment" of a man entirely "stripped of his original personality," experiencing "a living death" in "a sense of intense solitude accompanied by mistrust not of others but for all they do": "madness was close," Lawrence concluded when reflecting on Bedouin life, "harsh for those accustomed to it, terrible for foreigners." (*Seven Pillars of Wisdom*, 42–43 [editorial note: *Les sept piliers de la sagesse*, trans. Charles Mauron (Paris: Payot, 1936), 42–43])

Massignon went through the same experience but derived contrasting results: "When we think of the past, it is like a walk in the night . . . but from time to time we saw there a passing clarity, a key word thundered upon us, drilling down into a pure source and certainty within us" (*OM* II:613). He adds, "A foreign guest of the Arabs, I one day found this contact in their language, this communicable awareness of truth; by sharing their thought structure, seized by its linguistic 'profile of indentation.' I could have found it elsewhere, but the fact remains that it was in Arabic" (ibid.).

While Arabic placed Massignon "in a position of participation" with those before him, Lawrence used it as the language "of strangers," but "imitating them so well that they in their turn imitated him." And he then declared that "the man who behaves in this way abandons his own place: he lays claim to that of others; and the claims are in vain" (ibid.). "This admission of failure led Lawrence to depict the Arab world as a scene without nuance, one of brutal, almost cynical lucidity, but a masterpiece nevertheless. This appears in pages 49–56, which I have analyzed in detail since they are the broken mirror of the Arabic mysticism which Massignon reached by abandoning his own thought in order to host that of others" (Paul Nwyia, "Mystique musulmane," *École pratique des hautes études. Section des sciences religieuses* 85 [1976–77]: 275–84, at 279–80).

60. Gérard D. Khoury, "Robert de Caix et Louis Massignon: Deux visions de la politique française au Levant en 1920," in *The British and French Mandates in Comparative Perspectives/Les mandats français et anglais dans une perspective comparative*, ed. Peter Sluglett and Nadine Méouchy (Leiden: Brill, 2004), 165–83.

61. Charles Robert Ageron, "Un rapport inédit de Louis Massignon à la commission du centenaire de l'Algérie," *Cahiers de Tunisie* 23 (1985): 37–47.

62. See Albert Thibaudet, *La république des professeurs* (Paris: Grasset, 1927).

63. Henry Laurens, "La politique musulmane de la France," *Maghreb-Machrek* 152 (1996): 3–12.

64. Henry Laurens, "La place de Louis Massignon dans la politique musulmane de la France sous la IIIème République," *Bulletin des Amis de Louis Massignon* 2 (1995): 13–46.

65. Allan Christelow, "Louis Massignon et les intellectuels musulmans algériens: Domination coloniale et absence de confiance," in *Louis Massignon au cœur de notre temps*, 195–210.

66. Henry Laurens, "Le Chatelier, Massignon, Montagne: Politique musulmane et orientalisme," in *Orientales II: La IIIe République et l'islam* (Paris: CNRS Éditions, 2004), 251–80.

67. E. Méténier, "Massignon et l'Égypte," in *Louis Massignon au cœur de notre temps*, 153–72.

68. Waardenburg, "Louis Massignon (1883–1962) as a Student of Islam," 325.

69. Ibid.

70. Hourani, *Islam in European Thought*, 97. Massignon and Claudel had a reserved but engaging encounter regarding the consequence of conversion and vocation. Claudel wished Massignon to follow his vocation, possibly in the direction of Charles de Foucauld; Massignon rejected this but remained a man of scholarship animated by the spirit. See Hourani, *Islam in European Thought*, 97–98. Claudel doubted Massignon's decision to become a priest in the Melkite Church; see Olivier Théon, "Paul Claudel et Louis Massignon: Une amitié tourmentée," in *Louis Massignon et ses contemporains*, 63–92.

71. R.-L. Moreau, OP, "Une experience de Badaliya à Dakar," in Borrmans, *Badaliya*, 355–58.

72. Julian Baldick writes, "It is to some extent his Gallicanism, which, he tells, was well known in the Vatican. It was doubtless his hostility to the Ultramontane element in the Catholic Church in France that led him to be secretly ordained as a priest in the Melchite rite, within the Catholic communion, in 1950. To be anti-clerical and a priest might seem contradictory: but it is rather a question of pressing for the reform of a corrupt clergy, in a long French Catholic tradition" (*Religious Studies* 23, no. 1 [1987]: 29–39).

73. Mehmet Ali Mulla-Zadé was born in Iraklion (Candia) on the island of Crete, then still part of the Ottoman Empire. His father was a Turk, his mother Egyptian Albanian. While studying at the university of Aix-en-Provence he met the philosopher Maurice Blondel (1861–1949), who was to mark his religious and intellectual outlook deeply. When Mulla was baptized in 1905, Blondel became his godfather, and Mulla chose the name Paul. In 1911 Mulla was ordained priest. In 1924 Pope Pius XI charged him personally with teaching Islamic studies at the Pontificio Istituto Orientale in Rome, where he remained until his death in 1959.

74. Caspar, "La vision de l'islam," 136. Philippe Chenaux suggests Massignon influenced Giovanni Battista Montini on his wider understanding of the religious and political situation in the Middle East: Chenaux, *Paul VI et Maritain*, 45. According to Maurice Borrmans, Montini had been a member of Badaliya sometime between being appointed as archbishop of Milan and being elected as Pope Paul VI; see M. Borrmans, "Lettres de Mulla-Zadé à Louis Massignon," *Orientalia christiana analecta* 292 (201):

253–369, at 335n207. See also Jacques Prévotat, "Les sources françaises dans la formation intellectuelle de G. B. Montini (1919–1963)," in *Paul VI et la modernité dans l'église: Actes du colloque de Rome* (2–4 June 1983), Collection de l'École française de Rome 72 (1984): 101–27.

75. Oissila Saaïdia, *Clercs catholiques et oulémas sunnites dans la première moitié du XXe siècle: Discours croisés* (Paris: Geuthner, 2004).

76. Mayeres, "L'influence de Louis Massignon," 76–77.

77. Ibid., 77. See also Maurice Borrmans, "Vivre à la place de l'autre: La Badaliya selon Louis Massignon," *Christus* 230 (2011): 214–18.

78. Mayeres, "L'influence de Louis Massignon," 76–77. See also Pierre Rocalve, "Louis Massignon et Abraham," *Luqman* (Paris-Tehran), 13. no. 2 (1997): 27–36.

79. A. O'Mahony, "Catholic Theological Perspectives on Islam at the Second Vatican Council," *New Blackfriars* 88, no. 1016 (2007): 385–98; however, as Sidney Griffith rightly comments, the council fathers "nevertheless clearly recognized the importance of Abraham in the self-understanding of Muslims, and thereby they provided Catholics with a theological and biblical point of reference in which to esteem Muslims" ("Sharing the Faith of Abraham," 193). It is often held that the Second Vatican Council spoke to Muslims and not of Islam; see Unsworth, "The Vatican, Islam and Muslim-Christian Relations," in *Christian Responses to Islam: Muslim-Christian Relations in the Modern World*, ed. A. O'Mahony and Emma Loosley (Manchester: Manchester University Press, 2008), 54–65.

80. Mayeres, "L'influence de Louis Massignon," 77–78.

81. Guy Harpigny, "Le sacrifice d'Isaac, et le signe de la Palestine," in *Islam et christianisme selon Louis Massignon*, 92–102.

82. Mayeres, "L'influence de Louis Massignon," 77; quotation from a letter from Mulla to Pacelli, 28 October 1935, Segr. stato, rubr. 256, Archivio Segreto Vaticano. I would like to thank Dr. Paolo Maggiolini (Milan) for acquiring a copy of this letter for me.

83. F. Jacquin, "Louis Massignon et le groupe judéo-catholique (1936–1938)," *Bulletin des Amis de Louis Massignon* 12, 22–31.

84. David Lazaer, "Louis Massignon, le sionisme et l'état d'Israël," in *Les intellectuels français et Israël*, ed. Denis Charbit (Paris: Editions de l'Éclat, 2009), 81–96; Catherine Nicault, *La France et le sionisme, 1897–1948* (Paris: Calman-Levy, 1992).

85. Louis Massignon, "La Palestine et la paix dans la justice," *Dieu vivant* 12 (1948): 79–90, at 84–85.

86. Dominique Bourel, "Six lettres de Louis Massignon à Martin Buber," *Pardès* 2 (1985): 173–81.

87. Dominique Bourel, "Massignon face à Israel," in *Louis Massignon: Mystique en dialogue*, ed. Marc de Smedt (Paris: Albin Michel 1992), 67–75; Olivier Danino, "La France et le question de Jérusalem, 3 avril 1949–7 juin 1967," *Relations internationales* 122 (2005): 47–62.

88. The British were in fact divided on what policy to pursue; for example, Churchill, among others, was resolutely pro-Zionist. See A. O'Mahony, "Les chrétiens palestiniens: Politique, droit et société, 1917–1948," in *De Balfour à Ben Gourion: La France, L'Europe occidentale et la Palestine, 1917–1948*, ed. Dominique Trimbur and Ran Aaronsohn (Paris: Éditions CNRS, 2008), 351–95.

89. Destremau and Moncelon, *Massignon.*

90. Agathe Mayeres, "Massignon face au sionisme," *Bulletin du Centre de recherche français de Jérusalem* 20 (2009): 1–15.

91. Maurice Borrmans: "Louis Massignon, témoin du dialogue islamo-chrétien," *Euntes docete*, 37 (1984): 383–401.

92. The earliest example of such a response is probably the substantial article by Jules Monchanin (1895–1957), "Islam et christianisme," *Bulletin des Missions* 1 (1938): 10–23. A spiritual brother of Massignon, Monchanin died in India, where he had engaged with Hindu mysticism in the context of Christian contemplation. In this article we can already see the emergence of the idea of Islam as having a mediating function in terms of the taking up of a prophetic announcement, which had meaning only before Christ but which takes its sense from the notion of a Muslim, Adam-based, prophetic, and eschatological time. See also Françoise Jacquin, "Pour une compréhension des cultures: Louis Massignon et l'abbé Monchanin," in *Louis Massignon et le dialogue des cultures*, 341–56. Massignon was a leading personality in the extraordinary ecumenical review *Dieu vivant*, which emerged after World War II seeking new religious engagement in the world; *Dieu vivant* also published works by Jewish writers such as Martin Buber. A range of thinkers developed renewed spiritual theology with a sharp political edge, which redefined thought in their own denomination: Catholic, Orthodox, Anglican, and Jewish; see Étienne Fouilloux,

"Une vision eschatologique du christianisme: *Dieu vivant* (1945–1955)," *Revue d'histoire de l'église de France* 57, no. 158 (1971): 47–72.

93. J.-P. de Menasce, "Contemplative Life and Missions," *International Review of Missions* 56 (1967): 330–37, at 331–32. Massignon and Charles de Foucauld remain important influences; see Étienne d'Escrivan, *Un monastère cistercien en terre d'Islam? Notre-Dame de l'Atlas au Maroc* (Paris: Cerf, 2010), 140–55.

Contributors

Katherine Davies held lectureships in modern European history at Magdalen College Oxford and at Manchester, following which she became an independent researcher including consultancy work at the Humanitarian and Conflict Response Institute and the Overseas Development Institute. Her publications include "A Third-Way Catholic Intellectual: Charles Du Bos, Tragedy and Ethics in Interwar Paris," *Journal of the History of Ideas* (2010), and "Continuity, Change and Contest: Meanings of 'Humanitarian' from the 'Religion of Humanity' to the Kosovo Wars" (2012).

Joseph Dunlop completed his PhD in history at St. Antony's College, University of Oxford, in 2013. His previous publications include "'Une amitié fondée dans la Vie': Catholic Conceptions of Friendship at the French Canadian Review *La Relève*, 1934–1950," *History of European Ideas* (2014), and "The 'Christian Society' of Garret FitzGerald and Pierre Elliott Trudeau," *Eire-Ireland* (2009).

Toby Garfitt is tutorial fellow of Magdalen College, Oxford. He works on French literature of the last hundred years, with a particular interest in Catholic writers such as Mauriac, Bernanos, Patrice de La Tour du Pin, and Sylvie Germain. His latest books include *Jean Grenier. Un écrivain et un maître: contribution à l'histoire intellectuelle du vingtième siècle* (2010) and *Jean Grenier-Jean Guéhenno, Correspondance 1927–1969* (2011). Among recent articles, "Newman at the Sorbonne, or, the Vicissitudes of an Important Philosophical Heritage in Inter-war France" was published in *History of European Ideas* (2014), and "The Embodied Philosophy of Jean Grenier" in *Embodiment: Phenomenological, Religious and Deconstructive Views on Living and Dying* (2014).

Paul Gifford is Emeritus Buchanan Professor of French, University of St. Andrews, where he was director of the Institute of European Cultural Identity Studies. He has been a visiting research fellow at the Girard Foundation ('Imitatic'), Stanford. His books include *Reading Paul Valéry, Universe in Mind* (edited with Brian Stimpson, 1998), *Love, Desire and Transcendence in French Literature: Deciphering Eros* (2005), and *Europe and its Others: Essays on Interperception and Identity* (edited with Tessa Hauswedell, 2010). Paul is continuing to work on René Girard's 'fundamental anthropology' in evolutionary perspective. His forthcoming collections of edited essays: *Can We Survive Our Origins*? and *How We Became Human* (with Pierpaolo Antonello, preface by Rowan Williams).

Michael Kelly is professor of French at the University of Southampton where he is director of the Centre for Languages, Linguistics, and Area Studies. He has published books on Emmanuel Mounier, Modern French Marxism and the reception of Hegelian philosophy in France. His most recent book is *The Cultural and Intellectual Rebuilding of France After the Second World War* (2004). He is coeditor of a book series on Languages at War. He is the editor of *Synergies Royaume Uni et Irlande* and of the *European Journal of Language Policy/ Revue européenne de politique linguistique*, and is a member of the editorial board of the journal *French Cultural Studies*, which he helped to found. He is currently working on debates around atheism and secularism/*laïcité*.

Florence de Lussy was conservateur général at the Bibliothèque nationale, Paris, France, where she was responsible for the archives of Paul Valéry and Simone Weil, among others. Her research originally focused on poetry and poets, including Valéry, Henri Michaux, and Yves Bonnefoy, before she devoted herself to editing the complete works of the philosopher Simone Weil. The first ten volumes in the series (1988–2010) came out under her editorship, as did the one-volume edition of Weil's works in the Gallimard Quarto series (1999). Her publications on Valéry include *La Genèse de* 'La Jeune Parque' (1975) and a genetic study of *Charmes* (her thesis, in two volumes, 1990 and 1996). She has published widely on Weil in edited collections and journals including the *Cahiers Simone Weil*. She is currently pursuing projects on Simone Weil, Joë Bousquet, and Paul Valéry.

Brenna Moore is assistant professor in the Department of Theology at Fordham University. She is currently working on projects on the "ressourcement" in early twentieth-century France and the relationship between friendship and religious subjectivity. Her book, *Sacred Dread: Raïssa Maritain, the Allure of Suffering, and the French Catholic Revival* was published in 2012. She has also published articles in *Spiritus*, the *Catholic Historical Review, HDS Cult/ure*, and *Commonweal*.

Anthony O'Mahony is reader in theology and the history of Christianity at Heythrop College, University of London. He has published extensively on the modern history of Christianity, especially Eastern Christianity, and Christian-Muslim relations in contemporary contexts. His books include *Eastern Christianity in the Modern Middle East* (edited with Emma Loosely, 2010) and *Christian Responses to Islam: Muslim-Christian relations in the Modern World* (edited with Emma Loosley, 2008), and he has published articles in the *International Journal for the Study of the Christian Church*, *Aram*, and *New Blackfriars*.

Stephen Schloesser is professor of history at Loyola University, Chicago. He is the author of *Jazz Age Catholicism: Mystic Modernism in Postwar Paris, 1919–1933* (2005), which won the John J. Gilmary Shea prize from the American Catholic Historical Association, and *Visions of Amen: The Early Life and Music of Olivier Messiaen* (2014). In 2008, he curated the exhibition and edited the catalogue entitled *Mystic Masque: Semblance and Reality in Georges Rouault, 1871–1958,* for which he received the Valley Foundation's "Curatorial Excellence Award."

Brian Sudlow is lecturer in French with translation studies at Aston University. His book *Catholic Literature and Secularisation in France and England 1880–1914* was published in 2011. He edited *National Identities in France* (2011) and has published articles and book reviews in *Literature and Theology, Modern and Contemporary France, The Chesterton Review,* and *Nottingham French Studies.* His article "Agamben, Girard and the Life that Does Not Live" appeared in *Intensities: Philosophy, Religion and the Affirmation of Life* (edited by S. Shakespeare and K. S. Moody, 2012).

Index

Abdallah ibn al-Torjoman (Anselm Turmeda), 321n17
Abd el-Jalil, 318n5
Abhishiktananda. *See* Le Saux, Henri
Abrahamian, Ervand, 234
Académie française, 52, 130, 262
Action catholique, 179
Action française, 4, 5, 31–32, 52, 54, 107, 138, 175–79, 214, 219, 311n18
Aeschylus, 82
Aeterni patris (1879), 65, 76
Alain (Chartier, Emile), 69, 73, 80
Albert, Henri, 58
Al-Hallâj, 233, 235–39, 321–26
Ali Shariati, 232–35, 322n21
Altermann, Jean-Pierre, 109, 111–12, 127
Alverny, Marie-Thérèse d', 25, 188, 189, 201–8, 305, 307
Ancelet-Hustache, Jeanne, 188
Angela of Foligno, St., 192, 194, 198
Anselm, St., 78
Anti-Semitism, 54, 67, 73–74, 204, 206, 208, 213, 248, 310nn11,14, 318n7
Antliff, Mark, 207–8
Apocalypse of St. John (Revelation), 155, 159, 165, 170–2, 184
Aquinas, St. Thomas, 5, 24, 26, 37, 66, 76, 77, 126, 149, 150, 153–59, 194, 196, 197, 201, 207, 225, 273n26, 295nn88,90
Arbre, L', 221–24
Archambault, Paul, 274n29
Archives d'histoire doctrinale et littéraire du moyen âge, 202
Aristotle, 66, 143, 157, 158, 159
Arland, Marcel, 286n30
Aron, Robert, 290n53
Association des libertés civiques, 223
Association internationale des écrivains pour la défense de la culture, 90
Aube, L', 7
Aubray, Thérèse, 286n28
Augustine, St., 78, 115, 143, 149, 287n34
Avicenna, 202, 208
Axworthy, Tom, 316n95

Baas, Émile, 220
Balfour Declaration, 249
Balthasar, Hans Urs von, 1–3, 26, 27, 81–83, 87
Bannister, Peter, 292n71
Barré, Jean-Luc, 213

Barrès, Maurice, 51, 261n2
Barthes, Roland, 29
Baudelaire, Charles, 167
Baudrier, Yves, 147
Baudrillart, Alfred-Henri-Marie, 52
Beaulieu, Paul, 212, 220–21
Beauvoir, Simone de, 29, 205
Béguin, Albert, 226
Benda, Julien, 88, 99, 124–25
Benedict XVI, 268n50, 328n51
Benedictines, 52, 200
Benjamin, Walter, 197
Berdyaev, Nikolai, 99, 216–17
Bergson, Henri, 53, 119, 138, 141, 195, 196, 203
Berl, Emmanuel, 116
Bernanos, Georges, 16, 18, 19, 24–25, 52, 162–85, 219, 310n15
Bernard of Clairvaux, St, 186–88, 191, 192, 195, 197, 207, 208
Bernard, Victor, 263n5
Berque, Jacques, 235
Bianchi, Enzo, 84–85
Bidault, Georges, 8
Blondel, Maurice, 45, 109, 110, 124, 231, 332n73
Bloy, Léon, 162, 167–68, 195–98, 203
Blum, Léon, 124, 147, 224
Borgese, Giuseppe Antonio, 224
Bosco, Henri, 92
Bosson, Abbé, 52
Bossuet, Jacques-Bénigne, 275n53
Boulanger, André, 72
Bourbaki group, 69
Bourget, Paul, 51, 114, 261
Bouyer, Louis, 280n8
Bradley, Francis Herbert, 119, 121
Braque, Georges, 95
Bremond, Henri, 52, 109–11
Breton, André, 151, 263n14
Breton, Stanislas, 86
Bruckberger, Raymond, 179
Brunschvicg, Léon, 119, 120
Buber, Martin, 334n92
Buddhism, 189, 199, 200, 206, 208
Bunlet, Marcelle, 295n85
Burnouf, Émile, 97

Camus, Albert, 93, 94–95, 100, 103
Canadian Commonwealth Federation (CCF), 214
Cancouët, Lucien, 69
Caspar, Robert, 239, 250
Casti connubii (1930), 149
Caussade, Jean-Pierre de, 125
Céline, Louis-Ferdinand, 162
Celsus, 74
Centre catholique des intellectuels français (CCIF), 6, 9, 21
Certeau, Michel de, 279n5, 280n8
Chabot, Jacques, 165
Charbonneau, André, 308
Charbonneau, Robert, 212–13, 216–29, 312n38
Charcot, Jean-Martin, 131
Chateaubriand, François-René de, 286n30
Chenu, Marie-Dominique, 26, 187, 188, 202, 231, 307n80
Cholvy, Gérard, 6
Christoflour, Raymond, 99
Churchill, Winston, 334n88
Cistercians, 186
Claudel, Paul, 31, 51, 54–55, 66, 87, 105, 244, 262n14, 310n15, 332n70
Clausewitz, Carl von, 183

Clemenceau, Georges, 241
Clement of Alexandria, St., 83
Clement of Rome, St., 83
Cloitre, Jules-Désiré-Gabriel, 131
Cocteau, Jean, 147, 160, 307n80
Commitment. *See* Engagement
Commonweal, 222
Communism, 44, 70, 89, 91, 123, 137, 160, 212, 217–19, 221, 223, 235. *See also* Marxism
Congar, Yves, 26, 207, 231
Conseil national de la résistance, 8
Constable, Gilles, 202
Constant, Benjamin, 113–15, 125, 127
Corbin, Henri, 121, 235, 277n84
Cornick, Martyn, 88
Coutrot, Jean, 290n53
Couturier, Marie-Alain, 74, 80
Crémieux, Benjamin, 286n30, 288n38
Crépu, Michel, 128
Critique sociale, La, 70
Cuypers, Michel, 233
Cyprien de la Nativité de la Vierge (André de Compans), 58

Daladier, Edouard, 98
Dalí, Salvador, 151
Dall'Oglio, Paolo, 327n46
Dandieu, Armand, 290n53
Daniel-Lesur, 145–47
Daniélou, Jean, 83, 97, 126, 127, 187, 188, 193, 200, 236
Daniel-Rops, Henri, 134–39, 141, 147, 160
Daudin, Claire, 162
Davies, Katherine, 14–17, 19
Davy, Marie-Ma[g]deleine, 17, 25, 186–208, 306n76
Dawson, Christopher, 325n37
De Gaulle, Charles, 52, 101, 222, 249, 262n8
Delbos, Claire. *See* Messiaen, Claire
Delbos, Victor, 138, 288n42
Déléage, André, 40
Delvaux, Paul, 174
Descartes, René, 56, 138
Desjardins, Paul, 115, 275n59
Didier, Béatrice, 117
Dieu vivant, 334n92
Divino afflante spiritu (1943), 267n43
Dollfuss, Engelbert, 217–18
Dominicans, 7, 52, 71, 74, 84, 92, 187, 194
Doms, Herbert, 150
Doughty, Charles Montagu, 330n59
Dreyfus Affair, 5, 30, 31, 48 51, 53, 173
Drieu La Rochelle, Pierre, 34–35
Drogoul, Fernand. *See* "F. D."
Drumont, Édouard, 163, 179
Du Bos, Charles, 14, 16, 17, 19, 23–24, 104–28, 265n20, 286n28
Duhamel, Roger, 215, 217
Dukas, Paul, 140, 289n51
Dunlop, Joseph, 13, 17, 18, 21, 25
Duplessis, Maurice, 224
Dupré, Louis, 11
Durand, Jean-Dominique, 10
Durkheim, Émile, 62

Eckhart, 191–92, 197, 206, 208
Economie et humanisme, 84
Einstein, Albert, 55
Élie, Robert, 218, 225, 226
Eliot, Thomas Stearns, 216
Éluard, Paul, 138, 151, 286n28, 289n44

Engagement, 17–20, 37–49, 69–71, 81, 84, 89, 94–103, 126, 219, 222–29
Esprit, 7, 40, 42, 45, 93–94, 98, 100, 226, 234–35, 290
Estève, Michel, 162, 180, 185
Etiemble, René, 90–91
Etudes, 99, 126
Europe, 91
Eusebius, 83
Existentialism, 93, 94, 108, 119–21, 225

Faisal I of Iraq, 241, 330n59
Fanon, Frantz, 235, 322n21
"F. D.", 135–40, 286n28, 288n37
Fédération nationale catholique, 8
Fernandez, Ramon, 105, 116–18
Festugière, André (Jean), 92
Fichte, Johann Gottlieb, 73
Fontoynont, Victor, 83
Ford, Henry, 137
Foucauld, Charles de, 229, 230, 238, 250, 317–18, 324, 327, 332, 335
Foucault, Michel, 29, 206, 235, 322n21
Fouchet, Max-Pol, 93, 98–101
Fouilloux, Étienne, 6, 8, 30, 230
France, Anatole, 30
Franciscans, 267–68n48
Franco, Francisco, 147, 163, 211, 219–20
Friedmann, Georges, 91, 96, 100
Fulcher, Jane, 130
Fumet, Stanislas, 79
Furfey, Paul Hanley, 218–19

Gallimard, Gaston, 89, 91, 92
Gandhi, Mahatma (Mohandas), 43, 236
Gandillac, Maurice de, 83
Garfitt, Toby, 14, 16, 17, 19, 23
Garneau, Saint-Denys. *See* Saint-Denys Garneau
Garrigou-Lagrange, Réginald, 9, 76, 90, 205–6, 257n28
Geffré, Claude, 268n51
Gertrude, St., 196
Gide, André, 19, 26, 89, 91, 104, 114, 116–18, 120, 126, 261n4
Gifford, Paul, 12, 17, 22
Gillet, Martin-Stanislas, 52
Gillouin, Charles, 138
Gilson, Émile, 26, 97, 186, 189, 201–2, 205, 220, 231, 307n80
Girard, René, 24, 53, 61–62, 162, 172–85
Gnosticism, 72, 75
Goebbels, Joseph, 176
Goethe, Johann Wolfgang von, 117
Goldziher, Ignaz, 324n81
Görres, Joseph von, 130
Gregory of Nyssa, St., 83, 197
Grenier, Jean, 14, 16, 17, 19, 20, 23, 88–103, 287n30
Griffiths, Richard, 240
Groulx, Lionel, 311n18
Groupe d'éducation sociale, 69
Grunenwald, Jacques, 146
Guéranger, Dom Prosper, 130
Guéhenno, Jean, 91–95
Guillemin, Henri, 92
Guilloux, Louis, 92, 94
Guitton, Jean, 92, 101
Gurian, Waldemar, 222
Guyon, Madame (Jeanne), 280n9

Habermas, Jürgen, 10, 268n50
Halévy, Daniel 89

Hallâj. *See* al-Hallâj
Harpigny, Guy, 236, 324–25n34
Hegel, Georg Wilhelm Friedrich, 29, 73, 119, 121, 264n13
Heidegger, Martin, 3, 16, 26, 119, 120, 121, 276n83, 277n84, 286n29
Hello, Ernest, 198
Henriot, Philippe, 8
Hilaire, Yves-Marie, 6
Hildebrand, Dietrich von, 149–50
Hinduism, 199–200, 334n92
Hitler, Adolf, 34, 134, 151, 159, 193, 266n31
Hobbes, Thomas, 183
Honnert, Robert, 220
Honnorat, Hélène, 265n26
Hopkins, Gerard Manley, 58
Hourani, Albert, 231, 318–19n8
Hügel, Baron Friedrich von, 131
Hugh of St. Victor, 153
Hugo, Victor, 262
Humanism, 95–99, 105–6, 115–19, 121, 123, 218–20
Hurtubise, Claude, 213–29, 308, 316n94
Huysmans, Joris-Karl, 51, 52, 139, 141

Institut catholique, Paris, 32, 205
Irenaeus, 83
Islam, 18, 20, 21, 25, 26, 189, 199, 200, 202, 206, 208, 230–51
Istrati, Panaït, 88
Izard, Georges, 40

Jacob, Max, 92
James, William, 2, 119, 131
Jarrety, Michel, 51
Jaspers, Karl, 119
Jaurès, Jean, 48, 235
Jerome, St., 184
Jesuits, 8, 83, 85, 99, 125, 126, 187, 205, 212, 221, 240
Jeune-Canada, 212–23, 217
Jeune France (1940–42), 101
Jeune France, La (1936–38), 147, 149, 292n69
Jeunesse ouvrière chrétienne (JOC), 218
Joan of Arc, 326n44
John XXIII, 38, 245
John of St. Thomas (João Poinsot), 194
John of the Cross, St., 58, 192, 267n38
John Paul II, 227
Jolivet, André, 146–47
Jolivet, Hilda, 146
Journet, Charles, 194, 196, 304n40, 306n80
Jouve, Pierre-Jean, 286n28
Jouvenel, Bertrand de, 35
Judaism, 20, 21, 25, 72–87, 189, 200, 203–4, 206, 208, 235, 240, 246, 247–49
Judt, Tony, 40, 199
Julliard, Jacques, 30
Justin Martyr, St., 83
Juvenal, 122

Kahil, Mary, 240
Kant, Immanuel, 5, 61, 73, 119
Keats, John, 121
Kelly, Michael, 8, 13, 15, 16, 18, 22, 25
Khomeini, Ayatollah Ruhollah, 323n28
Kierkegaard, Søren, 121, 235
Klee, Paul, 197
Kleinberg, Ethan, 276n76
Kojève, Alexandre, 121
Koyré, Alexandre, 119, 121

Kraemer, Joel, 324n31
Kraus, Paul, 324n31
Küng, Hans, 227

Lagrange, Marie-Joseph, 321n17
Lamartine, Alphonse de, 159, 284n19
Lambert, Edmond, 94
Lambeth Conference (1930), 149
Lamennais, Félicité-Robert de, 126
Langlais, Jean, 146
Lash, Nicholas, 67
Laugier, Henri, 222–23
Laurendeau, André, 220
Laurens, Henri, 241–42
Laval, Pierre, 89
Lawrence, Thomas Edward (Lawrence of Arabia), 81, 329–31n59
Lebey, Édouard, 52
Lebret, Louis-Joseph, 84
Lefebvre, Henri, 34, 235
Leiris, Michel, 88
Le Moyne, Jean, 220, 225–28, 316nn92,95
Leo XIII, 4, 36, 76, 225
Lequier, Jules, 93
Le Roy, Édouard, 109
Le Saux, Henri (Abhishiktananda), 200
Levinas, Emmanuel, 264n13
Lévi-Strauss, Claude, 75
Lévy-Bruhl, Lucien, 131
Ligue des droits civiques, 223
Loew, Jacques, 84
Loisy, Alfred, 109
Lowenthal, David, 166
Lubac, Henri de, 26, 83, 126, 187–97, 200, 207, 208, 227, 307n80
Lukács, György, 235
Lussy, Florence de, 15, 17, 20, 23
Maggiolini, Paolo, 333n82
Mallarmé, Stéphane, 58, 103
Malraux, André, 89, 95, 97
Mao Zedong, 225
Marxism, 21, 26, 34, 72, 89–90, 98–100, 225, 235. *See also* Communism
Marcel, Gabriel, 2, 14, 15, 16, 22, 31, 38, 45, 47, 53, 77, 93, 105, 116–20, 125, 126, 136, 265n20
Marcotte, Gilles, 211
Maritain, Jacques, 4, 9, 13, 14, 22, 25, 31–33, 37–39, 40–47, 51–52, 66, 77, 97–98, 101–2, 105, 109, 110, 116, 120, 123, 127, 138, 141, 147, 167, 193–95, 205, 210–14, 218–29, 231, 257n28, 265nn23,24, 273n17, 274n32, 316nn94,95, 321n17
Maritain, Raïssa, 25, 52, 53, 66, 101, 188–208, 210, 226, 306n67, 310–11n18
Mark of Toledo, 202
Marmion, Dom Columba, 134, 142–46, 159, 285n25, 290–91nn54,58–59, 296n107
Maspero, Gaston, 326n44
Maspero, Henri, 326n44
Massignon, Daniel, 320–21n17
Massignon, Louis, 17, 18, 26, 199, 230–51, 317–35
Massis, Henri, 93, 138, 214, 311n18
Matisse, Henri, 264n15
Mauriac, Claude, 52
Mauriac, François, 12, 45, 52, 104–5, 111, 112, 138, 141, 219, 310n15
Maurras, Charles, 4, 31, 32, 51, 52, 54, 93, 107, 138, 167–68, 175–79, 184, 214, 274n29, 311n18

Mayeres, Agathe, 245
Méhémet-Ali Mulla-Zadé. *See* Mulla, Paul
Mellers, Wilfred, 129
Melo Franco, Virgilio de, 181
Menasce, Jean-Pierre de, 235, 250, 324n32
Mercure de France, Le, 58, 90, 99
Messiaen, Claire, 133, 145, 148, 150
Messiaen, Olivier, 15, 24, 129–61, 278–97
Mettepenningen, Jürgen, 126
Michon, Jacques, 224, 314n64
Migne, Jacques-Paul, 83, 131
Migot, Georges, 145
Miró, Joan, 151
Mohammad V of Morocco, 241
Monchanin, Jules (Swami Paramarubyananda), 319n13, 334n92
Monde, Le, 29
Mondésert, Claude, 83
Montagne, Robert, 243
Montherlant, Henry de, 94
Montini, Giovanni Battista. *See* Paul VI
Moore, Brenna, 16, 17, 20, 21, 25
Morin, Edgar, 73
Mounier, Emmanuel, 7, 18, 22, 35, 38, 40–44, 46, 47, 53, 93, 101, 147, 234, 292n69, 316n95
Mouvement international des intellectuels catholiques, 6
Mouvement républicain populaire (MRP), 6, 8
Mugnier, Abbé (Arthur), 52
Murry, John Middleton, 121
Mussolini, Benito, 7, 44, 48, 152

Neo-scholasticism, 2, 5, 9, 17, 21, 76, 108, 188, 230. *See also* Thomism.
Neo-Thomism. *See* Thomism
Newman, John Henry, 97
Nicholas of Cusa, 78–79, 83
Nietzsche, Friedrich, 51, 56–59, 167, 209
Nizan, Paul, 34
Noce, Augusto del, 82
Nord, Philip, 130
Nordau, Max, 131
Nougat, Noël (Noël Vesper), 93
Nouvelle Relève, La, 222–24. See also *Relève, La*
Nouvelle revue française, La (*NRF*), 35, 51, 88–104, 179
Nouvelle théologie, 9, 21–21, 77, 97, 108, 126, 187. *See also* Ressourcement
Nous, 212
Nwyia, Paul, 330n59

O'Mahony, Anthony, 17, 18, 20, 21, 25, 26
Onfray, Michel, 100
Opus Dei, 316n92
Ordre nouveau, 39, 136, 141, 149, 290n52
Ordre nouveau (Quebec), 221
Origen, 74, 83, 197
Orphism, 72

Pacelli, Eugenio. *See* Pius XII
Pacem in terris (1963), 38
Padberg, Magdalena, 170
Parain, Brice, 92
Pascal, Blaise, 27, 56, 135, 196, 287n31
Pasteau, Rémy, 306n80

Paul VI, 245, 327n45, 332n74
Paul, St., 74, 75, 109, 117, 118, 154, 155, 291n59,62
Paulhan, Jean, 88–89, 91, 94, 97, 102
Péguy, Charles, 31, 41, 48, 51, 53, 99, 194–97, 207, 232, 288n39, 310n15
Pernoud, Régine, 188
Perrin, Joseph-Marie, 71, 72, 76–79, 84
Pétain, Philippe, 53, 101, 211, 220, 262n9
Pétrement, Simone, 70, 72, 265n26
Phenomenology, 44–46, 108, 119
Philo of Alexandria, 83
Picasso, Pablo, 151
Picot, Georges, 241, 320n17
Pius X, 4
Pius XI, 31, 36, 41, 52, 54, 215, 245, 247, 332n73
Pius XII, 245, 247, 265n19, 267n43
Plato, 73, 75, 79, 82, 264n17
Plotinus, 196
Pontigny, 115, 123, 125, 275n59
Porcher, Jean, 206
Pouget, Père (Guillaume), 92

Quadragesimo anno (1931), 36–37
Quebec, 13, 25, 210–29

Rainaldo di Piperno. *See* Reginald of Piperno
Ratzinger, Joseph. *See* Benedict XVI
Raymond, Marcel, 226
Recherches philosophiques, 119
Reginald of Piperno, 295n88
Reinhold, Hans Asgar, 222
Relève, La, 25, 210–29. See also *Nouvelle Relève, La*
Renard, Pierrette, 162, 165–70, 180, 181, 185
Rerum ecclesiae (1926), 247
Rerum novarum (1891), 36
Ressourcement, 20, 25, 27, 126, 186–209. *See also* Nouvelle théologie
Revelation of St. John. *See* Apocalypse of St. John
Révolution prolétarienne, La, 70
Revue dominicaine, La, 311n18
Revue du moyen âge latin, La, 193
Revue philosophique, La, 53
Revue thomiste, La, 99
Revue universelle, La, 311n18
Riccardi, Andrea, 85
Ricci, Matteo, 85
Ricœur, Paul, 35
Rideau, Émile, 52
Rimaud, Jean, 27, 99
Rimbaud, Arthur, 58
Robert of Kelton, 202
Roche, Déodat, 81
Rocher, Guy, 310n15
Rolland, Romain, 92
Romains, Jules, 84
Roosevelt, Franklin Delano, 134
Rougemont, Denis de, 35
Roussel, Raymond, 88
Ruysbroeck, John of, 86

Sabanegh, Édouard (Brother Martin), 237
Sadoul, Georges, 90
Said, Edward, 320n14
Saint-Denys Garneau, Hector de, 214
Salazar, António de Oliveira, 217

Salman Pak, 233
Sangnier, Marc, 30
Sanson, Pierre, 287n34
Sant' Egidio community, 84
Sarraut, Albert, 89
Sartre, Jean-Paul, 28, 29, 48, 49, 277n84
Sauvage, Cécile, 283–84n19
Schaeffer, Pierre, 101
Schloesser, Stephen, 10, 15, 17, 24
Schola Cantorum, 145–46
Schwager, Raymund, 184
Scouting, 212
Schwob, René, 112
Sept, 7
Serge, Victor, 224
Serry, Hervé, 5
Sertillanges, Antonin-Gilbert, 52
Sforza, Carlo, 222
Shariati. *See* Ali Shariati
Sillon, Le, 30
Simon, Yves, 220
Smith, Bonnie, 197
Sophocles, 82
Sources chrétiennes, 83, 193, 200, 267n43
Sources et feux, 200
Souvarine, Boris, 70
Spaier, Albert, 119
Spengler, Oswald, 34, 216
Spinoza, Baruch, 73
Spirale, La, 145–49
Stalin, Joseph, 225
Stavisky Affair, 33, 141
Steiner, George, 264n16
Storelv, Sven, 164–66, 170–72, 177
Sturzo, Luigi, 222
Sudlow, Brian, 16, 18, 19, 24
Suleiman, Susan, 100
Surin, Jean-Joseph, 194, 196
Surrealism, 100, 137, 138, 151 160, 289n50, 297n113
Sykes, Mark, 241, 320n17

Talbi, Mohamed, 321n20
Taylor, Charles, 19, 168–70
Taylorism, 137
Teilhard de Chardin, Pierre, 52, 54–55, 226–27, 316n95
Témoignage chrétien, 8, 192
Teresa of Avila, St, 192, 194
Thibaudet, Albert, 91, 104, 107
Thomas à Kempis, 140, 143
Thomas Aquinas, St. *See* Aquinas
Thomism (Neo-Thomism), 4–5, 9, 13, 14, 16, 17, 23, 24, 50, 62, 65, 66, 76–77, 90, 98, 99, 101, 105, 108, 110–11, 126, 127–28, 143, 159, 205–6, 214, 225–26, 230, 274n32, 278n112. *See also* Neo-scholasticism
Tournemire, Charles, 132, 133, 153, 160, 284–85n22
Trent, Council of, 76
Trilling, Lionel, 106
Troisième Force, La, 40, 42, 93
Troll, Christian, 240
Trudeau, Pierre Elliott, 229, 316n94
Turmeda, Anselm. *See* Abdallah ibn al-Torjoman

Underhill, Evelyn, 131
Union pour la vérité, 120
Urs von Balthasar, Hans. *See* Balthasar, Hans Urs von

Valensin, Auguste, 52
Valéry, Paul, 12, 17, 22, 34, 50–68, 261n4, 262n8–9,14
Van der Meer de Walcheren, Christine, 206
Van der Meer de Walcheren, Pierre, 206
Vatican I (First Vatican Council, 1869–70), 61, 76
Vatican II (Second Vatican Council, 1962–65), 6, 9, 26, 38, 61, 187, 211, 225, 227–28, 240, 241, 246, 250, 333n79
Vesper, Noël. *See* Nougat, Noël
Vie intellectuelle, La, 7
Vie spirituelle, La, 194
Vigile, 111–12
Vincent d'Indy, 286n28
Viollet, Jean, 149
Voltaire (François–Marie Arouet), 56

Wagner, Richard, 58
Wahl, Jean, 1–3, 16, 27, 119–20
Waite, Arthur, 131
Wardenberg, Jacques, 244
Weber, Max, 14
Weil, André, 69, 72, 78
Weil, Simone, 17, 20, 22–23, 68, 69–87, 192, 263n5, 264n16, 265nn18,26, 266nn32,34, 267nn38,40
Weizmann, Chaim, 247
Whitehead, Alfred North, 2, 119
William of St Thierry, 191, 192, 207
Winter, Jay, 208
Wittgenstein, Ludwig, 121, 264n16
Woodsworth, James Shaver, 214–15

X-Crise, 290n53

Yad Vashem, 76